NetObjects
Fusion Handbook

TIM WEBSTER

Hayden
Books

Hayden Books

Publisher
Lyn Blake

Publishing Manager
Laurie Petrycki

Managing Editor
Lisa Wilson

Marketing Manager
Stacey Oldham

Acquisitions Editor
Michelle Reed

Development Editor
Kezia Endsley

Copy Editor
Marta Partington

Technical Editors
Mike Goos
Jeff Kawski

Publishing Coordinator
Rachel Byers

Cover Designer
Sandra Schroeder

Book Designer
Anne Jones

Manufacturing Coordinator
Brook Farling

Production Team Supervisor
Laurie Casey

Production Team
Cindy Fields
Daniela Raderstorf
Elizabeth San Miguel
Scott Tullis
Megan Wade

Indexer
Kevin Fulcher

NetObjects Fusion Handbook

©1996 Hayden Books

Library of Congress Catalog Number: 96-77852

ISBN: 1-56830-327-0

Copyright © 1996 Hayden Books

Printed in the United States of America 1 2 3 4 5 6 7 8 9 0

Warning and Disclaimer

About the Author

Tim Webster's career as a computer scientist began long, long ago, when he taught himself assembly language on his truly underpowered Timex-Sinclair. He has contributed to several books for Hayden, including *Mastering Netscape Navigator 2.0 for Macintosh* and *Teach Yourself Java in 21 Days for Macintosh*. This is his first solo project.

Currently, Tim is employed as a digital imaging specialist (whatever that means) at the Office of University Publications at the University of Chicago. He has no spare time. Tim lives with his wife, Chris Corcoran, on the south side of Chicago—the baddest part of town.

Trademark Acknowledgments

All terms mentioned in this book that are known to be trademarks or service marks have been appropriately capitalized. Hayden Books cannot attest to the accuracy of this information. Use of a term in this book should not be regarded as affecting the validity of any trademark or service mark. NetObjects Fusion is a trademark of NetObjects, Inc.

Dedication

This book is dedicated to my wife, Chris Corcoran. I could not have written the *NetObjects Fusion Handbook* without Chris's collaboration. She did the bookkeeping, made the screenshots, critiqued the chapters, looked up esoteric information, and kept me sane, all while on summer vacation from her own grad school career.

Acknowledgments

Special Thanks to:

Jim Azim, who will practice law for food; Cindy Bold, my art director, design mentor, and advisor in all things; Dee and Patrick Corcoran, who waited out my slacker period; Joe Gallagher, Shockwave guru and all-round Mac stud; Jack Green, who, as usual, figured out the hard parts at the last minute; Jeff "talented *and* sexy" Hall, who drew the thumbnail in Chapter 4, and did my real job during my writing vacations; Karl Heino, who did the dancing; Greg Holden, *il miglior fabbro;* Greg Lewis, best man, Eagle scout, who helped in thousands of ways; Ann Lindner, the always-undercredited office muse and technophobe, who really does shriek when you say "set the preferences;" Ralph and Sue Webster, my parents, who taught me even more than they or I ever suspected; the folks at NetObjects for their prompt answers and rockin' software; and the hard-working, ever-patient crew at Hayden, especially Kezia, Laurie, Michelle, and Steve, all of whom politely endured my incoherent and paranoid phone calls and e-mail.

Hayden Books

The staff of Hayden Books is committed to bringing you the best computer books. What our readers think of Hayden is important to our ability to serve our customers. If you have any comments, no matter how great or how small, we'd appreciate your taking the time to send us a note.

You can reach Hayden Books at the following:

Hayden Books
201 West 103rd Street
Indianapolis, IN 46290
317-581-3833

Email addresses:

America Online:	Hayden Bks
Internet:	hayden@hayden.com

Visit the Hayden Books Web site at http://www.hayden.com

Contents at a Glance

Table of Contents

ix

x

xi

Part III: Getting Fancy   257

Introduction

HTML is dead.

Just a few years ago, when the NCSA Mosaic and Netscape Navigator browsers were first introduced, the only way to create Web pages was to write HTML by hand, using a text editor. You may have written some HTML yourself, and if you have, you know that it's a tedious, boring, error-prone business.

Within a few months, HTML-friendly text editors and text editor extensions began to appear on both the MacOS and Windows platforms. These products, such as WebWeaver and HoTMetaL, made the process of editing HTML a little less painful by providing services like automatic tag-creation and page templates. The basic problem remained, however: Web page designers were creating page layouts—a visual process—with text-editors—that is, non-visual tools.

Soon, the WYSIWYG (what-you-see-is-what-you-get) HTML editors began to arrive. These applications, such as Adobe PageMill and Hotdog, represent the second generation of Web design tools: visual HTML editors. PageMill and its peers allow Web authors to create pages more intuitively, by allowing users to edit text, pictures, and links in an environment that previews the resulting page. For the most part, tags are added behind the scenes by the application.

WYSIWYG editors are a significant improvement over text editors, but they aren't quite everything that a Web developer needs. These tools are handy for designing individual pages, but don't offer any support for designing *sites* as sites—that is, collections of pages that share a consistent look-and-feel, are organized in a logical way, and work together.

You've probably seen plenty of sites on the Web with great looking entry-points (or "home pages") that fall to pieces once you're deeper inside. Perhaps the sub-levels use a different style of typography, or a different color scheme, and they seem like pages that belong to another document. (It's like finding a few pages from *W I R E D* magazine spliced into *TIME*, or vice-versa—very disconcerting.)

Creating a hierarchy of linked pages is also very time-consuming, and difficult to maintain. A set of five pages with internal links to each other requires 20 separate connections. If you're using a second-generation editor, you must create these links manually, even if you actually code them in HTML. You've surely seen sites where some of the internal links don't quite work correctly...they point to the wrong pages, or to documents that have been moved or deleted.

Enter NetObject Fusion. Fusion introduces a third generation of Web design tool: you can design entire Web sites *as sites.*

- Sites are designed visually—you add new pages by editing a tree or outline style map of your site.

- Links are handled automatically and painlessly. Fusion automatically generates navigation tools based on the site map.

- Each page can contain its own unique information, and yet shares a consistent look and feel with other pages on the site.

- Site design is abstracted from page implementation, so an entire site can be instantly reconfigured with a new page style or for the capabilities of a particular Web browser.

Just for laughs, the folks at NetObjects have improved—or rather, reinvented—WYSIWYG design at the page level:

- Fusion supports the full gamut of modern (circa mid-to-late 1996) Microsoft and Netscape extensions to HTML: tables, embedded Java applets and ActiveX controls, background colors, everything—except, mercifully, frames and blinking text.

- Fusion uses a drafting table–style interface, similar to page-layout packages like Adobe PageMaker and QuarkXPress. Essentially, you place elements wherever you like on the page. This is a revolutionary departure from flow-style interfaces derived from word-processing programs, as we'll see in Chapter 1.

Things change, and traditionally Web sites are much more difficult to maintain than they are to build in the first place. NetObjects Fusion is built to help you present your information dynamically, making it easy to update and reorganize your site without tedious link-debugging sessions. In fact, NetObjects can update your site automatically!

If all this sounds complicated, it's not. Fusion is very easy to use, and it collects in one package just about everything you'll need to put a site together. NetObjects Fusion was designed by a designer, Clement Mok, and it shows in the elegance of Fusion's interface. If you've spent any time working with desktop publishing tools, like QuarkXPress or Adobe Illustrator, Fusion will seem familiar. If you've done any programming with Visual Basic (on the Windows platform) or Hypercard (on the Mac), Fusion will ring a few of those bells, too.

Who Can Use Fusion?

One of the great things about NetObjects Fusion is that it's a good tool for a wide range of users. No matter what your background and level of technical expertise, you will be able to use NetObjects Fusion to create professional-looking pages and to make your site work more smoothly.

Novices Using Fusion

Let's say you've never done any kind of Web page design at all, and all of this Internet stuff is new to you. You'd like to learn something about the way the Web works, and create your own home page, but you're not interested in spending a lot of time figuring out how to make a Web page. Maybe you're even a little afraid of technology, like my friend Ann Linder, an otherwise rational person who shrieks with fear whenever someone says "set the preferences."

NetObjects Fusion is definitely for you. Using Fusion, you create pages by drawing boxes where you want pictures and text to go. To put a picture in its box, you use a simple file dialog. To add text, you simply type it in. (We'll take a little tour of Fusion in the next chapter. Figure I.1 shows you a little peek at how easy the interface is to use.)

FIGURE I.1

Creating a Web page with Fusion is as easy as drawing and typing.

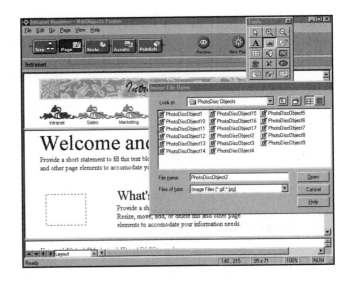

It's not much harder to add things like links to your pages, or to add things like ready-made animations, sounds, and even Java Applets. The NetObjects Fusion package comes bundled with some of these goodies already, and there are even more on the *NetObjects Fusion Handbook* CD-ROM that comes with this book. Just in case that's not enough, I'll show you where you can find all sorts of Web page gee-gaws that are freely available on the Net.

HTML Experts Using Fusion

Some of you may have experience with HTML...some of you may have been building pages from the very beginning. You have a good idea how time-consuming it is to build pages with something as simple as a margin or a couple of tables.

NetObjects Fusion makes these difficult elements very easy to handle. You can add things like complex tables, ActiveX controls, Shockwave presentations, and Java applets simply by drawing a box and entering a few parameters into a floating palette like the one shown in Figure I.2. Even if you prefer coding your HTML by hand, you may want to use NetObjects Fusion to generate the complicated tags for these kinds of elements.

FIGURE I.2

You can easily build complex tags with a simple dialog box.

NetObjects Fusion also relieves you of the tedium of creating a complete set of links between the pages on a site. I've coded a lot of HTML by hand, and it still takes me hours to set up a complete set of links for every page of a fairly modest site. I promise you—you won't want to code any more HTML by hand once you've seen Fusion create a Navigation bar!

Webmasters Using Fusion

Even if you're an experienced HTML author, and you don't want to add anything too fancy to your site, you've probably spent more time than you'd like designing the basic structure of your site: how pages are related to one another, how they link together, and how they look as a cohesive whole. NetObjects Fusion provides an innovative set of tools that you can use to plan the way your pages work together by organizing them into a site tree, like the one shown in Figure I.3.

Furthermore, NetObjects Fusion can help a Webmasters to organize a files, repair broken links and missing images, and to update and maintain a whole site with very little effort. (The feature set is something like the site management tools found in Adobe SiteMill, if you're familiar with that—but Fusion adds a few tricks of its own.)

FIGURE 1.3

NetObjects Fusion provides an easy way to plan a site.

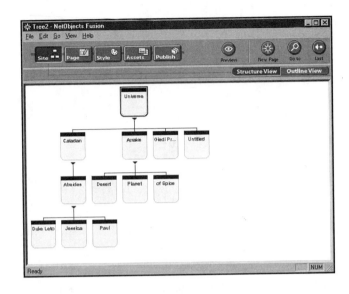

Database Gurus Using Fusion

There are probably a few of you out there with databases that you'd like to serve up on the Web. After all, you've spent a lot of time and energy creating your database—why duplicate that effort by re-creating the same forms and reports in HTML? What if you don't know HTML, and you're too busy to learn a new language?

NetObjects Fusion is very database savvy, and you can use it to automatically generate a Web site from your ODBC-compliant database. Furthermore, you can use all of Fusion's site and page design tools to add whatever features you like to your database-derived sites. All it takes is a few clicks in NetObjects Fusion to update your database as well.

JavaScript Developers Using Fusion

If you've tried to do any JavaScript development, you know that there are just no tools to aid you. There are no integrated development environments, no debuggers—you simply write the JavaScript into the HTML with a text editor, and load it with Netscape Navigator.

Alas, NetObjects Fusion isn't a JavaScript development kit, but it's the closest thing we've got. If you're writing JavaScripts, Fusion offers a convenient way to attach JavaScripts to Web page elements by simply entering them into a dialog box like the one shown in Figure I.4. (It's just as easy to add a Script for a whole page as it is to add a script to a particular element.) Fusion automatically inserts the JavaScript in the HTML code—you never need to leave the comfort of the graphical page editor.

FIGURE I.4

It's easy to attach JavaScripts to Web pages with NetObjects Fusion.

Publishers Using Fusion

If you're a traditional publisher with extensive art and editorial resources, you will want to be able to reuse your materials for the Web with a minimum of fuss. NetObjects Fusion provides not only easy tools to edit sites and pages—the Fusion package also provides a very diverse range of site and page templates that will allow you to quickly adapt your present materials to the Web, and a multitude of styles that you can use to further customize your pages. One such template page is shown in Figure I.5. Adding your own material is as easy and cutting and pasting your own stuff into the appropriate fields.

(Even if you don't have a lot of digital imagery in the can, you'll find that NetObjects Fusion includes some nice clip-art to get you started.)

FIGURE 1.5

One of the many page templates included with NetObjects Fusion.

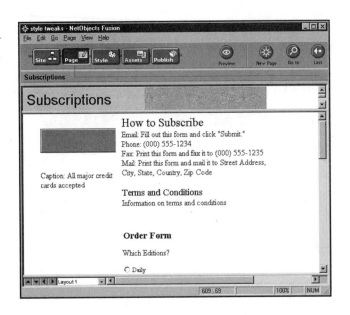

What You'll Need to Know to Use Fusion

You certainly don't need to know any HTML to use NetObjects Fusion, or to learn Fusion from this book. From time to time, we might look at HTML tags in passing, but if you're a code-a-phobe, you can safely skip over these sections. If you do know some HTML, great! You can always peek at the HTML that Fusion creates for you, and in one or two spots, I will suggest a few ways you might fine-tune your pages with a little bit of raw HTML.

Likewise, you don't need to know anything about Java, JavaScript, ActiveX, or Shockwave to put these kinds of interactive elements into your NetObjects-based site. I'll tell you all about what these things are, and what they do, and how they work. You won't be able to create these kinds of elements yourself after reading this book, but you'll be able to use NetObjects Fusion to add ready-made interactive elements to your pages.

You *will* need to have a basic working knowledge of your preferred Web browsers—if you have some sort of Internet connection and you know how to look at Web pages, download software, install plug-ins, and set your browser's preferences, you'll be fine.

I also assume that you've mastered the day-to-day operation of your MacOS or Windows system. You should be able to do simple things like install software, perform searches, and copy files. I won't dwell on the finer details of things like dialog boxes and moving windows around—I'll just say things like: "pick the file that you want from the dialog box."

I will discuss things like graphics and sound file formats, but creating such files—by scanning, recording, or whatever, is up to you. Fortunately, Fusion comes bundled with some basic building blocks, and the Web offers many storehouses of clipart and clip-sounds to get you started building your page if you don't have the resources to create images yourself.

Who Can Use this Book?

NetObjects Fusion is a tool that Web developers of all sorts—Web page designers, Webmasters, and content creators—will find useful.

The *NetObjects Fusion Handbook* contains thorough instructions for using Fusion to create complete, consistent professional-looking sites. If you are responsible for creating Web sites, you'll find everything you need in this book to design your site.

This isn't a book about content development, and NetObjects Fusion isn't a content development tool. Rather, the *NetObjects Fusion Handbook* describes how to add content to sites that you build with Fusion.

Conventions Used in this Book

NetObjects Fusion is a Mac/Windows cross-platform product, and this is a cross-platform book. In most cases, the procedures to perform a task are the same on both platforms. In situations where things are slightly different from platform to platform, the text will be marked with a cross-platform icon, like so:

In the spirit of platform neutrality, I have not included keyboard shortcuts, accelerator keys and the like. It's just too cumbersome to add all of the many possibilities for every single command.

(By the way, I apologize to all of my Mac compadres for all of the Windows screen shots—the Windows version of Fusion was available months before it came out for the Mac.)

Sometimes the software will have hidden commands, or shortcuts or nice features that aren't immediately obvious. When we point out these little doodads, the notice will appear in a sidebar, marked with a "tip" bar:

TIP

I'll also use tips to point out some labor-saving devices and workarounds for common problems.

WARNING

Certain procedures or decisions are potentially dangerous: they may cause your computer to crash, compromise the security of your Web site, or just cause an enormous headache. These sections are marked with a warning bar.

For your convenience, all of the URLs and net.references from each chapter are included in the "URL Roundup" section at the end of each chapter, and on the *NetObjects Fusion Handbook* CD-ROM. (I stole the URL round-up idea from rocket scientist and Hayden author Tobin Anthony, by the way.)

As you probably know, URLs never end with a period. English sentences do. If you see a period after an URL, it's there for punctuation, and you shouldn't enter it when you're fetching the URL with your browser.

In a few places, we'll take a look at code: mostly little snippets of HTML and JavaScript. Code will always be set in a separate font, like this:

```
alert("Hello, World!");
```

Where to Go From Here

In Chapter 1, you learn what NetObjects Fusion is, how it can help you design great pages, and how to best use it.

In Chapter 2, we'll take a tour of NetObjects Fusion, and you'll build your first Web site with Fusion.

In Chapter 3, we'll look at some basic Internet principles, and how these issues may affect your site's design.

In Chapter 4, we'll look at Fusion's Site View mode, and you'll learn how to design your site's architectural framework.

In Chapter 5, we'll look at Fusion's Page View mode, and you'll learn how to add basic elements to your pages.

In Chapter 6, we'll look at Fusion's Style mode, and you'll learn how to apply and to create the basic building blocks used to construct your site.

In Chapter 7, we'll look at Fusion's Asset View mode, and you'll learn how to manage the files and other resources that Fusion creates and uses.

In Chapter 8, we'll look at Fusion's Publish mode, and you'll learn how to transfer your site to a Web server, and even set up a very simple server of your own.

In Chapter 9, you'll learn about imagemaps, and how to add them to your site.

In Chapter 10, you'll learn about multimedia content like sounds, video, and Shockwave, and how to add such content to your site.

In Chapter 11, you'll learn about forms and form components, how to add them to your site, and what you'll need to handle your forms on the server end.

In Chapter 12, you'll learn about databases, and how you can use NetObjects Fusion to publish a database on the Web.

In Chapter 13, you'll learn about programs that run inside Web pages, like Java Applets, JavaScripts and ActiveX controls, and how you can add such components to your site.

xxix

Introduction to NetObjects Fusion

Third-Generation Web Design

In the introduction to this book, I suggested that NetObjects Fusion represents the first product in a new, third generation of Web design tools. Previously, Web authors coded HTML by hand using text editor software (the first generation) or using page-level WYSIWYG Web editors (the second generation.)

What Is NetObjects Fusion?

Now that we've established that NetObjects Fusion is really versatile and that it's useful to just about everybody, let's take a minute to look at Fusion's many capabilities, and see what you can (and can't) do with Fusion once you've mastered the program.

At the simplest level, NetObjects Fusion creates HTML, just like a second generation Web page editor such as Claris Homepage. Fusion doesn't create the HTML for a single page at a time, however. Rather, it generates a complete set of HTML documents—one for every page in the site—and creates all the auxiliary files required to complete the site.

This is a radical approach, and it integrates a new set of functions, including image-editing, file management, and database handling, into the Web site editor. Let's compare the basic procedures for creating a site with Fusion and creating a site with a second generation authoring tool.

Suppose you're working on a little two-page site. That seems simple enough, doesn't it? Let's call the pages in the site, oh, "Home" and "Away." Figure 1.1 and 1.2 show what these two pages might look like in the browser window.

FIGURE 1.1

One page of a very simple two-page site.

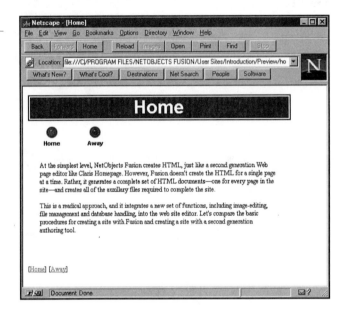

There's not much to these pages, and they look pretty simple to construct. Let me point out the features that we're interested in:

- Each page has a banner with its name at the top of the page

- Each page has a navigation bar showing each page on the site underneath the banner

- Each page has text links to each page on the site at the bottom of the page

- The text on each page is in a block in the middle of the page, with margins on either side

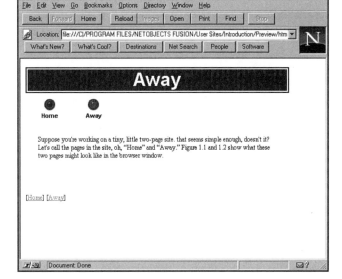

FIGURE 1.2

The second page of the simple site.

If you're working with NetObjects Fusion, the basic procedure goes something like this:

1. Add a new page to the site by adding a new icon to NetObjects Fusion's diagram of the site.

2. Name each page by typing the name into the page's icon in the site diagram.

3. Pick a "look" for your site from a set of ready-made buttons and banners.

4. Add the text by drawing a text box on the page and adding text to it.

5. Publish the site.

(Don't worry—you'll learn the specifics of these procedures in the next few chapters. For now, all you need to do is compare the complexity of the two procedures.) To create a site with a second-generation authoring tool, you need to do the following:

1. Create banners for each page in an image editing program. (If you've got a ready-made template for the banner, you'll still need to add the page's name to each.)

2. Create a set of buttons for each page in the image editing program. (Again, you'll need to add text to the buttons, even if you've got a ready-made button.)

3. Create the "Home" page in the authoring program. Import the banner and buttons for the page and place them. Create a table (if your program supports tables), edit the table so that its border doesn't show (if your software supports this aspect of tables), and place your text in the table.

4. Repeat step 3 to create the "Away" page. (Remember, it uses a different set of buttons and banners, so you'll need to start from scratch.)

5. Link the "Away" button on the home page to the "Away" page.

6. Add the word "Away" to the bottom of the "Home" page, and link the text to the "Away" page. To put the text at the bottom of the page, you'll probably need to add a few cells to your table and a tall, skinny, transparent image to one of the cells to keep the table from collapsing.

7. Repeat steps 5 and 6 to link the button and text on the "Away" page to the "Home" page.

8. Find all of the components that you used to create your site (hopefully, you put them all into the same folder, and somehow labeled them as essential files) and transfer them to the Web server.

I hope you get the basic idea: NetObjects Fusion takes care of all the little tasks, like labeling buttons, creating navigation bar links, and managing files so that you can focus your energy on the creative tasks, or just go home on time.

NetObjects Fusion Is a Site Design Tool

First and foremost, NetObjects Fusion is a site editor that allows you to create an entire set of linked pages as a single site with a consistent look and feel. Using Fusion's site-editing features, you can:

- **Plan the way your site is organized.** NetObjects Fusion displays the site in an intuitive tree-structure diagram. You can see your site's organization, and how its pages work together in a single glance.

- **Add and remove pages with a click of the mouse.** Adding a new page to the site is as easy as adding a page icon to the site map. New pages are linked to the rest of the site with automatically generated navigation bars.

- **Reorganize the pages of your site as needed.** Pages in the site can be moved to new locations with drag-and-drop ease. All changes are automatically updated in each page's navigation bars.

- **Link pages together with Navigation tools.** You can supplement NetObjects Fusion's automatically generated bars and easily add custom links between the pages of your site.

- **Add standard components to every page of a site.** You can create standard "header"0 and "footer" material that NetObjects Fusion automatically adds to all of the pages in your Fusion site.

- **Make global changes to the style of all of the pages in the site at once.** Changing the style of your site—the way the buttons and banners look and the colors used—can be handled with NetObjects Fusion's SiteStyles feature. SiteStyles allows you to globally change all the pages in your site with one dialog box.

- **Save the entire structure of a site as a template for other sites.**

NetObjects Fusion Is a Page Design Tool

Fusion also offers comprehensive page design features. You can use Fusion to do these things:

7

- **Create and manipulate text within text boxes.** NetObjects Fusion's text-handling capabilities are similar to the types of text tools found in programs such as QuarkXPress or Adobe PageMaker. Designers and desktop publishers will find these tools familiar and easy to use.

- **Add and manipulate images using image boxes.** Similarly, NetObjects Fusion handles images with image boxes. This approach will be familiar to anyone with traditional desktop publishing experience.

- **Draw basic shapes directly on Web pages.** NetObjects Fusion offers a novel feature that's new to Web page design software: drawing tools. You can use Fusion to draw basic shapes such as squares, ovals, and polygons directly on your pages.

- **Add multimedia to pages.** Adding components such as sound files, video clips, and Macromedia Shockwave presentations is nearly as easy as adding image files. Fusion uses the same basic picture-box metaphor, and allows you to fine-tune the way multimedia files are presented to the reader.

- **Add scripts to pages.** You can enter HTML, JavaScript, or VBScripts directly into your page. This makes it easy to add custom scripted features to your page, or even tweak the page's basic HTML.

- **Add forms to pages.** NetObjects Fusion supports all the basic form components: text entry fields, radio buttons, check boxes, list boxes, and buttons. You can add these components by simply adding them onto your page.

- **Add links to other sites.** Linking text or an image to an external site is as easy as typing an URL into a dialog box. NetObjects Fusion can link to newsgroups and email addresses as easily as it can link to Web pages.

- **Import existing HTML pages and edit them with Fusion's advanced tools.** If you have pages that you've already created with another application, you can open them with NetObjects Fusion, and use Fusion's superior text, image, and multimedia pages to add new components and apply Fusion's SiteStyles.

NetObjects Fusion Is a Site Management Tool

After you've completed a site design, there's still a lot of maintenance work to be done. Fortunately, NetObjects Fusion does much of it for you. Specifically, Fusion can perform the following tasks:

- **Generate a complete list of documents used in your NetObjects Fusion site.** This makes file management easy to handle, and helps you to fix problems with your site.

- **Generate a complete list of links within the site.** This makes it easy to test the links on your site and easy to update them as necessary.

- **Generate a list of database connections used on your site.** This function makes it easier to keep track of the way databases are linked to your site.

- **Organize and store copies of all files internally.** NetObjects Fusion makes its own copies of all the necessary files so that you can keep the originals where you want them.

- **Create a set of preview files on your local disk.** You can use the Preview files created by NetObjects Fusion to view your site or raw material for your own hand-tweaked pages on your local machine before you publish it.

- **Create a copy of your site on a test server.** NetObjects Fusion automatically FTPs all of the necessary files to the Web server—you don't need to collect the files and send them.

- **Update all components of your site on the server.** When you update your site with NetObjects Fusion, updating your site is as simple as re-publishing the site with a single click.

In the real world of Web publishing, updating and managing a site is as complex and time-consuming as creating the site in the first place. NetObjects Fusion doesn't do everything for you (it can't handle server maintenance), but it goes a long way toward making site updates as easy as possible.

NetObjects Fusion Is a Database Front End

Technically speaking, NetObjects Fusion isn't quite a database front end—you *can* use it to take a look inside a database, but that's not really what it's built for. Rather, NetObjects Fusion creates an easy way to move information from a database to a Web site. Fusion can perform the following functions:

- **Connect to an ODBC database.** You can import data from any database or any other application that understands the ODBC protocol.

- **Connect to many common database systems (without ODBC).** NetObjects Fusion can import data from many commonly used database systems, even if the database doesn't provide its data via an ODBC driver.

- **Create an index of all the records in a database.** NetObjects Fusion automatically indexes imported databases, and presents that index as a table of links on a Web page.

- **Create a unique page for each record in a database.** NetObjects Fusion builds a separate page for each record in a database, using a common template for each page.

- **Display any field or table on the record's page.** Any field in the database can be displayed in a text or picture box. These "windows" to the data can be manipulated as desired so that you can present your data in whatever format you like (see Figure 1.3).

FIGURE 1.3

*NetObjects Fusion
enables you to
customize the way
you display your
database data.*

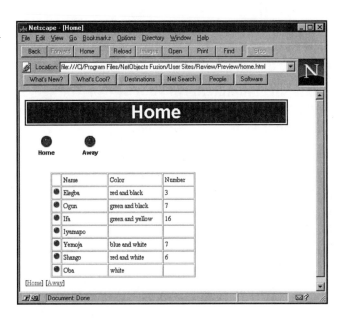

What NetObjects Fusion *Is Not*

NetObjects Fusion is a powerful package, and you can use it to design and
implement a Web site from start to finish. However, there are a few things that
Fusion won't do for you.

NetObjects Fusion Is Not a Web Server

NetObjects Fusion can create your site and transfer it to the appropriate place in
your server's file directory, even if the server is on another machine. However,
Fusion won't actually serve your files on the Web. (I'll discuss what a server is in
Chapter 3, so don't worry if you're not quite sure what this distinction means.)

In many cases, you probably don't need a Web server anyway. You can pass off
your site to your Internet Service Provider or Network Administrator, and she or
he will put your files on the Web for you. Just in case you *don't* have someone to
take care of this for you, I'll provide a brief introduction to server administration
in Chapter 8.

NetObjects Fusion Is Not an HTML Editor

NetObjects Fusion does generate HTML code for you, but it's not an HTML
editor in the sense that you can open your pages and monkey around with the

raw source code. Personally, I have mixed feelings about not having an easy way to look at the source HTML. Although you can add *extra* HTML to the page easily enough with Fusion, there's no easy way to alter the HTML that Fusion generates if you'd like to tweak it just a bit.

NetObjects Fusion generates some pretty darn complicated code, so it's probably just as well that you can't touch the code. There are plenty of tables within tables within tables, and a tiny change at a critical junction can make the whole page look like it went through a shredder.

I know, I know, some of you will find this disappointing. It's a little inconvenient, but if you really want to edit the code by hand, you can use a text editor. However, most of the time, it's a relief that all of the HTML is safely behind the scenes.

Summary

In this chapter, you learned about the specifics of NetObjects Fusion's feature set and what Fusion can do for you and your site. Specifically, you learned the following:

- How NetObjects Fusion is different from second-generation WYSIWYG editor.

- What Fusion's side-editing features can do.

- What Fusion's page-editing tools can do.

- What Fusion's site management features can do.

- What Fusion's database publishing tools can do.

In Chapter 2, you'll take a tour of NetObjects Fusion and see some of these tools in action as you build your first Fusion site.

URL Roundup

- Adobe PageMill (second-generation WYSIWYG editor):
  http://www.adobe.com

- Claris HomePage (second-generation WYSIWYG editor)
  (This is the one I've been using lately when I need such a thing):
  http://www.claris.com

A Tour of NetObjects Fusion

In this chapter, you'll work through all the stages of creating a full, working Web site with NetObjects Fusion. In later chapters, you'll look at each of these steps in greater detail; for now, the idea is to get an overview of the entire process and to see how easy publishing with NetObjects Fusion can be.

If you haven't already done so, install the NetObjects Fusion software, following the instructions in the README file on the book's CD-ROM. If you're using a commercial version of the software, follow the instructions that came with your distribution.

Taking Inventory

Let's take a look at the basic directory structure in the NetObjects Fusion package. Your final distribution copy might look slightly different than the figures here, but the basic components should be pretty much the same. Figure 2.1 shows the contents of the NetObjects Fusion directory.

FIGURE 2.1

The NetObjects Fusion package (Windows '95 version).

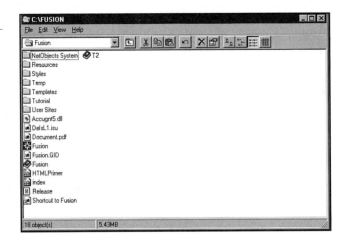

WARNING

Sorry, Mac lovers—the Mac distribution wasn't released in time to put a screen shot in the book. The NetObjects Fusion folder should look pretty much the same, but in glorious Mac OS-version.

In both cases, the folders contain the following special goodies:

- **Templates.** The Templates folder contains templates for sites at the content architectural level. In the AutoSites folder, you'll find templates of whole sites designed for particular communications needs, such as marketing or online publishing. In the Pages folder, you'll find templates for commonly used pages, such as guestbook pages or personal home pages.

- **Styles.** The Styles folder contains collections of harmonized banner, button, and rule art that you can apply to all or some of the pages in your site. Fifty SiteStyles are included with 1.0.

- **User Sites.** The User Sites folder is a repository for sites that you create. (Of course, you can store them somewhere else if you want. NetObjects Fusion won't grind to a halt if it can't find your site in the User Sites folder.)

- **Parts.** The Parts folder contains Web page clip art (dingbats, arrows, and so on) that you can add to your pages as desired. They're in ordinary GIF format, and you can use them with any Web page construction tool you like.

TIP

The *NetObjects Fusion Handbook* CD-ROM contains templates designed by Clement Mok, especially for this book. If you're using the commercial version of the software, be sure to copy these templates from the Book Templates folder into the appropriate folders in the NetObjects Fusion folder.

Looking around the Fusion Interface

Enough bookkeeping. Fire up the software!

If you're launching NetObjects Fusion for the first time, you'll be presented with the New Site dialog box, as shown in Figure 2.2. When you type a site name (for example, My First Site) into the Site Name field, you'll notice that the dialog box adds your site's name to the pathname in the Save site to field. Choose Blank Site from the list (or if you're using a Mac, choose from the pop-up menu) and click Create. Voilá.

15

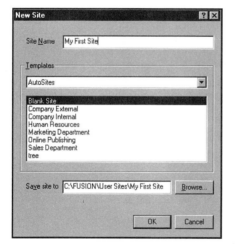

FIGURE 2.2

The New Site dialog box.

After you've dismissed the dialog box, NetObjects Fusion presents its main window. This window may change form slightly as you perform different tasks, but most of its tools will stay with you throughout your authoring session. Let's take a moment to look around and identify the various widgets built into the window.

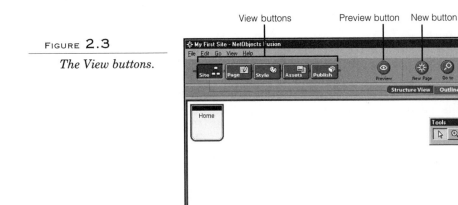

FIGURE 2.3

The View buttons.

The View Buttons

A basic idea behind the NetObjects Fusion interface is that of multiple site views: You can look at your site from an architectural perspective, page by page, examine the site's design theme, or inventory and organize the files that comprise the site. Each of these views is represented by one of the buttons at the top left of the main window.

By default, NetObjects Fusion starts in Site view. The current view mode is represented as a pressed button. To change views, click a new button. View buttons behave like standard "radio buttons"—you can be in only one view mode at a time. (If you prefer, you can also change between views by using the Go menu, which contains menu items for each of the page views.)

Let's try it. A blank site consists of a single home page, represented in Site view as a page icon. Click the Page view button, and NetObjects Fusion shows you just what the blank home page looks like. Click the Style view button, and a list of Site styles appears. Choosing styles is discussed in more detail under "Style View" later in this chapter. Click the Assets view button to see a list of the files that the site already contains. Click the Site view button again to return to the basic site view.

> **TIP**
>
> Sometimes, NetObjects Fusion changes modes automatically when it makes sense to do so. For example, if you double-click a page's icon in Site mode, NetObjects Fusion loads the target page in Page mode.

The Preview Button

The Preview button, located at the top of the control bar, is available in all view modes. When you click the Preview button, NetObjects Fusion generates all the HTML and auto-generated images (like banners and navigation bars) of your site, stores it in the Preview folder, and launches your Web browser of choice to view the page. Click it now. Depending on the number of pages your site contains, previewing takes a few seconds (for most sites) to a few minutes (for gargantuan sites).

> **WARNING**
>
> I'm assuming, of course, that you have some kind of browser —preferably Netscape Navigator (2.0 or later) or Microsoft Internet Explorer (2.0 or later)—installed on your machine. If not, you won't be able to preview your site. If you have both browsers installed, use the **Edit→Preferences** command to pick your browser of choice. You need to make this choice only once; NetObjects Fusion will use the same browser for previews until you reset your preferences. Browsers must be capable of reading tables because NetObjects Fusion-generated HTML make extensive use of table tags and attributes.

The New and Navigation Buttons

The three buttons at the top right of the NetObjects Fusion window are used for adding to the site and navigating within the site's pages. The New button (labeled "New Page" in Site view) changes function according to the view mode; the Go To and Last buttons aren't affected by mode changes.

The New button creates different kinds of new objects, depending on the current view mode. We'll return to the function of this special button several times in Chapters 4–7, which discuss each of the view modes in detail.

The Go To button searches the current site for any named object or page you specify. When you click it, NetObjects Fusion presents a dialog box for you to enter your search term and parameters.

If there's a single match to your search, you'll go directly to the matching object. Try searching for "home" to see how this works. If more than one object matches your search string, NetObjects Fusion presents a list of matches. Click a list item to go to that item. If no items match, NetObjects Fusion presents an alert box to tell you no matches were found.

The Last button behaves much like a Web browser's "back" button, taking you to the previous view. If you tried the search button experiment in the last paragraph, Last will take you from the home page to the view that you searched from. If you were in Site view, you will return to Site view. Last toggles you back and forth between the current and previous views.

The Go menu contains menu items—equivalents and keyboard shortcuts to the five Views, Preview, Go To, and Last buttons. It also adds a third navigation command, called "Recent." The Recent command presents a list of recently visited pages and views; selecting any item from the list takes you to that page or view.

The Secondary Control Bar

The Secondary control bar is located directly below the control bar. This toolbar changes dramatically when you change from view to view, providing easy access to view-specific tools. In Site mode the Secondary control bar includes the Structure view and the Outline view buttons. You'll learn how to use these tools in a later chapter.

For now, it's useful to notice that in Site mode, the very top of the control bar displays the name of the current site, and in Page mode, the Secondary control bar displays the name of the current page. In all modes, a dotted blue rule connects the toolbar's buttons to the current view button, to remind you that the toolbar buttons are view-specific.

Adding Pages in Site View

Most sites have more than one page. Let's add a few pages to make our example site more interesting, and to show you just how easy it is to design sites at the architectural level.

First, make sure you're in Site view. Now, click the New Page button. A page icon for the new, untitled page appears directly below the Home page in the blank site. Click the name of the Untitled page. The name of the page is automatically selected when you click it; give it the name "Hotlinks" or a name of your choosing. Figure 2.4 shows the resulting Site view.

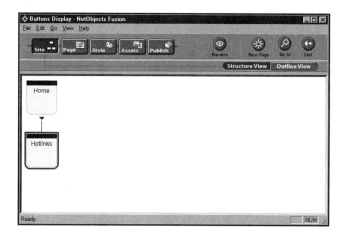

FIGURE 2.4

Adding a new page to the site.

Double-click the Hotlinks page. NetObjects Fusion has automatically added a banner with the page's name and a navigation bar with a button for the Home page and the new page. If you take a look at the Home page in Page view, you'll see that a link to the new page has been added to the navigation bar there, too.

(I don't think it's an overstatement to say that this is pretty astonishing. When I first saw this feature of NetObjects Fusion, I knew that Web page authoring would never be the same—don't be surprised if you feel the same way when you see it in action.)

You don't need to limit yourself to adding blank pages to the layout. Let's add a predesigned page from the set that comes bundled with the NetObjects Fusion package. Use the following steps:

1. Go back to Site view and click the Home page icon.

2. Choose Insert from the File menu.

3. Use the Open File dialog box to navigate to the Pages folder inside the Template folder.

4. Open the FAQ folder and select the FAQ file (Faq.nft).

NetObjects Fusion adds a preformatted FAQ page to your site as a "child" of the home page and a "sibling" of the hotlinks page. Double-click it to take a look at how a typical page template is set up (see Figure 2.5).

FIGURE 2.5

A predesigned FAQ template.

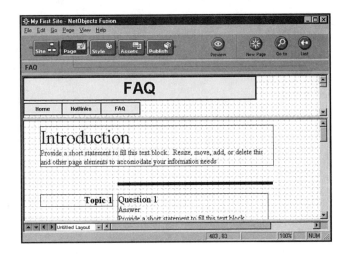

20

As you can see, the template contains text blocks with placeholder text where you can put your own information. Also note that even though the page is ready-made, its navigation bar is adapted to the particulars of the site that it belongs to, and the new FAQ page has buttons for the Home and the Hotlinks pages.

For the record, new pages are added as children of the page that is currently selected (as indicated with a blue border) in the Page view. If you want to add the FAQ page as a child of the Hotlinks page, rather than its sibling, you can select the Hotlinks page icon before choosing **File→Insert.**

You can read the site tree in the same way that you'd read a family tree. When one page is added beneath another page, and connected to the top page by a little line, the top page is called the parent of the bottom page, and the bottom page is called the child of the top page. All of the children of a single parent are called siblings of each other. (We'll cover this system of nomenclature in detail in Chapter 4.)

Be careful deleting pages with children. When you delete such a page, the children go with it, and there's no way to bring them back.

Be careful, object-oriented programmers—this is *not* a class inheritance tree. A parent/child relationship does not affect the contents or style of either page in any way.

To see how this works, click the FAQ page in Site view and click the New Page button two or three times to add a few new pages. As you can see, all the pages are added as children of the FAQ page, rather than as a chain of parents and children.

You don't really want to keep these new untitled pages; you added them so you could learn how to delete pages. Click one of the new untitled pages and select **Delete Page** from the Edit menu (or just press the Delete key). The selected page is removed from the site tree. *If a page to be deleted has any children, the child pages are deleted as well. NetObjects Fusion will warn you of this in a delete confirmation dialog box.*

WARNING

Although the Edit menu contains a standard Undo command, you can't undo page additions or deletions. Be very careful when deleting pages, *especially pages that have children!* There's no way to recover your work if you accidentally throw away the wrong page.

At this point, you might want to save the site to disk and use the Preview button to see how the pages work together in the real world of a Web browser. Remember, NetObjects Fusion builds the pages and launches your browser automatically; all you need to do is press the button.

All the navigation bars in the header and text links in the footer should be fully operational, including the Built with NetObjects Fusion icon in the footer of every page. Astonishing, isn't it? If you've ever built these kinds of navigation bars by hand, you might want to stop and pinch yourself.

Adding Content in Page View

The automatic links are cool, but so far the content is pretty meager. Let's add some material to the pages.

Take a look at the Tools palette. You may have noticed that the Tools palette changes from view to view; in Page view, the available tools are used to sling page content around. (Even if NetObjects Fusion didn't handle site architecture so masterfully, it would be an outstanding product for the richness of the Page view tool set, shown in Figure 2.6)

FIGURE 2.6

*The Page view tool
set.*

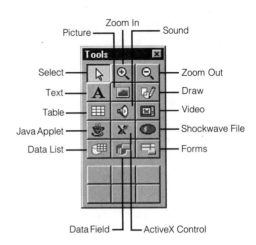

Adding a Picture

Let's start by putting a picture at the top. If you've got a favorite scan handy, you can use that; if not, you can use one of the Animated GIFs included with NetObjects Fusion.

1. Go to the Home page in Page view.

2   Click the Picture button (the middle of row two).

3. Use the crosshairs to draw a box where you'd like the picture to go. Select an area that's in the body of the page; that is, beneath the header divider—the thick gray line beneath the page banner and navigation bar.

4. NetObjects Fusion presents an image file dialog box; use it to navigate to /Parts/Design Parts/Animated GIFS/tv.gif (or whichever file you like).

Simple, wasn't it? Let's make the picture just a little bigger, just to see how it's done.

1. Click the picture to select it, if it isn't selected already.

2. Click the Picture tab in the Page Properties palette. (If the Page Properties palette isn't on-screen, choose **View→Page Properties** to make it visible.)

3. In the Settings section of the Picture properties palette, click the Stretch radio button.

4. Grab a corner of the picture's frame and drag. (Sorry, but there's no way to constrain the proportions of the picture as you resize.)

Naturally, you can make the picture smaller in exactly the same way.

TIP

If things get too weird, you can always recover by clicking the Normal radio button in the settings section to return the picture to actual size.

Adding Text

Let's add a headline to the picture.

1. Choose the Text tool (it's the first tool in the second row of the Tools palette).

2. Use the crosshairs to draw a text box to the right of the picture. Note that when you release the mouse button, an Insertion point appears inside the text box.

3. Type your headline. For this example, I've used "The Society For Self-Hypnosis."

4. Click the Text tab in the Properties palette.

5. Choose a paragraph style—say, Heading 1—from the Paragraph pop-up menu. Choosing a paragraph style applies the style to all the text in the paragraph that contains the insertion point.

6. To adjust the sizes of an individual character, select the character and choose a size from the Size pop-up menu. For this example, I've increased the size of the initial caps to 36 (+4) to create the illusion of small caps in the head.

7. Resize and reposition the text block, as necessary. To resize the box, grab a corner or edge control point and drag; to move the box, click inside it and drag. If you start highlighting text instead of moving the box, just click outside the box once then click inside the box to move it.

Figures 2.7a and b show how the picture and headline appear in NetObjects Fusion and Internet Explorer, respectively.

FIGURE 2.7A

*The sample home
page in Page view
mode.*

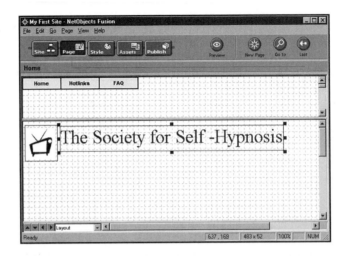

FIGURE 2.7B

*The sample home
page, as it appears
in the browser.*

Veteran designers, production artists, and lovers of page margins everywhere
who have struggled with HTML layout by using other tools can already see the
benefit to NetObjects Fusion's page tools: You can put the element where you
like on the page without messing around with tables, invisible boxes, and similar
kludgy solutions.

WARNING

As you may know, text size isn't completely under your control as a designer. The
user has a great deal of control over how text displays in the browser window, and
this example head won't necessarily appear in every browser window as it does in
Figure 2.7b. In Chapter 3, you'll find out which page elements are within your control
and which are not.

Next, let's add some body text below the head. Draw a new text block beneath the head and enter some text of your own. You can type it directly, or cut and paste it from an existing text document. If you cut and paste, NetObjects Fusion will retain the rich formatting.

After you've got a good-sized chunk of text, triple-click to select the whole paragraph. Copy and paste the paragraph a few times so that you have several paragraphs with which to work.

This will provide you with the raw materials you'll need to explore NetObjects Fusion's paragraph styles. If you've coded HTML before, or used an editor such as PageMill, you'll probably recognize some of the standard HTML styles, such as code (which renders the type in a monospaced font) and directory list (<DL> </DL>, which bullets the paragraph).

NetObjects Fusion goes one step further—you can define your own text style. This is another feature commonly found in word processors and page layout packages that have been heretofore mysteriously absent from Web page tools. When you define a set of styles, you can use your own styles throughout the site to ensure that the typography of all your pages is consistent from page to page. User-defined paragraph styles also make it easy to apply complicated type effects with a few clicks.

25

Let's try it:

1. Click the insertion point in a paragraph that is in normal style.

2. Click the center alignment text icon in the Text panel of the properties palette. (It's in the center of the first row of icons on the Format group.)

3. Triple-click the paragraph to select all the text in the paragraph. (This is necessary for step 6, below, but not for other paragraph operations.)

4. Click the Color button. Click a red color swatch and click OK. The selected text is now red.

5. Select Add from the Paragraph drop-down menu. Give the style a new name (like "centered, red") in the New Text Style dialog box.

6. To apply your new style to a new paragraph, click inside the target paragraph and choose the style's name that has just been added to the Paragraph drop-down menu.

Your new text style can be used on other pages throughout the site. It's *not* carried over into new sites, though, nor can you sneak it in with cut and paste.

Adding Links

What's a Web site without links to other pages? Of course, NetObjects Fusion creates internal navigation links automatically, but it's up to you to add links to interesting spots out on the Web. As you've probably guessed by now, NetObjects Fusion makes it easy.

Let's work on the Hotlinks page:

1. Create a text box.

2. Type some text, something like "Visit the NetObjects home page, and find out more about this amazing technology."

3. Select the text that you want to show as a link; for instance, "the NetObject home page."

4. Click the Link button at the bottom left of the Text tab in the Properties palette.

5. Click the external link tab in the Link dialog box.

6. Enter an URL (the NetObjects Web site is `http://www.netobjects.com`) and a name for the link in the Link dialog box. The name can be anything you like: it's used for bookkeeping later on. I'll use "NetObjects" in this example.

TIP

It's easy to mistype URLs, and it's good idea to make sure that you've got the URL right in the first place. For best results, load the page you want to link to in your Web browser, and cut and paste from the Web browser's location field to the Link dialog box.

You can test the link by clicking the Preview button and clicking the link in your Web browser. *Always* check that your external links are working before publishing your site!

The hypertext link appears as it will appear in the Web browser: underlined and in red type. (You'll learn how to change these defaults in Chapter 5.)

After you've created a link, you can easily edit or remove it:

1. Place the cursor somewhere in the link text. You don't need to select the whole link.

2. Click the Link button at the bottom left of the Text tab of the Properties palette.

3. To remove the link, click the Unlink button in the Link dialog box. You can also choose Remove Link... from the Text menu that appears when you are in a text box.

4. To edit the link, enter a new value in the desired field.

At this point, you can practice with the text tool and customize the information in the site: change the headline on the home page; write your own message; create your own set of links—make the site your own.

Style View

You may not care for the utilitarian square orange banners and buttons that NetObjects provides as a default. They're fine for a corporate site, but probably not quite right for a personal home page, an online magazine, or the Society for Self-Hypnosis.

27

In the bad old days of early 1996, creating elements such as buttons was inextricably tied up with the creation of links, and hence the architecture of the site. To create a button, you used an image–editing application like Photoshop to add type to a GIF or JPEG image, and manually created a link between the image and the page it linked to. To change the look of the button, you had to create a new button with new type, with your image-editor. Then you shuffled files around, making sure that the new button had the same name and location as the old button, and the old button was safely archived somewhere. In short, it was complicated and tedious.

NetObjects Fusion has changed all that. Because banners, buttons, and other page elements are generated automatically, you can change these elements with ease. Even better, NetObjects Fusion applies these page elements as complete sets, so that you can change all instances of these elements globally from one location—the Style view.

NetObjects Fusion 1.0 comes with a set of ready-made SiteStyles, appropriate for a wide range of design needs. (Don't worry if you don't see one that's right for you—you'll learn how to create your own style sets in Chapter 6.)

Let's take a look at NetObjects Fusion's ready-made styles. Click the Style button in the control bar. You'll see a screen similar to the one shown in Figure 2.8:

FIGURE 2.8

The Style view window.

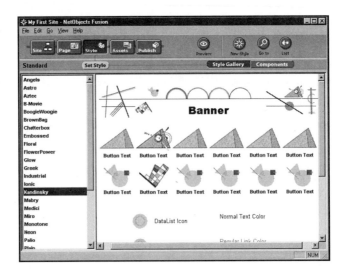

The column on the left shows a list of names of the styles that are available, and the pane on the right shows the elements of the style currently selected in the list—*not* the current style of the site. You can click down the list of names to examine each in turn.

Personally, I think that the Astro style works well with the jazzy little TV set I used earlier in this chapter. To make the Astro style the current SiteStyle, select it in the list, and click the Set Style button in the Secondary control bar. NetObjects Fusion updates all the pages in the site with the new look. Click the Page button and move the navigation bar in the header down a bit. Click the Preview button to see how Astro pans out in the real world of the browser window.

Figure 2.9 shows the example page with the new style applied.

As you recall, when you were working with text, you created a red text style. This creates a tiny problem—the color of followed links in the Astro style is also red, so it might be hard to spot such links in red text blocks. Of course, this is a problem only if you plan to put links in similar blocks (which you probably wouldn't). Let's take a moment to fix this problem so that you can see how flexible styles really are.

1. Click Styles view.

2. Click Astro in the left column.

3. Click the Components button in the Secondary control bar.

4. Note that the left column has changed to a list of all the elements in the Astro style. Double-click Visited Link Color in the left column.

5. Pick a new color from the Color palette. Click OK.

Changing buttons is only a little more work. You'll learn how to make that type of revision in Chapter 6.

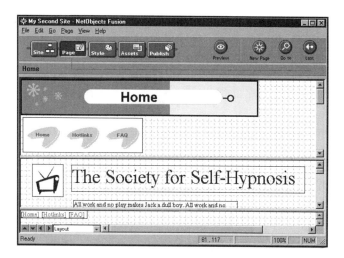

FIGURE 2.9

You can instantly change the look of your site in Style view.

29

Assets View

If you've worked a Web site or a traditional desktop publishing project before, you know that keeping track of files is a critical part of the process. If a picture file is moved from its proper place, or renamed, the browser (or imagesetter, in the case of desktop publishing) will display a gray box or missing-picture icon in its place, and if the file is in the wrong place, the browser won't be able to find it at all.

However, sometimes files do get moved around and renamed. For example, you might have organized a folder full of dozens of files into subfolders, included revision information in a file's name, copied files to another machine, or are trying to locate files that someone has moved to be mischievous. When these changes occur, you must repair the links in your site.

NetObjects Fusion refers to all the different kinds of files—picture files, video, Java applets, everything you can put into a Web site—as the site's *assets*. NetObjects Fusion keeps track of these assets for you, and provides tools to help you when your assets go bad.

Let's see how this works. First, you can simulate the problem by moving a file that's already in the site, and then fix the problem in Assets view.

1. Locate the picture file that you used on the home page. If you used the television GIF, it is "/Parts/Design Parts/Animated GIFS/tv.gif." Drag the file somewhere else on your hard drive.

2. Click the Preview button. NetObjects Fusion builds the site, but without the picture file. The result is shown in Figure 2.10. The browser displays the Webmaster's mark of shame, the missing-image icon, instead of the television set.

FIGURE 2.10

Missing files cause Web pages to display incorrectly.

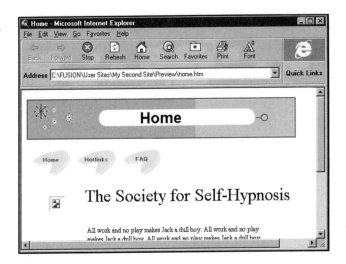

3. Click the Assets view button. Click the Files button in the Secondary control bar. The Assets view screen shows information about all the files used in your Web site. Your Assets view screen should look something like Figure 2.11, although the specifics will vary.

4. Locate the file that you moved in step 1 in the list. If you moved the tv.gif file, it's named TV. Double-click the file's name.

5. NetObjects Fusion presents a file dialog box. Click Browse... to navigate to the location where you stored the file in step 1, and select the moved file.

6. Click the Preview button.

7. Click your browser's Reload/Refresh button. (If you quit out of the browser after step 2, this step is unnecessary.)

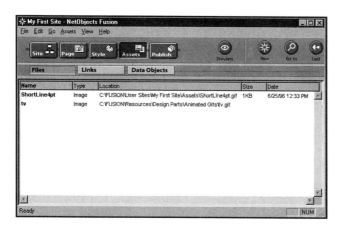

FIGURE 2.11

The Assets Files view provides a complete list of files used to build your Web site.

You can use exactly the same approach to re-establish connections with files that have been renamed. This is much handier than repairing links by replacing the file or editing the HTML directly.

Publishing Your Site in Site View

Let's publish your site.

It's common practice to load your site on a local server before you serve it to your intranet or the Internet at large. NetObjects Fusion refers to this precaution as "staging." Staging isn't quite the same as what you've done with the Preview button.

Staging tests your sites links and appearance by copying all assets, not just those generated by Preview to the LAN you have chosen. This way you can test your site with a closed group of people: clients, your team, your boss, and so on.

There are a few reasons to do this:

- To see if the server serves all the files correctly. For whatever reason, the server may have difficulty finding or recognizing a file, even if it's in the right place.

- To see how well the site's pages load over a network.

- To test CGIs—special applications that help the server process forms. (You'll learn about CGIs in detail in Chapters 3 and 11.)

- To allow proofreaders/beta-testers at remote sites to examine the site's content.

The procedures for staging and publishing your site with NetObjects Fusion are exactly the same. I suspect that you may not want to serve this little three-page site on your public Web server, so let's stage your site, rather than publishing it.

> **TIP**
>
> If you don't have a staging server set up, you can go ahead and set up your site on a server, if you have one. It's extremely unlikely, but not *completely* impossible, for someone to find your site if you don't tell anyone that it's there.

Some of you may not have access to a server at all—you're new to the Web publishing biz, or you hand off your files to someone who takes care of serving them for you, or you only have a dial-up connection to the Net. Never fear. Shareware server software for both Windows and Macintosh is easy to find on the Net, and basic instructions for downloading and setting the servers up in Chapter 8.

For this example, I'm going to use FolkWeb, a shareware server for Windows 95, running on my local machine without an Internet connection. Don't worry if you have trouble adapting these instructions to your particular configurations (see Chapter 8 for more details on Publish).

1. Make sure that your server software is running.

2. Click the Publish view button. NetObjects Fusion presents a screen similar to the one shown in Figure 2.12.

FIGURE 2.12

You can move your site to a server by using Publish view.

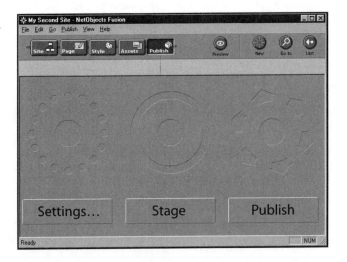

3. Click the Settings button or the Settings icon above it.

4. Click the Stage tab in the Configure Publish dialog box.

5. Click the Local radio button.

6. Click the Browse button. Use the Directory dialog box to choose the folder where your Web server looks for Web pages. FolkWeb uses the Pages folder inside the FolkWeb folder; your server may look in a different place.

7. *If you already have a file called Home.htm(l) on your server, pick a new name from the "Publish Home Page as" pop-up menu, so you don't overwrite your current home page.* You may need to change the name of the home page of the example site in Page view if none of the names in the pop-up menu are unused on your server.

8. Check the "Replace spaces with" check box. Although this isn't strictly necessary when using Mac or Windows 95 servers, it makes the files more portable to servers on other platforms.

9. Click OK.

10. Click the Stage button, or the Stage icon. NetObjects Fusion presents a progress bar as it moves the files to the server.

11. Launch your Web browser. In the browser's Location/Address field, type in your server's address (such as `http://www.selfhypnotix.com`), followed by a slash (/), followed by home.htm. (If you had to use a different name in Step 7, use that here instead of home.htm.)

That's it. If everything's set correctly, your Web browser will display everything as it did in Preview mode, but your browser's location/address field will show URLs that begin with http://..., rather than c:\... or File:\\\.... Call your friends, your boss, your client—whomever—and tell 'em to have a look.

If you click the Publish tab in the Configure Publish dialog box, you'll see that the Publish panel is identical to the Stage panel. This is logical enough: The only difference between staging and publishing is the location of the server—not the way that the files are set up and transferred.

By creating two sets of configuration settings, you don't need to change the details, such as your staging server address and your final server address, every time you want to switch from one server to another.

Summary

By now, you've got a basic idea of how NetObjects Fusion works, and you can do a few cool things:

- Create a complex hierarchy of pages visually without linking any pages by hand.

- Create pages that contains basic elements, such as pictures, styled text, and external links.

- Apply a consistent look and feel to all the pages in your site.

- Fix simple problems caused by missing or renamed files.

- Transfer your NetObjects Fusion site to a server.

This is already quite a bit more than what you can do with most Web page design packages, and you've only seen a small part of the NetObjects Fusion repertoire. You can add elements like tables, video, and Java applets to your Web site as easily as you added a simple picture, and it's not too much harder to add more ambitious components, such as forms and database information.

In Chapters 4–8, you'll look at each of the view modes in turn and learn about the choices, features, and tricks that each mode offers. But first, in Chapter 3, you'll learn some basic principals: How Web sites work and what you can and can't build into a Web page.

CHAPTER 3

Web Science

Before you start work on your Web site, let's have a little reality check, and talk about what can and cannot be accomplished within the framework of the Internet. There are lots of things you can do with a Web site, and new possibilities seem to arise every day, but there are pitfalls, too—things you can't do, things that are harder to do than you might think, and things that can get you into lots of trouble.

I'll start by explaining how a basic Web transaction takes place: what a browser does, what a server does, and what each of these players needs to perform its task. Next, I'll talk about fancier stuff—forms, plug-ins, and applets. Then I'll cover issues that are still troublesome, such as fonts and color, and wind up with a look at security and how you can protect yourself and your readers.

Some of you more experienced Webmasters probably have a basic knowledge of this stuff already. You can skip ahead to the next chapter if you like, but you may find something new here, too.

How Basic HTML Pages Work

The raw material of a Web site is HTML. Fortunately, when you're working with NetObjects Fusion, all the HTML is hidden from you, so you can think about issues such as design and content, rather than checking to see whether that <H1> tag has a matching </H1> end tag, and how to build a table inside a table inside a table without going completely nuts.

So what is HTML? It's an acronym for HyperText Markup Language, and it's a way of specifying how text and pictures are to be displayed by a Web browser.

HTML Is Not Programming

You'll sometimes hear people talking about "programming" in HTML. I am by no means a technoweenie, or language purist, but HTML is not just a programming language, folks. HTML is complicated. It requires skill, attention, and planning, but there are no variables and no flow control statements—in other words, none of the headaches that is the hallmark of the programmer's art. Writing a cookie recipe is closer to writing code than HTML is.

As the name suggests, HTML is a system for "marking up" text, in much the same way as an editor might write "A- Head" next to a headline, or a designer might specify that a block of text be set in 10-point Garamond. Some of the old programs from the dawn of the word processing era use the same basic techniques as HTML: the instructions, or tags, are included right inside the text, set off with pointy brackets <like this.> (The ancient and venerable *runoff* program for the VAX/VMS, which I used in college to write papers about what Mr. Melville meant by "Hey, Hey, Jenny get your hoe cakes done," used this format.)

For example, to specify italics with HTML, you use the <I> tag, like so:

```
NetObjects Fusion is <i>soooo<i> easy to use!
```

And it is rendered like this in a Web page:

```
NetObjects Fusion is soooo easy to use!
```

Nowadays, there are a zillion tags that let you specify the text's column, the size of picture, and how many columns the page has. HTML tags can control just about every aspect of the appearance of every element that appears in the browser window.

A modern (c. 1995-96) Web page might use many tags to create its look. Sometimes the tags take up more room than the text does, and they're tangled up with each other in a way that's hard to decipher. Figure 3.1 shows a fairly modest Web page created by NetObjects Fusion.

Figure 3.2, which shows Navigator's View Source window gives you a hint of how complex the underlying HTML is. (The whole code is just too long to include here—it would fill two pages!) Of course, it's possible to code this kind of page by hand, and many people have done so, but it's much easier to use Fusion to generate this kind of code.

FIGURE 3.1

A fairly simple-looking Web page.

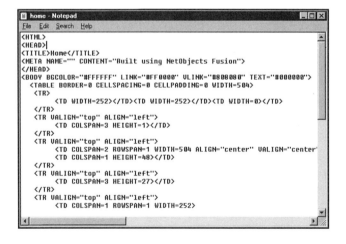

FIGURE 3.2

Figure 3.1 requires all this HTML — and there's more off-screen!

Web Pages

This raises the question: what is a Web page?

In the simplest of terms, a Web page is a block of HTML. It's not just any block of HTML: it has a beginning, a middle, and an end—marked off by HTML tags such as <HEAD></HEAD> and <BODY></BODY>.

In most cases, the HTML code that represents a particular page resides in a file. (However, this is not always the case. Some programs, such as the CGI programs I'll discuss later in this chapter, create HTML on the fly.) The file has an Internet address, called its *URL*. When your browser loads an URL (meaning that you've typed the location into the browser, or it's pointed to by a link on another page), the browser reads the HTML and creates a display based on the HTML's instructions.

Web Servers

But how does the browser contact the HTML file in the first place?

This is what Web servers do. A Web server is a simple software package that "listens" for requests from Web browsers for files, and, after checking a set of Webmaster-defined rules about who may download files, sends the file to the browser that requested the file. A Web server may do a few special chores, such as check to make sure that the requester has permission to read the file, add some kind of "macro" to parts of the HTML, or serve documents other than Web pages. For the most part, however, servers simply dish up whatever is asked for, without doing any heavy CPU work.

How is this different from getting files from a server on your local area network? It's not, really. Most non-UNIX LANs use a proprietary networking system: Macs use AppleTalk, for example. The Internet and intranets use a non-proprietary UNIX-based TCP/IP protocol. TCP/IP is an "open" protocol, meaning that its specifications are freely distributed. Currently, there's a movement underway to use TCP/IP in all kinds of LANs. TCP/IP is used on the Internet for historical (and cyberpolitical) reasons, and also because it works well with the gigantic network called the Internet, but it's just another protocol.

What this amounts to is a conversation between the browser and the server that goes something like this:

Browser: OK, what does that darned reader want now? He's clicked on the anchor that's associated with the URL http://www.selfhypnosis.com/home.htm. Let me look that up in DNS*...OK, there it is. *(dials phone)* www...selfhypnosis...com. *(taps foot impatiently)*.

Server: Hello! Would you like a cookie?

Browser: Sure, I'm looking for the file home.htm.

Server: OK. Say, you're not from that evil.com or uchicago.edu, are you? *(examines browser's credentials)*.

You: What's taking so long? I hate the Web.

Server: OK, here's the file. Enjoy!

Browser: Yeah. See ya, chump. *(Hangs up)* OK, tag tag tag-tag tag, I understood all that—here's what the page looks like.

You: Ah, the Society for Self-Hypnosis home page.

TIP

DNS stands for Domain Name Server. It's a sort of database of Internet addresses that usually resides on your gateway to the Internet, rather than on your personal machine.

What Is HTTP?

You've almost certainly heard of HTTP, if only by virtue of seeing it in the address of Web pages. What is HTTP, and how is it different from HTML?

HTML, as you saw in the preceding section, is a language used to control the way the browser displays a page. HTTP stands for HyperText Transport Protocol, and it's a system of conventions for transporting Web documents from machine to machine.

HTTP is a step further behind the scenes than HTML. You might think of HTTP as the procedures that the server and the browser follow so that each one knows that it's a Web page (and not something else) that the reader wants to download from the server.

HTTP isn't the only Internet protocol, of course. The most common protocols other than HTTP are summarized in Table 3.1.

TABLE 3.1

The most common Internet protocols.

Protocol	Use
ftp	File transfers
gopher	Gopher sites—a kind of pictureless forerunner of the Web
HTTPS	A secure version of HTTP, used for transporting encrypted information
NNTP	Newsgroups
SMTP	Email

The Anatomy of an URL

You have probably seen dozens or hundreds of URLs. Just for the record, let's examine the construction of URLs and what each part means. (If you didn't know already, URL stands for Universal Resource Locator, and it's simply the address of a page or other resource on the Internet.)

> **TIP**
>
> You will sometimes see the expression URI, which stands for Universal Resource Indicator, in places where you'd expect to see URL. It's just a more all-encompassing term for the same thing: every URL is also an URI. More than anything else, the distinction is about precision of language—not a difference in the syntax or content of the URL.

An URL may consist of several different parts, including the following:

- **Protocol Specification.** The protocol section of the URL tells the net-surfing browser how to handle a file. (The browser is usually, although not necessarily, a Web browser.)

  For example, the protocol `http:` tells the browser that the file is a Web page, and the protocol `ftp:` tells the browser that the location is a file that can be downloaded to disk. The browser handles these two kinds of files differently—by loading the file in the browser window in the case of `http:`, and by saving the file to disk if the protocol is `ftp:`.

  The protocol is always the first section of an URL. In the following examples, the protocol specification is italic:

  ```
  http://www.netobjects.com
  file:///home.html
  ```

- **Server Address.** Almost all URLs also contain the address of the server machine, usually as the machine's human readable nickname (such as `www.netobjects.com`) or occasionally by IP address (a sequence of four numbers, separated by periods, like this: `127.0.0.1`). URLs that specify a file on your local machine (such as `file:///home.html`) don't contain a server address.

  The server address follows the protocol name in the URL. In the following examples, the server address is italic:

  ```
  http://www.netobjects.com
  http://www.mcp.com/hayden
  ```

- **Port number.** Sometimes, a server machine is handling several different Internet services at once. For example, a single machine might serve one Web site to the Internet at large and another Web site to an Intranet of private users.

  Because the server has the same address in both cases, the fiction of port numbers was invented. (You might think of port numbers as similar to apartment numbers, which are used to distinguish different residences that share the same street address.) Port numbers are an extension to the server address, and they help the server know which software process should handle a particular request.

  Often, port numbers are left off URLs because each kind of server software "listens" for requests on a default port. If, however, you find a port number in an URL that you want to link to, it's important to include it when you enter the URL in the Links dialog box.

  The port numbers are italic in the following URLs:

  http://www.netobjects.com:*80*
  http://www.uchicago.edu:*80*

- **File Paths and Name.** In many cases, the URL specifies the path and name of the file to be served. (If the filename isn't specified, most servers send out some sort of default file.) Almost all servers allow some sort of directory structure within the folder that contains the files to be served, so that any path information is included with the filename.

  For example, if you're using MacHTTP "out of the box," your files that need to be served reside in a folder called "MacHTTP Software & Docs" along with the MacHTTP application. If you're serving a file called "page.html" that's in this folder, no path name needs to be specified, and the page's URL resembles the form here:

  http://www.your_organization_name/page.html

  If, however, you're serving the same file from inside a folder named "pages," the URL must include the file's path, like so:

  http://www.your_organization_name/pages/page.html

Forms

You've probably seen a few forms in your net.travels. Forms, like the one shown in Figure 3.3, are special Web page elements that enable readers to enter data and send it back to the server. They're often used for online purchases, member applications, and subscriptions to mailing lists. You'll also see forms when you download free software. Beware: before you get the goods, you'll need to provide some basic marketing information, and you'll probably get stuck on a few mailing lists.

FIGURE 3.3

A form that enables readers to send information to a Web server.

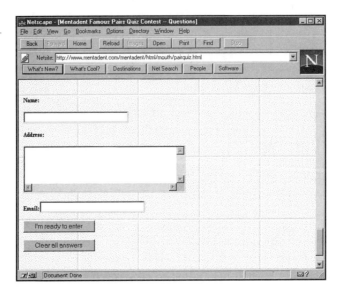

How Do Forms Work?

After a reader has entered information into a form and clicked the appropriate send button, the Web browser packs up the user's information and sends it to the URL specified in the form's HTML. (I'll cover how the address is specified and how information is coded in Chapter 11.)

As I mentioned earlier, almost all Web server software provides one basic set of functions: to send files to authorized requesters. Servers aren't designed to handle the data submitted by forms. They must pass it along to another application on the server's side of the connection that will handle the task of data processing.

The applications on the server side that handle the data processing are called CGIs. A CGI program accepts data from the form (and perhaps from a few other sources as well) and does something interesting with it. Common CGI functions include the following:

- Storing the form information in a database

- Mailing the form data to a specified address (usually the Webmaster)

- Mailing a confirmation message to the user

- Generating a new page on the fly, based on the form data

- Searching a database or file system on the server side

CGIs

CGI stands for Common Gateway Interface, and a CGI program or script is any application that can be invoked and controlled by the server software. The term CGI stands for the protocol by which the server and the application "talk" to each other.

It's a little misleading to suggest that a CGI is nothing more than a forms processor. Many CGIs are actually programs that generate Web pages on the fly, without handling any sort of form data.

The applications that process imagemaps are also CGIs—although these applications are crunching data of a sort, and it's not form data.

Figure 3.4 shows my favorite CGI of all time. You can find it at `http://www.scifi.com`, the Web site of the world's most perfect cable network, the Science Fiction channel. You can fill out a simple form at `http://www.scifi.com/schedulebot/`, and the CGI consults the site's database and creates a listing of all programs shown on the date entered in the form.

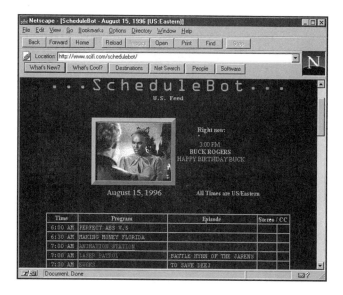

FIGURE 3.4

The schedule-making CGI at the Science Fiction channel—a brilliant use of CGIs.

In the bad old days, there weren't many ready-made or generalized CGIs—you had to write your own from scratch. It's still quite common for Webmasters to create their own CGIs for special purposes, and the capability to do so clearly separates weenies from wannabes, but there are plenty of CGIs that you can add to your site without doing a lick of programming. (We'll look at a few in Chapter 11.)

What this All Means for Web Site Designers

Serving Web pages can put a load on your server, especially if your site is getting thousands of "hits" every day, but it's nothing like the burden that CGIs add.

After all, a server is just chugging out files, not calculating your income tax or rendering a scene in 3D. File transfer is resource intensive, but it's not memory or CPU intensive. However, a CGI might possibly be calculating someone's income tax or rendering a scene in 3D for a reader. This kind of activity does eat up a lot of RAM and CPU time.

If the CGI is *asynchronous* (meaning the server doesn't wait for the CGI to send a response to one task before sending it another job), it may be calculating several readers' income taxes or rendering several scenes at once. If there are many CGI tasks going on simultaneously, everything will be slowed significantly because all the tasks are competing for the machine's resources. If a CGI is *synchronous,* it can only field one request from the server at any one time, but other readers will have to wait for the first one to finish.

There are ways to set up servers to alleviate this problem, such as splitting up CGI processing across many machines and limiting the number of connected users, whether they're using CGIs or not. You may never need to deal with this directly, but *you should know that forms and other CGI-based effects can require substantially more resources than conventional pages, especially on high-traffic sites.* If you're serving everything from a 386 to a Mac IIsi, you should probably limit the use of CGIs on your site. If you've got a couple of Sun Netras lying around, shoot for the baroque.

Client-Side Processing

One way around the problem of server overload is to move as much processing as possible from the server to the browser. After all (the reasoning goes), a high-traffic server has plenty to do anyway, and the reader is just running a browser. After the browser has downloaded and displayed the page, it's just sitting there—why not put it to work?

This is one of the big ideas behind JavaScript (*not* Java—I'll discuss Java in the executable code section next).

JavaScript is a scripting language that enables you to create little self-running programs that you build into your Web page, and it can do many activities that a CGI might do—display different pages based on the reader's address or the time of day, for example.

You can also use JavaScript to ease the load on your CGI when the form is submitted by preprocessing the form information.

For example, assume that a form entry will be entered into a database after it's sent to the CGI, and the database will be displayed somewhere else in the site. (This is how a guestbook works, for instance.) You can use a JavaScript script to make sure that a number entered into a phone number field has seven or 10 digits, or that a text entry doesn't contain any unusual characters that might munge (read: ruin) your database.

Of course, a CGI can perform the same checks—but why should it, if it has a dozen other forms to process at the same time? (JavaScript can do some activities that weren't meant to take the load off a CGI, and there are other ways to move the load onto the client machine, albeit unconventional. I'll talk about these techniques in the section, "Executable Code" later in this chapter.)

Plug-Ins (and Helper Applications)

It's likely that there won't be Web browsers in a few years. (Wait! Keep reading! You will still need NetObjects Fusion!) The folks at Netscape have been calling Navigator a "platform" or an "environment" for more than a year now, and it's rumored that Netscape employees are fined for uttering the word "browser." Microsoft has promised to integrate Internet Explorer into the Windows operating system so that it won't be a separate application.

What this amounts to is a change in the way that we think of browsers. Rather than applications that can be used to retrieve remote documents, browsers become an environment wherein programs can run, just as regular programs run in the MacOS, DOS, and Windows 95 operating system environments. (Earlier versions of Windows weren't operating systems in the strict sense of the term.)

Operating systems have certain built-in capabilities, such as the capability to copy, move, and rename files. Likewise, browsers have certain innate capabilities, such as the capability to retrieve and display files. You may also add new functionality to an operating system with a system extension, or you can run programs that do their own *thang* with the operating system's help. Likewise, you can use plug-ins to extend the browser's capability, or to run programs inside the browser window.

How Does a Plug-In Work?

Plug-ins arrived on the scene in the Fall of '96 with the release of Netscape Navigator 2.0. Microsoft quickly followed suit with Internet Explorer, and now, the browsers are more or less completely plug-in compatible. This means that a plug-in that extends Navigator will extend Internet Explorer in the same way.

Let's look at a more concrete example. Browsers aren't set up to read word processor files. Like an HTML document, something like a Microsoft Word document has invisible tags that tell the word processor how to format and display the text. (You've probably seen these tags if you've ever opened a WordPerfect document with Word, or vice-versa, using the wrong filter.) A Web browser doesn't know anything about word processor tags and characters, and it can't use them to control the display—it will show them as garbage if it shows them at all (see Figure 3.5).

FIGURE **3.5**

How an ordinary word processor document appears in the browser window: mangled.

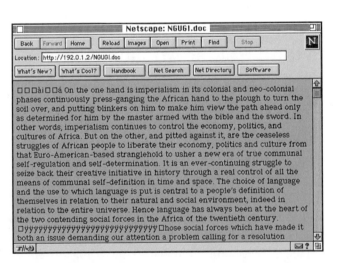

However, a plug-in can extend a Web browser's capabilities and enable it to interpret, or parse, kinds of content that it couldn't handle before. The

Word Viewer Word plug-in enables the browser to read Word documents that have been embedded inside Web documents or loaded as a file inside the browser window.

TIP

Windows users can find the Word Viewer plug-in at `http://www.browserwatch.com/` or http://www.inso.com/plug.htm. Inso, the plug-in's maker, promises a Mac version soon. In the meantime users can write a desperate note to `wordplug@inso.com`.

The Word plug-in is a fairly modest example of what plug-ins can do. Other plug-ins enable the browser to handle new image file formats, such as Macromedia FreeHand files, as well as movie formats, such as QuickTime and MPEG. The Shockwave plug-in, which you'll look at in detail in Chapter 10, can run interactive presentations created by Macromedia Director. The Adobe Acrobat plug-in allows the full version of the Adobe Acrobat Reader program (which has plug-ins of its own!) to run inside the browser window, almost exactly as if it were running in a window of its own.

What this Means for Web Site Designers

Many of the multimedia elements that you can add with NetObjects Fusion, such as Shockwave presentations, movies, and sounds, require that the reader install some sort of plug-in software. If the reader doesn't have the appropriate plug-ins installed, all the elements on the pages of your site will not be readable.

Certainly, the use of multimedia elements can make your site more appealing, which will attract attention to your site and encourage visitors to return. (Presumably, these are your goals.) On the other hand, many readers may not have the appropriate plug-in when they first visit your site. If readers can't figure out that they're missing a necessary plug-in, or they don't feel like interrupting the browsing session, they're not going to see your whole message.

It's a common practice to put some sort of notice at the top of pages that contain elements that require plug-ins (see Figure 3.6) as well as a link to a place where the reader can download the plug-in. Some people use a note in the body text of the page; some provide some sort of icon; some provide a big old horsy headline. This is an aesthetic decision you'll have to make.

FIGURE 3.6

*You should notify
readers that a page
or site contains
elements that
require a plug-in.*

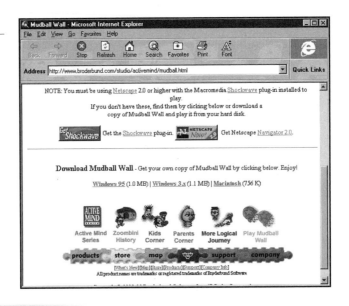

48

TIP

Every plug-in I've ever seen has been freeware—software companies make their money selling the software that creates the stuff that the plug-ins read. As long as the plug-in is free, you might as well provide links to the sites where users can download the plug-ins required by your pages. With the vendor's permission, you can also provide the plug-in from your own pages, but if you do, be sure to provide complete installation instructions.

You should also seriously consider limiting the number of different plug-ins required to read your pages. (Several elements that all use the same plug-in are OK.) Even if the reader already has copies of all of the appropriate plug-ins— and they probably don't—each plug-in requires additional memory on the user's machine. Netscape Navigator is a complete memory hog already (12MB? Come on!), and it's doubtful that most readers on home machines will have space for a few MB more.

How Does a Helper Application Work?

Before the advent of plug-ins, there were helper applications. Like a plug-in, a helper application handles the kinds of files that the browser doesn't understand. However, helper applications don't run in the browser window; they're separate applications with their own windows (see Figure 3.7) that are remotely controlled by Navigator or Internet Explorer.

FIGURE 3.7

*A helper applica-
tion runs in its own
Window.*

For the most part, the browser's interaction with the helper application consists
of passing off the file. The browser gives an image to an image-handling program
to open and a text document to a text-handling document, and that's the end of
the transaction. The helper application doesn't usually send any information
back to the browser or interact with it after the file has been loaded.

Helper applications aren't widely used anymore, because the helper applications
can't usually interact with the browser or make Web transactions. Plug-ins,
which *can* interact with the browser, can handle most of the commonly used file
formats that helper applications used to take care of. With one notable exception—decompression utilities for downloaded files—none of the many browsers I
use on several different platforms has launched helper applications in the last
six months or so.

The bottom line: unless you're serving compressed files on your site, you may
never serve up media in a format that requires the use of helper applications by
your readers. In any case, NetObjects Fusion doesn't provide an easy way to
present files in this way: it's geared toward the plug-in approach, as it should be.

Executable Code

Plug-ins are a great system for extending the capability of the Web browser, but
they have certain limits and disadvantages:

- Plug-ins are adapted to handle particular kinds of files and can't be extended without updating the plug-in. Take the example of the Word file plug-in that was discussed previously. When Microsoft releases a new version of Word, the plug-in must be updated, and the new plug-in installed on reader's machines, before the browser can read the new kind of Word file.

- Although plug-ins are easy to install, it's disruptive to browsing sessions if the reader must go to another site, download a file that can be as large as 2MB, install the plug-in, and then restart the browser (or perhaps even restart the computer).

- Plug-ins work only in browsers that support the plug-in architecture. (As of this writing, this is probably not a significant issue—Navigator and Internet Explorer have a near-monopoly on the browser market.) However, why shouldn't an application be able to run inside the browser *and* inside an ordinary operating system window?

What Is Executable Code?

The disadvantages of plug-ins mentioned above have lead to the current wave of development in Web page technology. Webmasters are beginning to put *executable code* into Web sites—programs that run like applications inside the browser environment.

How is this different from plug-ins? Actually, plug-ins and executable code cover pretty much the same turf—they both run like any other application. The difference is where the files reside and what they do. A plug-in lives on the reader's computer and handles incoming files. Executable code is embedded in Web pages and runs itself—it *is* the incoming file. Some of the major differences between plug-ins, applets, and helper applications are summarized in Table 3.2.

TABLE 3.2

Helper applications, plug-ins, and applets.

	Helper Applications	Plug-ins	Applets
Platform-dependent	yes	yes	yes
Capable of running in browser window?	no	yes	yes
Capable of running as standalone application	yes	no	sometimes
Interacts with browser	Almost never	yes	yes
Where is it stored	reader's machine	reader's machine	server

Running executable code that you find in a Web page raises some questions about security. What will stop such an application from doing something stupid or malicious, such as deleting random files, or making a run on NORAD's computers from the reader's machine, or spying on the reader's activities and sensitive information like system passwords or credit card numbers?

WARNING

This isn't an issue that's unique to executable code embedded in a Web page. Any code that you download is potentially dangerous and can do stupid or malicious harm. If you don't know who wrote a piece of software, and you run it on your machine, you're putting yourself at risk. Web pages may make it a little easier to accidentally run a suspect file, but the principles are the same.

To address these issues, new tools have begun to appear that allow a reader to run software from Web pages with the assurance that their files and information are safe. Such tools include Sun Microsystems's Java programming language, Netscape's JavaScript language, Microsoft's ActiveX technology, and emerging technologies such as Sun's Tcl/Tk language.

How Does Java Work?

Java was designed by Sun as a programming language that is:

- **Small.** Java programs use minimal system resources and can run with a tiny budget of RAM. Thus, the applet can run on a wide variety of client machines, even machines with scant memory resources.

- **Simple.** C++, the language that Java is based upon is way too complicated. There are many features of C++ that are for historic, rather than practical, reasons. Java is meant to be a new language without the baggage or benefits of backward compatibility with other language.

- **Safe.** C++'s wide range of commands and capabilities enables the programmer to control the computer at a low, fundamental level (it also makes it easy for one mistake to mess up the computer at a fundamental level). Java's more limited command set makes it (theoretically) impossible for a program to invade the memory allocated to the system of other applications. This makes it safe for readers to run Java applets without crashing their systems.

51

- **Secure.** A Java applet cannot (in theory) do anything potentially harmful to the machine that it's running on. It can't read or write to the hard disk, or make network connections to machines other than the one it came from. It also cannot read system information.

Java programs are written in the Java language and compiled into a special kind of intermediate code that is interpreted by a Java Virtual Machine. "Java Virtual Machines" can be built into just about anything—a browser, an operating system, or even a microchip. Because the virtual machine has been ported to a number of platforms, and the Java program runs on the virtual machine, Java programs are effectively cross-platform.

Compiled Java programs are stored in a separate file from the Web page that contains them. The special <APPLET> tag is used to add applets to pages, and any situational information is passed to the applet via parameters of the tag (see Figure 3.8).

FIGURE 3.8

A Java program running in a browser window.

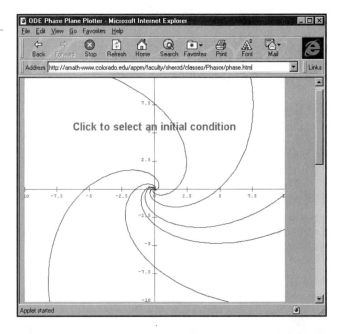

Java has extensive libraries for creating a graphic user interface and for communicating with Web sites, other applications, and databases. Although Java *is* relatively simple compared to C++, it's still too complex for casual programming. It's better suited for large, complex applications systems than for small, Web-based projects. (There are still plenty of small, Web-based applications out there, however.)

How Does JavaScript Work?

JavaScript, originally called "LiveScript," was developed by the folks at Netscape. JavaScript has security features similar to the features implemented in Java, and its syntax is remotely similar to that of Java. Otherwise, it's a completely different language with different uses and capabilities.

As discussed in the section on CGIs earlier in this chapter, JavaScript programs are particularly well-suited for tasks such as error-checking form entries, since JavaScripts can be attached to form entries so that they execute when a form component is manipulated by the reader. JavaScript doesn't provide support for graphics and network connections, so its scope of influence is limited to the text that appears in a single Web page.

In fact, JavaScript doesn't provide some of the basic tools available in most other programming languages. JavaScript doesn't even have array or list data structures, one of the most basic building blocks of most programs. In short, JavaScript is not actually meant for building complicated programs—it's used for attaching snippets of code to other Web page elements to make those elements more flexible and adaptive.

Figure 3.9 shows a relatively rare instance of a JavaScript program that shows up on-screen (most of it is behind the scenes work). It's a game called "The Incredible JavaScript Maze Game," developed by Steven Weinberger, and the idea is to use the buttons at the bottom of the form to navigate through a maze of asterisks in a text box. Of course, text boxes and buttons are standard form components, but this clever JavaScript has co-opted these parts for a non-form application.

Unlike Java, JavaScript isn't compiled—the source code is interpreted directly by the Web browser. There's no virtual machine involved, so a JavaScript script runs only browsers that support the JavaScript language. However, a JavaScript script runs the same way in any browser on any platform. As of this writing, Navigator and Internet Explorer are the only such browsers on the market that support JavaScript scripts.

How Do ActiveX Controls Work?

ActiveX controls is a technology developed by Microsoft to distribute executable code on the Web. ActiveX is derived from Microsoft's OLE (Object Linking and Embedding) 2.0 technology, which allows application developers to move functionality between applications.

53

FIGURE 3.9

The Incredible Java-Script Maze, a simple game written in JavaScript.

For instance, OLE technology can allow a software developer to paste an OLE-compliant spell checker from a Word processor program into a custom database application, in pretty much the same way you cut and paste text or an image. ActiveX is an extension of this technology that enables you to paste snippets of Visual Basic, Visual C++, or other code created with Microsoft Development tools into Web pages.

ActiveX components are created in Microsoft's Visual C++ development environment and other Windows-based development kits. There are many freely available ActiveX components that you can use and customize for your pages without doing a lick of programming. (You'll see in Chapter 13 how easy it is to manipulate ActiveX components with NetObjects Fusion.)

As of this writing, ActiveX controls work only inside the Internet Explorer browser—Navigator simply ignores any ActiveX controls that it finds. Netscape's plans regarding support for ActiveX in Navigator are still unknown.

What this Means to the Web Site Designer

Delivering executable code to users over the Net gives you more flexibility and makes it easier for readers, too. Executable code runs by itself inside the browser window so that you can include these kinds of elements without worrying about whether the reader has the correct plug-ins installed.

You *do* need to worry about whether the reader has the correct version of the right browser. Often, you'll see notices or icons on pages that recommend the use of a particular browser. Figure 3.10 shows an example of such a notice.

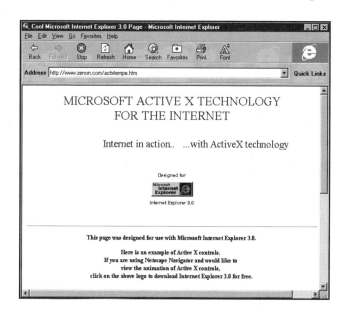

FIGURE 3.10

Typical notice that a page needs a particular browser to display executable code properly.

55

The main issue that many designers and Webmasters will face is the question of who will code the executable code to be included on the site. Granted, there are now many ready-made Java applets and ActiveX controls that you can add to your page, but there's no way around programming if you want to develop a totally new element.

(This is quite a bit different from the situation with plug-ins. The kinds of files that plug-ins process, like movies and alternate picture formats, can be created by a non-programmer, and many people already have the skills to develop these kinds of documents.)

Although there are plenty of programmers around, they aren't usually part of a standard PR/advertising agency/design studio team. If you've already hired a programmer as part of your design team, you're all set. Otherwise, you'll need to find someone to do your coding for you, or confine yourself to ready-made applets and controls. If you plan to learn to program custom elements yourself, plan on investing at least six months and several hundred dollars to get up to speed!

Bandwidth

How much time have you spent waiting for pages to load? Personally, I think I've spent nearly a month doing nothing but watching browsers' progress bars crawling across the screen.

In fact, I thought 9600 baud modems were quite zippy until I started using the original image-friendly Web browser, Mosaic. It quickly became clear that even the fastest modems can't load an average Web page as quickly as you can read it. Even today, a 28.8 modem can handle pictures and text adequately, but it's still too slow to download large files such as video and sound files at an acceptable pace.

The speed of the connection isn't the only issue, however. My connection to the Internet at the University of Chicago is very fast. Apple's site is connected to the Internet by an equally fast connection. However, when I recently downloaded version 7.5.3 of the Mac operating system, the transfer rate was *slower* than many modem connections. The problem wasn't the potential speed of the connection, but, rather, the number of people who were downloading from the Apple site at the same time.

This is what bandwidth is all about: how much information an Internet connection can carry and how quickly it can carry it. Bandwidth is often likened to a pipeline; only so much water can fit through the pipe at a time.

I've spent much more time on the highway than doing plumbing, so I tend to think of bandwidth in terms of traffic on an expressway. When information is sent over the Internet, it's broken into little discrete packets that are analogous to the cars on my metaphorical highway. The number of cars that can pass over a particular stretch of highway in an hour is influenced by a number of factors: the condition of the road, the speed limit, and the number of lanes on the highway.

Likewise, the bandwidth of a particular connection is influenced by factors such as the quality of the connection and the number of simultaneous signals the physical wiring can handle.

Although a stretch of highway might be able to handle a certain number of cars in an hour, that doesn't mean that a particular car or group of cars will be able to traverse that stretch in an hour. If there's bumper-to-bumper traffic, an individual car can't travel at full speed. Likewise, if a Web site is producing outbound information at the peak of its connection's capacity, even a reader with a fast connection to the Internet will experience slow downloads of pictures and other files from the site.

For this reason, it's prudent and "net.citizenly" to reduce the size of files that you serve from your Web site. This includes, but is not limited to, images, movie, sound, and other multimedia files.

What Can I Do to Limit Bandwidth?

There aren't any specific quantities or file sizes that I am prepared to recommend. Rather, the basic idea is to trim the size of files whenever possible. This can be accomplished in a number of ways:

- Make images smaller. (See Chapter 5 for a chart that relates the dimensions of images to their file sizes.)

- When saving line art in GIF format, use a small palette size—two bits or four bits, instead of eight bits.

- Limit the number of pictures in the document.

- Use compression utilities such as StuffIt and PKZIP to compress files that won't be viewed in the browser window, such as application files served via FTP.

- Make video and sound clips as short as possible.

- When possible, combine images into a single image. The images in Figure 3.11, for example, should probably be combined into one large image, rather than two separate files. (Technically, this is saving on the number of connections, rather than the size of the files. It's not actually saving bandwidth, but it's a good thing.)

TIP

There are some more esoteric precautions you can take to limit the bandwidth of your pages, such as looking at the direction of color gradients in GIF files. (Really!) If you're interested in net.ecology, you can find out more at the Bandwidth Preservation Society home page at `http://www.infohiway.com/faster/index.html`.

What this Means to the Web Site Publisher

Conserve bandwidth!

The longer it takes to load the pages in your site, the more readers you'll lose. For this reason alone, it's in your interest to make your sites as parsimonious as your muse allows.

Smaller file sizes will take a load off your server. This will also speed up the site for readers and make them happy.

Color Matching

You may have had the experience of looking at the same site on more than one monitor. Did it look the same? Sometimes colors will look the same from machine to machine, and sometimes they will look drastically different. (My PC's monitor, which I suspect had been dropped down a flight of stairs before I bought it, seems to add a strange greenish-brown cast to every color.)

I'm afraid that I'm not here to tell you the good news about monitors and color matching. Nowadays, expensive monitors can sometimes achieve almost adequate consistency under controlled lighting conditions. I suspect that most high-end monitors in expensive lighting booths are *not* being used to surf the Net, and so it follows they are not in the hands of your readers.

In short, you can't be sure what the colors you choose will look like on readers' monitors. It's a good idea to preview your site on as many machines as possible in order to get an idea of the range of variations with which you're working.

TIP

One of the areas you should be careful about is light colors against a light background. Recently, I worked on a site that used a gold color for text links so that the links could both show up against a white background and reverse out of dark colors. I settled on a color that worked fine on my monitor, only to discover that it was nearly illegible on every other machine I used to look at the page.

For the most part, colors will be in the same ballpark, or at least the same time zone, from machine to machine.

Resolution and Bit-Depth

Apart from the general issue of color-matching, there is a fairly wide range of resolution and bit depth between machines. Strictly speaking, this depends on the video card driving the monitor more than the monitor itself, but both are involved, so it's practical to discuss the two as one system.

Resolution (in this context, anyway) refers to the number of pixels that the monitor can display. This is usually measured for the whole display: that is, the video driver can be configured to display a screen of 400×600 pixels, or 600×800 pixels, or 1000×1200 pixels. Most machines can be configured to display at more than one resolution setting.

Closely related is the issue of bit-depth. Each pixel in the display can be set only to a certain number of colors or levels of gray: most machines support 16 or 256 colors, quite a few support thousands of colors, and many machines used in desktop publishing environments support millions of colors. In most cases, the user must make a compromise between resolution and bit depth—a machine might show thousands of colors at a 600×800 resolution, but only 256 colors at 1000×1200.

Web pages will vary in size according to the resolution of the display. The lower the resolution of the display, the larger and blurrier the image will appear. The difference is usually fairly subtle, but it can be noticeable.

Bit depth can be a bit more problematic. A solid color that looks fine with your $4,000 monitor and video card may not display properly on screens that support only 256 colors. In fact, it can look pretty darn bad. To have the best preview of what a color will look like on a reader's screen, set your monitor to 256 colors, even if it can support more colors. The basic color-matching issues described at the beginning of this section will still apply, but your monitor will be closer to the reader's if it's set to a modest bit depth.

What this Means to the Web Page Designer

The Web is a great tool for delivering color pages at low cost—you certainly can't achieve the same effect that you can on the Web on paper with the same budget. However, when you use the Web, you lose control over how closely the finished project will match the colors (and even dimensions!) of what you designed.

For most people, the color match will be close enough. If you're very discerning (read: picky), do your pages in black and white, or repeat this handy mantra: "Let it be."

If you're creating a catalog Web site for a clothing or art supplies manufacturer, you probably should include some sort of disclaimer underneath pictures of illustrations of merchandise, something like *All computer monitors display colors differently. Product may not appear exactly as shown on-screen,* so that potential buyers are aware of the color issues.

Typography

I love typography, and sometimes it makes the Web frustrating. The features that I look for in good type—correct spacing between letters and between lines, columns of the right width, justified text, or a nice even rag—are pretty much ignored by Web browsers, who just dump the text on-screen and go on to other issues. Although NetObjects Fusion tries to address some of these problems, it can't add nuances that the browsers don't yet support.

Let's take a look at what you can control, what you can't control, and what you may be able to control in the future.

Screen Fonts, PostScript Fonts, and TrueType

As you may know, there are three major kinds of font formats used to display and print type with computers. They include the following:

● Screen fonts

● PostScript fonts

● TrueType fonts

The way these fonts are used to create and display Web pages varies from machine to machine. You might use a TrueType version of Times to create a Web page with NetObjects Fusion on your machine, but the reader's machine might use a combination of screen fonts and PostScript fonts to create the display.

Screen Fonts

As the name suggests, screen fonts are used to display type on-screen. Screen fonts have the following characteristics:

- They are made of bitmaps.

- They come in particular sizes, such as 10 pt. or 12 pt.

- They don't scale well.

- They print with jaggy edges when sent to a laser printer.

- They aren't capable of being copyrighted, and are freely distributed.

PostScript Fonts

PostScript fonts are used to print fonts with a PostScript-compatible laser printer. Usually, a computer displays a PostScript font on-screen with its screen font equivalent, and when the page is sent to a laser printer, it substitutes the PostScript font. PostScript fonts have the following characteristics:

- They are made up of tiny programs that describe how to draw the characters.

- They are too complex to display on-screen on all but the fastest machines.

- They don't have particular sizes—there's only one PostScript file for each font.

- They can be scaled to any size without distortion.

- They print smoothly when sent to a PostScript-compatible printer.

- They are able to be copyrighted, and are usually sold as commercial software.

TrueType Fonts

TrueType fonts were developed by Apple. The idea behind TrueType is that the same font should be used to both display the font on-screen and to print the font with a laser printer. As it turns out, TrueType isn't widely used on the Mac, but is widely used on Windows machines. TrueType fonts include the following characteristics:

- They don't have a particular point size.

- They scale smoothly.

- They print smoothly to a laser printer.

61

- They aren't very good for producing high-end output for conventional printing.

- They are capable of being copyrighted, and are usually sold as commercial software.

You can see the problem: there are several possible ways that a user's machine can be configured, and there are good reasons for each kind of configuration. Furthermore, because the most flexible kinds of fonts are commercial software, they can't be freely distributed for readers.

As a result, there's no way to create a page that's guaranteed to appear with type in a particular font and size. Although proprietary tags enable Web designers to specify a particular typeface in an HTML tag, many browsers will still substitute another face in its place.

Leading, Tracking, and Justification

There are some basic attributes of type that cannot be controlled in the current implementation of HTML. There are no tags to control these aspects of the type's layout, and browsers simply use default settings for these values. (Figures 3.11 and 3.12 illustrate these concepts.)

The attributes that can't be controlled include the following:

- **Leading.** The vertical space between lines of type.

- **Tracking.** The horizontal space between characters. Tracking refers to extra space added to a range of several characters, and it is closely related to kerning.

- **Kerning.** The process of adjusting the space between a particular pair of letters. Kerning can be done manually, to adjust words that just don't look right, and many PostScript fonts also contain automatic "kerning pairs" that adjust space between a problem pairs of letters, such as T and y.

- **Justification.** The process of adding space between characters and words so that each line of a column of text has exactly the same width.

- **Hyphenation.** Most page layout software provides fairly sophisticated control over hyphenation. Typesetters can control the maximum number of consecutive lines that are hyphenated, the minimum length of words that can be hyphenated, and similar settings. Browsers don't provide any hyphenation at all, so there's clearly no control over how hyphenation works.

11 pt. type with 13 pt. leading

There are some basic attributes of type that can not be controlled in the current implementation of HTML. There are no tags to control these aspects of the type's layout, and browsers simply use default settings for these values.

11 pt. type with 15 pt. leading

There are some basic attributes of type that can not be controlled in the current implementation of HTML. There are no tags to control these aspects of the type's layout, and browsers simply use default settings for these values.

11 pt. type with 22 pt. leading

There are some basic attributes of type that can not be controlled in the current implementation of HTML. There are no tags to control these aspects of the type's layout, and browsers simply use default settings for these values.

FIGURE 3.11

Leading: beyond the scope of HTML.

63

Loosely tracked text

There are some basic attributes of type that can not be controlled in the current implementation of HTML. There are no tags to control these aspects of the type's layout, and browsers simply use default settings for these values.

Tightly tracked text

There are some basic attributes of type that can not be controlled in the current implementation of HTML. There are no tags to control these aspects of the type's layout, and browsers simply use default settings for these values.

FIGURE 3.12

Tracking and kerning—beyond the scope of HTML.

Type
book
flood
Kerned characters

Type
book
flood
Unkerned characters

There aren't compelling technical reasons why things like tracking, justification, and other typographical issues can't be controlled in a Web page. HTML was meant to be simple, so no one anticipated the need for this kind of refined control over type. (Indifference to ergonomic and aesthetic issues is part of the UNIX creed, anyway.)

In fact, it's likely that future implementations of the HTML specifications will offer support for some or all of these attributes of the way type is set.

Typographical Attributes You Can Control

Some attributes of type are not included in the HTML specification, but *are* supported via special tags developed by Netscape or Microsoft. These attributes include the following:

- **Font.** Despite the technical difficulties detailed previously, it's possible to use Microsoft's <FONT> tag to specify the typeface of text displayed by Internet Explorer.

- **Size.** Netscape's implementation of the <FONT> tag enables the Web page designer to have some control over the size at which type is displayed. You can't display type at any arbitrary size, but you *can* make a font four notches bigger and smaller. Different browsers may implement a +2 size in different ways. Internet Explorer supports this special tag.

- **Color.** Netscape's <FONT> tag also enables you to select the color of type. Internet Explorer also supports this tag.

(You'll see how to control these attributes by using NetObjects Fusion in Chapter 5.)

What this Means to the Web Page Designer

The race is on to develop new font technologies for the Web, and by the summer of 1997, this section will probably be out of date. Adobe, the largest manufacturer of PostScript fonts, and Microsoft, champion of TrueType, have announced a new font technology called OpenType tailored to the needs of Web page designers.

Now that a whole generation of WYSIWYG HTML editors has arrived, it's likely that most humans will get out of the HTML-editing business. Such a change makes it even more likely that Netscape and Microsoft (who each offer their own WYSIWYG editors) will introduce tags to control leading and tracking, even if such tags never make it into the official HTML specification.

In the meantime, you'll just have to let your site's typography be less than perfect. (At least NetObjects Fusion offers you the easiest control over the effects you *can* control.)

Security

The messages that travel over the Internet—your Web pages and information that readers submit via forms, for example—pass through a variety of public and private machines that act as relay stations. Each machine in the chain receives packets of information and routes them along to another machine. This structure makes the Internet robust because messages can be routed around damaged or missing pathways. The same structure makes your messages vulnerable because anyone who controls a relay machine can read your message.

How real is this threat? There are billions of packets out there, and the bad guys can't read 'em all. The odds are probably in your favor: an eavesdropper has to sort through `alt.imploding kibo` and the Olivia Newton John page to zero in on your credit card number.

On the other hand, there are some bad guys out there, and they're messing with *somebody's* stuff. The only way to be sure that you and your readers are protected is to take precautions.

Protection from Eavesdropping

65

Let's suppose you're designing a site for a retail company that wants to sell products over the Internet, and your client wants customers to be able to make credit card purchases by using forms on the site.

If you've ever submitted a form with Netscape, you've probably seen the dialog box shown in Figure 3.13. This is bound to discourage people from sending credit card numbers over the Net. What can you do to assure customers that their personal information is safe?

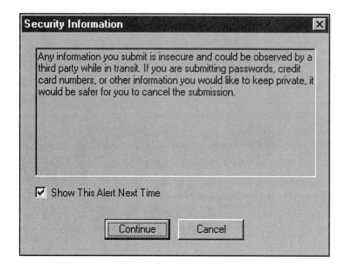

FIGURE 3.13

The biggest barrier to commerce on the Web.

You can use a secure server. When a browser communicates with a secure server, all messages between the browser and the server are encrypted with a (presumably) unbreakable code. Even though eavesdroppers can still read your packets, they can't decode them.

Netscape's Folly

You may have read about a bug in Navigator's implementation of this security model. Although the form of encryption used by Navigator is powerful, Netscape used a predictable random number generator to create code keys, which compromised the power of the technique. This bug has been fixed.

When Navigator is engaged in a secure session, similar to the one shown in Figure 3.14, the browser displays a blue bar at the top of the window's content area, and the broken key icon at the bottom of the Navigator window turns into a solid key icon. Furthermore, Navigator presents a reassuring alert box when the user submits a form securely, rather than the warning shown in Figure 3.13.

FIGURE **3.14**

Navigator offers a secure mode so that readers can safely transmit credit card numbers and other sensitive information.

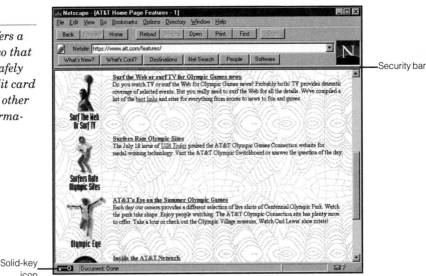

Security bar

Solid-key icon

Protection from Fraud

Ambitious villains can do more than eavesdrop on your conversation— savvy bad guys can masquerade as a server and fool a browser into thinking that a page coming from the bad guys is a page coming from you! As you can imagine, there's plenty of trouble to be caused here.

Use of a secure server solves this problem. When a reader connects to a site that is being served with a Netscape-style secure server, the reader may examine the site's certificate (see Figure 3.15). Certificates cannot be forged, so a reader can know with absolute certainty where a secure site is coming from and who it belongs to.

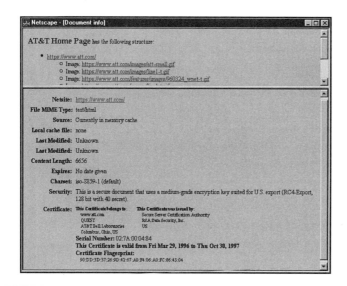

FIGURE 3.15

A site's certificate: an iron-clad guarantee to the reader that the site is what it claims to be.

67

TIP

To look at a site's certificate from Navigator, choose **View→Document Information.** Remember, this applies only to secure sites.

Passwords

Many sites require the reader to enter a name and password to enter the site or to view certain pages on the site. There are two main points to remember about passwords:

- Passwords don't provide any security measures! Just because the reader uses a password to enter a site doesn't mean that the transactions between the server and the browser are protected. *Only a secure server can encrypt a session.*

- Passwords are there to protect your site, *not* your readers. The idea is to keep track of who logs onto your site and to prevent unauthorized users from looking at your pages. For example, you might use a password to protect pages that serve alpha versions of an application so that only authorized testers can get to the pages and download the software.

What this Means to the Web Site Designer

Site security is implemented by the server software—not in the site design. To encrypt transactions and provide certificates, you need to set up a secure server. Most server software has built-in support for passwords. You can't implement these features with NetObjects Fusion or in HTML.

This doesn't mean that you can't design with security in mind. Here are a few ways you might adjust your site if you're using security features:

- As of this writing, Microsoft's plans for security are still under development. If you want to serve your site securely by using Netscape's secure server, you should think twice about adding Internet Explorer-specific components, such as ActiveX controls, to your pages.

- The encryption and decryption process takes time, and secure sites load more slowly than other sites. Thus, you'll want to design your site so that as few pages as possible are served securely. You may want to consider creating a separate site tree for each set of pages.

- You may also want to refer your readers to documentation on Network security so that they can make informed choices about sending personal information via a net connection. Point your readers to http://home.netscape.com/comprod/server_central/config/secure.html or http://www.rsa.com for introductory tutorials on the security features of Netscape Navigator.

Summary

In this chapter, you covered enough about the workings of the Web to help you make some decisions about your site's design. Specifically, you learned the following information:

- How Web pages are comprised.

- How servers and browsers work together.

- How forms are handled, and what a CGI is.

- The difference between server-side and client-side processing.

- What plug-ins are, and what they do.

- What helper applications are, and how they work.

- How executable code (applications) can be delivered via Web pages.

- The current limits of color matching on the Web.

- The current limits of typography.

- How Web security works.

In the next section of the book, we'll examine each of NetObjects Fusion's view modes in turn. Chapter 4 begins with a look at Site view.

URL Roundup

- The world's grooviest CGI:

  http://www.scifi.com/schedule.pl

- The Microsoft Word reader plug-in, Word Viewer:

  http://www.browserwatch.com/

- The Bandwidth Preservation Society:

  http://www.infohiway.com/faster/index.html

- Security Information:

  http://www.netscape.com/comprod/server_central/config/
  secure.html
  http://www.rsa.com

PART

II

Five Ways to Work with Your Web Site

Using Site View to Plan and Organize Your Site

Site view is the simplest of the five view modes. There isn't a huge array of tools to choose from, and the basic currency of Site view (page icons) is easy to understand and manipulate.

This doesn't mean that Site view isn't important. You'll probably make your most important design decisions here, for this is where you'll decide upon your site's overall organization, its themes and agendas, and how the information you present connects together and to the world outside.

Structure View and Outline View

Many designers start work on a new project by creating a thumbnail sketch of the project on paper. Each thumbnail represents a page or spread of the publication, and shows the format and content of the page. A complete set of thumbnails serves as a guide for adding the project's content to the proper position in the project's layout. Figure 4.1 shows a thumbnail created by my designer friend Jeff Hall, who did my so-called real job while I was writing this book.

Likewise, writers usually develop writing projects by outlining. For example, I outlined this book by deciding on the section titles (introduction, view modes, and advanced topics), then the chapter titles, and finally the chapter section heads. After the outline was completed, I started filling in the actual content. The titles and heads that you see in this book are taken directly from the original outline.

FIGURE 4.1

A designer's thumbnail used to plan the layout of an application.

Thumbnails and outlines are a sensible way to organize a huge amount of material, and it makes sense to develop a Web site—especially one that contains more than three or four pages—with the same kind of technique.

In fact, many Web site designers have used pencil and paper to create thumbnail sketches of Web sites before any actual HTML was coded. Figure 4.2 shows my notes from a meeting at which a complicated Web site, containing several independent paths through the site, was designed.

Using NetObjects Fusion, you can create this kind of thumbnail on-screen, and NetObjects Fusion creates the pages and links that comprise your site by using your thumbnail sketch. Even if you "think with a pencil," NetObjects Fusion makes it easier to transfer your design from paper or a chalkboard to a working Web site.

TIP

You don't have to publish all the pages that you include in your thumbnail/outline, as you'll see in the "Editing Niceties" section. So plan big and include everything you want to put in your Web site in the outline, even if you're not ready to implement every page right away. You can leave unfinished pages out of the published site until they're ready.

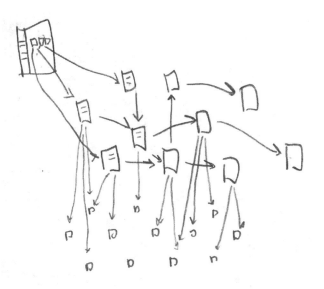

FIGURE 4.2

A pencil and paper sketch of a Web site design.

Nodes, Parents, and Children

You've already been introduced to NetObjects Fusion's handling of pages in Chapter 2. In default mode (when the Structure view button in the Secondary control bar is clicked), ordinary pages are represented by yellow, shield-shaped icons. If you click the Outline View button (also in the Secondary control bar), you can see the site structure in a form that may be familiar to you: a file tree list that looks suspiciously like something you'd see in a Windows 95 explorer window or a Mac Finder window in Outline mode (see Figure 4.3).

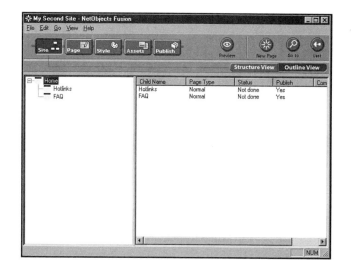

FIGURE 4.3

The site in Outline View mode looks much like a simple file directory.

> **TIP**
>
> This similarity between the diagram and a file directory isn't too surprising. Both Macintosh and Windows file systems—in fact, all modern file systems—are based on tree structures. What's special about a tree structure is that it's recursive: any part of the tree looks like the whole tree. Thus, you can put any folder inside any other folder, which is in turn inside another folder.

Changing between Structure View mode and Outline View mode doesn't change the structure of the site at all. They are just two different ways of looking at the same set of relationships.

The items that make up a hierarchy diagram (in this case, Web page icons) are called *nodes*. A node can have several connected nodes below it in the diagram; these nodes are called the node's children. The connected node above a node in the diagram is the node's parent. A node can only have one parent, but many children. (It's similar to a file system: a folder can contain several folders, but it can only be inside one folder at any time.)

All the children of a particular node are called *siblings* of one another. Rows of nodes, whether they are siblings or not, are called *levels*. The top node of the tree is called the *root*.

These relationships are illustrated in Figures 4.4a and 4.4b:

- Node a is the root.

- Nodes b1, b2, and b3 are the children of node a.

- Node a is the parent of nodes b1, b2, and b3.

- Nodes b1, b2, and b3 are siblings.

- Nodes b1, b2, and b3 are all members of the first level.

- Nodes c1 and c2 are the children of node b1.

- Node b1 is the parent of nodes c1 and c2.

- Nodes c1 and c2 are siblings.

- Nodes c1 and c3 are *not* siblings. Nodes c5 and c6 are *not* siblings.

- Nodes c1, c3, c5, and c6 are all members of the second level.

- Node d1 looks a little funny…it's a special case that you'll learn about later in the "Kinds of Nodes" section in this chapter.

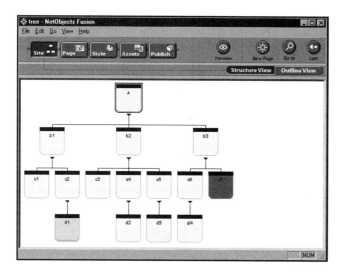

FIGURE 4.4A

A complex hierarchy diagram in Structure View mode.

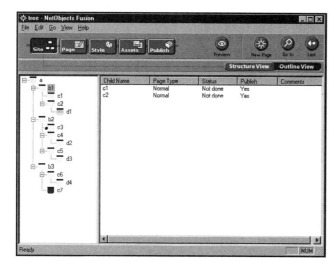

FIGURE 4.4B

A complex hierarchy diagram in Outline View mode.

77

Editing the Site Structure

If you're experimenting with site design, you'll probably want to try different structures to see which best suits your site's particular needs. Fortunately, it's as easy to move pages around in the tree diagram as it is to create them in the first place.

I've included a copy of the site shown in Figures 4.4a and 4.4b on the *NetObjects Fusion Handbook* CD-ROM. It's called tree.nod, and you can find it in the folder / Book/Sites/Tree. You can use this file to practice tree-pruning—just drag the whole tree folder to the NetObjects Fusion folder on your hard drive. Follow these steps:

1. To move a node in Structure View mode, drag it onto its new parent or one of its new siblings—let's call this the target node.

   When the node that you're moving is over the target node, the target's outline turns red, and a red arrow appears to show the moving node's new location.

2. When you've got an arrow that points to where you want the new node to go, let go of the mouse button. The new node pops into its new home automatically.

   For example, let's say that you want to move node d3 so that it's the child of node c7, rather than c5. Grab node d3 by the yellow part (not the title or the black bar at the top) and drag it onto node c7. Notice that as you move the node over c7, you can make the red arrow point left, right, or down. When the arrow points down, let go; d3 is now the child of node c7.

3. To move a node in Outline View mode, drag the node to be moved onto its new parent. For example, you can move node d3 back where it was by dragging it onto node c5. *Don't* move the node onto a prospective sibling; all nodes are added as children to the target node in Outline View mode. (For this reason, I think it's a little easier to edit in Structure View.)

4. When you move a node that has children, the children move along with the parent. For example, if you want to promote node c6 to a b-level node, drag it onto node b3 and drop it when the arrow points to the right. As you can see in Figure 4.5, node c6's child, d4, has been promoted to a c-level node.

As you may recall from Chapter 2, you can delete nodes by selecting the node and choosing **Edit→Delete Page** and by clicking the Delete key on your keyboard after selecting the node. When you delete a node, all its children are deleted with it. *You can't undo node deletions with **Edit→Undo**, so be careful!* However, NetObjects Fusion gives you a reminder dialog box each time.

Editing Niceties

NetObjects Fusion has many special features that make designing and project managing large, complex sites a little easier. You can specify nonpublishing pages, add comments or color-coding to pages, or hide pages that are in your way in Site view.

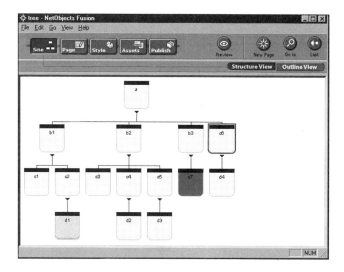

FIGURE 4.5

Editing the site tree — the children of a moved node move with it.

Designating Nonpublished Pages

As I mentioned in the introduction to this chapter, you don't have to publish all the pages in the site tree right away. In fact, you can designate which pages preview or publish on a page-by-page basis. Fusion will only add printing pages to your final site: nonpublishing pages will remain in the Fusion layout, but will not appear in navigation bars or be transferred to the Web server.

To turn off a page (mark a page as nonpublishing), do the following:

1. Click the page's icon in Site view.

2. Click the Don't Publish radio button in the Page tab of the Properties palette. A red dot appears in the black bar at the top of the page icon.

When you mark a page as nonpublishing, the name of the page is removed from all navigation aids on other pages, and no HTML page is generated by the Preview button or in Publish mode. However, the page stays in the site tree, and you can turn it on whenever you like. *The node's children are not affected, and are still published, although there may not be any links to the child nodes.*

WARNING

If you've already published your site on a Web server, turning off a page in NetObjects Fusion doesn't remove the page from the server. The page's HTML file must be removed by hand.

79

Marking Nodes

You can use colors to mark each of the nodes in your site tree. Marking a node in Site view doesn't change the appearance of the page, it's simply a tool to help you organize pages when you're designing your site. Node colors appear in both Structure View and Outline View modes.

For example, you might represent nonprinting pages with red nodes, pages that need corrections with blue nodes, and pages that contain forms with green nodes. Such a system can help you identify problem areas at a glance.

Or, you might want to mark different categories with different colors. Suppose that you're working on an online music magazine. You could mark feature story pages with blue, recording review pages with green, performance review pages with red, and so on. If you decide to juggle pages around later, you won't accidentally add a page to the wrong department.

To mark a node with color, use the following steps:

1. Click the page's icon.

2. Click the Page tab in the Properties palette.

3. Click the Color button. Click a color swatch in the color dialog box.

Adding Page Information

You can annotate your pages with more information, to help you plan and organize your site, and to make it easier to collaborate with others.

You can designate a page's status as "Done" or "Not Done." (By default, pages are marked as "Not Done.") A page's status is displayed when you view the page's parent in Outline View mode, and when you look at the page's information in the Properties palette. That's it...the page's status doesn't affect whether the page is published. It's just there to help you recognize problem areas. You can view or change a page's status in the Page tab of the Properties palette.

You also can add comments to a page. Comments appear only in the NetObjects Fusion site file. They're *not* included as comments in the page's HTML file, so you don't need to worry about your audience seeing information that you included for yourself and your collaborators. You might use this space for credits, a to-do list, or notes about special information that the page contains. The comments field is located in the Page tab of the Properties palette. You can add your name into the HTML generated by NetObjects Fusion by entering it in the Author field of the site tab.

Collapsing/Expanding Nodes

Large trees can be ungainly to work with, so you can hide all of a node's descendants without deleting them by collapsing the node. To hide a node's descendants in Structure View mode, click the black arrow that points down to the node's children. The node's children are hidden from view, and a tiny plus sign icon appears below the node to signify that the node contains hidden children. In Figure 4.6, node b3's children have been hidden. To make the descendants reappear, click the plus sign icon and the node expands. Hiding pages in this way doesn't remove the children from the site or "unpublish" them—it only hides them in Site view, so you can get an undistracted view of other parts of the site.

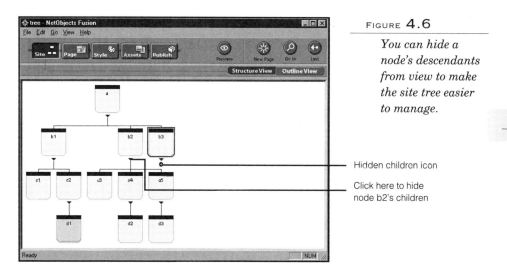

FIGURE 4.6

You can hide a node's descendants from view to make the site tree easier to manage.

81

Hidden children icon

Click here to hide node b2's children

To hide a node's children in Outline View mode, click the minus sign marker to the left of the node's name. The minus sign changes to a plus sign. To restore the descendants, click the plus sign. (It's exactly like closing and opening a folder in the Explorer window.)

Changing Magnification

After you have more than a few nodes on the site tree, it can be difficult to get an idea of the general layout of your site. Of course, you can scroll around as necessary, but it's helpful to see the whole site at once.

To solve this problem, NetObjects Fusion provides a set of magnifying glass tools that enable you to zoom in and out while in Site view. When you zoom out, you can see your site from a global perspective. A fully zoomed-out site can accommodate sites that are 40 nodes wide in a maximized window on a large screen, which should be quite adequate for almost all applications (see Figure 4.7).

To zoom out, choose the Zoom Out tool from the Tools palette and click within the site. To zoom in, click the Zoom In tool. (There aren't any special shortcuts or tricks, at least in early versions of the software.)

FIGURE 4.7

Maximum zoom.

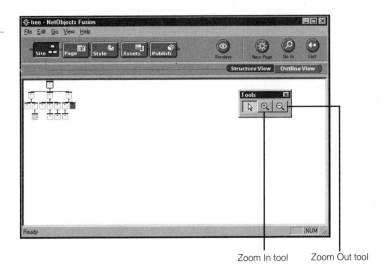

Zoom In tool   Zoom Out tool

Changing Orientation and Background Color

You can further customize the way that NetObjects Fusion displays the site tree. These controls are located in the View tab of the Properties palette.

- You can look at the site tree sideways, with the root at the left and child nodes to the right of their parents. (Structure View mode looks more like the Outline View mode this way.)

- You can change the background color against which the site tree is displayed by picking a new color from the palette.

Kinds of Nodes

Almost every node looks and behaves exactly the same way. However, there are a few special cases with which you should be familiar:

- **The root node.** The root node, or the site's home page, can't be moved—it's always the root. When you move a node, all the children of the node move with it, and all the nodes in the site are descended from the root.

- **Form pages.** You may recall from the discussion of forms and CGIs in Chapter 3 that CGIs are programs that handle forms and perform other tasks on the server side. Although CGIs are not Web pages, some CGIs generate Web pages on the fly—usually things like error-message pages and acknowledgment pages. Because these on-the-fly pages are generated by the CGI, rather than by NetObjects Fusion, they don't appear in Site view—they are, practically speaking, invisible nodes. Links from these pages to other pages in your site must be handled manually, by configuring (or rewriting) the CGI.

- **Data pages.** As mentioned earlier in Chapter 1, NetObjects Fusion can easily create a set of pages, called *data pages*, that share a common framework and automatically generate an index of all the pages in the set. Data page nodes are automatically generated when you create an index for a set of pages, and the data page node is represented with a special stacked-page icon in Structure View mode (see Figure 4.8). Don't worry about the particulars of data pages right now. You'll learn more about them in Chapter 12.

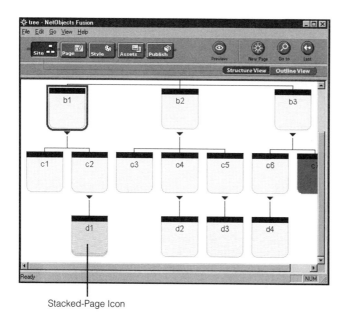

Stacked-Page Icon

83

FIGURE **4.8**

Data pages are represented with a special icon in Structure View mode.

For now, let's get a grip on what the data page icon represents:

1. Double-click the c2 page icon.

2. The little box on this page is called a data table, and it shows where an index of the data pages will appear on this page.

3. Return to Site view. Double-click the d1 page icon.

4. Notice that the Secondary control bar contains a new group of buttons with the label "Stacked Page___of___." Every one of these data pages has the same layout, but each page has its own data. Click the right and left arrow buttons in the Secondary control bar to flip through the pages in the stack.

5. Return to Site view. Click the c2 page icon.

6. Click the preview button. When page c2 is viewed in the browser window, it contains a complete index of the stacked pages contained in data page d1 (see Figure 4.9). You can navigate through the data pages by clicking on the square orange bullets in the index.

FIGURE **4.9**

NetObjects Fusion automatically generates an index to the contents of data pages.

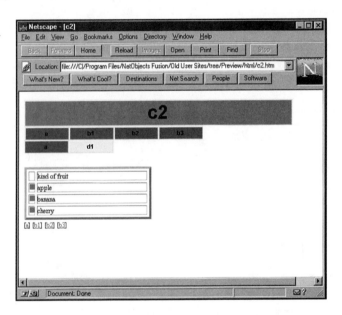

As you'll see in Chapter 12, data pages are automatically added to the site tree as children of the page that contains the data table, which indexes the data pages. That doesn't mean that they need to stay there, however, you can move a data page node anywhere you like in the site diagram, using the same drag-and-drop method you used to move ordinary nodes.

Creating Navigational Aids

After you've got a rough outline of your site's shape, you'll want to start thinking about how your users can navigate from page to page. As you saw during your tour of NetObjects Fusion in Chapter 2, visual navigational aids that link the pages of the site together are automatically generated for each page in the site.

The assignment of navigational aids to each page is based on the page's position in the site tree. As a result, the site's ease of navigation is closely related to the design of the site tree, and you'll want to look at each page's navigational aids as you design the site's structure.

NetObjects Fusion offers you some choices about how it creates navigation tools. Technically, you implement these sorts of choices in Page view, but because site design is inseparable from navigational issues, I will introduce navigation aid construction here.

Headers and Footers

Go to Page view. When you were goofing around with NetObjects Fusion in Chapter 2, you probably noticed that each page was divided into three sections. The home page (node a) of the tree site is shown in Figure 4.10.

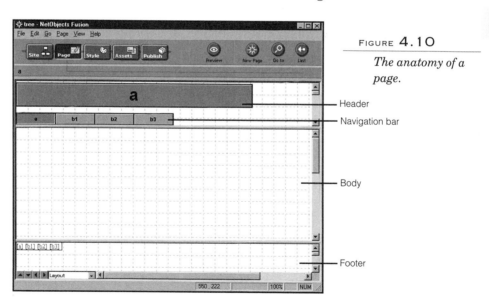

FIGURE 4.10

The anatomy of a page.

The topmost area (above the first horizontal bar) is the page's header, and the bottommost area (below the second bar) is called the footer. You can move each of the bars by dragging them up and down with the selection tool. Only one section of the page is selected at any given time: to select an area, click inside it with the mouse. (You can see the tabs in the Properties palette change as you select different sections of the page.)

All of the header and *all* of the footer are included in the final page, even if parts of the header and footer are hidden in Page view. By default, headers and footers are included as a common element of every page. If you add a picture or text block to the header while you are viewing the home page, you add it to every page in the site.

TIP

The use of a single header and single footer for every page of the site is Fusion's default behavior. In fact, you can have a set of several headers and several footers and use different headers and footers on different pages. (You'll see how this relates to navigation, in particular, later in this chapter.)

In the simplest sense, a navigation bar is an object with properties similar to a text block or a picture. However, it's an object with a special property—the navigation tool varies its appearance according to the page that it's on.

For example, the navigation bar in the header of page b1 contains buttons that link to pages a, c1, and c2, while b2's navigation bar contains links to a, c3, c4, and c5. Although these appear to be different elements, they are really the same navigation bar, magically altered from page to page.

Skeptical? Try this experiment:

1. Select the navigation bar in the b1 page's header by clicking on it once.

2. Cut the navigation bar with the **Edit→Cut** menu command.

3. Take a look at other pages in the site. As you can see, the navigation bar has been removed from all the pages in the tree.

4. Go to page b2 in page mode.

5. Click in the header portion of the page. *This is very important!* If you paste into the body section of the page, the navigation bar will only appear on page b2.

6. Paste the navigation bar with **Edit→Paste**.

7. Look at the rest of the sites—the navigation bar has returned.

Adding a Navigation Bar

There isn't a navigation bar tool. All the site templates included with the NetObjects Fusion package include navigation tools in sensible places, so you may never need to create one, but it's possible if the need arises.

Although the navigation bar is an object like a picture or a text box, you can't automatically create a navigation bar by drawing it on the page. Rather, you must use a special, somewhat nonintuitive procedure:

1. Go to any page.

2. Click inside the header area.

3. Click the header tab in the Properties palette.

4. Click the Navigation Bar button in the Add to Header group.

Modifying the Navigation Bar

Navigation bars are customizable, which means that you can control the look of the navigation bar and how the navigation bar links to other pages. You can change button style and link style, for example.

Button Style

A navigation bar can take several different forms. Usually, the navigation bar appears as an array of buttons, similar to the headers in the example pages that you looked at, or as text links, as in the footers of the example pages.

You can further customize the look of button style navigation bars by picking between "primary buttons" and "secondary buttons." Both styles of buttons function in exactly the same way: the only difference between primary and secondary buttons is the button's appearance.

To see what a style's primary and secondary buttons look like, click the Styles view button and pick the style's name from the list on the left. The primary buttons appear in the second row of the style window, directly below the style's banner. The secondary buttons appear in the third row beneath the primary buttons. Figure 4.11 shows the primary and secondary buttons of the Industrial style.

FIGURE 4.11

*Primary and
secondary buttons
of the Industrial
style.*

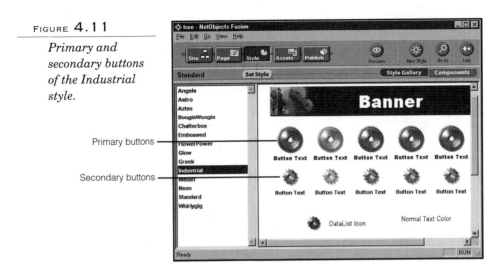

Primary buttons ———

Secondary buttons ———

Both primary and secondary buttons offer a highlighted buttons option. If a navigation bar is configured to use highlighted buttons, the current page's button appears in a special format—usually in a different color or a different style. (A button set's highlighted button appears as the second button on the left in the Style view display.)

If a navigation bar doesn't use highlighted buttons, all of the bar's buttons are identical, regardless of the page that contains the navigation bar.

You may also display a navigation aid as a series of text links. Very often, text-style navigation aids are included at the bottom of Web pages, as a compact way to reproduce the navigation bars at the top of the page. (If a user is reading a modest-sized Web page in a modest-sized browser window, it's likely that the navigation bar will scroll out of the window by the time the reader gets to the bottom of the page.)

WARNING

Button-based navigation aids are, in the end, images, and some users may view your pages with automatic image loading turned off, or even with one of those rare browsers that does not support images. If the only links on your page are button-based, readers who don't see your images can't navigate to other parts of your site...so it's a good idea to put text-based links somewhere on your page.

To set the navigation aid's appearance, use the following steps:

1. Click the navigation bar.

2. Click the Nav. Bar tab in the Properties palette.

3. Select Primary Buttons, Secondary Buttons, or Text from the Buttons group.

4. Click the Use Highlighted Buttons check box, if you want to use highlighted buttons.

5. Click the Include Home Page check box if you want to give visitors access to your site's root regardless of shown level.

Link Style

You can also control which level of the site tree appear in the navigation bar. Each of the four basic choices is shown with an icon in the Nav. Bar tab of the Properties palette, as illustrated in Figure 4.12

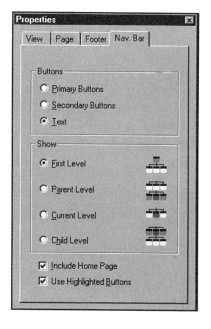

FIGURE 4.12

89

NetObjects Fusion enables you to control which page levels in the site tree appear in the navigation bar.

Let's relate each of these link styles to the example site shown in Figure 4.4a:

- **First Level.** When this option is selected, the navigation bar shows the first level of pages under the root node (nodes b1, b2, and b3 in the example site). Under this plan, every page in the site will use the same navigation bar because the links are not relative to the current page.

- **Parent Level.** When this option is selected, the navigation bar shows all the parent's sibling pages, *not* all the pages on the parent's level. For example, page d2's navigation bar includes links to c3, c4, and c5, but *not* to c1 or c6.

- **Current Level.** When this option is selected, the navigation bar shows the current page and its siblings, *not* all the pages on the current page's level. For example, page c4's navigation bar includes links to c3, c4, and c5, but *not* to pages c1 or c6.

- **Child Level.** When this option is selected, the navigation bar shows the children of the current page. Other pages on the children's level are *not* shown. For example, page b2's navigation bar includes links to c3, c4, and c5, but *not* to c1 or c6.

The decision to show the home page of the site (the root node) is independent of this choice. To show the site's home page in the navigation bar, click the Include Home Page check box in the Nav. Bar tab of the Properties palette.

Putting Navigation Bars to Work

Now that we've got the basics down, I've modified our abstract site tree so that it represents an online newspaper. (You can find it in the folder /Book/Sites/Newspaper.) Each b-level node represents one of the sections of the paper: the news section, the entertainment section, and the classifieds section. Each of these sections is made up of its own components: for example, the news section contains pages for national news and local news. Figure 4.13 shows the site tree of our online newspaper.

FIGURE **4.13**

Site tree of the net.gazette.

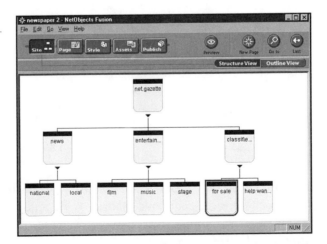

I have set the link style of the navigation bar to "child level." If you spend much time clicking around in the newspaper, you'll notice that the reader is directed down toward the bottom nodes of the tree. I'd like the reader to be able to browse each section by using the navigation aid, and to be able to switch between sections of the paper without going to the front page.

You don't need to limit yourself to a single set of link styles when you're designing your site. There are two ways you can extend a page's set of navigation aids:

- A header can contain more than one navigation bar. Each navigation bar can have its own link style.

- As I hinted earlier, NetObjects Fusion allows you to create more than one header style, and you can assign these headers on a page-by-page basis. Using a mix of navigation bars, it's possible to create a richly structured site.

TIP

One of the simplest and most elegant ways to add a second layer of links to a site is to use text links at the bottom of each page. The navigation bar in the footer is independent of the navigation bar in the header, and can have its own link style. In fact, NetObjects Fusion adds a first-level style navigation bar to the site's footer as a default. I've removed this navigation aid from the newspaper site to show how difficult it is to navigate with a one-way set of buttons.

Let's say that you want to add the section titles at the top of each page, rather than at the bottom.

1. Double-click any page in Site view.

2. Click inside the header area.

3. Click the Navigation Bar button in the Add to Header group in the Header tab of the Properties palette. A second navigation bar appears below the first.

4. Click the first navigation bar. Let's make this the navigation bar that points to sections of the paper. In the Nav. Bar tab of the Properties palette, make sure that the Primary button, First Level, and Include Home page are checked.

5. Click the second navigation bar. Let's use this button to navigate to particular pages within each section. In the Nav. Bar tab of the Properties palette, make sure that the Secondary button and Child Level are checked and that Include Home page is unchecked.

6. Depending on the style you choose for your site, you might want to nudge down the second navigation bar so that it's not bumping into the first.

7. Click the Preview button.

Figure 4.14 shows the resulting entertainment section page. The top row of navigation buttons enables the reader to navigate from section to section, and the lower level enables the reader to navigate to each of the entertainment subsections.

FIGURE **4.14**

Two layers of buttons at the section level—this looks great.

This is an improvement over the single set of buttons, but to be honest, it's still a pretty awkward solution. If you navigate down to the bottom level (say, the music page), there are no links to siblings. It would be nice if you could move from music to movies to stage without jumping back to the classified section. Even worse, both rows of buttons on the home page point to the section pages—it looks pretty stupid (see Figure 4.15).

What you'd really like is something like the following:

*   The home page contains navigation buttons to each of the section pages.

*   Each section page contains links to each of the subsections within the section and to the other main sections of the paper.

*   Each of the subsections contains links to the other subsections in the section and to each of the main sections.

FIGURE 4.15

The same set of navigation bars at the home page level. The two rows are redundant here.

Because each level of the site needs a special set of navigation bars, let's use multiple headers—one header for each level, each with the appropriate set of navigation bars.

93

1. Go to one of the pages on the middle level of the site tree, such as the "news" page.

2. Click the middle section of the page.

3. Click the Layout tab.

4. Take a look at the Header/Footer group at the bottom of the Layout tab. As you can see, the Header pop-up menu contains one entry—the default, Header1.

5. Most of the nodes in the diagram are at the bottom (subsection) level, so let's set up Header1 for subsections. There should be two navigation bars in the header already; make sure that the link style of the top navigation bar is set to First Level, and the link style of the bottom bar is set to Current Level with Show Home Page unchecked.

6. Let's create a new header. You're still in the news page, right? Click in the middle section of the page and click the New button next to the Header pop-up menu. Call the new header Header2.

7. Click inside the header section of the page. There should be just one navigation bar in the new header; click on the Navigation Bar button in the Header

tab of the Properties palette to add a second navigation bar. Click the Banner checkbox to add a banner. Set the link style of the bottom navigation bar to Child Level and make sure that Show Home Page is unchecked.

8. Go to the entertainment and classified pages and choose Header2 from the Header pop-up menu for each page.

9. Go to the home page. Click the New button next to the Header pop-up menu.

10. Click in the header area of the page and make sure that Banner is checked in the Header tab of the Properties palette.

11. Make sure that the navigation bar link style is set to First Level and Include Home Page is unchecked.

12. Click the Preview button.

Now the links at the top of the site point down, and the links at the bottom of the site point up so that maneuvering through the paper isn't a one-way trip.

TIP

Here's another practical use for tagging pages with color in Site view—you can use different colors to indicate different headers used by each page. You could even name the headers things like "red" and "blue" to make the relationship easier to remember.

You probably noticed the Footer pop-up menu when you were juggling palettes around in the last exercise. For the record, footers work in exactly the same way as headers; you can have more than one footer in your site and assign them to pages in exactly the same way. The Footer pop-up menu is located in the Layout tab in the Properties palette—this tab is visible when the middle section of a page is selected.

Handcrafting Links

The automatic links created by NetObjects Fusion are easy to work with, and they provide an easy way for users to navigate around your site. Sometimes, however, you may want to do special things with links: things like linking to pages on other sites in the Web or creating links between pages that aren't structurally related in the site tree.

As with automatic navigation aids, the procedures to build custom links into your site really takes place in Page view, rather than in Site view. However, you'll want to know how custom links work when you're designing at the architectural level, so I'll introduce the subject now.

Adding Links to Specific Pages

Suppose that the local news page in our newspaper site contains a story about the opening of a new movie theater. You might want to add a link from the news story to the theater's listings on the movie page. Because the pages aren't siblings on the site tree, no set of link styles will automatically connect these pages.

You can, however, manually link the pages together. I added a sample external link to the NetObjects Web site in Chapter 2, and it's just as easy to add internal links to one of your own pages.

Links can be associated with text, pictures (scans or line art created in other programs), and drawings (shapes created directly in NetObjects Fusion). You'll learn all about the finer points of creating and manipulating these elements in Chapter 5. For now, let's deal with simple instances of these objects—they all link in the same way, anyway.

Let's use a text string for our link:

1. Draw a text block on the local news page. (The text tool is the first icon in the second row of the tool palette.) Type in some text, something like: "Strand Theatre baffles a new generation of moviegoers with weekly showings of *Last Year at Marienbad.*"

2. Select the words "Strand Theater."

3. Click the Text tab in the Properties palette. Click the Link button.

4. Click the Page Link tab in the Link dialog box. (Actually, it's the default, so you probably don't need to click it.)

5. Enter the name of the page in the Page Name field. (If you're feeling lazy, you can enter "f" and get a listing of all the pages that start with the letter "f.")

I told you it was easy.

Adding Smart Links

Sometimes you'll want to add links to pages that have a structural relationship to the current page, without using a navigation bar to do so.

This kind of approach is widely used in online journals and literary magazines that use a strict page metaphor. Stories are divided into screen-sized pages, and each page features navigation tools at the bottom that enable the reader to move forward and backward in the manuscript. (Take a look at http://www.word.com for a look at this approach in action.)

Navigation bars wouldn't make a lot of sense in this kind of context. You probably *don't* want readers to jump from page 1 to page 3, so you don't want to provide links to all of the pages at once. On the other hand, you don't want to code all your links by hand, either.

NetObjects Fusion provides the "Smart Links" feature to solve this problem. Smart Links allows you to specify a custom link by using page relationships, rather than specifying a particular page. The example below shows exactly how this works.

Figure 4.16 shows what the site tree of such a literary magazine might look like. Each story has its own introductory page, and a series of pages, called page 1, page 2, and so on, which contain the actual content of the story. The reader can click through each of the pages without using a navigation bar at the top of the page. (You can find this site on the *NetObjects Fusion Handbook* CD-ROM in the folder /Book/Sites/Story.)

FIGURE 4.16

Site map of a page-based literary magazine.

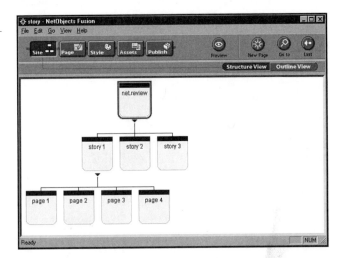

This time, let's attach our links to pictures, rather than text:

1. Draw a picture box in the footer area of the page. (The picture tool is the second icon in the second row of the Tools palette.)

2. NetObjects Fusion will present a file dialog box. Navigate to the folder /Fusion/Parts/Design Parts/Arrows/ and pick one of the left arrows from the list.

3. Draw another picture box and put a right arrow in it. (I've aligned the boxes with the left and right edge of the banner, but you can put them wherever you like.)

4. Select the left arrow picture box.

5. Click the Picture tab in the Properties palette.

6. Click the Link button.

7. Click the Smart Links tab in the Links dialog box.

8. Select Previous Page from the Link Types list in the Smart Links tab.

9. Using the same procedure as in steps 4–8, assign Next Page to the right arrow picture box.

10. Click the Preview button.

Try it—the reader can navigate back and forth through the story by using only the arrow key. (The example text shown in Figure 4.17 is stolen directly from Lewis Carroll's *Hunting of the Snark.)*

This approach allows a great deal of flexibility. If you decide that you want to separate the story into five pages, rather than four, you don't need to do anything to configure the arrow links—they rebuild themselves automatically.

NetObjects Fusion supports several kinds of smart links: to the site's home page, to the current page's parent page, to the current page's sibling pages (as you saw in the example above), and to adjacent pages in a data pages stack. (See the introduction to data pages in the "Kinds of Nodes" section earlier in this chapter, and an extended discussion in Chapter 12.)

FIGURE 4.17

A page with Smart Link navigation tools.

Linking to External URLs

As you saw in Chapter 2, linking to an external URL is as simple as typing the URL into a dialog box. If you're familiar with URLs and how they work, you can skip this section and go on to the "About Anchors" section that follows. If you're not sure what an URL is, or if the details are a little fuzzy, this section will be of interest to you.

URL is an acronym for Universal Resource Locator, and as this name may suggest, it's a location—like a Post Office address. In Chapter 2, I described the Internet as a giant file system. An URL is simply the address of a file and instructions about what to do with the contents of the file.

As a general rule of thumb, if you can load an URL with your Web browser by typing the URL into the browser's location field, you can link to the URL from your Web site. Naturally, there are a few special cases:

● Although you can load local files from your machine by using the `file://` (or in Internet Explorer, `c:/`) protocol, you can't use the external links dialog box to link to URLs of this type; the reader's browser will look for the files on the user's machine, and they won't be there.

● Browsers sometimes use URLs as a sneaky way to send information to CGIs: For example, if you search for the word "NetObjects" using the Infoseek search service, you'll notice that the browser loads the URL: `http://guide-p.infoseek.com/Titles?qt=netobjects&col=WW&sv=IS&lk=noframes`, or something similar. The stuff after the question mark is information that the browser sends to the server as part of the query. Although you *can* link to this URL, search data and all, you shouldn't. Part of the data contains information about the configuration of your browser, and users who submit the same string with a different browser may well get unintended (that is, weird) results.

- Some browsers, such as early versions of Netscape Navigator, load news articles in the browser window and include an URL for the article. (Such URLs take the form nttp:*seemingly-random-string-of-letters and numbers.)* You can link to such URLs, but they will almost certainly expire within a few days.

About Anchors

Some of you who have created Web sites with other tools are probably wondering about anchors. An anchor is like a bookmark in the middle of a long page. You can create links to anchors so that the reader doesn't need to scroll down to the particular section of the page that she or he is interested in.

You can find a good example of this at the following location:

`http://www.ncsa.uiuc.edu/general/internet/www/htmlprimer.html`

This page is an introduction to the basics of HTML, and it's easily several dozen screens long. The page contains a table of contents at the top, and every entry in the table of contents is linked to an anchor on the page. This makes it easy to skip down the section on fill-out forms without searching through all the material above the forms section.

Here's the thing: giant, multi-screen Web pages are an anathema to the NetObjects philosophy, and you can't create anchors with NetObjects Fusion, at least not in version 1.0.

If you find this disturbing or inconvenient, keep in mind that anchors were invented to solve a specific problem: big, shapeless blobs of text. Before NetObjects Fusion came along, it was time-consuming to break a giant text block into a series of linked, digestible-sized pages. As you've seen in this chapter, NetObjects Fusion makes it easy.

There's another advantage to anchor-based pages that NetObjects Fusion doesn't address—it's much easier for a user to save a single page to disk than to save a series of pages. This isn't a terribly serious problem, but it may be important to some of your readers. If you have long documents, and you'd like your readers to have the option to read them or download them, you have a few different options.

Providing Information in Adobe Acrobat Format

Personally, I think Adobe Acrobat is the most sensible and hassle-free solution. If you have a long document that you want to serve, chances are you have it in a word processor or page-layout format; it's often as easy to save these kinds of documents in Adobe Acrobat format as it is to print the document to a laser printer.

Adobe offers a free Acrobat Reader plug-in for Netscape Navigator and Microsoft Internet Explorer. (You can freely distribute the plug-in on your site for readers who don't already have it.) Using the Acrobat plug-in, readers can read Acrobat documents in the browser window, using Acrobat's built-in navigation features, or save the document to disk with a single keystroke (see Figure 4.18).

FIGURE 4.18

Readers can easily view Acrobat documents in a browser window by using the free Acrobat plug-in.

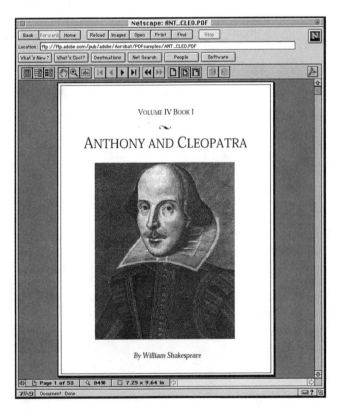

To find out more about Adobe Acrobat, take a look at `http://www.adobe.com/` or check out *Beyond Paper: The Official Guide to Adobe Acrobat* (Adobe Press, 1993).

Adding Anchors by Hand

This procedure isn't tough, but you'll need to add some raw HTML. You don't need to know any HTML tags other than what is shown here:

1. Go to the home page of a new, blank site. Draw a text box and enter the phrase "a link to an anchor." Select the word "anchor."

2. Click the Link button in the Properties palette. Click the External tab in the Links dialog box. In the URL field, enter the code

   `#myAnchor`

3. In the Name Field of the Links dialog box, type something like "anchor 1."

4. Put some stuff on the page under the link—pictures, text, whatever you like—so you'll have something to jump past.

5. Choose the spot where you want to put the anchor. Remember, this will be the top of the page when the reader jumps to the anchor by clicking the link. Select the object that you want at the top of the page, and choose **Page →** **Element** Script.

6. NetObjects Fusion presents the Script dialog box. In the Before Element field of the Script dialog, insert the code:

   `<A NAME="myAnchor"></a>`

7. Click your browser's reload/refresh button. Click the text link at the top of the page, and the browser will jump to the object that you picked in step 7.

Get it? In general, the name of the link goes in the URL field of the Links dialog box, preceded by the # character (#myAnchor in the example) and the anchor is of the form:

`<A NAME=<A NAME="name-of-the-link-here"></a>`

Make sure that your anchor's name is one word, and that it doesn't contain any special characters (like #) in the middle. It's best to confine yourself to numbers, letters, and the underscore (_) when you're creating anchor names.

Site Templates

You don't need to build site trees from scratch. You can use a template for the basis of your site, or you can add templates as an extension to sites that already exist. Any site you design can be saved as a template, and NetObjects Fusion comes with a wide selection of ready-made site outlines.

You've already seen a list of the standard NetObjects Fusion templates. Remember the New Site dialog box from Chapter 2? Each of the sites listed in the dialog box represents a site template. The blank site that I chose is simply a template that consists of a single page.

To see this dialog box again, choose **File→New Site**. Let's take a look at an example of a complex site diagram: choose Company Intranet from the list, give the new site a name, and click OK.

Figure 4.19 shows just how complex the Intranet site is. The corporations' Human Resources, Sales, Marketing, and R&D departments are each represented on the first level, and each of these departments has a set of children, or a hierarchy of descendants, below it. If you look at individual pages of the site in Page view, you'll see that placeholder pictures and text have been included on each page as well.

FIGURE 4.19

The site tree of the "Corporate Intranet" template.

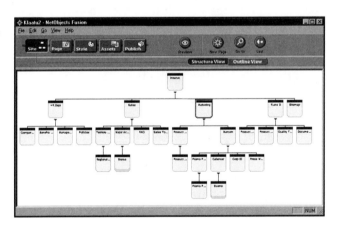

Of course, after you've loaded such a template, you can alter it as you desire. For example, you might drag the Policies page from under the Human Resources Department page and put it under R and D instead. A site created from a template is just as flexible as a site that you built from scratch.

You can also add a template to a site that already exists. The whole template will be added as a child of the current site tree.

To see how this works, delete the Human Resources page from the Company Intranet site. (As you've seen before, NetObjects Fusion will remove the children of the Human Resources department node as well.) Now, add the Human Resources subhierarchy back to the site, using the Human Resources department template:

1. Select the node that you want as the parent of the template to be imported. In this case, it's the Intranet page because you want to add Human Resources as a sibling of the other departments.

2. Choose **File→Insert**. NetObjects Fusion presents a file dialog box. Navigate to the /Templates/Autosites/Human Resources folder and select the Human Resources.nft file.

3. NetObjects Fusion adds the Human Resources hierarchy as a child of the Intranet page (see Figure 4.20).

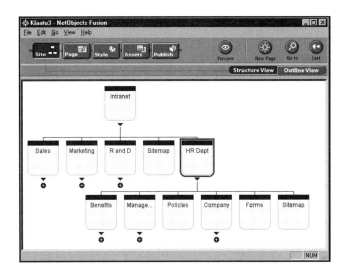

FIGURE 4.20

The revised "Corporate Intranet" site.

103

I suspect that this gives you some ideas about what you might want to save in a library of site templates. Let's say that you're a freelance site designer, and you routinely add a few pages of information about your services to each site—with your clients' permission, of course—say, a page about how the site was created, a page about NetObjects Fusion, and a page about your business (see Figure 4.21).

FIGURE 4.21

Creating a new template: a colophon subtree for site designers.

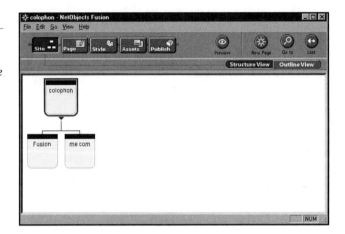

To save this little subtree as a template that you can add to all the sites you work on, simply choose **File→Save As Template**. You can save the template anywhere you like, of course, but if you save it in the /Templates/AutoSites/ folder, the template will appear in the list of templates next time you use the New Sites dialog box.

Design Principles

Page design is an ancient and time-honored discipline. Styles may change, but the underlying principles really haven't changed for hundreds of years.

There are certain precedents—online page design as well as traditional book design can lend some guidelines—but its three-dimensional hierarchy and hypertext approach are pretty much all new.

This is really exciting—it's an opportunity for you to participate in the creation of the new art and science of site design. However, as with any unexplored territory, there are no maps and no signposts.

This doesn't mean that there aren't plenty of people who will claim expertise in the area of site design, and many of these people do have as much experience as is possible in this young field. However, until we've had some time to take a look at how users interact with complex sites, we can't really establish general principles, and anyone who tells you otherwise is just makin' stuff up.

With that as a preface, let me share a few ideas with you.

Width versus Breadth

One of the first ideas about site design that has gained widespread acceptance is the notion that the site tree ought to be balanced. What this means is that the tree shouldn't be substantially wider than it is tall (Figure 4.23a), or taller than it is wide (Figure 4.23b), or contain branches that are substantially different in size than other branches (Figure 4.23c).

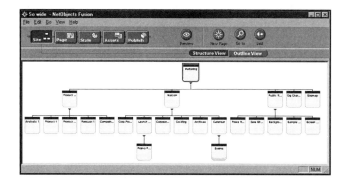

FIGURE **4.22**A

A wide tree.

FIGURE **4.22**B

A tall tree.

FIGURE 4.22C

A lopsided tree.

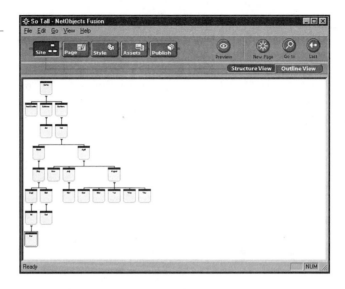

This probably isn't necessary. Where did this idea come from? When an application is storing information in a tree structure inside the application, searches are usually faster when the tree is balanced. The program traverses the tree in an orderly fashion, and if the tree is balanced, it's more likely that the program will find what it's looking for in the middle of the search, rather than at the end.

Tree structures in programs aren't the same as tree structures in Web sites. Readers can't even *see* the tree in most cases, and in any case, they almost certainly won't search the site for a particular page by loading it page-by-page.

Even if you provide a search CGI for readers to find things on your site, the CGI won't use the site tree to traverse the site—it will use the directory structure of the folder(s) that contain the site. The site tree is there to help you, a human, organize the site conceptually—not to contain the site's data in the machine's memory.

I don't mean to discourage you from balancing the site tree, or encourage you to make crazy, lopsided sites. All I'm suggesting is: *don't fret about the tree's shape.*

Attention Span

It seems fairly obvious that readers would like to limit the number of clicks on navigation bars before they get to the content that they're interested in. For example, let's say a reader wants to read an article that's on page c1 of the abstract site tree that we first looked at in Figure 4.4. To get to the page that contains the desired content, the reader must choose from the navigation bars of two intermediate pages (a1 and b1) before they get to the stuff they want to read, assuming that they started at your home page in the first place. (For that matter, perhaps people secretly enjoy clicking links and navigation bars—after all, they seem to like the Web in the first place.)

Although this seems obvious, there are no real hard and fast rules about how many clicks are too many. So the rule seems to be: Put the content as close to the top of your site as possible.

Site Organization Fits Message

Web sites seem to be curiously representational. For example, the corporate intranet site looks quite a bit like a corporation's organizational chart. Likewise, it's pretty easy to map one-to-one correspondence between the newspaper site's sections and pages and the sections pages of an actual, physical newspaper.

This isn't surprising. Because readers have notions of how corporations and newspapers are organized, they can make some pretty good guesses about how to find their way around Web sites based on these models.

107

This doesn't mean that new formats won't emerge that aren't specific to the needs and capabilities of the Web. Primordial sites that feature a "web-o-centric" design— not based on metaphorical representations of real world objects—have begun to appear, and it's likely that these pioneering sites will engender a new generation of site designs that have little to do with newspapers, magazines, or other paper-based publications. (Take a look at http://www.slate.com to see a site that's reaching for a nonrepresentational design based on pure Web logic.)

Naturally, not all sites will take this approach, and it's not always appropriate. After all, why shouldn't a company's Web site be organized like the company? Then again, why should it? This is really an aesthetic decision, and it's yours to make, based on the organization's needs, and the motivation for creating the site in the first place.

Ease of Navigation

I find it frustrating to try to navigate a site that doesn't contain any type of descriptive navigation aids. Maybe I'm just claustrophobic, but I usually bail out of a site as soon as I loose sight of guideposts that tell me where I am and where I can go.

Fortunately, the NetObjects Fusion engineers seem to feel the same way, and as we've seen in this chapter, you need to do some work to *remove* banners and navigation aids. Unless you're looking for some kind of special effect (like a '94 nostalgia site), *leave these elements in place.*

Let me suggest that you always add a link to the site's home page somewhere on your page, if only in a little text link in the footer. Such a link provides the reader with an escape hatch that's still on your site. Otherwise, the reader might bail right off your site. (I usually go straight to Infoseek when I panic.)

Summary

In this chapter, you learned about the tools NetObjects Fusion offers for designing a site on an architectural level, including:

- How Web sites are represented as tree diagrams.

- How to create and manipulate site trees.

- How headers and footers work.

- How NetObjects Fusion creates automatic navigational aids.

- How to create your own custom navigational aids.

- How to use and create site templates.

- Some design issues to think about when you're developing your site.

In the next chapter, you'll learn how to work on the site at the detail level by manipulating the design and content of individual pages.

URL Roundup

- Word (on-line literary magazine):
  `http://www.word.com`

- Introduction to HTML (and an example of anchors):
  `http://www.ncsa.uiuc.edu/general/internet/www/htmlprimer.html`

- Slate (a "non-representational" Web site):
  `http://www.slate.com`

CHAPTER 5

Page View

So far, you haven't really worried about the content of Web pages—how to include the stuff that readers are actually interested in. In this chapter, you'll learn how to add content in Page view mode and how to handle the basic elements of text, pictures, and drawings.

Some elements that are added in Page view—multimedia content and content such as Java applets—are fairly simple to add, but require a little more background information about how the content itself works and is handled. Section III of this book covers these more advanced topics.

The Anatomy of a Page

When you design a print publication, you need to make certain decisions about what the pages will look like. You pick a page size, a paper stock, the margins of each page, and so on. It's possible to vary these attributes on individual pages in special circumstances, but usually these decisions affect every page of the document.

When you design a Web publication with NetObjects Fusion, you will need to make similar decisions about the pages that make up the site. How big are they? What color are they? Which headers and footers go on which pages?

NetObjects Fusion stores your decision about each of these issues in the page's *layout*. The layout is associated with the middle section of the page—the area between the header and footer when you're looking at the page in Page view. You can view information about each page's layout in the Layout tab of the Properties palette (as shown in Figure 5.1).

FIGURE **5.1**

Information about each page's layout is stored in the Properties palette.

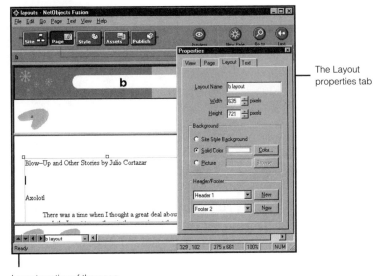

The Layout properties tab

Layout section of the page

Just as you can create sets of multiple headers and footers to assign to each page, you can create a set of layouts to choose from, as well. Each page can use the layout unchanged, or it can modify any particular element of the layout.

To see how this works, open the site /Book/Sites/Layouts on the *NetObjects Fusion Handbook* CD-ROM. The site is a simple chain of four identical pages, labeled a, b, c, and d.

Go to page a. It's a basic page, created with the default attributes that NetObjects Fusion assigns to every page: 800 pixels wide by 600 pixels high, with a background color that matches the color specified by the sites style in Style view, using the default header Header1 and the default footer, Footer2.

Go to page b, and tweak it a little:

1. Change the layout size to 550×500 in the Layout tab of the Properties palette.

2. Change the background color. In the Layout tab of the Properties palette, click the Solid Color radio button in the Background group, click the Color button, and choose a color swatch. (This is getting familiar by now, isn't it?)

3. Change the footer. Click the New button next to the Footer pop-up menu in the Layout tab of the Properties palette. Change the footer's navigation bar style from text link to secondary buttons.

4. Give the layout a name: type "b layout" (or whatever) in the Layout Name field in the Layout tab of the Properties palette.

Figure 5.2 shows the new layout. You may have noticed the little pop-up menu at the bottom of the window—it has changed from Layout to reflect the name of the new layout.

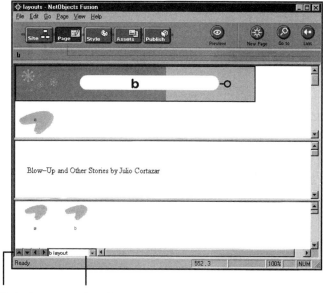

FIGURE **5.2**

A modified version of NetObjects Fusion's default layout.

111

Navigation arrows   Layout pop-up menu

TIP

Look at the four little navigation buttons next to the Layout pop-up menu. They're called the page navigation controls, and they enable you to navigate from page to page without leaving Page view. As you might guess, the Up button takes you to the current page's parent, the Down button to its leftmost child, and the Left and Right buttons take you to the pages on the same level as the current page. (All the pages—not just the siblings.)

Page Size

Although you can set a page's size attribute in the Layout tab, and NetObjects Fusion will show the layout in Page view at the size you designate, the page's size has little impact on what readers see in the browser window.

For example, set the page size to 550 or so, drag something like the page banner so that it's off of the grid, and click the Preview button. The element is still there in its entirety—it's *not* truncated, cropped, or missing in Preview mode.

The page size is there to remind you where the reader's browser window will be set—especially if you're working with the kind of gigantic 20" or 21" monitor commonly found in design studios. Of course, you don't have any control or influence over the window size on a reader's screen, but the default—800 pixels by 600 pixels—isn't too far from what you'd expect from a typical reader with a typical monitor and video card.

You've been to the Color dialog box several times by now, gentle reader, and have not yet learned how colors are chosen or how custom colors are defined. The time has come.

By far, the easiest way to pick a color is to use the color matrix and slider provided in the Color dialog box:

1. Click the Define Custom Colors button. The Colors dialog box changes to its wider, extended form (see Figure 5.3).

112

FIGURE 5.3

The Custom Color dialog box.

Color matrix

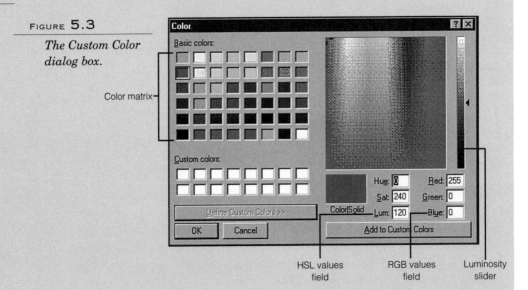

HSL values field

RGB values field

Luminosity slider

2. The easiest way to pick colors is to click a color in the Hue-Saturation map, adjusting its brightness as necessary with the Luminosity slider. (The Hue Saturation map shows all the colors in the color wheel along its east-west axis, and shows each color, from fully saturated to gray, along the north-south axis.)

The two dimensions of the Hue Saturation map aren't quite enough to specify every possible color; each spot on the Hue Saturation map can be made lighter or darker with the Luminosity slider.

3.   To add your new color to the site's palette of custom colors, click the Add to Custom Colors button.

As you change the colors by using these controls, you'll notice that the numbers in the HSL and RGB values field change as the colors change. What do these values mean?

A computer monitor breaks down color into its primary red, green, and blue (RGB) components. Each pixel in the monitor contains a separate element for each of these colors, and each element can glow at 256 different levels of brightness.

Because red, green, and blue are primary colors, they can be combined to create a wide range (but not all) of the colors in the visible spectrum. The computer mixes colors by varying the brightness of each of the red, green, and blue components of the pixel.

The brightness of each channel is specified with a number from 0 to 255, where 0 is darkest and 255 is brightest. So, a pixel set to the values of

113

red = 0

green = 0

blue = 0

is black because none of the three pixel components is glowing at all. Conversely, a pixel set to

red = 255

green = 255

blue = 255

is white because all the pixels are glowing at their brightest, and the three primary colors combine to make white light.

Another common way to specify colors is the HSB model. H stands for Hue, a value from 0 to 360 that specifies the angle of the color on a color wheel; S stands for saturation, a value from 0 to 100 that specifies the grayness of the color; and B stands for brightness, also measured on a scale from 0 to 100. (HSB is used for the convenience of humans—many designers find it more intuitive to specify colors with HSB than RGB. Monitors still use red, green, and blue pixel components, no matter how the color is specified in software.)

In both cases, it's unlikely that you'll get to know the numbers well enough to be able to enter them directly or to recognize the numerical values of colors when you see them. It's much easier to use the matrix and slider controls to pick colors. Using the numbers is handy for "nudging" colors in a certain direction or transferring colors between applications.

Nudging is simple enough. Let's say that you want to make the color just a little brighter, but you're having trouble making fine adjustments with the mouse on the slider. You can enter values directly into the luminosity field—if the luminosity is set to 75, you can type in 76 or 77.

Matching colors is a little more complicated. Let's say that you want the background color of a page to match the color of some object in a picture that you've scanned—say, the color of someone's shirt in a group photo. If you've got a scanner, I'm assuming that you have some sort of image-editing software program—such as Adobe Photoshop, Fractal Design Painter, Color-It, or a Corel package—that came bundled with your scanner. (If not, there are shareware image editors, such as NIH Image, that will do the job.) I'll use Photoshop to show you how this works. Although each of these packages handles the details in its own way, they're similar enough that you'll be able to figure it out from this example:

1. In Photoshop, open the scan that contains the color you'd like to match.

2. Choose **Palettes→Show** Info from Photoshop's Window menu.

3. Choose Palette Options from the pop-up menu at the top right corner of the Info Palette.

4. In the First Color Readout group in the Info Options dialog box, choose RGB color from the pop-up menu. In the Second Color Readout group, choose HSB from the pop-up menu. Click OK.

5. Choose the eyedropper tool from the Photoshop tool palette. Position the eyedropper over the color you want to match.

6. Look at the readouts in the Photoshop information palette. The readouts show the RGB and HSL (called HSB in Photoshop) data for the target color. Make a note of these values (see Figure 5.4).

7. In the NetObjects Fusion colors dialog box, enter the RGB values from Photoshop in the RGB field, or the HSB values in the HSL fields. (You don't need to do both.)

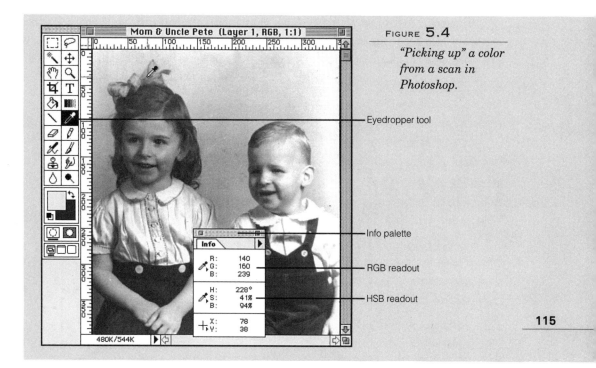

FIGURE 5.4

"Picking up" a color from a scan in Photoshop.

Eyedropper tool

Info palette

RGB readout

HSB readout

115

The Grid

By default, NetObjects Fusion shows a grid on the page's layout. No doubt you've already noticed this and discovered that the grid doesn't appear in the final version of the page in the browser window.

If you're a designer, you already know that a grid is a great thing, and that every element on a page ought to align to *something*, unless you have a very good reason to let it "float." (My art director and design mentor, Cindy Bold, hits me with a big stick when things don't look neatly aligned.) The grid that NetObjects Fusion provides makes it easier to line things up and to organize your page.

By default, the grid is a purely visual tool that helps you figure out where objects lie with respect to each other. You can use the grid to see whether edges line up and to make sure that text blocks are the same width as the banner—that sort of thing.

You can control the size of the squares that make up the grid in the View tab of the Properties palette. Simply enter new sizes into the Width and Height fields of the Grid Size field.

Suppose that you want to organize your page into columns that are 150 pixels wide. Rather than counting out six little 25-pixels squares—personally, I always miscount this kind of thing anyway—you can specify a grid width of 150 pixels. The resulting grid shown in Figure 5.5 is much easier to work with.

FIGURE 5.5

The basic grid, reconfigured for working with columns.

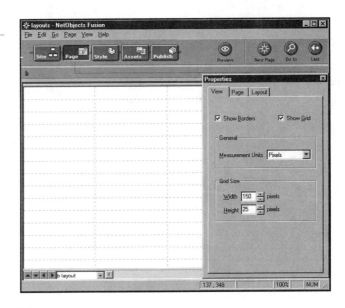

116

You can also use the grid as a more active participant in the layout process. If you've used page layout packages such as PageMaker or QuarkXPress before, you're probably familiar with this feature: it's called "snap to grid," and it makes the grid exert a kind of magical magnetic influence on the elements of a page.

Here's how it works: when you draw a box with the text tool, the picture tool, or anything that draws a box, the top left corner appears at the nearest intersection of grid lines, no matter whether you started on the grid or not. Likewise, the bottom right corner is positioned at the closest grid intersection, even if that's not where you released the mouse button.

If you resize a box, the size of the box is constrained in the same way. If you're moving an element that doesn't fit the grid (such as a ready-made banner), the top left corner of the element will jump to the nearest grid intersection, no matter where the place the element.

To turn on snap to grid, choose **Edit →Preferences** and check the Snap to Grid checkbox in the Layout Preferences tab of the Preferences dialog box. (Go ahead and try it: It's easier to see than it is to read about.)

As useful as the grid is, sometimes you'll want to see the page without the distraction of the grid. You can turn off the grid's display in the View tab of the Properties palette. If you've got snap to grid on, boxes will still snap to the grid, even if the grid isn't visible.

Body Text

Type is probably the biggest headache you'll deal with when you're designing a Web page. As you saw in Chapter 3, there are plenty of things about type that designers are used to having control over—fonts, leading and tracking, and justification—that are just not in your control when you're designing for the Web.

NetObjects Fusion makes the handling of type easier, but it can't change the way that browsers work. You'll need to make certain compromises about the way the page is laid out.

Text Blocks versus Shapeless Globs

As I've mentioned a few times before, NetObjects Fusion has made a significant advance in the handling of text blocks by introducing text boxes to the world of Web design. (I keep saying this because it's so exciting to find software that does what I want it to do!)

I don't know about you, but I really missed page margins in the early days of Web design. Before the HTML 2.0 specification, almost all Web pages had type that went from one edge of the browser window to another, like the page shown in Figure 5.6.

You don't see too many books without margins. The eye needs a place without type in it to rest while it is reading, and the white space of the margin provides that resting place. Web pages shouldn't be any different.

Furthermore, I was raised to believe that the width, or *measure*, of a block of type should only be so long—maybe 50 or 60 characters—and that allowing the text to be as wide as the browser window made the measure too long and the text hard to read.

FIGURE 5.6

From the bad old days, before page margins were possible on Web pages.

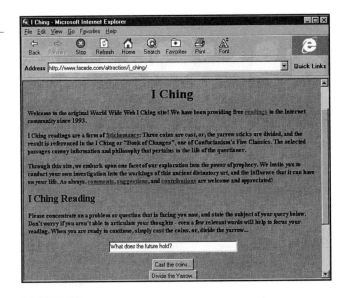

TIP

A nice little book about the aesthetics of type is *Stop Stealing Sheep: and Find Out How Type Works* by Erik Spiekermann and E. M. Ginger (Adobe Press 1993). Both designers and nondesigners will find it an interesting introduction to the art and science of typography.

The HTML 2.0 specification allowed for tables, which allowed elements to be placed in specific parts of the page. Suddenly, it became possible to create margins and control the size of blocks of type. As an added bonus, text in tables doesn't move when the browser window is resized, so any line breaks that are added by hand stay put.

After tables were introduced, many Web page developers spent a lot of time flowing text into tables. Unfortunately, even relatively advanced second-generation page design tools, such as Adobe PageMill 1.0, did not support tables, so margins had to be hand-coded in HTML. Creating tables by hand in HTML is fairly easy to screw up, especially if you need to present another table within the table that contains the text.

Perhaps you can begin to understand my enthusiasm for NetObjects Fusion's text-box approach. NetObjects Fusion puts in all of those tables automatically, behind the scenes, so you can fret about other problems.

Character Styles and Paragraph Styles

You can control the attributes of text in the Text tab of the Properties tab. Before I get into specifics, I want to make a distinction between two different ways to style text:

- **Character styles.** Changes made at the character level affect only the text currently selected. Character-level attributes include things like text style (italic, roman, bold), size, and color.

- **Paragraph styles.** Changes made at the paragraph level affect the text that contains the insertion point or selected text, even if all of the text in the paragraph isn't selected when the change is made. Paragraph-level attributes include alignment, indentation, and "paragraph styles"—shortcuts that change the text style of an entire paragraph at once.

These categories should be familiar to just about everyone: most word processors and page layout packages make these kinds of distinctions, although they may use different terms for each level. For example, Microsoft Word handles the character level with the **Format →Font** command, and the paragraph level with the **Format→Paragraph** and **Format→ Style** commands.

Logical and Physical Styles

HTML also introduced a distinction that's unique to Web pages: logical and physical styles. This distinction, which appears only at the character level, can allow the reader even more control over how text is displayed.

Logical styles allow text to be tagged according to certain conceptual categories, such as emphasis, citation, and source code. The Web browser marks each logical style with some kind of character style: it might mark emphasis with bold type, a citation with italics, and source code with a different font.

Logical styles are marked with special typographic treatment. Then again, it might not. The idea behind logical styles is that they give the reader control over how such text is displayed. Some browsers (*not* Navigator or Internet Explorer) allow the reader to control how each style is displayed, so that emphasis is marked with a different font, and source code with italics.

Surrendering control over the type in this way is horrifying to designers, but that's the way UNIX weenies think; they want to be able to hack every single element of software so it's customized to their tastes. If you ever look at HTML manuals online, many weenies will recommend that you use logical styles, rather than physical styles, whenever possible. This is the UNIX-weenie party line. Forget it.

> **TIP**
>
> Before any of you UNIX weenies mail bomb me, I'm a believer—really! I've got Linux running *right now* on my PC. But as a designer, I think things like the <EMPHASIS> tag interfere with good design.

Fortunately, HTML also provides physical styles, which allow you to spec type as you want it to appear: in italics, or bold, or whatever. Readers don't have the option to remap italic onto bold, or bold onto strikethrough, or any other crazy configuration.

As you'd suspect, NetObjects Fusion uses physical styles almost exclusively. There are a few logical styles that make sense—logical styles for email addresses are one—that appear in the paragraph styles pop-up menu.

120

Text Styles

NetObjects Fusion offers controls for manipulating text at the character level at the top of the Text tab in the Properties control tab (see Figure 5.7) and in a special Text menu in the main NetObjects Fusion menu bar. The Text tab and the Text menu appear only when something they affect—text or a text box—is selected in Page view mode.

FIGURE **5.7**

The Text tab of the Properties palette.

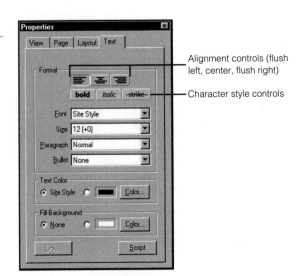

Alignment controls (flush left, center, flush right)

Character style controls

Using the Format Buttons

The six buttons at the top of the Format group enable you to apply paragraph and character styles to text. Both groups will probably look familiar to most readers:

- The alignment button controls function at the paragraph level, and sets the alignment of the current paragraph to flush left, centered, or flush right. For the record, you can't justify text in a Web page—at least until the current HTML is revised.

- Of course, only one alignment style can be applied at any time: text can't be both flush right and flush left simultaneously.

- The bold, italic, and strikethrough buttons function on the character level and add these styles to the currently selected text. These buttons can also be accessed through the usual keyboard shortcuts—Control-B for bold and Control-I for italic in the Windows version, and Command-B and Command-I in the Mac OS version.

- These character styles can be added "on top of" any other style: characters can be both bold and italic, and these styles can also be applied to characters that have any other style changes discussed in the next sections.

121

Changing the Font

You can't spec the font of the body type that will appear in the browser window—at least not with any assurance that it will appear.

When you pick a font from the Font pop-up menu in the Text tab, NetObjects Fusion uses that font to display the font in the layout, and adds the name of the face to the block's HTML. However, many browsers, including the most widely used browser, Netscape Navigator, don't support the FACE parameter of the <FONT> tag. Navigator uses its default font, no matter what the tag specifies.

Even if the reader is using Internet Explorer, which does support the FACE parameter, the specified font must be installed on the reader's system. There's no way of telling which fonts the reader has installed, and no way to guarantee that the correct font will appear.

TIP

Adobe and Microsoft are collaborating on a new technology, called *OpenType,* that may allow fonts to be embedded in Web pages. Whatever OpenType becomes, it won't be ready in time to be supported by NetObjects Fusion 1.0, but future versions of Fusion will probably be OpenType friendly. Keep your eye on `http://www.adobe.com/type/opentype.html` for news about this emerging technology.

Adding Special Characters

Most browsers support the display of special characters like the trademark symbol (™) or registered marks (®). However, to be included in the page, they must be encoded in hexidecimal format and decoded by the browser. You don't want to mess around with encoding these things yourself—you want NetObjects Fusion to handle it for you.

To see the special characters supported by NetObjects Fusion, choose **Text→Insert Symbol**. NetObjects Fusion presents the Insert Symbol dialog box, chock full o' those special characters that make your site look professional, such as em and en dashes and smart quotes (see Figure 5.8).

FIGURE 5.8

Adding the right characters with the Insert Symbol dialog box.

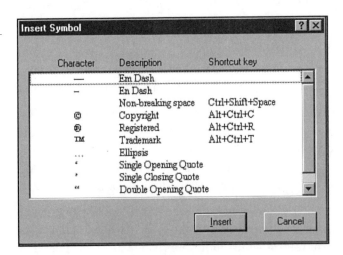

To insert a character, just choose it from the list. NetObjects Fusion adds the symbol at the insertion point. (If you've got text selected, the new symbol replaces the text.)

These touches really make a page look professional. Straight quotes are for typewriters, and that's that.

Changing the Size of Type

Changes to the size of type are applied on the paragraph level. To change the size, pick a new font from the Size pop-up menu. You'll notice that there are only a few pre-sets. These few are all that are available. You can't specify sizes, other than those in the menu.

Keep in mind that these sizes are relative to the size that the reader has set in the browser preferences. NetObjects Fusion assumes that the reader uses the Navigator default size of 12 points. This isn't necessarily true—there's nothing stopping a reader from setting the point size to 9, or 14, or 72 points.

Also, keep in mind that fonts vary in size. A 12-point font isn't 12 points high on the screen or on a page—and the difference in size between two fonts set to 12 points can be substantial. (Compare Times and Impact (Windows) or Times and Helvetica (Mac) to see the difference.)

123

The lesson: just because you can read a font on-screen when you're designing it doesn't mean that the reader will be able decipher it when it loads in the browser's window. Of course, this may be the reader's fault for setting up his or her browser with screwy font preferences, but placing the blame on the reader doesn't make your type any more legible. More precisely: *Don't make your type too small*. Save the small sizes for stuff you don't want people to read. And always look at your page in a few different browsers, with a few different browser font settings.

Paragraph Indentation

NetObjects Fusion provides support for paragraph indentation: this is a unique feature among Web page design packages. You won't have complete control over the way indentation works—you can't set the indentation in pixels or indent only the first line of a paragraph—but it's possible to structure your text into several different layers of indentation.

The indentation controls are located in the Text menu, under the separate commands Indent and Unindent. Both commands work on the paragraph level and move the entire paragraph about 5 or 6 characters (37 pixels) to the right and left, respectively (see Figure 5.9).

FIGURE 5.9

NetObjects Fusion supports automatic indentation of text.

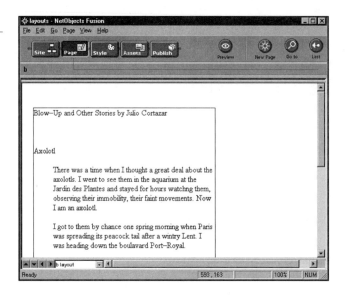

Indentation is particularly practical when used in conjunction with bullets, as described in the next section.

Adding Bullets

You can use the Bullet pop-up menu to add bullets at the paragraph label. You have a wide choice of bullet styles, including automatic labeling with Arabic numerals, Roman numerals, and upper- and lowercase letters. Bulleted paragraphs are indented, and the bullet hangs to the left of the paragraph's indent (see Figure 5.10).

FIGURE 5.10

A selection of bullet styles.

WARNING

When NetObjects Fusion adds a character-based bullet to a paragraph, it creates the character by using the default paragraph style that's been set up in Style view— no matter what the size, color, or style of the type in the current paragraph is. This doesn't always look good. You *can't* apply any character styles to character bullets—you'll have to live with them as they are.

When you use character-based bullets in consecutive paragraphs, NetObjects Fusion automatically numbers each paragraph at the same indentation level with consecutive characters. Each level of indentation can have its own bullet style.

For example, let's experiment with this list:

```
aardvark
baboon
chicken
donkey
elephant
```

125

1. Type this list into a text box, making sure that the Bullet pop-up menu is set to None for each paragraph.

2. Select all five paragraphs and select 1, 2, 3 from the Bullets pop-up menu. NetObjects Fusion automatically numbers the list from 1 to 5.

3. Select just one line of the list—any line—and choose I, II, III from the Bullets pop-up. Notice that all the paragraphs change, even the unselected ones.

4. Select the lines that contain baboon and chicken, and indent them with **Text → Indent**. The list has now been renumbered as shown:

    ```
    I.aardvark
    I. baboon
    II. chicken
    II. donkey
    III. elephant
    ```

5. Select line 1 and choose 1, 2, 3 from the Bullets pop-up. Notice that lines 1, 4, and 5 (aardvark, donkey, and elephant) have changed to the new format, but the indented lines keep their Roman numeral format.

6. Add a new line, such as

   ```
   fruitbat
   ```

   after line five. NetObjects Fusion gives it an Arabic numeral, consistent with the level that it is on. Then indent this line. Notice that it keeps its Arabic numeral format, but is renumbered from 4 to 1. Notice that it doesn't share either format or numbering with the previously indented section, even though it's on the same level of indentation (see Figure 5.11).

FIGURE 5.11

Bullets and inden-
tation are closely
connected.

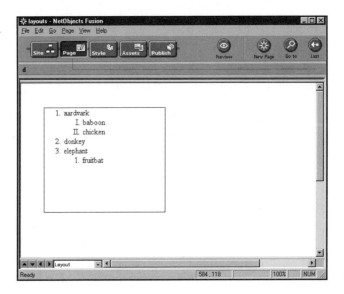

If, for some reason, you need to start an outline with a number other than one, or a letter other than "a," do the following:

1. Select a paragraph at the level to be renumbered.

2. Choose **Text→Set List Start**.

3. Enter a new starting value in the Set Start Value dialog box.

If you're feeling especially daffy, you can renumber subsections of the outline, rather than the main level so that it looks like:

```
A. aardvark
     23. baboon
     24. chicken
B. donkey
```

…although its hard to imagine why you'd want to do this.

Text Color

Text color is set at the character level. To change text's color, select it, click the Text Color button in the Properties palette, and pick a color from the color dialog box. It's the same dialog box that was covered earlier in the chapter, and the same techniques for selecting custom colors apply here.

> **WARNING**
>
> Make sure that you check any text color choices you make with the text link colors that are set up in Style view. If you make your regular text the same color as text links, the links will be hard for your readers to see.

Text color is another one of those attributes that are under the reader's control. Netscape Navigator enables a reader to set the colors that are used to display text and allows the reader to override any color choices made for the page.

Built-In Paragraph Styles

NetObjects Fusion provides a set of 15 ready-made paragraph styles. Most of these styles are based on the logical styles defined in the HTML 2.0 specification. (See the previous physical versus logical style discussion.)

Naturally, paragraph styles are applied at the paragraph level. All of the ready-made styles can be used in conjunction with character-level text treatments that I've discussed so far: you can make headlines italic, or green, or centered, or whatever you like. There's only one restriction—a paragraph can have only one paragraph style at a time.

Headline Styles

HTML provides for six levels of headlines, called "headings." Headings are defined in relative, rather than absolute, sizes. Heading 1 isn't any particular point size, and may be handled differently from browser to browser, but it's always the largest head size. Heading 1 through Heading 3 are (usually) larger than body type, Heading 4 is the same size as body type, and Heading 5 and Heading 6 are *smaller* than the default size of body text. Headings are always rendered with bold type (see Figure 5.12).

127

FIGURE 5.12

The varying sizes of headings compared with one another.

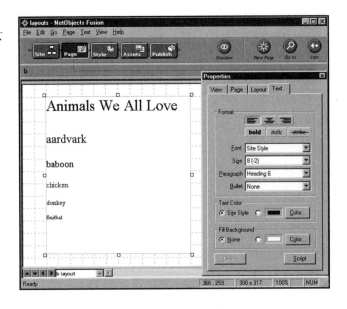

Body Text

NetObjects Fusion also provides a set of ready-made body text styles. These styles provide a library of commonly used HTML body text styles. They are the following:

Address. The address style is normally used for setting email addresses—very often the address of the Web page designer. By convention, email addresses are set in italics.

TIP

The address style *doesn't* use the HTML <ADDRESS> tag—it substitutes a physical italic style for the logical style, so the address will appear in italics in *all* browsers, no matter how they're configured.

Here's the down side: because the <ADDRESS> isn't used, the reader can't click the address to automatically send email. In fact, version 1.0 of NetObjects Fusion doesn't provide a way to add this feature to a page.

Bulleted List. The Bulleted list style places a round, filled bullet at the beginning of the selected paragraph, using the standard HTML style for making bullets. The standard HTML style is different from bulleted paragraphs created by NetObjects Fusion—standard HTML bullets don't "hang."

Take a look at Figure 5.13. In the top paragraph, created with the NetObjects Fusion Bullet pop-up menu, the whole text of the bulleted paragraph is indented, and there's nothing but white space underneath the bullet. In the second paragraph, created with the Bulleted Text style in the Paragraph pop-up, only the first paragraph is indented; the second line begins underneath the bullet.

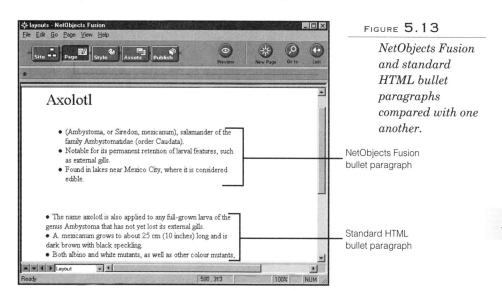

FIGURE 5.13

NetObjects Fusion and standard HTML bullet paragraphs compared with one another.

NetObjects Fusion bullet paragraph

Standard HTML bullet paragraph

Which style you use is up to you and the demands of your page design. I prefer hung bullets, but my art director Cindy likes the clean, straight edges of inline bullets.

Code. The code list style is used to set program code. You've probably noticed that your Web browser asks you to set two fonts in your preferences: a proportional-width font (like the typeset text of this book) and a fixed-width font (like this--the kind of type made by typewriters). The code style sets the paragraph in a fixed-width font (see Figure 5.14).

Why is code set in a fixed-width font? Because it's a good idea to pay careful attention to indentation when writing source code, and the easiest way to line things up in the bad old days (before fancy code editors) was to use a font whose characters were all the same width.

You can use the code style for purposes other than setting code—use it anywhere that you'd use a fixed width font. Tables of numbers usually look best set in a fixed-width font, for example, and sometimes the second font can work as a design accent, if used properly.

FIGURE 5.14

Most browsers use both proportional-width and fixed-width fonts.

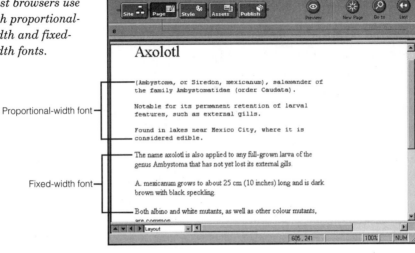

Proportional-width font —

Fixed-width font —

130

TIP

Here's another case of NetObjects Fusion pullin' the old switcheroo: although there's a <CODE> tag, it's a logical style. NetObjects Fusion actually uses the <TT> tag, the physical style specification for fixed-width fonts.

Comment. The Comment style is exactly like the Code style, except the type is green, rather than black.

Directory List. The directory list style creates a bulleted list. It's exactly like the Bulleted List style.

Format. The Format style sets the current paragraph in the browser's fixed-width font. It's exactly like the Code style.

Using the <PRE> Tag

The <PRE> tag (short for preformatted) is arguably the most commonly used tag for specifying a fixed-width font when writing HTML by hand. Normally, a browser ignores things like line breaks and extra spaces in an HTML's text, but the <PRE> tag instructs the browser to keep the text exactly as it is, extra spaces and all.

NetObjects Fusion takes care of all this stuff for you—it uses a million little tricks to make your text look the same in the browser window as it does in NetObjects Fusion's window. You don't really need the <PRE> tag.

And in fact, the Format style doesn't use the <PRE> tag, either, despite what the name may suggest. That's right—it uses our old pal, <TT>. The Format style's name is just there as a mnemonic for all of us "old HTML curmudgeons."

Menu List. The Menu List style acts in exactly the same way as the Directory List and Bullet List styles.

Numbered List. The Numbered List style numbers the paragraph with an Arabic numeral. Adding numbers with this style is different from using the Bullets pop-up menu:

- All paragraphs in the Numbered List Style are numbered consecutively.

- Numbered List style paragraphs are not indented with hung numbers; numbered paragraphs created with Bullet pop-ups use hung numbers.

- If you change the style of a paragraph in the middle of a series of paragraphs that use the Numbered List style, the numbers resume after the unnumbered paragraph (see Figure 5.15a).

If you use the Bullet pop-up menu to change the paragraph, the second group of numbered paragraphs starts again at 1 (see Figure 5.15b).

131

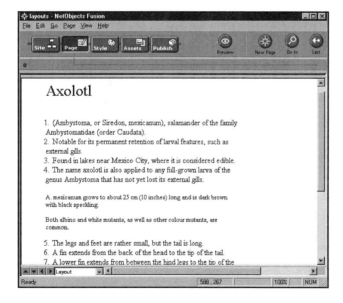

FIGURE 5.15A

Interrupting a numbered list by using a new Paragraph style.

FIGURE 5.15B

*Interrupting a
numbered list by
using the Bullet
pop-up menu.*

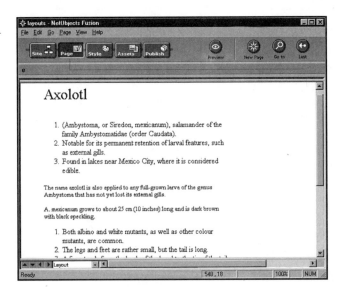

Creating Your Own Paragraph Styles

You can create your own paragraph styles that work in exactly the same way as
the preset styles. After the style is established, the style can be applied to new
paragraphs, and all of the attributes of the original paragraph are applied to
new paragraphs. (You've already seen an example of this feature in Chapter 2,
and you may be familiar with styles if you've used them in a page layout or word
processing application.)

FIGURE 5.16

*Paragraph styles
make setting up
outlines easier.*

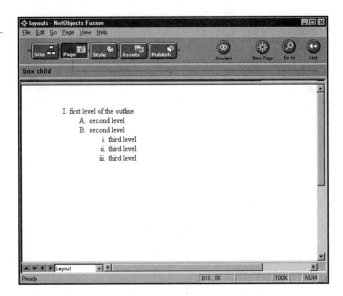

Example 1: Let's say that you want to set up an outline with three different levels of indentation, like the outline shown in Figure 5.16.

Each level of the outline should have its own numbering system. As you saw in the section on bullets, you can achieve this effect by repeated use of the **Text→Indent** command, but you can save yourself some time by setting up each level as a paragraph style.

1. Start with the list.

    ```
    a head
    b head
    c head
    ```

2. Select the "a head" line. Choose I,II,III from the Bullet pop-up menu.

3. Select Add from the Paragraph pop-up menu in the Properties palette. Name this style "a head" in the New Text Style dialog box.

4. Select the "b head" line. Choose **Text→Indent** *twice* and then choose A,B,C from the Bullet pop-up menu. Select Add from the Paragraph pop-up and name this style "b head."

5. Select the "c head" line. Choose **Text→Indent** three times and then choose 1,2,3 from the Bullet pop-up menu. Select Add from the Paragraph pop-up and name this style "c head."

6. In a new text box, enter the text that you want to outline.

7. Select the level one outline items and then select "a head" from the Paragraph pop-up menu. Follow the same procedure to apply the b head and c head styles to level two and level three items in the outline.

You can see how this can save you considerable effort, especially if you're developing an outline that's 20 or 30 lines long.

Example 2: Let's say you're designing a page that contains an interview in question and answer format. You'd like to use bold red type for the questions and indented black type for the answers (see Figure 5.17).

This is another perfect use of the Styles feature. After you've set up the question paragraph as you like it, define it as a style. Likewise, once you've got an answer style you like, add it to the Style list. In general, it's a good idea to establish styles for any type that isn't one of NetObjects Fusion default styles—it's easier in the long run, and it helps to make the site look consistent from page to page.

133

FIGURE 5.17

*Another practical
use of style.*

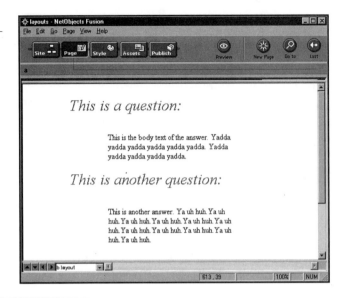

TIP

I find that it's easier if styles that go together appear next to each other in a style menu. Styles are added to the Paragraph pop-up menu in alphabetical order, so you can force them to appear together by using a leading character like *, -, or ~ in the style's name. In the real world, I give styles names such as *question and *answer.

Pictures

There's very little doubt that pictures made the Web what it is today. After all, the original Web browser, Lynx, was around for years without getting anyone too excited. It was Mosaic, with its support for inline graphics, that really made the Web explode.

(One of the wryest acknowledgments of this idea is the home page of Mosaic mastermind and Netscape kingpin Marc Andreessen—Andreessen's page, shown in Figure 5.18, is nothing but a GIF.)

If you've ever spent any money having color documents printed, you're probably already pretty excited about the idea of adding color pictures to your Web page. Traditional color printing is still pretty expensive, and doing basic scanning and creating color separations at a professional quality level is much more difficult than the scanner salesperson would have you believe.

Producing quality scans for Web pages is much easier and cheaper than print production. You can use a fairly inexpensive desktop scanner, rather than sending out for drum scans at 25–40 dollars a pop, and you don't have to worry about things like screen angles, dot gain, or expensive proofing systems.

Of course, there are new issues unique to Web publishing, but, honestly, they're not nearly as complicated as print stuff. We can cover most of the basics in a few pages.

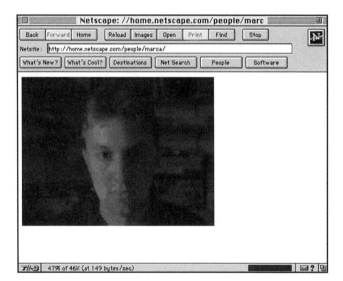

FIGURE 5.18

Marc Andreessen's home page. Load the URL into Netscape to see it.

135

TIP

Looking for information about clickable maps? They're covered in detail in Chapter 9. Much of the discussion that follows also applies, so if you're a complete image novice, read on.

Image Resolution

Creating images at the correct resolution is an important part of making sure that your Web site works as efficiently as possible. If your images are too large, it will place an unnecessary strain on your Web server software, and cause your pages to load slowly, especially when readers are loading your pages over a slow connection.

Mac monitors display 72 pixels per inch, as do most SVGA monitors on multimedia PCs. Image resolution is measured in samples per inch (s.p.i.). (This is very commonly, and incorrectly, stated as "dots per inch.") When you're creating images for Web pages, you want the image resolution to match the monitor resolution—that is, you want the image's final resolution to be 72 s.p.i. If the resolution is any higher, the extra samples are essentially thrown away.

Image resolution is very closely related to file size, which is in turn related to how quickly the file can be transferred to the reader's machine. Let's say that the reader is using a 22.8 modem. Table 5.1 shows the various file sizes and optimal transfer times per square inch of the file, when the file is scanned at various common scanning-software presets.

TABLE 5.1

Optimal transfer times per square inch of a file.

Resolution (s.p.i.)	File Size (kilobytes)	Transfer Time (seconds)
72	16	5
150	66	23
300	264	91
1200	4,200	1,448

Note: Resolution refers to file sizes and transfer times per square inch at various image resolutions.

Transfer times depend on a lot of factors, but the bottom line here is that if you scan an image at your scanner's maximum resolution, a one-square inch image will occupy a significant chunk of your server's hard disk. It will also take at least half an hour to download—assuming that readers will wait around to see the image (they won't), and your server will have fewer CPU cycles to devote to other connections.

To help you avoid this pitfall, NetObjects Fusion displays placed images at 72 s.p.i., no matter what their actual resolution may be. Every single pixel in the image is displayed, so if the resolution is greater than 72 s.p.i., the image will be larger than its correct size.

Take a look at Figure 5.20. These images, created with Adobe Photoshop, both have an image size of 1" × 1." The image at the left has a resolution of 72 s.p.i., and the image at the right has a resolution of 150 s.p.i. As you can see, the 150 s.p.i. image is about twice as big as the 72 s.p.i. image.

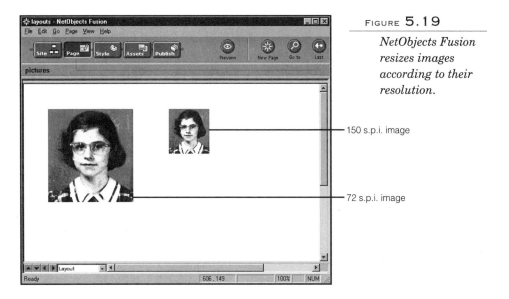

FIGURE 5.19

NetObjects Fusion resizes images according to their resolution.

This procedure makes sizing images a little more intuitive because it works in a way that's similar to the approach used in Adobe Photoshop and other image editors. The image will appear in NetObjects Fusion and on the finished page at exactly the same size as it does in the image editor's 1:1 view ratio. (See your image editor's manual for specifics on how view ratios work. In Photoshop, the view ratio is displayed in the window's title bar, directly after the filename.)

137

File Formats

If you use image files for traditional desktop publishing, you're probably used to using files in TIFF and EPS format. Casual users may be familiar with the PICT and BMP files created by applications like SuperPaint or Windows Paint. The most common file formats found on the Web are GIF and JPEG.

NetObjects Fusion enables you to work with all these graphics file formats. If you create your files in GIF or JPEG format yourself, you can simply place them in your Web page layout without any fuss. If you want to import a file that's in another format, NetObjects Fusion converts the file, giving you a choice between GIF and JPEG as target formats.

GIF Files

GIF stands for Graphics Interchange Format. GIFs were developed by the folks at CompuServe as a compact file format that CompuServe users could quickly transfer via modem.

Most common graphics file formats represent a color image as a set of layers—each layer represents one of the component colors that make up the image. Each pixel in the image is represented in each of the layers: a cyan pixel might have a brightness value of 255 in the green and blue layers, and a brightness value of 0 in the red layer.

GIFs *don't* work this way. Rather, the GIF defines a palette of colors to be used in the image and assigns each pixel one of the palette's color. A GIFs palette can contain a maximum of 256 colors—if the image contains more than 256 colors, the GIF-creating program does its best to fake, using the closest possible color or eye-fooling combinations of colors in adjacent pixels.

TIP

You don't ever need to mess around with converting files to GIFs yourself—NetObjects Fusion handles this for you automatically. However, if you're interested in seeing the palette that comprises a GIFs color, open it up with an application like Transparency, which displays the GIF's palette in...well...a palette.

Because the number of colors used in a GIF is limited, and because all of the GIF file's color information is stored in a single layer, GIFs are substantially smaller than TIFFs or EPS files. Of course, the image quality of a GIF isn't comparable to that of a TIFF, either, especially when you're printing.

JPEG Files

The JPEG file format was developed by the *J*oint *P*hotographer's *E*xpert *G*roup, and JPEGs were developed as a way to create very compact color image files. JPEG takes a completely different approach to trimming file sizes: It's based on compression.

You're probably familiar with common file-compression utilities such as StuffIt (Mac) and PKZip (Windows). These compression techniques manage to "abbreviate" the information in a file and can reduce a file's size by a factor of 25 or even 50 percent.

These kinds of file compression utilities are *lossless*. When you decompress your file, all of the original information—every single byte—is restored. JPEG uses similar techniques to reduce the file's size, but it uses *lossy* compression: some of the file's information is thrown away, and it can never be restored. This compromise allows JPEG files to be *very* small—sometimes only five or ten percent of the original file size.

Fortunately, JPEG-savvy programs are very clever about what they throw away and how they reconstruct the lost information. In fact, although JPEG images are degraded from the original, it's sometimes hard to see any difference at all between the original and the JPEG.

I'm not promising that you won't ever see the side effects of the compression process. JPEG offers several levels of compression, and the more space you save, the more you'll see blurring, weird shadows, and other artifacts. (See Figure 5.20 for a side-by-side comparison.) Even at the same level of compression, the extent of distortion depends on the image: Different images yield different results.

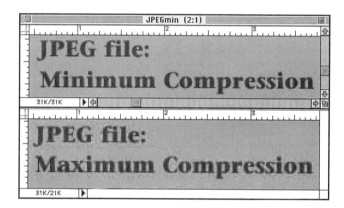

FIGURE 5.20

The image quality of a JPEG file depends on the compression level.

Special File Formats

There are a few special kinds of files that you'll see when you're surfing the Web. The ones I'll discuss—transparent images, interlaced, or "fade-in" images, and animated images—are variants of the GIF format.

- **Transparent GIFs.** A special flavor of the GIF format, called GIF89, supports transparent pixels that show the color of the Web page underneath. You can make parts of a GIF transparent in NetObjects Fusion, which handles the conversion to GIF89 automatically.

- **Interlaced GIFs.** You've probably seen the kinds of Web page images that appear blurry when first loaded and gradually come into focus. These are called interlaced GIFs, and for technical reasons, they're not used much nowadays. NetObjects Fusion does not support interlaced GIFs.

- **Animated GIFs.** There are many ways to add animation to a Web page, and animated GIFs are probably the simplest and easiest. An animated GIF is just a sequence of GIFs that the browser loads one by one, usually in rapid succession. You'll learn how to make animated GIFs in the next sections.

There is support for other file formats out on the Web—ways to put things like FreeHand and BMP files directly into Web pages—but these kinds of tricks require the reader to have a plug-in loaded, and they aren't supported by NetObjects Fusion. It's really fairly uncommon to see these kinds of things in a typical surfing session.

JPEG versus GIF: Which Is Better?

At some point, you'll need to decide which file format to use for an image. If your image-editing software supports JPEG and GIF, you can make the decision when you save the file. Otherwise, you'll decide when you import the file into NetObjects Fusion. Fusion immediately presents a dialog box when you import the file (see Figure 5.21).

FIGURE 5.21

The Unsupported File Format dialog box.

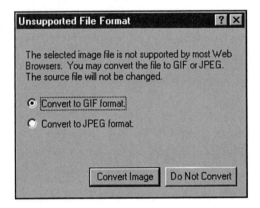

Neither GIF nor JPEG is correct for every situation. Otherwise, why would NetObjects Fusion present a dialog box, right? Here are a few factors to think about when you're picking an image format:

- GIFs are more widely supported. Nowadays, when Netscape Navigator and Internet Explorer share about 90 percent of the browser market between them, most users will have a browser that can load JPEGs. However, there are some browsers out there that don't support the JPEG format and won't display JPEGs at all. As with all technical minutia, the use of JPEGs can become a political issue on the Web, but the furor over JPEGs has pretty much died down by mid-1996.

- GIFs support transparency. If you want to make part of an image transparent, it must be a GIF file. Transparency is not supported in the JPEG format.

- JPEGs generally provide better image quality. A JPEG file is made out of layers, so it can display a wide gamut of colors, unlike GIFs. Consequently, JPEGs often look better than GIFs on-screen.

- Not always, however. You're more likely to see JPEG "artifacts" in line art, especially at small sizes. This is especially evident when scanned images contain type, which can get quite fuzzy when stored in a JPEG (see Figure 5.22).

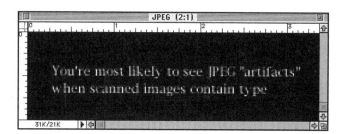

FIGURE 5.22

JPEG compression can make small type look fuzzy.

141

The GIF-JPEG gundown

	JPEG	GIF
Size	Small to very small	Small
Color gamut	Full	Limited
Sotware tool availability-good	Excellent	
Overall image quality	Varies according to amount of compression	Consistently good, especially for images with few colors

Sometimes it's just best to try it both ways, and see what looks best when you load the page in the browser window. The Unsupported File Format dialog box makes this relatively easy. Just save the file as a PICT in your image-editing program and place it in your layout twice, once as a GIF and once as a JPEG. (Be sure to check it in the browser window, not just in NetObjects Fusion.)

Placing and Sizing Images

Now that you've got an idea what sort of file you'll need, and at what size, let's look at how NetObjects Fusion handles image files: how you can place, size, and otherwise manipulate images in your layout.

There are three basic steps to the picture-placing procedure:

1. Use the Picture tool to specify where the image will go.

2. Use a file dialog box to specify the image to be placed.

3. Use the Picture tab in the Properties palette to adjust the image's properties, as necessary.

Let's work through this with one of the sample images included with the NetObjects Fusion package. I'm going to use one of the free samples of the PhotoDisc Objects that's included with the NetObjects Fusion beta distribution; the same file may or may not be included with your copy of Fusion. (Look in the /Parts/Design Parts/PhotoDisc Media Resources/PhotoDisc Objects folder to see what you've got.)

You can use the picture tool (the second icon in the second row of the tool palette) in two ways:

- If you're going to use the picture at its actual size, you can simply click the Picture tool cursor where you'd like the top left corner of the image to appear.

- If you want the picture to be a particular size, you can use the Picture tool to draw a box that's the size you want the picture to be. Drag with the picture tool to create the box, and release the mouse button when the box is the size you want it to be.

It doesn't really matter which approach you use—you can easily resize the image after it's been placed. I tend to click to position the box, as I would in Adobe PageMaker, but Quark users will probably instinctively draw boxes.

After you've specified the location by clicking or drawing a box, NetObjects Fusion presents the Image File Open Dialog box, as shown in Figure 5.23. This dialog box works pretty much like a standard dialog box, but allows you to preview the image to be placed.

By default, NetObjects Fusion filters the display of filenames so that only files with the .JPEG and .GIF extension to the filename appear in the window. If there are text files, or TIFFs, or anything else in the current folder, they won't appear in the display. (This is a fairly common convention in file dialog boxes and is probably familiar to you.)

You can set the filter to different file types, or remove the filter and show all files regardless of type, by choosing the appropriate option from the file type pop-up menu. Naturally, it doesn't make much sense to place something like a text file or an application as an image. NetObjects Fusion will give you a hint by leaving the preview box empty if it can't handle the selected file. If you try to place it anyway, NetObjects Fusion will put an empty placeholder box in the layout (see Figure 5.24).

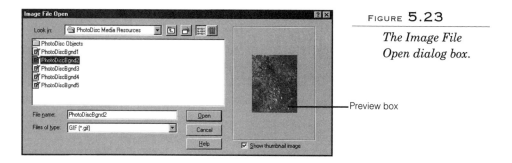

FIGURE 5.23

The Image File Open dialog box.

Preview box

WARNING

If you preview or publish a page that contains a placeholder icon, the browser substitutes a broken image icon for the placeholder.

After you've selected the image in the file dialog box, NetObjects Fusion places the image in the layout. *An image is always in an image box.* When an image box is selected, it shows eight handles around its edges and no borders; an unselected image box has a border, but no handles.

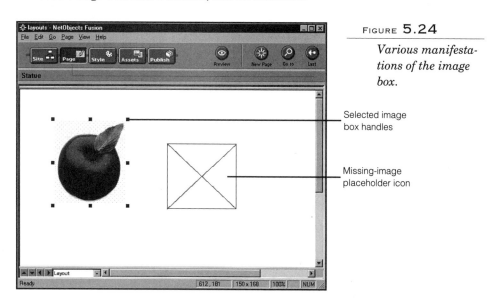

FIGURE 5.24

Various manifestations of the image box.

Selected image box handles

Missing-image placeholder icon

No matter what size box you draw with the Picture tool, an image's image box begins exactly the same size as the image, although you can resize the image box without resizing the image—in fact, this is the default. To resize the box, grab a handle and drag it. If the resized image box is larger than the image, the extra space will be left blank, as in the left of Figure 5.25; if the box is smaller than the image, the image will be cropped, and only the top left corner will appear, as in the right side of Figure 5.25.

FIGURE 5.25

The image box size and the image can be two different sizes.

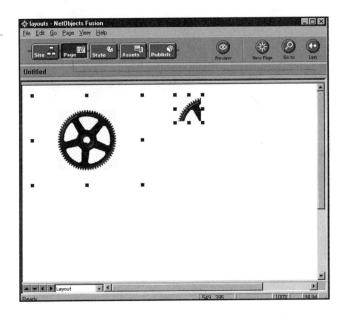

To control the relationship between the image and its image box, use the Picture tab in the Properties palette, shown in Figure 5.26. Like all the object-control tabs you've looked at, the Picture tab only appears when an image is selected.

There are three basic modes in the Settings group. When the Normal radio button is selected, the image appears at actual size, no matter what the size of the image box. To control the image's position *within* the image box, click the Align button and choose the appropriate settings in the Alignment dialog box.

When the Stretch radio button is selected, the image is resized to fill the image box, as shown in Figure 5.27. The image will fill the box from right to left and top to bottom, even if the image and image box have different shapes. If the image and image box have significantly different proportions, the picture will be significantly distorted.

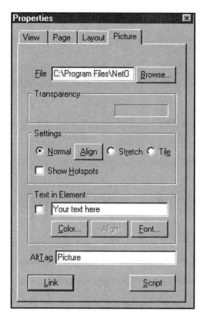

FIGURE 5.26

The Picture tab.

145

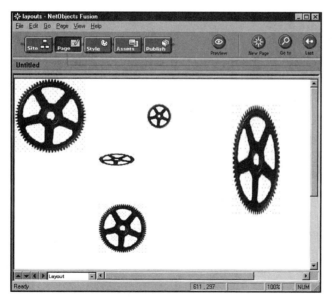

FIGURE 5.27

Images can be stretched to fill the image box.

When the Tile radio button is selected, the image is tiled, or repeated side-by-side to fill the image box. Each tile is exactly the same size as the original image: the tiles at the right and bottom edges are cropped, if necessary, to fit them inside the window (as shown in Figure 5.28).

FIGURE 5.28

Images can be tiled to fill the image box.

146

Adding Alt Tags

Some readers on slow connections may surf with their browser's automatic image-loading feature turned off; a few Luddites out there use Web browsers that don't support images at all! Alt tags are a way to let such users know what they're missing by providing a short text description of what the image contains.

By default, NetObjects Fusion adds alt tags to each image. However, the default text substitute for the picture is "Picture"—not terribly descriptive. If you want, you can specify a more descriptive alt tag by typing it into the Alt Tag field at the bottom of the picture tab.

Making Images Transparent

It's easy to use NetObjects Fusion to make part of an image transparent. This effect is commonly used to outline a form, so that it creates an interesting shape—rather than a box—on the page (see Figure 5.29).

As I mentioned in the GIF versus JPEG discussion earlier in this section, transparent images are in special file format, called GIF89. If your image is already a GIF, or in a file format other than JPEG, you're all set—just be sure to convert the file to a GIF when you place it in your layout, if it's not a GIF already. NetObjects Fusion will handle the conversion from GIF to GIF89 automatically.

The techniques described next won't work with placed JPEG files. If your image is a JPEG, you'll need to do a little work outside NetObjects Fusion because you won't have the option to convert the file to a GIF when you import it. (Fusion just assumes that you want it to stay in JPEG form.) Before you place the file, use a utility like PolyView (Windows), Transparency (Mac), or an image-editing package like Photoshop to convert the file from JPEG to GIF.

FIGURE 5.29

The background of this image has been made transparent to let the back-ground color of the page show through.

147

> **TIP**
>
> You can find a link to PolyView at `http://www.pcwin.com/graphic.apps.html` and many other large Windows ftp sites. You can find Transparency at `http://wwwhost.ots.utexas.edu/mac/pub-mac-graphics.html` and many other Mac ftp sites.

After you've got a GIF on the page, it's easy to drop out sections of the image:

1. In the Layout tab of the Properties palette, set the background color of the page to a bright color, such as red, so that it's easy to see where the back-ground shows through the transparent image. Although this step isn't necessary, it makes the "proofing" process easier.

2. Click the image's image box to select it.

3. Click the Use Current Color checkbox in the Transparency group in the Picture tab of the Properties palette. (If you don't see the Use Current Color checkbox in the Transparency group, you haven't selected a GIF.)

4. Choose the Picture tool in the Tools Palette. Notice that a set of secondary tools appears at the bottom of the Tools palette. Choose the Eyedropper tool from the Secondary tools section of the palette (see Figure 5.30).

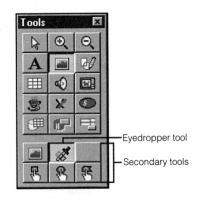

Eyedropper tool

Secondary tools

5. Click inside the image on the color you want to drop out. Notice that the selected color appears in the color swatch inside the Transparency group in the Picture tab. You *won't* see a preview of the effect in NetObjects Fusion.

6. Click the Preview button. Only the selected color will be transparent and all the pixels of that color will change, even if the color isn't contiguous with the color patch that you sampled with the eyedropper. You may need to try a few different sample points to get the effect you want.

7. Change the background color of the page back to its original color if you changed it in step one.

Sometimes, you just can't seem to make the transparent the way you want. Usually, this is because areas within the foreground are the same color as the color of the background, and these parts of the foreground drop out. In cases like this, you may need to go in and retouch the image with an image editor. Let's say you're working with an image that's got a white background and white highlights within the image's shape, such as the statue shown in Figure 5.31. You'd like to outline the shape on a Web page that has a blue background.

If you sample the white color in the image's background to make the background transparent, the highlights below the statue's neck and the white thunderbolts that he's holding will turn blue, too. This is a bad thing.

To correct this, you need to paint the background a different color. You can use any color that's not in the image already, but it's easier to use a color that's similar to the color of the Web page that the image will appear on. In this particular case, you could probably use a paint-bucket style tool to slop in the color with a single click, but more difficult images may require closer work.

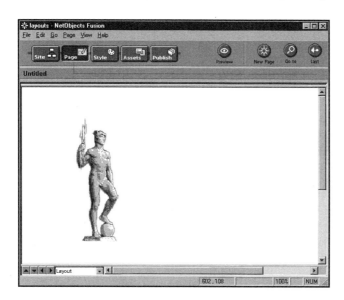

FIGURE 5.31

A problem image.

Adding Type to Images

NetObjects Fusion enables you to easily add type to images. This is a very convenient feature to have around—most image-editing software packages have mediocre type-handling capabilities anyway, and it's difficult to make revisions to type that you've added manually.

The type that we discussed in the "Body Text" section earlier in this chapter is *really* an instruction to the Web browser to display a blob of text in a certain style. This kind of type is searchable, cut-and-pastable, and very, very compact. However, the reader and the browser have some control over how this type is displayed, and it may appear in a font, size, or style that you didn't specify.

Text in an image, on the other hand, is a picture of type, and it appears the same way in the browser window as it does in your layout. However, the picture of the text *isn't* the text, and the reader can't do anything with it.

(Confused? You might think of body text as being like email, and the type in an image as being like a FAX. You can edit an email document, or put it into Microsoft Word and search it, or lay it out in PageMaker in 36 pt. Arnold

Böecklin. You can't do any of these things with a FAX, but the receiver of the FAX knows that it looks like what went into the FAX machine at the other end.)

Let's say that you want to add some type to the tiled image that you saw in Figure 5.27.

1. Select the image's image box.

2. Check the *Your Text Here* checkbox in the Text in Element group. Replace *Your Text Here* with, well, your text.

3. Click in the color button to set the text's color with the standard NetObjects Fusion Color dialog box.

4. Click the alignment button and use the standard NetObjects Fusion alignment dialog box to position the type within the image. (The type is bounded by the image, *not* the image box.)

5. Click the Font button to set the type to your tastes. Remember, you can use any font or size you like here—you don't need to worry about what readers have installed on their systems.

That's it! The result is shown in Figure 5.32. If you want to change the type in the image, just edit the text in the *Your Text Here* field. (If you've ever created buttons with text by hand, you know how tedious these kinds of corrections can be—especially positioning the type consistently from button to button. This feature is another thing I really like about Fusion.)

FIGURE **5.32**

Type added to an image.

Creating Animated GIFs

There are many ways to add animation to a page, and I'll cover some of the more sophisticated ways—such as Shockwave and Java—in Section III of this book. However, if you want to add a small, simple, noninteractive animation, the easiest way is via an animated GIF.

To create an animated GIF, you must first create the individual frames of the animation. Although it's not strictly necessary, it's best if all the frames are the same size (to avoid jerkiness) and share the same background color (if not, it may introduce flicker). I've included a set of GIFs on the NetObjects Fusion Handbook CD-ROM for you to play with—you can find them in the /book/Animated GIFs/Frames folder.

TIP

It's very helpful to put all of your animation frames in the same folder, and name them consecutively with names like a.gif, b.gif, c.gif or ball01.gif, ball02.gif, ball03.gif. If you use numbers, use leading zeros to keep 02 between 01 and 10.

151

You'll also need some special software to build Animated GIFs. There are a few different packages available as of this writing: I prefer Yves Piguet's freeware GifBuilder for the Mac, and the shareware GIF Construction Set for Windows 95.

TIP

You can find GIF Construction Set at http://www.mindworkshop.com/alchemy/gifcon.html and GifBuilder at http://iawww.epfl.ch/Staff/Yves.Piguet/clip2gif-home/GifBuilder.html.

If you use GIF Construction Set, be sure to pay the very reasonable shareware fee.

See the instructions that come with the software for the details on how to use the software's extended features. In short for GifBuilder:

1. Drag the GIF files to be included in the Animation into the GifBuilder window.

2. Choose **Option→Loop** if you want the animation to play repeatedly.

3. Choose **File→Build** to create the animation.

4. Drag the finished GIF onto Netscape Navigator, or load it with Internet Explorer's **File→Open** command.

5. If you like, use the **Option→Interframe Delay** to adjust the speed of the animation. (You'll need to rebuild and reload after this step to see the results.)

For GIF Construction Kit:

1. Choose **File→Animation Wizard (Control-A)**.

2. Answer the wizard's questions about where the image will appear, the style of the image, and the delay between frames. (The default, 100 hundredths, is a good starting place.)

3. Select the image files to be used: navigate to the folder where they reside, and select them, in order, from the file dialog box. When you've selected all of the files to be included, click Done.

4. Drag the finished GIF onto Netscape Navigator, or load it with Internet Explorer's **File→Open** command.

5. Although there are subtler ways to adjust the animation, the easiest way to change the speed of the animation is to rebuild the GIF with a new frame delay.

After you've completed your Animated GIF, you can place it and use it like an ordinary GIF. You can even tile it, but if you do so, only the first frame of the GIF will be used—there will be no animation.

Embellishments and Dingbats

There's another type of image that you often see in Web pages: things like customized rules, bullets, buttons, and the little flourishes called *dingbats*.

Although you may think of these elements as a separate category from scanned images, these kinds of images are exactly the same as scanned images. They're stored in GIF or JPEG format, and the same kinds of rules and techniques apply. You can resize them, tile them, make' em transparent—whatever you'd do with a scan.

NetObjects Fusion provides you with a library of these little Web page embellishments. In the /Parts/Design Parts folder you'll find the following:

- **Animated GIFs.**

- **Arrows.** Arrows are handy for using as buttons, as you saw in Chapter 4. There are many different arrows styles to accommodate a variety of site styles.

- **Alphabets.** NetObjects Fusion includes a complete alphabet of characters in a nice script face. You can use them as drop caps, for headlines, or to spell out messages in animated GIFs (see Figure 5.33).

FIGURE **5.33**

Building a drop cap with the alphabet clip art included with NetObjects Fusion.

153

- **Dingbats.** Fusion includes a few dingbats that you can use to dress up your pages. It's easy to create your own dingbats with dingbat fonts like Carta or Wingdings—just insert them into a blank picture, using the Text in Element group in the Picture palette.

- **Flourishes.** You can use calligraphic flourishes in place of ordinary rules.

- **Motif shapes.** The motif shapes folder contains dingbat-like clipart with Web and Web-related themes: checkboxes, mail and postage icons, and my favorite, puzzle pieces.

- **Navigation buttons.** There are two sets of navigation buttons, "oval" and "salsa," that you can use in conjunction with the Smart Links feature that I discussed in Chapter 4. The buttons are just image; you'll need to add the links yourself.

● **Symbols.** The symbols folder contains some miscellaneous dingbat-type clipart.

Drawing Tools

Yet another innovation that NetObjects Fusion has introduced to Web design at the page level are basic drawing tools. Using these tools, you can generate simple graphics on the fly while you're working in Fusion. Elements that you create by drawing behave like other image objects in Fusion.

NetObjects Fusion's drawing features enable you to create rectangles, circles, lines, polygons, and rounded/beveled rectangles (see Figure 5.34).

Each of these shapes has its own handles and can be reshaped after it has been placed on the page. Although shapes can overlap in the NetObjects Fusion layout, they will *not* overlap in the browser window. As you might suspect, these graphics are GIF format files that NetObjects Fusion generates on the fly when you preview or publish your site.

TIP

You can use the Rectangle tool anywhere you'd ordinarily create a solid block of color. One practical use of the Rectangle tool would be to make simple buttons to external URLs.

The main drawing tool is the third icon in the second row of the Tools palette. When this tool is selected, five secondary drawing tools appear at the bottom of the Tools palette. Each of these tools is used to draw one of the basic shapes supported by Fusion. Figure 5.35 identifies each of the secondary drawing tools by shape.

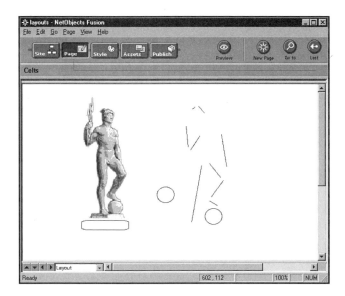

FIGURE **5.34**

Some basic shapes supported by Fusion's drawing tools.

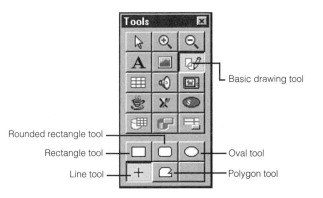

Basic drawing tool

Rounded rectangle tool

Rectangle tool

Line tool

Oval tool

Polygon tool

FIGURE **5.35**

155

The basic drawing tools.

Rectangles, Ovals, and Rounded Rectangles

Drawing rectangles and ovals is as simple as drawing a picture box, and by now, most of these shapes' attributes will seem pretty familiar. NetObjects Fusion's rounded rectangles are a little different from the kinds of rounded rectangles you might be accustomed to using in drawing programs like Adobe Illustrator, but they're easy to work with, and they're kinda cool as rounded rectangles go.

To draw a regular rectangle, choose the Rectangle tool, pick a corner, and drag. NetObjects Fusion draws the rectangle's box with a dashed line until you let go of the mouse. After the rectangle is the size you want it to be, let go. Conventional rectangles have eight handles—one on each side and one at each corner—and you can resize the rectangle by dragging any of these points.

You draw an oval in exactly the same way by using the oval tool. Like a rectangle, an oval has eight handles. You draw rounded rectangles in the same way by using the rounded rectangle tool. A rounded rectangle has *nine* handles: one for each corner and edge, and a curve handle that controls the rectangle's shape.

The curve handle is inside the rounded rectangle. It can be moved freely within the lower-right quadrant of the rectangle. The closer the handle is to the right edge of the rectangle, the straighter the rectangle's horizontal lines; the closer to the bottom edge of the rectangle, the straighter the rectangle's vertical lines. If the handle is at the center of the rectangle, the rectangle is so rounded that it becomes a circle, and if the control is at the extreme lower right, the rectangle looks almost as square as a conventional rectangle (see Figure 5.36).

156

FIGURE 5.36

Four different flavors of the rounded rectangle.

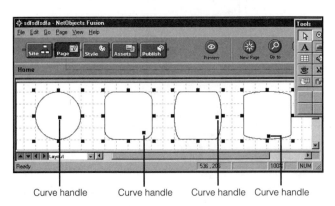

Using the Rectangle, Oval, or Round Rectangle tab in the Properties palette, you can set the basic attributes of the shape:

- To set the fill color, click the Color button to the right of the Fill label. NetObjects Fusion presents its standard color dialog box.

- To set the stroke color, click the Color button in the Border group. To set the stroke weight, enter a value from 1–20 in the Size field.

- To add type to the shape, use the Text in Element group. Adding type to a shape is *exactly* like adding type to a scan, as described earlier in this chapter.

- Remember, the shape is stored as a GIF, and so it may not appear in some reader's window. To customize the alternate text displayed when the image doesn't load, type your own message into the Alt Tag field.

Lines

Lines are a little simpler, and a little more complicated. To draw a line, pick the Line tool from the secondary drawing tools and draw. You'll see a preview of the line as you draw. A line has two handles, one at each end. You can move the line as you want by moving the handles.

The only attribute of a basic line is its color. To change it, click the Color button in the Options group in the Line tab. NetObjects Fusion presents the standard color dialog box.

However, you can choose to use a special line in place of a simple rule; the picture that has been defined as the "picture line" for the current style. Usually, the picture line is stylized to harmonize with the other components of the style, such as the page banner and navigation bars (see Figure 5.37).

157

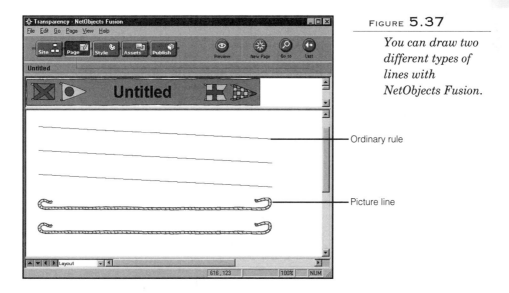

FIGURE 5.37

You can draw two different types of lines with NetObjects Fusion.

Ordinary rule

Picture line

To see what the picture line for the current style looks like, click the Style view button and scroll down to the bottom of the page. The style's picture line appears just below the Data List Icon and Visited Link Color icons. To choose the picture line, click the Default Line Style radio button in the Options group in the Line tab.

The big limitation to this kind of line is that it must be horizontal. It can't be rotated, even 90 degrees. Fortunately, NetObjects Fusion remembers the angle and size of the line you drew in the first place, so if you switch to the picture line and switch back, your line isn't lost.

Polygons

OK...OK...I know: A rectangle *is* a polygon. What the polygon tool draws are irregular polygons: Arbitrary shapes that you can specify point by point.

To draw a polygon:

1. Select the polygon tool from the secondary drawing tools.

2. Click in the layout to position the first point in the polygon.

3. Click somewhere else to specify the second point.

4. Continue clicking at different points in the layout to add points to the polygon. (It's OK if the lines cross.)

5. When you're ready to draw the last point, double-click instead of single-clicking. NetObjects Fusion adds the last point and releases you from polygon-drawing mode.

Each of the points that you added when you drew the polygon becomes a handle, and you can reshape the polygon as you want by dragging the handles around.

After you've built the polygon, you can set its attributes—fill color, stroke weight, etc.—in exactly the same way you'd set the attributes of a rectangle.

Page Geometry

When all of the elements are on the page, you might find that you want to adjust the layout, to make sure everything lines up nicely. NetObjects Fusion provides alignment and sizing commands that make this job easier and the results more precise.

To see how this works, try setting up a set of scattered elements like the rectangles shown in Figure 5.38. (Hint: Use copy and paste to quickly build something like this.) Now, use the selection tool to select all of these elements at once.

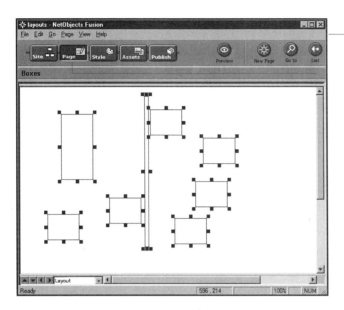

FIGURE 5.38

A random scattering of rectangles.

Now, choose **Page→Align Elements →Bottom**. All the selected elements move up on the page so that the bottom of each element aligns with the bottom of the topmost element.

Here's something that's really interesting about NetObjects Fusion: You can undo this group move item by item. Choose **Edit→Undo**. Note that a single element moves back to its own place. Now choose **Edit→Undo** again—another element returns to its original position. (It looks a little like a game of Tetris if you do it quickly enough.)

As you can see, there are several alignment options. You can try each of them out to see how they work.

You can resize multiple elements in a similar way. To try this out, draw two rectangles (or whatever) of different sizes and select them both. When you choose **Page →Size Elements →Height**, the taller element is resized to the height of the shorter element. Similarly, choose **Page→Size Elements→Width** to reduce all elements to the width of the narrowest element.

Importing Pages

This is all very nice, you may say to yourself, but what about the pages that you've already struggled to create in HTML? Are you supposed to throw those away now?

159

No, probably not. NetObjects Fusion enables you to import HTML pages into your layout, whether those pages were created with Fusion or not. Under ideal conditions, the page will look the same in your layout as it did in the original HTML.

Unfortunately, it doesn't always work correctly, at least not in the early betas that were available when this book went to press. In general, you'll find that simple pages made up of text and graphics import smoothly. Pages that contain more complex elements, such as tables or Java applets, don't always fare so well.

Hopefully, this problem will be fixed by the time you read this—the NetObjects R & D crew is hard at work on fine-tuning the software. Be sure to keep an eye on http://www.netobjects.com for news.

To import a page:

1. Click in the section of the layout—the header, body, or footer—where you'd like the imported page to go.

2. Choose **File →Import Page**.

3. If you want, cut and paste elements to move them to other sections of the page. (You might want to put a page banner in a header, for instance.)

Summary

You've learned quite a bit in this chapter—it's the longest one in the book. You have learned:

- The parts of a page.

- How to customize NetObjects Fusion's layout controls.

- How to set a page's attributes.

- How to control type.

- How to use and create paragraph styles.

- How to place and size images.

- How to make transparent images.

- How to make animated images.

- How to handle dingbats and other embellishments.

- How to draw basic shapes.

- How to fine-tune the alignment of your page.

- How to import pages.

In Chapter 6, you'll look at SiteStyles: what they are, how to use 'em, how to make 'em, and how to fine-tune 'em.

URL Roundup

- OpenType (Technology to embed fonts in Web pages):
  `http://www.adobe.com/type/opentype.html`

- PolyView (Windows file conversion utility):
  `http://www.pcwin.com/graphic.apps`

- Transparency (Mac file conversion utility):
  `http://wwwhost.ots.utexas.edu/mac/pub-mac-graphics.html`

- GIF Construction Set (Windows tool for animated GIFs):
  `http://www.mindworkshop.com/alchemy/gifcon.html`

- Gifbuilder (Mac tool for animated GIFs):
  `http://iawww.epfl.ch/Staff/Yves.Piguet/clip2gif-home/`
  `GifBuilder.html`

161

Style View

How often have you seen sites where every page has its own look, its own color scheme, and its own typography? The way that first- and second-generation Web page editors emphasize page design, rather than site design, encourages this kind of inconsistency. I'm probably a *little* over-sensitive because I work in a design studio, but most readers will notice that something is wrong—even if they can't quite put their finger on the problem.

Style view is one of the special features that sets NetObjects Fusion apart from the competition. By using Site view, you can apply a consistent look to all of the pages in your site, with a single application of a "SiteStyle." What's even better, it's just as easy to change the SiteStyle as it is to apply it.

Examples: What You Can Do

I love Style view—it's the icing on the NetObjects Fusion cake. It's not too hard to believe that visual site-builders and layout-style page editors were inevitable, but the style editor features of Fusion were a surprise to me. SiteStyles enables automatically generated components to have personality and...well...style.

As you saw in the tour in Chapter 2, Site view enables you to quickly change the overall look of all of a site's pages at once. Figure 6.1 shows the "Front Section" page of the ready-made Online Publishing site outline bundled with NetObjects Fusion.

FIGURE 6.1

The Online Publishing front page, out of the box.

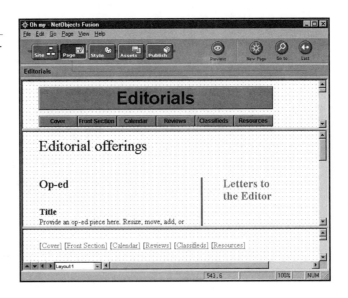

This seems a little drab for an online magazine. With one click in Site view mode, you can give your online magazine a completely different look, as shown in Figure 6.2.

FIGURE 6.2

The same page with a new SiteStyle applied.

This is the very same page, with the Chwast SiteStyle applied. It's quite a bit livelier than Figure 6.1, isn't it? It's perfect for, say, an online children's magazine, or a whimsical sailing magazine (if there are such things), or a literary magazine for snide crypto-yuppies.

Suppose that this isn't quite right—you want something a little less exuberant, but not quite as utilitarian as Figure 6.1. Another click, and you can change SiteStyles again, as shown in Figure 6.3.

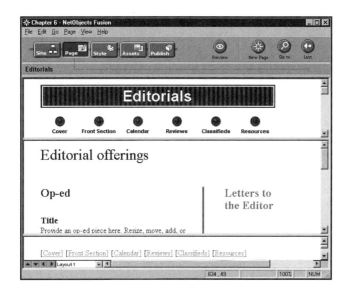

FIGURE 6.3

The same page in a third SiteStyle.

165

Here's the same page in the "Uptown" SiteStyle. Don't these look like three completely different sites?

What's really incredible is that these changes are applied to every page of the site at once. Making these kinds of changes in HTML, or even with a tool like Adobe PageMill, might take *weeks* with a medium-sized to large site. Actually, each of these changes took about 15 seconds with NetObjects Fusion, and all of these SiteStyles, and many more, come bundled with the Fusion package.

Suppose that none of the ready-made SiteStyles is quite right for your project. You can make your own SiteStyle and apply it to pages as quickly as you apply the bundled SiteStyles. Suppose that you're working on a magazine that features African Literature. Figure 6.4 shows the same page again, featuring a SiteStyle based on Yoruba *adire* cloth.

FIGURE 6.4

*The same page with
a homemade
SiteStyle applied.*

(By the way, this SiteStyle was designed by my wife, Chris Corcoran, who is, in the real world, a linguist specializing in African languages and a connoisseur of African fabrics.)

Creating your own SiteStyle takes a little time, but it's design time, not book-keeping time. Most of the work involved is in creating the style components, not defining the SiteStyle in NetObjects Fusion. After you've created the basic components, it's very easy to make them into a SiteStyle.

Applying SiteStyles

Let's take a look at the Style view. There are two basic modes in Style view:

- The SiteStyle Gallery, which enables you to look at each SiteStyle one by one

- Components, which enables you to adjust the individual components of the SiteStyle

You can switch between modes with the buttons in the Secondary control bar, as shown in Figure 6.5.

Set Style button   Mode Change buttons

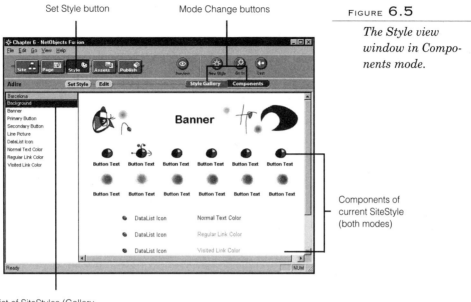

FIGURE 6.5

The Style view window in Components mode.

Components of current SiteStyle (both modes)

List of SiteStyles (Gallery mode) or list of components (Components mode)

TIP

> You can switch from Gallery mode to Components mode by double-clicking anywhere in the right panel. Oddly enough, you can't go back to Gallery mode by using the same shortcut.

In both modes, the right panel of Style window displays all the components of the current SiteStyle. If the Style Gallery button is selected, the left panel shows a list of available SiteStyles. If the Components button is selected, as it is in Figure 6.5, the left panel lists the names of the components that make up a SiteStyle.

Let's take a look at these individual components, which include banners, primary buttons, secondary buttons, the DataList icon, text color, rules, and backgrounds.

Applying a SiteStyle to Your Site

As you saw in our tour of the "NetObjects Fusion" section in Chapter 2, applying a SiteStyle to your site is as easy as clicking a single button. Let's review the basic procedure.

1. Click the Site view button to go to Site view.

2. Make sure the mode is set to Style Gallery in the Secondary control bar. (It should be in this mode already because it's the default setting.)

3. Scroll down the list of SiteStyle names in the right panel of Style view. To look at a style, select its name in the list. (This does *not* apply the SiteStyle to your site; it only displays it in the right panel of the Style View window.)

4. To apply a SiteStyle to your site, click the Set Style button in the Secondary control bar when the desired style is selected in the left panel. NetObjects Fusion applies the style to every page of your site.

Remember, a SiteStyle is a *collection* of components, and when you apply a SiteStyle, it affects every style element—banners, buttons, lines, and so on. You can't change just banners, or change just buttons, because SiteStyle is a package deal. If you really want to mix and match elements from different ready-made SiteStyles, you'll need to create a new style of your own, and borrow the components from other SiteStyles. (See "Creating Your Own SiteStyles" later in this chapter.

Banners

A SiteStyle's banner appears as the top element in the right panel of the Style window. You've seen a zillion banners by now. All the sites included with NetObjects Fusion have banners in their headers by default.

This doesn't mean that you need to confine the use of banners to the header, although that is their most natural location. Let's say that you're working with the Industrial SiteStyle. I love this banner, but I'm not sure that I'd want to put it on every page of the site—it's just a little too ornate as a recurring element.

Figure 6.6 shows an alternative use of banners. I've cut the banner from the header and pasted it to the top of the home page. Notice that it still retains the page's name. Because it's not in the header any more, it won't appear on any of the other pages. Basically, it's being used as a one-shot illustration that fits in quite nicely with the rest of the elements on the page.

(There's no special reason why I've changed the Navigation bar in the header to text—it just seemed more natural when it's above the header.)

FIGURE 6.6

An ordinary banner that is pressed into service as an illustration.

Primary Buttons

169

A SiteStyle's primary buttons appear directly below the SiteStyle's banner in the Style window. There are actually two kinds of primary buttons: ordinary buttons and highlighted buttons. The SiteStyle's highlighted button is the second button on the left in the SiteStyle display (see Figure 6.7).

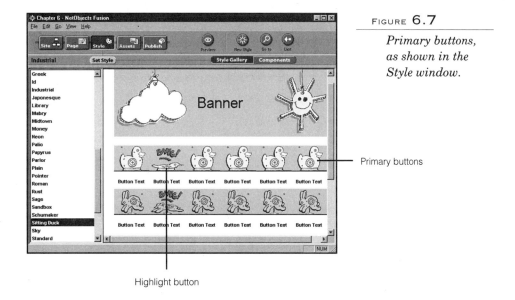

FIGURE 6.7

Primary buttons, as shown in the Style window.

Highlighted buttons are used when a page's navigation bar shows the page itself; for example, when the bar's link style is set to Current Page and siblings. The use of highlighted buttons is optional, and it can be set in the Nav. Bar tab of the Properties palette, as discussed in Chapter 4.

Every site template included with NetObjects Fusion has a set of primary buttons in its header. As with banners, you can move these elements out of the header by cutting and pasting them, if you like.

Secondary Buttons

A SiteStyle's secondary buttons appear directly below the primary buttons in the Style window's display. Like primary buttons, a set of secondary buttons includes a highlight button, which appears as the second button on the left in the display (see Figure 6.8).

You learned about secondary buttons in Chapter 4. Secondary buttons function just like primary buttons, but have a different look. They're useful when you have two (or more) tiers of buttons in the header, or when you want to use buttons, rather than text links, in the footer.

FIGURE 6.8

Secondary buttons.

Secondary buttons

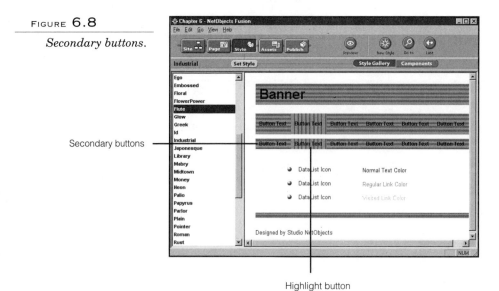

Highlight button

TIP

If you like a SiteStyle's secondary buttons better than the primary buttons, you can certainly use them instead. The design police won't come and get you. You don't need to change the SiteStyle—just check the secondary buttons radio button in the Buttons group of the Nav. Bar tab of the Properties palette while the Navigation bar is selected.

Most of NetObjects Fusion's ready-made SiteStyles don't include secondary buttons by default—they're used only if you add them.

DataList Icons

A SiteStyle's DataList icon appears in the left column directly below the secondary buttons in the Style window. There's only one DataList icon for each SiteStyle—the same icon is repeated three times in the display (see Figure 6.9).

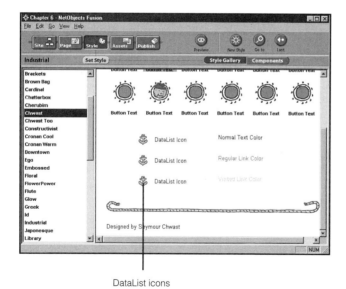

FIGURE 6.9

171

DataList icon.

DataList icons

You had a glimpse of how DataLists work in Chapter 4, and you'll look at them in detail in Chapter 12. Here's the basic idea: NetObjects Fusion creates a set of identical pages and automatically generates an index of the identical pages on the parent page. The DataList icon is used to bullet each item in the list.

The Online publication site uses stacked pages for features, and indexes these stacked pages on the Front Section page. Figure 6.10 shows how the index is displayed in the layout.

FIGURE 6.10

A DataList icon, as it appears in the layout.

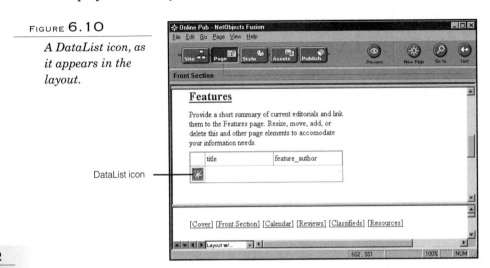

DataList icon

Let's add a few pages to the stack to see how this pans out in the browser window:

1. Go to the "Features" page (in Style view mode).

2. Click the "+" icon next to the words "Stacked Page" in the Secondary control bar. In fact, click it a few times.

3. Go back to the "Editorial" page.

4. Click the Preview button. Figure 6.11 shows how DataList icons display in the browser window.

5. After you're in the browser, click one of the DataList icons. The browser takes you to the page that is indexed in the same line as the icon. For example, the icon is a link to the indexed page.

WARNING

Some of the DataList icons built into the ready-made SiteStyles don't really look like navigation buttons, at least not to me. The orange rectangle in the Standard SiteStyle strikes me as especially non-buttonlike. You might want to alter such

DataList icons by using the techniques described later in this chapter, or put some sort of explicit instructions (such as, "push the orange buttons") along with the index.

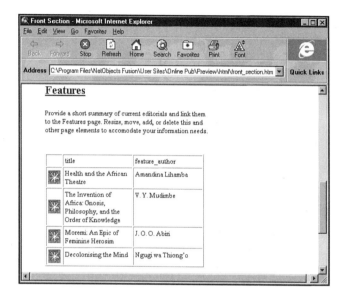

FIGURE 6.11

DataList icons, as they appear in the browser window

Text Color

A SiteStyle's text color set appears in the column to the right of the Data List icons in the Style window. Three different text colors are specified in each SiteStyle: a color for body text, a color for Regular links, and a color for Visited links.

In your Web surfing sessions, you've probably noticed that text links to other pages or sites are usually rendered in a color other than regular text. By default, body text is black in the browser window, whereas links to places you've never been before are blue. After you've visited a site, links to that site are displayed in red, rather than blue—even if the links are in pages you've never visited before.

You've probably been to sites where this color scheme has been altered. It's not too uncommon to see white type reversed out of a black background. Often, the text links on such pages use pastel colors, rather than blue and red. Web page designers can specify any color they like for both body text and links.

TIP

Remember that the user has control over how color elements appear. Most Web browsers, including Navigator and Internet Explorer, enable the reader to override any color scheme built into the page with the reader's own choices.

In Chapter 5, you learned how to change the colors of particular paragraphs of text, and it's a useful technique for making special words or paragraphs stand out. The text color in the Style view is simply the default text color for all the rest of the text throughout the site. (Don't worry—paragraphs that you've colored by hand or with paragraph styles will be unaffected by change of SiteStyle or by editing the SiteStyle's text color.)

Rules

A site's line picture is displayed at the bottom of the Style window (see Figure 6.12).

FIGURE 6.12

A SiteStyle's line picture.

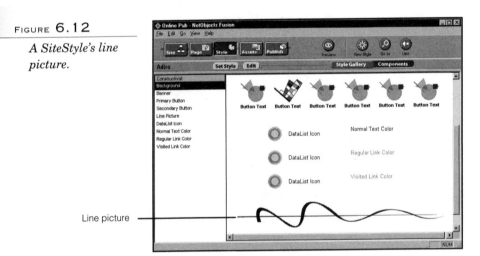

Line picture

You've already had a look at line pictures in Chapter 5, when you looked at the Line Drawing tool. A line picture can be used as a rule anywhere that you draw a line, with the restriction that line pictures are always horizontal.

Remember, a line picture is just a picture, and pictures can be altered and placed by hand. If you want to use the site's line as a vertical or even diagonal rule, you can do it.

Assume you're working with the Standard SiteStyle, and you want to use the picture line vertically on both sides of a page. You can do the following:

1. Find the file /Styles/Standard/Lines/StandardLine and make a copy of it. Put the copy in the same folder as the rest of the art for the project, rather than in the file /Styles/Standard/Lines/ directory, and call it something like "vertical line."

2. Open the new file with your image editor and rotate the image 90 degrees. (Every image editor handles rotation in a different way. In Photoshop, use the **Item → Rotate→ 90° CW/CCW** menu commands. If you're using another program, consult the program manual.) Save it and close the image file.

3. Use the NetObjects Fusion Picture tool to place the new image. (See Chapter 5 for specifics on using the Picture tool to add pictures to your layout.)

175

Of course, you can rotate the line by any angle you want—it doesn't need to be 90 degrees. However, some image editors may not support free rotation, or may produce unacceptably jagged results if you try something like 22 degrees.

Now, this is a hack, and NetObjects Fusion doesn't know that the new image is made from a picture line. If you change SiteStyles, the line *won't* change to the picture line of the new SiteStyle. This is just a sneaky way to get free clip art that matches the look of the site after you've decided on a SiteStyle.

Background

The background displayed behind the elements of a SiteStyle in the Style view window is the default page background used in the SiteStyle.

The background happens to be solid white in almost all the SiteStyles included with NetObjects Fusion, but it's possible to specify another color, or even a picture, as the style's background (see Figure 6.13). You'll learn how to edit the background color or add a background image in the "Creating Your Own SiteStyles" section.

FIGURE 6.13

A SiteStyle with a picture as a background.

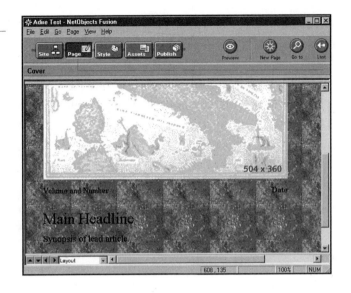

Creating Your Own SiteStyles

Because most SiteStyle components are essentially images, creating your own SiteStyle is as simple as creating a set of images and assigning each image to a component in NetObjects Fusion. (I've included the parts that my wife designed for her *adire* SiteStyle on the *NetObjects Fusion Handbook* CD-ROM in the folder /Book/Styles/Adire if you want to try this out before you build your own components.)

Creating Components

First, you need to build the parts that will make up your SiteStyle. You'll need to make (or borrow) the following items:

- One banner
- One regular primary button
- One highlighted primary button
- One regular secondary button
- One highlighted secondary button
- One DataList icon
- One line picture

You can build these elements in any image-editing program that can save files in a format that NetObjects Fusion can read. (If you can place a file format as a picture, you can use it as a StyleElement.)

Image-Creation Software

When I'm creating buttons for a Web site, I usually start working in Adobe Illustrator's drawing program. (It's much easier to make sure that everything's consistently sized, lined-up and centered in a program that has a ruler and the right tools!) When I'm finished in Illustrator, I save my work as an EPS and drop it onto Photoshop, apply any texturizing filters or drop-shadows in the 'shop, and save it as a GIF. (Nowadays, you can rasterize your image right in Illustrator 6.0.) You can use other drawing programs such as Macromedia FreeHand or Deneba Canvas in the same way.

Of course, you don't need to add any kind of text labels to these elements—NetObjects Fusion automatically adds the correct labels. All you need to worry about is the component's basic appearance.

When NetObjects Fusion puts buttons into a Navigation bar, it butts them up against each other so that their edges touch. Take a look at Figure 6.14—the buttons seem to be evenly spaced under the banner. The edges of the buttons don't seem to touch, but there's a trick here, as you'll see in the next section.

177

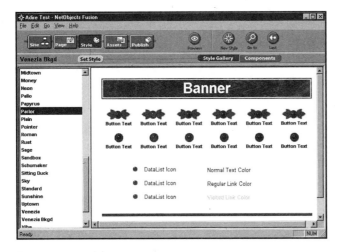

FIGURE 6.14

The space between buttons is an illusion.

In fact, the image file that contains the button has included substantial white space on either side of the button image. The entire image is about 75 pixels wide, but the button itself is only about 25 pixels in diameter. Figure 6.15 shows what the button really looks like in an image-editing program.

FIGURE 6.15

The space is part of the buttons, not between the buttons.

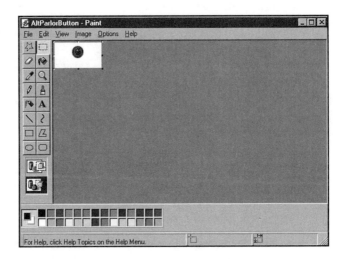

That white space at the bottom of the button is there to accommodate the button's label. If you want the button's label to overprint the button's image, this large margin isn't necessary.

Similarly, DataList icons benefit from a few pixels of "air" on each side—the amount will vary, according to the image, but five pixels or so should be about right in most cases. You might want to add a few pixels above and below rules, but it doesn't need any space on the left and right edges. Banners don't need any margin at all.

Table 6.1 shows some suggested sizes for SiteStyle components. These sizes *include* space added for margins. You can certainly vary from these sizes—NetObjects Fusion doesn't have any limits about the sizes or proportions of SiteStyle components—but these sizes work well with the way that navigation bars and DataLists are set up, and make for a compact Web page that won't take forever to load.

TABLE 6.1

Typical Sizes of Style Elements

Element	Height (Pixels)	Width (Pixels)
Banner	50-75	500
Button	50	75-100
DataList Icon	10-25	10-25
Line	10-50	500

Note: These sizes include space added for margins.

Building the SiteStyle

After you've created a set of components, you can assign each image to the component's name in the Style menu:

1. Assemble all the component images into a single folder. You can put the folder anywhere you like.

2. Click the New Style button. Give the SiteStyle a name—any name is fine, as long as it's not already used as a style name.

3. NetObjects Fusion enters Components mode, if you're not there already, and presents you with a fresh, blank right panel.

4. Double-click "Banner" in the left column. NetObjects Fusion presents the Banner dialog box.

5. Click the Browse button next to the Picture field and use the File dialog box to navigate to the picture that you created as your SiteStyle's banner.

6. Click the Font button and choose the attributes for the type to be added to the banner. This type will be built into the image, so you don't have to worry about which fonts readers may have installed on their machines.

7. Use the alignment controls to position the type within the banner. Click OK.

8. Double-click "Primary Buttons" in the left column of the Style window. The Primary Buttons' dialog box is similar to the Banner dialog box, but you must specify both the regular and highlighted buttons in the same dialog box.

9. Double-click "Secondary Buttons." The Secondary Buttons dialog box is exactly like the one for primary buttons. Don't forget to specify both regular and highlighted buttons.

179

10. Double-click "Line Picture" in the left column of the Style window. NetObjects Fusion presents an ordinary Image dialog box. (After all, you don't need to enter any text.) Navigate to your line picture.

11. Double-click "DataList Icon" and use the Image dialog box to specify the file for this component.

When you're done, look inside the Styles directory. You'll notice that NetObjects Fusion has created a new folder with the same name as your SiteStyle. Inside this folder is a set of subdirectories, each named for the components that make up the SiteStyle, and a file called "style.ssf." (See Figure 6.16.) These folders contain copies of all the component images of your SiteStyle, so you can throw away the folder you created in step 1, if you like. (Create an archive copy somewhere before you toss it, of course.)

FIGURE 6.16

Inside a SiteStyle's folder.

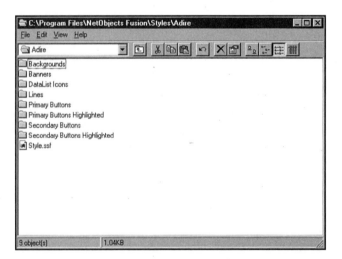

TIP

You can reuse elements from another SiteStyle if you don't feel like making a complete set of elements yourself. You *can't* copy elements directly from SiteStyle to SiteStyle in Style view, but you can use the same component file for more than one SiteStyle.

Finishing the SiteStyle

After you've set up the image components of the SiteStyle, you can set the colors of the text, regular links, and visited links. To do so, double-click the element's name in the left column of the Style window and pick a color from the standard Color dialog box. It's that easy.

Finally, you can set the SiteStyle's background, if you want it to be something other than plain white. Double-click "Background" in the left column of the Style window. NetObjects Fusion presents the Background SiteStyle dialog box.

If you want to use a solid color as the background, use the following steps:

1. Check the Color radio button.

2. Click the Color button and choose a color from the standard color palette.

If you want to use an image as the background, use the following steps:

1. Check the Picture radio button.

2. Click the Browse button. Use the File dialog box to navigate to the file you'd like as the page's background. The image you choose will be tiled at full size on every page of the site.

181

WARNING

There's really no way to make a background image that doesn't tile. If an image is behind other page elements, it tiles, and that's that. It's tempting to make a huge background image that's as big as the page so that it doesn't tile. At least, *I'm* often tempted to do so—but you really shouldn't. A page-sized image will be very large indeed, and take too long to download.

Fine-Tuning SiteStyles

As cool, intuitive, and magical as NetObjects Fusion may be, sometimes the built-in SiteStyles (or your own SiteStyles) don't quite work in the way that they should.

Take a look at Figure 6.17. The pages pointed to in the Navigation bar have fairly long names: "Meet the Boys from R & D" and "About Wrinkle Creams." Because these names are so long, they don't fit into the button, and the end of each label is missing. What's worse, these partial labels touch each other, so it looks as if everything has been squished together into one unreadable phrase.

FIGURE 6.17

When long page names meet narrow buttons.

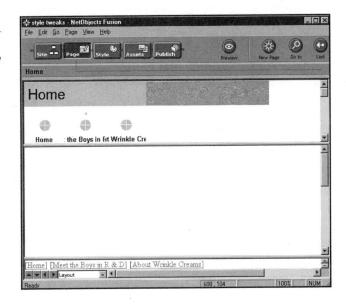

182

The quickest way to solve this problem is to try to make the labels a little smaller. If you're lucky, you can do this by editing the names of the pages (for example, "R & D" and "Wrinkle Cream").

However, you may not be able to make the page titles any shorter: maybe there's nothing you can cut, or your boss or your client insists that the long title stays. (It's in the nature of bosses and clients to make these sorts of demands.)

In this case, the next easiest solution is to reduce the size of the labels by reducing the size of the letters and using the following steps:

1. Double-click "Primary Buttons" in the left column of the Style window. (Make sure that you're in component mode, or you won't see the names of the components in the left panel.)

2. Click the Font button in the Primary Buttons dialog box.

3. If possible, reduce the size of the font in the Font dialog box. Remember, some fonts are narrower than others, even at the same point size.

Figure 6.18 shows the results of this change. The labels in Figure 6.17 used 10-point type, and the labels in Figure 6.18 used 8-point type. As you can see, it isn't enough.

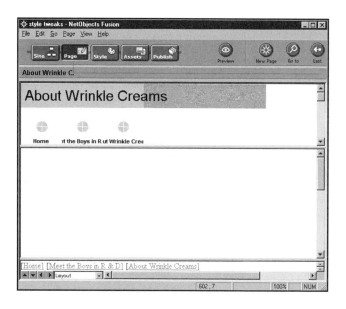

FIGURE 6.18

Reducing the button's point size can help—but not in this case.

What you need to do now is go in and do some surgery on the button images. *It's not hard, really*. Even if you don't want to create your own buttons, it's fairly simple to make these kinds of changes. Let's use a freely available tool: the Paint Program included with Windows 95. (You can use Mac tools, such as NIH Image, in almost the same way.)

1. Drag the icon of the image file of the button that you want to edit from Windows 95 *onto* the Paint application icon. The Paint window should look something like Figure 6.19.

2. As you can see, the white box has a set of control points around its edges. Position the cursor over the control point on the right edge of the box. (You'll know you've got it when the cursor turns into a double-pointed arrow.) After you've got the control point, click and drag to enlarge the box. Make it about one-and-a-half times as big as it was.

3. Then center the button in the box. Click the Marquee tool and draw a box around the button. Click and drag inside the selection box to move the whole selection around.

4. Save your work with **File→Save**.

5. Update NetObjects Fusion's SiteStyle description. Go to Style view and make sure that the component button is selected. Double-click "Primary Buttons."

183

6. The Paint application saves files only in .BMP format, so you'll need to set the File Type pop-up menu to BMP in order to find your new file. Do so and then navigate to the file. Figure 6.20 shows the improved buttons.

Marquee tool   Control points

FIGURE 6.19

Editing the component in Windows 95 Paint.

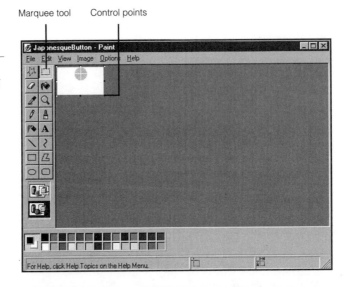

FIGURE 6.20

The improved buttons.

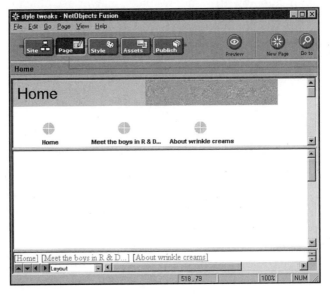

Of course, there are limits to this trick: if there are 15 buttons with long labels in one navigation bar, something will have to give: the site design and the page names might need your attention, rather than the width of the buttons.

Saving and Importing SiteStyles

NetObjects Fusion collects all a SiteStyle's information into the style.ssf file generated when the SiteStyle is created. So if you want to share your SiteStyles with other designers—your collaborators, or on a BBS or ftp site, or whatever— you can simply copy the entire SiteStyle folder, archive (or stuff) it with your favorite compression utility, and send it on its way.

If you receive a Style folder from someone else, you'll need to import the SiteStyle description manually—it won't show up if you just drop the new folder into the main Style folder. To import a SiteStyle, choose **File→Import Style** and navigate to the style.ssf file inside the new SiteStyle's folder.

Summary

185

In this chapter, you learned the following things:

- How to apply ready-made SiteStyles to your site.

- How to create new SiteStyles.

- How to fine-tune SiteStyles.

- How to import SiteStyles.

In Chapter 7, you'll learn how to take inventory on your site's assets and manage your Web support files effectively.

7

Assets View

Now that you've created the framework of your site, added content to each page, and given the whole site a consistent look and feel, it's time to stop, take a breath, and make sure that everything is in place for publication. Granted, doing a lot of double-checking isn't as exciting as some of the things you've done in previous chapters, but it's important to take inventory and make sure none of your files is missing.

If you're used to working in a conventional publishing environment, you might think of Assets view as something like the preflight procedure that you follow when you send your files to the printer. When you do a traditional preflight, you make sure that all your images and fonts are on disk, and that your document "knows" where they are. Doing a Web site preflight with NetObjects Fusion is exactly the same—you're making sure that all your images and other files are where Fusion thinks they are, and that your links point to the pages that you think they do.

Even a site that only has a few pages can contain dozens of links and use dozens and dozens of files. With so many parts in the puzzle of your site, it's easy for files to get misplaced or even deleted. When this happens, and you don't catch the problem before you publish your site, your pages show the mortifying missing-image icon (see Figure 7.1) and the dreaded page-not-found message (see Figure 7.2).

FIGURE 7.1

Assets view can help
you eradicate the
missing-image icon.

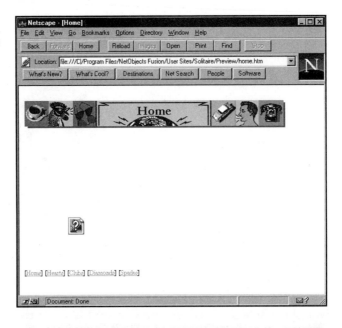

FIGURE 7.2

Assets view can help
you resolve missing-
page messages.

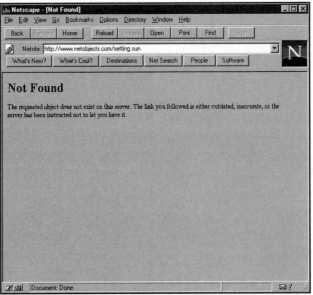

These kinds of blemishes are really frustrating, or, if you're showing a page to your supervisor or client, potentially dangerous to your business. Links that work the right way every time are the hallmarks of a professional-looking site.

The Assets view doesn't tell the whole story, so you'll also keep an eye on the Preview folder during this chapter. The Preview folder contains all the files that NetObjects Fusion generates on the fly, such as page banners and shapes that you've created with the drawing tool.

TIP

If you're one of those curmudgeonly HTML-hackers, and you plan to mess around with the HTML generated by NetObjects Fusion, the Assets view and the Preview folder are of special interest to you. Assets view will help you keep track of the components used to build the site and the Preview folder will contain the HTML files and other raw materials for your coding adventures.

Although this is the natural place to stop and discuss Assets view, and you should double-check your site before you go on to publish it, the discussion of assets must necessarily include things like applets and multimedia that I won't cover until Part III of the book.

Read through this chapter now, but don't worry too much if the discussion of advanced topics doesn't apply to your current site. After you've read through Part III, you might want to skim through this chapter again.

189

What Is an Asset?

Fusion defines assets in three different ways:

- Files that your site uses
- Links that your site provides
- Data Objects that your site presents by binding to internal or external data sources

You can switch between these Assets view modes by clicking the Files, Links, and Data Objects buttons in the Secondary control bar. Assets view displays a list of all the Assets of the current type and some basic information about these assets.

When Assets view is in Files mode, NetObjects Fusion displays a list of all the files that make up the site. These are the files that you've added to the site, not files that Fusion has generated automatically.

When Assets view is in Links mode, the display shows a list of all the links in the site. It's difficult, if not almost impossible, to check all the links in a site by transversing the site page-by-page, so it's helpful to have all the links in one place for testing (see Figure 7.3).

FIGURE 7.3

Assets view shows all the links contained in your site.

When Assets view is in Data Objects mode, NetObjects Fusion shows all the Data Objects that you've created (see Figure 7.4). (You'll learn the details of Data Objects and Database stuff in Chapter 13.)

FIGURE 7.4

Assets view shows all the Data Objects used in your site.

All three of these views (Files, Links, and Data Objects) share some common behaviors and shortcuts:

• You can choose to sort assets by any of the column headers in the current mode. For example, in Files mode, there are separate columns for each file's name, type, location, size, and modification date (see Figure 7.5). By default, the files are sorted by name, and the Name column header is in bold. If you want to sort the files by size instead, click the Size column header.

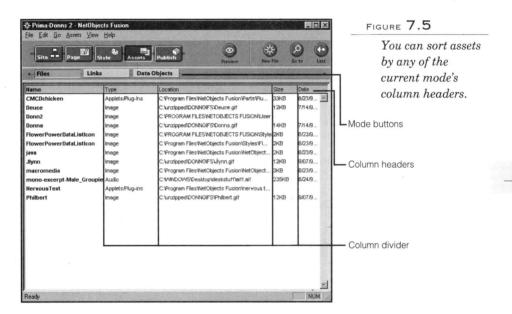

FIGURE 7.5

You can sort assets by any of the current mode's column headers.

Mode buttons

Column headers

Column divider

191

• You can resize any column in any mode. Position the arrow cursor over a column divider, and it turns into a double-arrow cursor. Then click and drag the column divider.

• In any mode, you can edit an asset by double-clicking on it in Assets view. (Each mode edits the asset in a different way, of course.)

• In any mode, you can add assets with **Edit→Add (File/Link/Data Object) Asset** and cut assets with **Edit→Delete (File/Link/Data Object) Asset**. (Adding assets in this way is a little odd; I'll talk about it more in the "Invisible Files" section later in this chapter.)

Files

Every site—even a brand spankin' new blank site that you haven't done anything with—consists of files. If nothing else, there's the HTML file of the page itself, the image file for the banner, and image files for each of the navigation buttons.

Not all of these files are assets. As you'll see next, in general, the files you add yourself are assets, and the files that NetObjects Fusion generates automatically are not assets (except for the built by NOF icon).

Images

Let's start by placing a file. I'm going to use the spade dingbat that comes with NetObjects Fusion, but the same principle applies with any image file.

Go ahead and place the image on a new page in a new site called "Solitaire." Then create a few variations on a theme by following these steps:

1. Place the image a second time.

2. Copy and paste the image to duplicate it. Stretch out the object's image box and click to the image.

3. Copy and paste the first image, and add some text to it.

Figure 7.6 shows a page that has all of these components. There are six separate images on this page: the banner, the home button, a tiled spade, two plain spades, and a spade with text.

FIGURE 7.6

This simple page already contains six images.

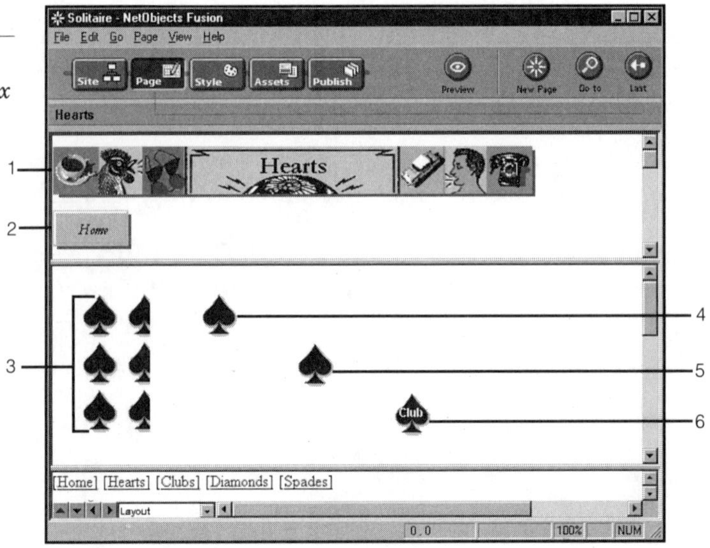

Now let's take a look at Assets view in Files mode. As you can see in Figure 7.7, the only thing that NetObjects Fusion lists as an asset is one instance of the spade file, which it has used as the base for all the other spade pictures.

FIGURE 7.7

NetObjects Fusion lists only the file that was placed by hand in Assets view — not the files that it creates itself.

193

Where, you may ask, are the other files? Take a look at the /Fusion/User Sites/ Solitaire/Preview/Assets/auto_generated_images folder. It should look something like Figure 7.8, but the filenames will be slightly different. You should have eight files in this folder: one for the banner, one for the home button, one for each tiled spade, the spade with type added, and one for each page. You can look at them with an image editor, file manager, or your Web browser, if you like.

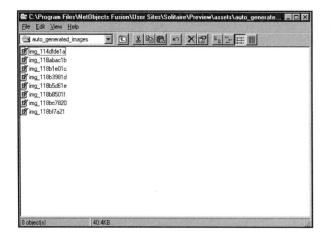

FIGURE 7.8

The files not shown in Assets view can be found in the Preview folder.

Multimedia Files

Now, let's see how a multimedia file shows up in Assets view. First, let's place a multimedia file. If you don't have a movie handy, you can use the Klassy Karl.qt file that you'll find in the /Book/Multimedia folder on the *NetObjects Fusion Handbook* CD-ROM. (That's my otherwise mild-mannered friend Karl Heino, by the way, doing his famous lard dance. Don't ask.)

You've never actually placed a movie before, but it's almost as easy as placing a picture:

1. Choose the video tool from the Tools palette. (It's the third tool in the third row.)

2. Draw an area on the page. NetObjects Fusion presents an Open File dialog box. Navigate to your movie file. It can be MPEG, AVI, MOV, or any other movie format.

3. Note NetObjects Fusion puts a default video placeholder image in your layout (see Figure 7.9). You can use this icon, choose you own, or click the Inline radio button. Inline lets the site visitor see the first frame of the video directly in your page layout.

194

FIGURE 7.9

Fusion represents the video file with a video placeholder.

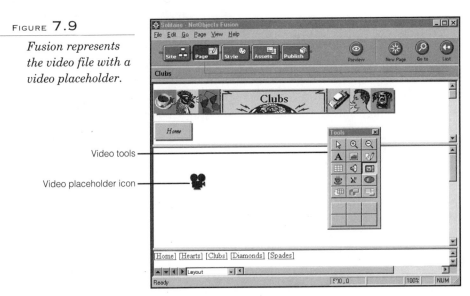

Video tools

Video placeholder icon

4. Click the Preview button. If you've got the appropriate plug-in, the movie will load inside the browser window. If not, the placeholder appears; double-click it to launch the appropriate helper application. (If it still doesn't work,

see Chapter 10 for instructions on configuring your browser for viewing video files.)

5. Go back to NetObjects Fusion and click the Assets view button. Click the Files button in the Secondary control bar. As you can see, NetObjects Fusion has added two files as assets: a video file that represents the movie, and an image file that represents the placeholder image.

    NetObjects Fusion includes an image file because you have some choices about the way the placeholder appears. (You'll learn about the finer points of movies and multimedia in Chapter 9.) Although Fusion automatically inserts the video placeholder icon shown in Figure 7.9, you don't need to commit yourself to the movie camera icon as the video placeholder.

6. Go to the Video tab in the Properties palette. Click the File radio button in the Display group. NetObjects Fusion presents a standard image dialog box. Navigate to the image file of your choice.

7. Go back to Assets view. The image file named *videoicon1* has been replaced with the image file you chose in Step 6.

Applets and Plug-Ins

Java Applets and Shockwave files (which are a little more complicated to add) appear in the File menu as type Applet/Plug-in. I'll cover these kinds of page elements in Chapters 10 and 13; for now, all you need to know is that there are external files involved, and only the file that you place appears in Assets view.

Editing File Assets

You can swap files around in Assets view to update any of the files that you may have changed *outside* NetObjects Fusion.

Let's say that you placed rough scans on several pages of your site early in the design process, and gave the scans names like apple.rough, banana.rough, and cherry.rough. The Assets view window would look something like Figure 7.10.

After you finalized your image choices, you went into your image-editing program and fixed the scans, saving the revised scans as new files called apple.final, banana.final, and so on. (I always keep old and new versions in separate files, in case I really mess up the image.)

Of course, you could go through your site page-by-page, double-clicking each image to update it, or deleting the old image and adding the new one. However, this approach is time-consuming, and it's easy to miss a file.

The much more elegant and surefire way to make this kind of bulk substitution is to use Assets view. Follow these steps:

1. Go to Assets view, making sure that the Files button is selected.

2. Click the Names column header. (This step isn't strictly necessary, but it makes the update easier.)

3. Double-click the first file with the .rough extension—in this example, apple.rough. NetObjects Fusion presents a file dialog box. Navigate to the corresponding .final file.

4. Proceed down the list, changing each .rough file to its .final counterpart.

FIGURE 7.10

Assets view shows that the images in your site are still rough scans.

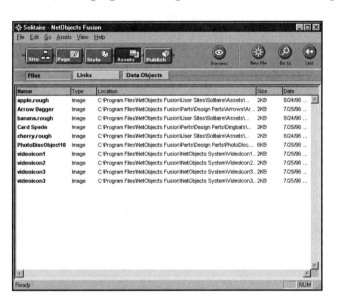

TIP

Some of you just feel more comfortable making changes by hand to be *absolutely sure* that all the files are updated. (I shouldn't, but sometimes I have these kinds of paranoid episodes myself.) Even if you do, you can check your work by looking for those telltale .rough extensions in Assets view.

Links

The Links mode view shows a complete list of the links in your site. As you'll recall from Chapter 4, NetObjects Fusion offers three basic flavors of links:

- Links to particular pages.

- Smart links to pages that are related to the current page in the site tree. (The link is defined as a link to the page's sibling, parent or other relative, rather than defined as a link to a particular page.)

- Links to external URLs.

TIP

Smart links are called "structural links" in Assets view. It's just an inconsistency in nomenclature. Smart links and structural links are the same thing.

 Links can be tricky to handle in Assets view because different kinds of links behave differently in Assets view. To illustrate how this works, I've included a site called Solitaire on the *NetObjects Fusion Handbook* CD-ROM. You can find it in the /Book/Sites directory.

Internal Links

NetObjects Fusion's handling of internal links in Assets view strikes me as confusing, but it's fairly easy once you understand it.

When the Links button is selected in the Secondary control bar, Assets view displays three column headers: Name, Link To, and Type. You can see this in Figure 7.11, which shows the Links Lab site's link assets. In the case of Internal Links, "Name" refers to the page that's pointed to by the link(s), rather than the page that contains the link(s).

If you double-click the name of an Internal link, NetObjects Fusion presents a special Links dialog box like the one shown in Figure 7.12. Click the link. Although this dialog box has the same name as the dialog box you used to build links in the first place, it acts quite differently. (It should probably be named something like "Internal Links Assets.")

FIGURE 7.11

The links assets of the Solitaire site.

FIGURE 7.12

The Internal Links Assets dialog box, called simply "Links."

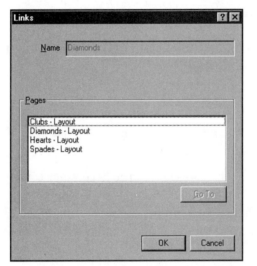

The Links dialog box shows a list of all pages that contain links to the page listed in the Name column of Assets view. Notice that unlike file assets, link assets display not only the links that you have explicitly added to the site, but also the links that NetObjects Fusion added automatically as part of the Navigation bar. You can jump to any of the pages listed in the Pages group by clicking it and clicking the Go To button. (Double-clicking the name *doesn't* send you to the page.)

TIP

Inexplicably, NetObjects Fusion adds the layout name of the page as well. I really have no idea how this particular morsel of information could come in handy at this stage of the process.

Structural Links

As you'll recall, structural, or smart links, connect a page to its relatives on the site tree: siblings, parents, or other stacked pages.

Because such links are dynamic, and don't point to any particular page, they can't be named for the target page. Take a look at Figure 7.13, which shows the site diagram of the Solitaire site.

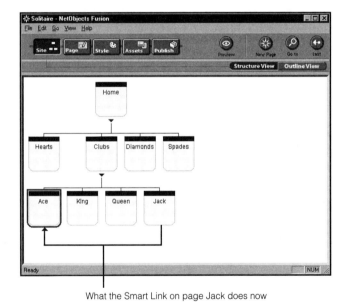

What the Smart Link on page Jack does now

FIGURE 7.13

The site diagram of the Solitaire site.

199

If you load this site into your browser with the Preview button, you'll see that the Next Page Smart Link on page "d" wraps around to point at page "a." If you add a new page "e" to the right of page "d", the Smart Link on page "d" will point to page "e," rather than page "a" (see Figure 7.14).

FIGURE 7.14

Adding a new page changes the page that the Smart Link points to.

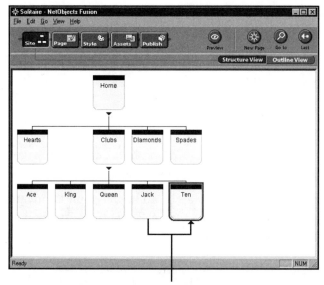

What the Smart Link does when the new page is added

It follows that you can't name the link after the page that it points to because the target page will change as the site changes. Thus, structural links are named after the kind of link that they are: Next Page, Previous Page, and so on.

You can double-click a structural link in the same way that you double-clicked an internal link, and you'll get a similar dialog box, also called "Links." Here's where things get a little strange. The page listed in this dialog box isn't the page that contains the link, or the page that's linked to. It's the first page in the group of pages that the Smart Link traverses.

In the Link Lab site, Next and Previous page links that are situated on the first level of the site tree will link to other pages on the first level. Thus, the page listed in the Structural Links Assets dialog box is the first page on this level.

TIP

If you think about it, you'll almost always add Smart Links to headers and footers, rather than to individual pages. This makes the way that structural links appear in the dialog box more sensible because they're not attached to, or pointing to, any particular page.

External Links

Every URL, mail to: address, or newsgroup that you link to has its own entry in Assets view.

As you'll recall from Chapter 4, when you create and add an external link, you give the link a name. This is the name that NetObjects Fusion uses in Assets view. This name isn't related to the page's URL, or to the text or image that is attached to the link on the page—it's a mnemonic device for your use alone.

This system assumes that you create a unique name for each unique URL for which you add links. If you don't, NetObjects Fusion will group together all the links to the same URL and give them the same name.

Let's say that you want to add links to the Pizzicato Five page at `http://www.matador.recs.com/bios/bio_p5.html` from several pages on your site. If you enter this URL on one page and give it the name "happy," and then enter the exact same URL on another page and give it the name "sad," the link will appear only once in Assets view with the name "sad." (These are pretty lame names for links—it's a Pizzicato Five joke, rather than an example of good link-naming practice.)

It doesn't work the same way in reverse: if you create links to both the Pizzicato Five page and the Stereolab page (at `http://www.hotwired.com.music/96/19/index2a.html`) and name them both "music," they appear as separate entries in Assets view.

Double-click an external link entry to edit it. NetObjects Fusion presents yet another variation on the Links dialog box. When you're editing an external link, you can readily change a link's URL and its name. The pages group shows the usual list of pages in the site that contain copies of the link.

Editing Links

Internal and structural links pretty much take care of themselves, and you can't change the way that they work from Assets view. The dialog boxes that you use to view their properties are essentially read-only.

You can, however, alter external links. Let's say that you made a link to the Stereolab page when it was at the front page of HotWired's pop music area, `http://www.hotwired.com/pop`. After the page was moved to the permanent, archival URL `http://www.hotwired.com.music/96/19/index2a.html`, your links no longer point to the Stereolab page.

This is why NetObjects Fusion collects all the links to the same URL under a single name in Assets view: when you want to make this kind of update, you can change all the links at once. (You could change them all if they had separate names, too, but it would be easier to miss one.)

You can also add external links with the **Edit→New Link** command when you're in Assets view and give the new link a name and URL. However, *there's no way to add such a link to any of your pages!* Although it's perfectly safe to create links in this way, it's a waste of your time.

Data Objects

Assets view also gives you a complete listing of all the Data Objects that you use in your site. (You'll learn about Data Objects in excruciating detail in Chapter 12.)

A Data Object is really just a slice of a database. It might be from a database that you've imported from a database program like Microsoft Access, or something that you've created yourself in NetObjects Fusion. In either case, a Data Object doesn't have attributes, *per se*. It doesn't appear on any particular page, and it's not so much a file as it is a set of instructions for looking at files.

Thus, the only thing that appears in Assets view when the Data Objects button is selected is a list of the names of Data Objects that your site uses.

You can edit a Data Object from Assets view. Don't do it now—wait until you learn more about how Data Objects work in Chapter 12.

TIP

A Data Object is a weird and nebulous thing, and you can't delete it from the Edit menu in the same way that you'd delete other assets. This is partly for your own protection, and partly because there isn't anything to delete. You might think of a Data Object as something like a Paragraph style or a Header style—you can't delete these kinds of things either, once you've made them. They're just part of the site's architecture.

The Preview Folder

That's about it for Assets view, and you still haven't seen all the files that make up your site. As you saw when you looked for the automatically generated images, the remaining files are in the Preview folder.

The Preview folder is the central warehouse for special files that NetObjects Fusion needs to preview the site and that it will use later to create your site on the Web server. There's no reason why these files aren't stored in a file called "Assets" or "Building blocks" or whatever, but Fusion needs some kind of consistent directory structure format—and the Preview folder is the convention created by the NetObjects engineers.

The way that NetObjects Fusion stores files is a part of its design that's still in flux, as you'll see when you take a look around inside these folders. Although you may see slightly different things inside the folders that a later version of Fusion creates, the same basic ideas still hold. You can use this tour to make some good deductions about what's going on inside your Preview folder.

NetObjects Fusion collects all the necessary files for a site into a folder with the site's name in the /User Sites/ directory. Inside a sites folder, you'll find the following information:

- **The site itself.** The site is stored in a single document, named with the extension .NOD.

- **An Assets folder.** This folder will be completely empty until the first time that you stage or publish your site.

- **A Preview folder.** This folder contains HTML files and everything else that Fusion needs to create your site. (Note that Fusion doesn't produce a Preview folder until the site has been previewed for the first time.)

Let's take a closer look at the contents of the Preview folder. It contains the following information:

- **An Assets folder.** The Preview folder contains its own Assets folder. Although it contains the same sorts of things that the first Asset folder contained, don't get them confused, and certainly don't replace one with the other. The two Assets folders are organized in different ways and *aren't* interchangeable.

203

- **An HTML folder.** The HTML folder contains the HTML files for every page in your site.

- **The site's home page.** The HTML code for the root of your site tree is stored at a different level than the rest of the pages. It's loose in the Preview directory, rather than in the folder with the rest of the HTML files.

Assets

There are some funny things in the /Preview/Assets directory. Some of the things that you'll find here seem to be here for historical, rather than functional purposes, and some of them are here as workarounds to problems that future versions of NetObjects Fusion will solve.

The Applets Folder

Even if you haven't placed any applets on any of the pages of your sites, you will find an HTML file (not an applet) in this folder. This is for SiteMapper, the navigation application included with NetObjects Fusion. Sitemapper is fairly cumbersome to add to a site, even with the tools provided with NetObjects Fusion.

Auto-Generated Images

As you saw earlier in this chapter, NetObjects Fusion keeps the image files that it generates on the fly, such as page banners and buttons, in the Auto Generated Images folder.

There are several basic cases where NetObjects Fusion must create an image file:

- NetObjects Fusion creates a new GIF file for each particular instance of the site's style elements. (A button that says "home," and a button that says "a" are two separate image files.)

- When you stretch or tile an image or add type to it, NetObjects Fusion keeps the original image untouched and creates a separate copy of the modified image.

- When you draw a shape, such as a line, rectangle, or a polygon, NetObjects Fusion creates a GIF image to send to the browser.

Because these files are generated automatically from a base image, you can easily alter all the modified files by changing the base file. Let's say that you want to change all those spades in Figure 7.6 back to clubs. (Maybe you just won a big poker game with a clubs flush or something.) When you change the base image, you cause NetObjects Fusion to update the automatically generated images as well:

1. Open the page that contains the spade images, or create a new one with several variations on the same image.

2. Go to Assets view. Double-click the spade image's name in the list of file assets.

3. NetObjects Fusion presents an Open Image dialog box. Navigate to the club image in the /Fusion/Parts/Dingbats folder.

Figure 7.15 shows the result—all the automatically generated images have been changed. If you look closely at the filenames in the Automatically Generated Images folder before and after you try this experiment, you'll see that these filenames change, too.

205

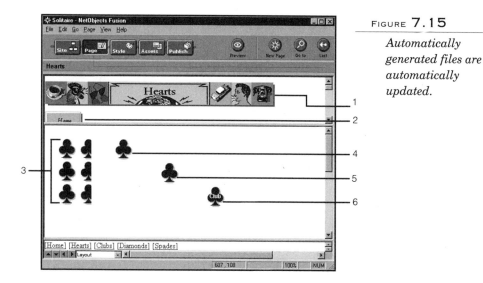

FIGURE 7.15

Automatically generated files are automatically updated.

CGI-Bin

NetObjects Fusion doesn't add CGIs to pages or sites—it's something you'll need to do yourself. If you do create a form that requires a CGI—and you'll learn how to do this when we look at forms in Chapter 11—you can install the CGI program in this folder by hand. (Bin, by the way, stands for binary, which in turn stands for binary executable, which means a program that runs. Damn Unix-weenie jargon!)

> **WARNING**
>
> As you'll see in Chapter 11, CGIs don't run like this in Preview mode—it must be activated by a server first. Don't be surprised if your CGI doesn't work if you simply drop it in this folder and click the Preview button.

Images

The Preview/Images folder contains folders named for each of the style elements—banners, primary buttons, and so on—but these folders are empty. (This is what I was hinting about when I said some things are in the Preview folder for historical reasons, that is, these folders were probably used in earlier versions of the software.) It's likely that they'll disappear, sooner or later. After you stage or publish, the pictures that you have chosen are copied to this folder.

This folder also contains a few special images:

- **BuiltByNOF** is a "created with NetObjects Fusion" button that Fusion automatically adds to sites.

- The cryptically named **dot_clear** is a tiny transparent image that NetObjects Fusion uses to cheat its way around a problem with the way Netscape Navigator makes tables.

- **Info** is a placeholder page, used only for previewing pages. If you have set NetObjects Fusion to preview the "current page" of your site in **Edit→ Preferences**, all of the links on the page point to this placeholder image. (See Figure 7.16.) This image will never appear when you publish your site.

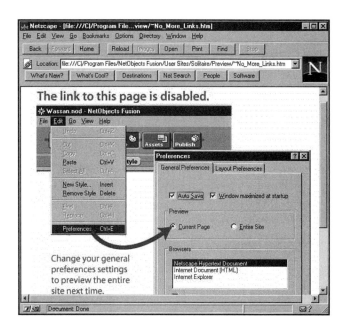

FIGURE 7.16

The Info file is only displayed when you preview pages with NetObjects Fusion.

207

Multimedia

The Multimedia folder will hold just about everything that isn't an image or an applet that you've added to your pages or an HTML file generated by NetObjects Fusion. This folder should be empty until you actually add some multimedia content to your site and stage or publish it.

HTML Files

The HTML files in this folder are exactly the same as the final HTML that will be published on your site. If you want to get in and fine-tune NetObjects Fusion's HTML, these are the files to work with. (By now, most of you are probably convinced that Fusion's HTML is finely tuned already.)

When NetObjects Fusion publishes a site on a server, it creates a directory structure identical to the structure of the Preview folder, with folders for applets, auto generated images, CGIs, images, and multimedia. This allows NetObjects Fusion to move the preview files onto the server without rewriting any of the HTML pages' link tags.

HTML uses link tags to specify links to page elements and other pages. When you're designing with NetObjects Fusion, you can use things such as page names and dialog boxes to designate your links, but when the site is actually implemented in HTML, Fusion must translate all of those fancy designations into plain old filenames. (In other words, Fusion must recognize that a page named "Diamonds" in Site view is contained in the file <Web-server-folder-file-path>/ HTML/Diamonds, and create the anchor using this filename.)

Consequently, if you open Fusion's HTML files with a text editor, or choose **View→Source** in your browser, you'll find that the links reflect the directory structure of the Preview folder. For example, a drawing might have a tag that looks like:

```
<IMG HEIGHT=74 WIDTH=72 SRC="./assets/auto_generated_images/img_516ab5c4.gif"
BORDER=0>
```

This snippet of HTML specifies the location of the drawing with respect to the page that contains the drawing. The tag tells the browser that the drawing's image is inside the folder called "assets," which is at the same level of the current page. The location is specified relative to the page, rather than as an absolute address in a particular folder. Consequently, it doesn't matter where exactly the files resides, as long as the two files maintain the same relationship. As long as the page and the assets folder are in the same folder, they can be in the Preview folder, or on a folder on the server, or on any folder on your hard drive in which you choose to store them.

Links to pages use the same kind of relative URL:

```
<A HREF="./html/front_section.htm"> </A>
```

In this case, the link specifies that the page is in the HTML folder, rather than the assets folder, but the principle's the same.

The only special case is an unmodified image files. When NetObjects Fusion creates HTML for the Preview folder, it specifies the image's location with an absolute URL, like this:

```
 <IMG HEIGHT=72 WIDTH=504 SRC="file:///c:/Netscape Fusion/Parts
    /Design Parts/Dingbats/Image.gif" BORDER=0>
```

When URLs are specified in this way, it doesn't matter where the Web page is relative to the file—the browser will always look for it in the folder specified.

However, when the site is published, NetObjects Fusion converts the URL to a relative format, like so:

```
<IMG HEIGHT=72 WIDTH=504 SRC="./assets/images/Image.gif"  BORDER=0>
```

This means that if you want to copy and modify these HTML files for your own fiendish purposes, you must do one of two things:

- Make sure that the /Preview/Assets/ folder, the /Preview/HTML folder, and the site's home (root) page always travel together, and none of the files is moved or renamed.

- Make sure that if you alter the directory structure of the Preview folder, or change any of the filenames, that you also alter all of the HTML tags accordingly.

In both cases, you must copy any unmodified image files to the Preview/Images/ folder, and edit the links that point to those pages. If you *really* want to edit NetObjects Fusion's HTML, you can save yourself some file copying and HTML editing by marking images as altered, even if they're not. To do this:

1. Select the image to be marked.

2. In the Image tab of the Properties palette, check the check box in the Text in Element group.

3. Delete everything in the Your Text Here field in the Text in Element Group.

NetObjects Fusion will think that it modified the image by adding text to it, but the image will remain unchanged.

209

"Invisible" Files

Some of the files and the applications that go into making your site work are not handled or monitored by NetObjects Fusion. These files don't show up in Assets view, and they're not automatically generated, so Fusion doesn't know that they're there. It's your responsibility to make sure that these files are up-to-date and in the right place.

These invisible files and applications include:

- CGI programs

- Dynamic pages created by CGIs

- Java helper files

- Special pages linked to the main site

- Source files for JavaScript

- Support files for JavaScript

- Source files for other kinds of applets

CGI Programs

As you learned in Chapter 3, a CGI is a kind of helper application for server software, and a CGI deals with data, such as form replies, that the server software is not equipped to handle.

If you are only designing pages, and not responsible for site administration, you don't really need to worry about where the CGIs go. Your site administrator will certainly take a very keen interest in the CGIs that are required to run the site anyway, and she or he will manage the particulars of getting the CGIs in the correct place.

If you do need to worry about this, or you need to set up a CGI on your test server, don't fret: there's a natural place to store CGIs—the /Preview/Assets/cgi-bin folder. You saw the cgi-bin folder when you looked at the Preview folder earlier in this chapter.

As you'll see when you look at forms in Chapter 11, you specify the address of the CGI when you create the form. As far as the HTML is concerned, there's no reason why a CGI can't go somewhere other than the ready-made CGI folder. However, on some server systems, especially UNIX-based servers, there are compelling security reasons to keep the CGIs in one place. Many servers expect to find a cgi-bin folder anyway, so you might as well put the CGIs in the folder that NetObjects Fusion has made for you.

Dynamic Pages Created by CGIs

A CGI can do more than crunch data—it can send HTML back to the reader via the server. When a CGI is processing a form, often the HTML is some sort of verification message that tells the reader that the form data was received. The verification message might even echo the form data.

Some clever Webmasters have used CGIs' HTML-generating capability to create dynamic Web pages. A dynamic page isn't an actual HTML file; it's a page made from HTML that is generated on the fly by the CGI program.

Dynamic Web Pages

Really, a CGI is just a program, and it can return whatever it likes to the browser via the server. Usually, CGIs are pretty simple, and return simple HTML pages that say things like "We received your form information. Thanks so much for filling out the form."

The CGI's output doesn't need to be this simple, however. For example, the CGI has access to information about the browser that the reader is using. A CGI might use this information to create a page with the headline "Howdy, *<browser name>*Users" at the top.

In fact, it can get quite a bit more complicated than this. A CGI could look at the day of the week for instance, take a look inside a database, and create a "this day in history" page to send to the browser. Individual pages for each day of the year need never be constructed—the CGI can write all the required HTML on the fly, when the request for a page is received from the browser.

This technique can be used to make a site more friendly to browsers of antique vintage. If the CGI detects that the browser can't handle a Java applet, for example, the CGI creates a page without an applet. It's also used to make sites change according to the time of day. For example, http://www.sony.com uses a different set of images in the morning and afternoon.

The actual HTML can be stored in a file outside the CGI program proper. This makes it much easier to update the CGI program. The CGI goes through a routine something like the following:

```
IF <the browser is Navigator 3.0 for MacOS>
    THEN
    <open the MacOS/Navigator 3.0 HTML file>
    <read the contents>
    <send the contents to the browser>
    END THEN
ELSE IF <the browser is Internet Explorer 3.0 for MacOS>
    THEN
    <open the MacOS/Explorer 3.0 HTML file>
    <read the contents>
    <send the contents to the browser>
    END THEN
    .
    .
    .
```

The idea here is that the server never serves any of the HTML files directly; rather, the CGI makes some decisions about which file is the right one to send and sends the contents of the file. Thus, all the different files appear under the single URL of the browser.

211

WARNING

The previous code example is *pseudocode,* a kind of outline of the way that a program works. It's not a real program, or even in a particular programming language, and you shouldn't try to type it into one of NetObjects Fusion script boxes or anywhere else.

Java Helper Files

Java is a modular language, and an applet can consist of more than one program file. When you add applets to your pages, as you'll learn to do in Chapter 13, NetObjects Fusion automatically adds the applet's main program file to the Preview/Assets/Applet folder, and the applet's name to the Assets menu. However, NetObjects Fusion can't tell if the applet "calls" (requires) one or more helper applets.

An applet may also require the use of image or audio files. NetObjects Fusion can't check to make sure that these files are in place, and the files *won't* show up in the Assets menu.

(If you've got any Java tools on your machine, your Java distribution must legally include a copy of the Java Development Kit, or JDK. Take a look at the Bouncing Head applet that is distributed with the JDK. After this applet has been compiled, it uses two separate program files: BounceImage.class and BounceItem.class. The applet also requires a folder full of images and a folder of audio files.)

How can you tell if an applet uses any external files? If you wrote the applet yourself, you'll know. If not, you'll need to consult any documentation that came with the code. If there's no documentation, contact the applet's author. (If you don't know who wrote the applet, or anything about it, you probably shouldn't put it on your Web site anyway.)

If you do find that your applet needs to use external files, store them in the Preview/Assets/Applets folder. Be sure to maintain the directory structure specified by the applet's documentation.

WARNING

Applets often use a folder called "images." Be sure to put this into the applets folder, too, *not* into the Preview/Assets/Images folder.

Special Pages Linked to the Main Site

Sometimes you might find that you have a page that wasn't created in Fusion, and it doesn't seem to import into Fusion very well, but you still want it to be part of your site. For instance, pages with Frames aren't ever imported properly by Fusion, which doesn't handle frames. Most pages with tables also are garbled by the import process. (It doesn't matter if you create such pages with another Web Page construction program or if you do it by hand.)

It's easy to add such a page to your site. Let's say the new HTML file is called special.htm:

1. Copy special.htm in the Preview/HTML folder.

2. Create an external link. Give the link any name you like.

3. Enter ./html/special.html into the URL field of the External Link dialog box.

This page *will* appear as a link asset when Assets view is in Link mode, but that's the limit of NetObjects Fusion's willingness to deal with the file. It won't show up in the site tree, it won't get automatic navigation bars, and it won't be affected by global changes to the site like SiteStyle changes. You're solely responsible for the upkeep of such pages.

213

Source Files for JavaScript

As you learned in Chapter 3, JavaScript is a special programming language that can be embedded directly into Web pages. Sometimes, however, it's convenient and less redundant to keep JavaScripts in a file that's separate from the HTML source.

For example, maybe you've developed a JavaScript that you want to use on more than one page of your site. It's easy to add and modify scripts right inside Web pages with NetObjects Fusion, but changing 10 pages requires that each page be changed individually. If each page simply contains a pointer to the JavaScript source file, all the pages will be updated when you update the single source file.

(Don't worry about how to add source files or pointers right now—you'll learn all about this in Chapter 13. For now, you just need to know that a JavaScript can be inside a page or stored externally.)

When you store a file externally, it's off the NetObjects Fusion map. You are responsible for making sure that the file is in the right place, and that its name

doesn't change. The natural place to store this kind of thing is in the Preview/
HTML folder, but you can put it anywhere you like.

Support Files for JavaScripts

Whether a JavaScript is stored in a page or in a separate file, the JavaScript can
write some raw HTML code. For example, a JavaScript attached to a button
might open a new window and write some HTML inside when the button is
pushed. (This is quite a bit like what happens with the dynamic CGIs mentioned
earlier in this section.)

Although you use NetObjects Fusion to add such scripts to your Web pages,
Fusion doesn't "read" the script, and doesn't know what resources the JavaScript
may require. A command such as

```
document.write("<IMG SRC='./images/image.gif>'");
```

instructs the browser to put image.gif into the browser window. Because you
didn't add image.gif to the page with NetObjects Fusion's image tool, Fusion
doesn't know or care anything about image.gif. It's not an asset, and it's not an
automatically generated file. You'll have to add it yourself and make sure that it
stays put.

This is probably the most complicated kind of problem of this sort because
there's all kinds of indirection possible. Let's say you have a whole bunch of
images, named image1.gif, image2.gif, image3.gif, and image4.gif. It's perfectly
legal for the JavaScript to split these names into parts and give an instruction
like

```
document.write("<IMG SRC='./images/image' & myVariable & '.gif>'");
```

Here the script is patching together filenames from a partial filename and a
variable, so this particular line uses the file image1.gif if the value of myVariable
is 1, image2.gif if the value of the myVariable is 2, and so on.

What this means is that you can't just look through the script for things that
look like filenames—JavaScript can build filenames on the fly. You must consult
the JavaScript's documentation or closely examine the JavaScript's code.

Where these kinds of resources go depends on the JavaScript. Although it seems
most sensible to write JavaScripts that use resources in the same folder as the
script itself, or in a folder with a particular name in the same folder as the script,
it isn't necessarily so. Again, consult the documentation, or go over the script with
a fine-toothed comb.

Source Files for Other Kinds of Applets

There are new kinds of scripting languages that are appearing on the Web, even as this book goes to press. Perhaps the most significant is Sun MicroSystem's Tcl/Tk plug-in, which allows you to write small applets easily with the graphics-friendly, simple scripting language, Tcl/Tk.

The example tcl-let shown in Figure 7.17 is about 10 times smaller than a Java applet that would do the same thing.

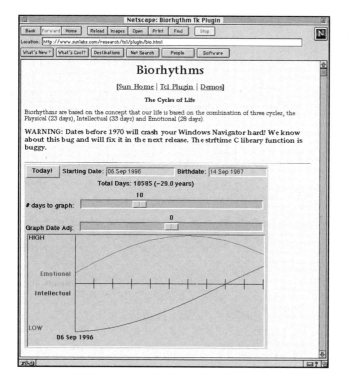

FIGURE 7.17

This new form of executable code, a Tcl / Tk tcl-let, is invisible to NetObjects Fusion.

It's likely that other new languages like this will arrive on the scene. (Perl in a Web page! Mmmm.) Both Navigator and Internet Explorer offer support for these kinds of new technologies via plug-ins. However, NetObjects Fusion will not be able to offer tool-based support for each new language as soon as the language is released.

Consequently, if you add Tcl/Tk or other scripts to your pages, you will need to manage the needs of the script—the source code, helper objects, graphics and audio support files—according to the needs of the language.

There aren't any firm guidelines for how these things will work. In fact, new tools and new approaches to Web publishing may work in a way that isn't appropriate for a NetObjects Fusion site. You don't need to use Fusion for *every* site that you create.

Troubleshooting in Assets View

NetObjects Fusion is remarkably smart for a software application. It's actually impossible to make certain mistakes in Fusion that are common when coding by hand or with page-based HTML tools. For example, you can't create an internal link to a page that doesn't exist.

Still, there are mistakes it's possible to make with Fusion. Even if you do everything exactly right, sometimes files mysteriously disappear or corrupt themselves. (It's in the nature of computer science for things to spontaneously go wrong—I routinely crash the CPU of my microwave oven.)

Stale Links

Many of the links that I try on Web sites that I visit don't go to the pages that they're supposed to point to. When the target page has been moved, renamed, or deleted, the link doesn't work any more.

Because NetObjects Fusion builds your whole site for you, you are protected from these kinds of problems with your internal and structural links.

Internal Links

Let's see NetObjects Fusion's automatic link management in action:

1. Open the Links Lab site. Go to Site view mode.

2. Create a new page called "target" as a child of the site's root page.

3. Add some text to the home and link it to the target page with an Internal link.

4. Go to Site view and rename the target page. I usually use "bubba" with this kind of experiment.

5. Go back to the home page and click Preview. Test your link; it still goes to the renamed page.

6. Now, let's really try to confuse Fusion. Return to Site view and drag the renamed page somewhere else on the site hierarchy.

7. Go back to the home page and hit the Preview button again.

8. Test the link in the browser. Again, the link should work perfectly.

9. Now, go to Site View. Select the target page and delete it with **Edit→Delete Page**.

10. Go back to the home page. NetObjects Fusion has automatically unlinked the text.

As you can see, it's impossible to create an Internal link that goes to a missing page. NetObjects Fusion either updates the link or removes it.

TIP

Automatic unlinking creates a new problem: regular text or images where the reader might be expecting links. (This looks especially bad if the links are attached to a button, or in a paragraph that starts "Follow this link.") To avoid this problem, take a look at the site's Assets in Link mode before you delete a page. If the page's name appears in the Name column, something somewhere will lose its link attributes.

Smart Links

Smart links are even smarter. If you experimented with Smart Links when they were first introduced in Chapter 4, you may have noticed that you can't create a Smart Link in the first place if the appropriate kind of target page doesn't exist. For example, you can't create a "Next Stacked Page" link if you're not on a stacked page already.

Furthermore, a Smart Link with nowhere else to go either loops around to link to itself, as in the case of Next, Previous, Next Stacked Page, and Previous Stacked Page, or unlinks itself, in the case of the Up Smart Link. The Home Smart Link always has a place to go.

WARNING

All these built-in safeguards won't help a bit if you tinker with the files in the Preview folder (or worse, with the Assets or HTML folder on your server). If you're not going to fine-tune NetObjects Fusion's HTML, you have no reason to ever move, edit, or rename these files. Don't touch 'em!

External Links

Alas, external links are not so easy to make foolproof. When you link to pages that aren't on your site, you have no control over what happens on those pages. It's always possible that the page could be renamed or removed entirely. In fact, it seems an ironclad law of Web design that one of the external links on any given page will go bad within 24 hours of the site's inception.

You can't lock external pages into place, but there are a few things you can do to monitor the freshness of external links.

Look at the Links by Hand

In the end, checking external pages with a browser is the only way to make sure that all of your external links are exactly right. To streamline this process, you can load the links directly from Assets view, rather than traversing your site page-by-page:

1. Go to Assets view and click the Links button.

2. Click the Type column header so that all the external links appear in one group.

3. Double-click the first External Link.

4. Select the text in the Link's URL field and choose **Edit→Copy**.

5. **Edit→Paste** the URL into the location field at the top of your browser's window or paste it into the **File→Load URL** dialog box.

6. Repeat Steps 3-5 for each external link in the list.

Monitor Your Links with Navigator

It's a very good practice to bookmark all the links in your site in your Web browser. (If you haven't done so already, bookmark them when you check the links by hand using the previous procedure.) If you use Netscape Navigator as your browser, you can use these bookmarks to automate the process of checking links. You should still take a look at your external links by hand from time to time, but checking your bookmarks allows you to look for trouble spots without looking at every page every time you search.

1. Open the bookmarks window with **Bookmarks→Go to Bookmarks**.

2. Use **Item→Insert Folder** to create a folder for the Web site's bookmarks. (The Item menu is in the bookmark window itself in the Windows version of Navigator and in the main menu bar in the Mac OS version.)

3. Add the site's bookmarks to the site's folder by dragging the bookmark's icons onto the folder's icon.

To automatically test bookmarks with Navigator follow these steps:

1. Open the Bookmark window with **View→Bookmarks**.

2. Select your site's bookmarks.

3. Choose **File→What's New**. (In the Windows version, use the Bookmark Window's File menu; in MacOS, use the main File menu.)

4. Check the Selected Bookmarks radio button.

5. Navigator presents a progress box showing how many bookmarks remain to be checked and the estimated amount of time required for the check. The check might take a few minutes, but you can do other things, even with Navigator, in the meantime.

6. As Navigator checks the bookmarked sites, it updates your bookmark icons. If a site has changed, Navigator uses the shiny bookmark icon shown in Figure 7.18, and if Navigator can't connect to the site, it displays the question mark icon, also shown in Figure 7.18.

219

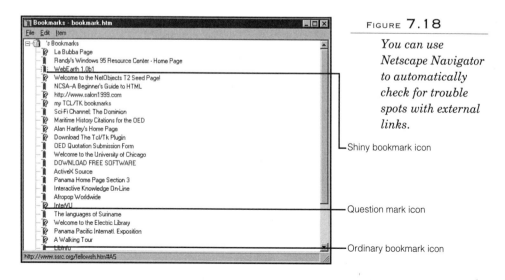

FIGURE 7.18

You can use Netscape Navigator to automatically check for trouble spots with external links.

Shiny bookmark icon

Question mark icon

Ordinary bookmark icon

Just because Navigator couldn't connect to a page doesn't mean that the page isn't there; perhaps the site is temporarily down, or perhaps network traffic delayed the connection long enough to cause Navigator to abandon the test.

Likewise, changes to the site are most often tiny corrections, rather than major revisions. Still, Navigator's What's New command is a good way to quickly find potential trouble spots.

Use a Robot

A few tools have appeared on the scene that can automatically search for changes to sites. These robots, or "intelligent agents," include the following:

- **Katipo.** Katipo is a freeware Mac OS-based application that scans Navigator's global history file (all the sites that you've ever visited with Navigator), checks each site, and creates a report about updated and missing files. Unfortunately, there's no way to limit the search to the links in your site—it will always scan and check your whole history file.

  You can find Katipo at `http://www.vuw.ac.nz/~newbery/Katipo/Katipo-doc.html`

- **Freeloader.** Freeloader is a freeware application for Windows 95 that automatically checks designated Web sites on a periodic basis and downloads any new content that it finds.

  Because Freeloader actually downloads the pages, all you need to do is set up Freeloader to check pages you're linked to and check the download area for problems. (See the Freeloader manual for specific instructions on configuring the software to check your sites.)

  You can find the Freeloader application (see Figure 7.19) at `http://www.freeloader.com`.

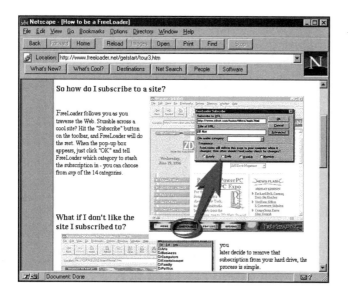

FIGURE 7.19

The freeware application Freeloader automatically downloads new material from pages you designate.

Missing Image Icons

221

When image files are missing, the browser substitutes the kind of missing image icon you saw back in Figure 7.1. Nothing quite tattoos your brain like seeing one of these things in a page that you have lovingly crafted and triple- and quadruple-checked for errors.

If you build your site with Fusion and leave the HTML files and the Assets folder alone, it's likely that you will never have problems with missing images.

There is one potential problem area. As you'll recall from your tour of the Preview/Assets folder, NetObjects Fusion leaves your image files exactly where they are until you publish your site. It doesn't make copies of the file, or keep track of them in any way: it trusts you to keep image files in the same place, with the same name, until you click the Publish button.

As you know, this doesn't always happen. In my workplace, a certain supervisor routinely shuffles files and renames them to make the names more descriptive. She knows this causes problems, but she can't resist this overpowering mania for organization. (It's a University of Chicago thing, I guess.) There are all kinds of crazy reasons why files get moved, and you can't rely on inertia to keep your files in place.

Assets view is a great tool to help you quickly determine whether any of your files are missing. All you need to do is look at the Size and Date columns in the Assets menu. If these columns are blank for a particular entry, NetObjects Fusion can't find the file. In Figure 7.20, the PhotoDiscObject10 file is missing.

FIGURE 7.20

Sign of a missing image file.

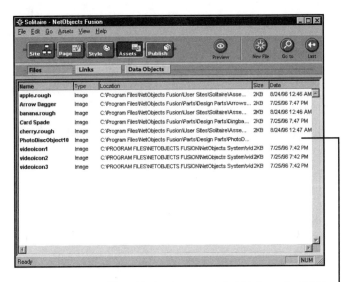

These blank columns mean that this image is missing——

TIP

Because the Size and Date columns are important for performing a quick inventory of your files, make sure that they're onscreen when you look at Assets view. Don't make the other columns so wide that Size and Date get lost.

WARNING

NetObjects Fusion won't figure out that a file is missing if the file is moved, renamed, or deleted while Fusion is running. If you're making a final check to make sure that your files are in place before you publish your site, quit Fusion and restart before you look at Assets view.

You'll have to find the missing image yourself. Start with your operating system's Find command (**Apple Icon**→**Find File** on Mac OS and **Start**→ **Find**→**File** or **Folder** on Windows 95) and gradually build your way up to frantic calls to your vacationing co-workers.

After you've found the missing file, you can use Assets view to put it back in place. Double-click the filename in Assets view and use the resulting dialog box to navigate to the missing file's new location.

TIP

If you put the missing file back in its rightful location while NetObjects Fusion isn't running, Fusion will find the file the next time it starts up.

Naturally, this technique applies to all the different kinds of file assets that NetObjects Fusion keeps track of—images, sounds, Java applets, and Shockwave components—in exactly the same way.

You don't need to worry about auto-generated images. NetObjects Fusion keeps track of them and keeps them hidden away in the Preview/Assets folder. However, keep in mind that if a base image is missing from Assets view, any changes that you make to the base image won't be applied to the automatically generated image until the base image is found by NetObjects Fusion.

223

WARNING

Again, NetObjects Fusion can make sure that everything's right *only if you don't mess around with the Preview folder.* Even if you want to mess around with the HTML inside, make a copy and leave the original alone!

Summary

In this chapter, you learned how to use NetObjects Fusion to keep track of the files and links that you use in your chart, and learned about the Preview folder, where Fusion stores its own files while it is preparing the site. Specifically, you learned the following information:

- What file assets are.

- How to use file assets to quickly update groups of files.

- What link assets are.

- How to edit link assets.

- What the Preview folder is, and what it contains.

- Which assets aren't tracked by Fusion.

- How to troubleshoot link problems using Assets view and other tools.

- How to troubleshoot file problems using Assets view.

In the next chapter, you'll learn how to publish your site!

URL Roundup

- Pizzicato Five page:
  `http://www.matador.recs.com/bios/bio_p5.html`

- Stereolab page, with samples:
  `http://www.hotwired.com.music/96/19/index2a.html`

- Sony Web site (look in the morning *and* in the afternoon):
  `http://www.Sony.com`

CHAPTER 8

Publish View

At last, it's time to serve your site.

You've built your site tree with loving care and added content to all the pages. Now you're ready to publish your site so that the Internet (or your intranet) has access to your site.

NetObjects Fusion makes it easy to transfer your site to a Web server. After you've set a few preferences in a dialog box, you can send your site to a test server with a single click, and when you're satisfied with the way the site performs on the test server, publish your site on a permanent server with another single click.

Once the site is transferred, some of you will be able to pass off the task of site maintenance to a Webmaster in your organization or at your Internet service provider. All the gritty details of making sure the site runs properly will be the responsibility of someone else.

Some of you, however, will need to maintain the site yourself, or at least need to set up the test server by yourself. I will provide some basic instructions and guidance in Appendix B of this book, but there are many aspects of site management. I'll try to point you toward some helpful resources to help you get your site running at peak efficiency.

If this server stuff is new to you, now is the time to look for help. There are plenty of books and Web sites with good information about running a server, but you shouldn't try to do this alone. You'll need to find the person who manages your connection on the Internet (or your intranet)—a system administrator or a network administrator—and work together with this person to make sure that your site is successful and that your network is safe.

Making a Preflight Checklist

Before you click the Publish view button, take a moment to make sure that everything is in place. Now is the time to make sure that everything is just perfect. I've developed the following preflight checklist as a starting point and included a copy in PDF format on the *NetObjects Fusion Handbook* CD-ROM so that you can print as many copies as you like. (You'll find it in the book folder.)

> **TIP**
>
> I never, ever proofread publications that I've laid out or written—I ask someone else to do it. After you've overlooked a mistake once, you can look at the same typo four or five times without catching it. I've never worked anywhere where designers and production artists were responsible for proofreading. We're usually terrible at it. Why should Web sites be any different? I've seen far too many typos on Web pages because Web page designers don't seem to ask for help.

Overall Issues

- Are readers notified of browser requirements, if any?

- Are readers notified of plug-in requirements, if any?

- Are links provided to the plug-in download site(s), if plug-ins are required?

Site View Issues

- Do all the pages have some sort of navigational controls?

- Do all pages have a link back to the site's home page?

- Is the navigation logical?

- Are all page names spelled and punctuated correctly?

Page View Issues

- Are all unfinished pages marked "Don't Publish?"

- Have all overlapping elements been separated?

- Has all text been checked for spelling, punctuation, and grammar?

- Are all image labels spelled correctly?

- Do all pages that need revision contain comments in the Page panel of the Properties palette?

- Do forms have CGIs to handle their data?

- How well does the text fit in the browser window?

- Do page elements align correctly?

Style View Issues

- Do all the buttons' labels fit inside the buttons?

- Is the site's style applied consistently to every page?

- Are the link colors different from the colors of any body text?

- Are link colors consistent with the background colors on the site?

- Are the text and links legible on the SiteStyle's background color?

Assets View/Preview Folder

- Are all file assets in place? (Look for blank date and size columns in the Assets window.)

- Are all external links current? (Check them with your browser.)

- Are all Java.class and support files in place?

- Are all JavaScript source files and support files in place?

- Are all plug-in support files in place?

- Are all auxiliary files named with a consistent and descriptive naming system?

Gathering Server Information

As you learned in Chapter 3, a Web Server is simply a software package that "listens" for requests for files from browsers and, when it receives a legitimate request, sends out the file.

By "software package," I don't necessarily mean an application that runs in the foreground, like NetObjects Fusion, Microsoft Word, or any of the other software tools you might routinely use. A server can run as an application, or it can run in the background as an invisible process. On some systems, this background process might be part of the basic operating system, and on other systems, it's an independent process. Also, Web server functionality can be added to other software packages—it's not uncommon to see databases that serve their contents as Web pages.

In this section, I'll look at some of the basic issues that you'll need to consider to configure your server for NetObjects Fusion. Ask your Webmaster or consult your software's documentation about these issues because they can vary according to the server's configuration. Being able to answer questions about your server's setup will be a critical part of transferring the site to the server!

(This assumes, of course, that your system administrator or ISP administrator has some sort of Web server software set up on a dedicated server machine already. If you're trying to set up a server on your own machine for the first time, see the sections "Setting Up the FolkWeb Server" [Windows] and "Setting Up WebSTAR" [MacOS] in Appendix B.)

The examples in the following section use the FolkWeb server for Windows 95 and the MacHTTP server for MacOS. The same kinds of controls and settings exist in some form on nearly all servers.

Determining Your Network Address

First, you must find the address of your server software's machine.

This is the same as the IP address that you learned about in Chapter 3. If you're setting up a server on your own machine, you don't need to have your own network address to set up NetObjects Fusion, but you'll need it to set up the server itself. If you're on a Mac, you can find your address by looking at the lower-left corner of the MacTCP control panel (see Figure 8.1).

If you're using Windows 95, follow these steps:

1. Open the Network Control Panel in the settings folder under the Start menu.

2. Double-click TCP/IP in the list of installed network components.

3. Click the IP Address panel in the TCP/IP Properties dialog box. Your IP address is the first line in the Specify an IP address group, as shown in Figure 8.2.

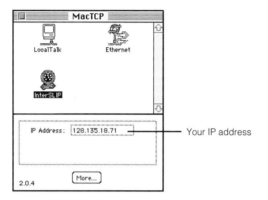

Your IP address

FIGURE 8.1

Mac users can find their IP address by looking at the MacTCP control panel.

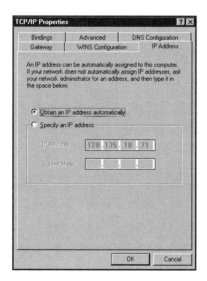

FIGURE 8.2

Windows 95 users can find their IP address in the Network control panel.

229

WARNING

If your connection to the intranet/Internet is via SLIP or PPP, your IP address may change every time you dial up the Net. Ask someone if you're not sure what type of connection you have. If your address changes with every dialup, you won't be able to serve from your machine—at least if you want anyone to find your pages.

Setting File Paths

Many server packages serve files from a limited set of directories: only the files that are in the same folder as the server software, or a certain designated folder, can be served via HTTP.

This restriction greatly enhances your security. You don't want to serve items such as commercial software, personal correspondence, or financial data to the Web at large, right? By limiting the directories that the server can serve, you can be certain that files that haven't been explicitly placed in the Web page folder won't ever be available via your Web server.

This is the way that the MacHTTP/WebSTAR server software package from MacOS works. The server software is a regular application, and only those files that are in the same folder as the application, or a subfolder thereof, can be served by MacHTTP or WebSTAR.

Other server packages may require you to explicitly configure software to serve particular folders in your directory. Typically, you open the software's preferences and type the folder's name into a field, or use some kind of server-administration application to control software that runs as a background application.

This is how the FolkWeb server works. FolkWeb runs in the background, so you must launch the administration application fcontrol in FolkWeb's bin folder and enter the server's directory in the Server Directory field in the Server panel (see Figure 8.3).

FIGURE 8.3

Setting the server directory for the FolkWeb server.

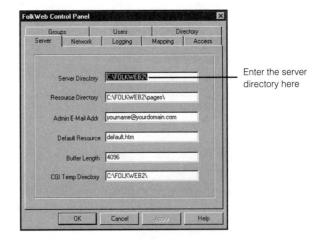

Enter the server directory here

No matter which server you use, or how it is set up, you must know the directory that the server uses to set up NetObjects Fusion.

Creating a Default Page

Most servers have some sort of default page that they send out when a browser connects to an address without specifying a particular file.

For instance, if you load the address http://www.uchicago.edu into your browser, the server sends the file http://www.uchicago.edu/default.html. In other words, the server automatically tacks the default filename onto any URL where the filename has not been specified.

MacHTTP sends the file default.html as a default. (If you like, you can configure MacHTTP to use a different name—say, home.html instead.) FolkWeb uses the similar default.htm (no L at the end) as its default. The default file is configurable in FolkWeb.

Here's a case where you might want to change the settings of the server, rather than adjusting your site to accommodate the server's configuration. If you don't want to use the rather bland "default" as the name of your root page, you can use your root page's name as the server's default.

231

To change the default file to home.html in MacHTTP, follow these steps:

1. Locate the MacHTTP.config file. (It should be in the same folder as the MacHTTP application.) Open it with a text editor such as BBEdit or SimpleText.

2. Find the line INDEX Default.html in the MacHTTP.config file. Change it to INDEX home.html.

3. Save MacHTTP.config.

4. Restart MacHTTP (if it was already running).

To change the default file to home.htm in FolkWeb, follow these steps:

1. Launch the fcontrol application.

2. Click the Server tab.

3. Replace default.htm with home.htm in the Default resource field.

Creating a CGI-Bin Folder

As you learned in Chapter 7, a CGI-bin folder contains the application programs that the server may use to help it handle forms and create other effects. Although particulars vary from platform to platform and server to server, CGI applications are often consolidated into a single folder for security reasons.

MacHTTP doesn't use a CGI-bin folder. You can put CGIs wherever you like inside the folder that contains the MacHTTP folder, including inside another folder. FolkWeb does use a CGI-bin folder, located at the first level FolkWeb directory hierarchy, that is, FolkWeb/cgi-bin.

Setting a Password

The FTP protocol, which is used to transport files over Internet and intranet connections, requires the use of a password to connect to remote servers. If you're going to transfer files to remote servers over a TCP/IP connection, you need to have a username and password to gain access to the server.

This is something that only the administrator of the server can give you. Ask nicely. When you have your password, take care of it. Don't write it on a Post-It note and stick it on your monitor or put it in your top desk drawer. Memorize it!

> **WARNING**
>
> It's possible to log onto some machines by using "anonymous" as a username and your email address as a password. If the server's administrator tells you to do this, you're in big trouble: anybody can upload anything they like to your Web sites, including Web pages you didn't design, or malevolent CGIs that can scan your disk or destroy your files. Unless you want to be the unwitting host of the *Stalking Mr. Belvedere* page, urge the site's administrator to reconsider this security procedure.

Configuring NetObjects Fusion

After you've proofed everything one last time, it's time to go to Publish view.

Publish view is the simplest of all of the view windows: it consists of three big buttons labeled Settings, Stage, and Publish.

- **Settings.** Enables you to configure the way that NetObjects Fusion sets up your site on the test and final servers.

- **Stage.** Sends your site to the test server.

- **Publish.** Sends your site to the final server.

WARNING

The Stage and Publish buttons send off your site without any kind of intervening dialog boxes, alerts, or confirmations. After you click the button, the files start moving to the server. You can cancel the transfer, but you can't bring back any files or pages that NetObjects Fusion manages to send before you cancel. Be sure you are ready before clicking these buttons.

Go ahead and click the Settings button. NetObjects Fusion brings up the Configure Publish dialog box, as shown in Figure 8.4.

FIGURE 8.4

The Configure Publish dialog box.

233

The Configure Publish dialog box has three panels:

- **Stage** enables you to specify the address of the test server and how the files are named on the server.

- **Publish** enables you to specify the address of the final server and how filenames are handled. You'll notice that the Publish panel is exactly identical to the Stage panel.

- **Modify** enables you to change files to accommodate any special needs of your audience. See the following section for more information.

Modifying Your Files for Specific Browsers

NetObjects Fusion enables you to tweak your site's files to accommodate your audience's needs. Because you can implement these kinds of changes at the point of publication, it's easy to bang out several versions of your site to several servers so that you can accommodate a wide range of users without redesigning and reimplementing your site each time.

Although most readers use up-to-date versions of Navigator or Internet Explorer, some readers will be using browsers that don't support the whole gamut of unofficial tags invented by Netscape and Microsoft. In fact, some moldy old figs use the original HTML browser, Lynx, which doesn't support pictures at all.

The Text-Only Option

When you click the Text-only check box in the Modify panel, NetObjects Fusion builds your site in the usual way, and builds a second copy of the site without any images, applets, or other modern accouterments. The text-only version of the site is simple enough that anyone with any browser can always read it (see Figure 8.5). Naturally, sites without images or other fancy features are significantly lower in bandwidth than a graphically rich site, and even a user with a slow 2400 baud modem can download pages in a moderate amount of time.

234

FIGURE **8.5**

A text-only page, as seen in a modern browser.

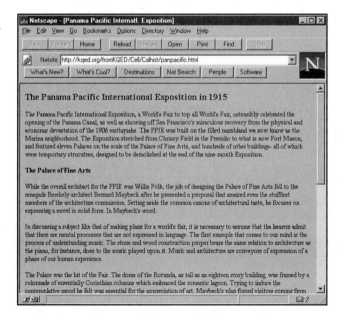

The Grayscale Option

When you build your site with the Grayscale check box selected, NetObjects Fusion builds an ordinary version of your site and a copy with grayscale (black-and-white) images.

Using grayscale images can save significantly on bandwidth in an image-intensive site. Recall from our discussion of color that a JPEG image uses three layers of color information: one each for red, green, and blue. A grayscale image uses only one such layer, so it is one-third the size of the corresponding color image. Besides, sometimes black and white just looks hipper, especially when you're aiming for a stark effect.

TIP

The grayscale option affects only placed images and drawings—not site elements like background colors, text colors, or link colors. Colors for these site elements require only a few bytes for the entire site, anyway.

235

WARNING

When you publish your site in grayscale mode, all your transparent GIFs will become opaque, and your animated GIFs will freeze. (D'oh!) *R I animated GIFs before you publish your site in grayscale.*

There isn't an easy formula for balancing color aesthetics against bandwidth decisions, but at least there's a fairly easy way to estimate how much bandwidth you'll save by converting to grayscale. Navigate to the site's Preview/Assets folder and take a look at the folder's size. The grayscale version of the site will be about a third the size of the Assets folder, and images will load about three times as fast. (This doesn't take into account unmodified images, but, hey, it's an estimate.)

The Low Bandwidth Option

The low bandwidth option builds a version of your site that is more compact than the regular site, but still uses color images.

To make images smaller, you must compromise image quality. Specifically, NetObjects Fusion reduces the palette of colors in each GIF to 128 colors, rather than 256, effectively halving the size of the GIF and reducing the image resolution of the JPEG files (and consequently the file size) in half.

How this affects images depends on the image, as always. A JPEG image of a big, fluffy cloud will probably still look like a big, fluffy cloud. A JPEG image with fine detail, like the one shown in Figure 8.6, will probably suffer. (In one experiment I did, half of a rectangle disappeared completely into a light gray fog!)

FIGURE 8.6

The low-bandwidth option can provide unacceptable results in JPEG images.

GIF images might fare a little better under the low-bandwidth plan. Colors might get a little funny, or even posterized or banded (see Figure 8.7) but it's unlikely that the image will get as fuzzy and pixellated as Figure 8.6.

WARNING

When you publish your site in low-bandwidth mode, your animated GIFs will freeze. Fortunately, your transparent GIFs will remain transparent.

As a general rule of thumb, you can expect that you will save about half of the size of your site's Preview/Assets folder by using the low-bandwidth option, and images will load about twice as quickly.

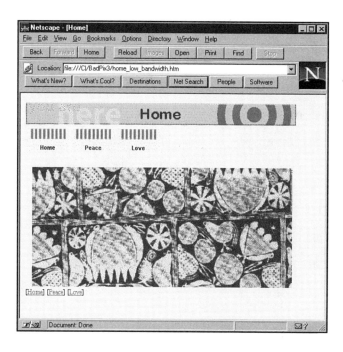

FIGURE **8.7**

Banding in GIF files caused by the low-bandwidth option.

Setting the Location of the Server

The Stage and Publish panels in the Configure Publish dialog box work in the same way, so let's cover both now. The settings that you enter in the Stage panel will be applied when you click the Stage button in the Publish window and the Publish panel entries are applied to the Publish button.

Here's where you'll need to use the file path information that you collected in the Gathering Server Information folder.

If the server is on the same machine as Fusion, or on the same LAN or AppleTalk network, follow these steps:

1. If the server is on the same LAN or AppleTalk network, but *not* the same machine as NetObjects Fusion, make sure that the server machine is mounted on your own computer.

2. Click the Local radio button in the Location group of the Stage or Publish panel of the Configure Publish dialog box.

3. Click the Browse button in the Location group.

4. NetObjects Fusion presents a directory dialog box. Use it to navigate to the desired folder within the server's file path and select it.

If the server is connected to your machine via the Internet or an intranet, follow these steps:

1. Click the Remote Radio button in the Location group of the Stage or Publish panel of the Configure Publish dialog box.

2. Click the Configure button.

3. Enter the IP address of your server in the Remote Host field.

4. Enter the file path to the folder that the server serves files from in the Base Directory field.

5. Enter the name of the server's CGI folder in the CGI directory field.

6. Enter your username in the name field.

7. Enter your password in the password field.

8. How safe is your machine? If you're the only person who has access to your machine, even when you're not at the keyboard, it's probably OK to click the Remember Password button. If there's any chance that someone you don't know or someone you don't trust can sit down at your machine, *don't* click Remember Password.

9. Click OK.

Adjusting the Filenames

Although Fusion manages the filenames of your HTML files automatically, giving each page the same filename as the page's name in Site view, you may need to make some adjustments to filenames to make everything work.

Home Page Name

In the Collecting Server Information section, I suggested that you may want to configure the server so that its default file has the same name as the root page of your site. This is probably the best solution in most cases, but it's not possible in every situation. Some server packages may not allow you to configure the default filename. Some servers may be serving several sites at once, with each site in a separate folder, and may require that the default name of each home page in each site be the same.

Fortunately, NetObjects Fusion gives you some flexibility about the filename used for your home page. Even if your home page is named something like "Bubba" or "Not a home page" in Site view, you can specify that the page be named something other than Bubba.html or Not a home page.html in the server's file system.

To change the filename, click the Stage [Publish] Home Page as pop-up menu and select one of the alternate names—Current Page Name, Index, Default, or Home—based on your server's default file setting. After you've selected the filename, click the Extension pop-up menu and pick the extension (.html or .htm) that your server requires.

Underscore Substitutions in Filenames

When you're creating a site on a Windows 95 or MacOS machine, you can use filenames that contain spaces, like "my file" or "be bop a lu la." However, some server's platforms, most notably UNIX machines, don't support the use of spaces in filenames. To make it easier to transfer your site to such machines, Fusion can automatically substitute underscores for spaces in filenames when the site is published.

239

If you're planning to serve your machine from a Windows 95- or MacOS-based server, you can serve up the file without worrying about spaces in filenames. If you're sending files to a Unix, Windows 3.x, or Plan 9 server, be sure to check the Replace spaces check box.

Of course, you can certainly use underscores if you are using a Windows 95 or MacOS server, and doing so makes your site more portable to other machines. Why, then, would you ever *not* substitute underscores for spaces?

So the short answer is: always check the Replace spaces check box. It can't hurt, and it might solve problems on the server end.

Transferring Your Site to the Test Server

After you have the configuration set up in the Stage panel, you can send your file to the test server. Click the giant Stage button in the Publish window and the transfer commences. NetObjects Fusion presents a progress bar, similar to the one shown in Figure 8.8.

FIGURE 8.8

The Staging Site dialog box.

Staging the site can take a while longer than building a preview. If a fair-sized site is being transferred to a remote server, the transfer might take as long as several minutes. The staging process can go on in the background while you're doing other things. If necessary, you can cancel the transfer at any stage of the transfer. Canceling the transfer will *not* remove any files that have already made it onto the server.

If your site uses any of the "invisible" files that I covered in Chapter 7, you must manually transfer these files to the staging server. If the server is on the same machine, or the same LAN as your machine, you can simply copy the file from its place in the Preview folder hierarchy to the corresponding place in the server folder hierarchy.

Let's say that a site uses a JavaScript source file that's stored in the site's Preview/HTML folder, and your server software is FolkWeb, running on a machine on your local network that's mounted on your machine as the F: directory. In this case, you would copy the JavaScript to the F:/FolkWeb/pages/HTML directory. If the support file were a folder of images in the Preview/Assets/Applets folder, you would copy the image folder to F:/FolkWeb/pages/Assets/Applets.

If the server is running on a remote machine, you'll need to transfer the files to the server via FTP. This isn't too complicated, but you'll need an FTP client application, like Anarchie (for MacOS) or Ws_ftp (for Windows 95).

TIP

You can find the freeware Windows 95 FTP application Ws_ftp at http://www.csra.net/junodj/ws_ftp.htm or at most major Windows shareware sites. You can find the Mac shareware application Anarchie, or the freeware application Fetch, at http://www.ots.utexas.edu/mac or most other large Mac sites. (I much prefer Anarchie to Fetch.)

Why Use a Test Server?

Setting up a test server can seem like a big hassle. It *is* a big hassle. However, it's the best way to see how your site works under real-world conditions.

When you look at your site with the Preview button, you're loading the files that make up the site right off the hard drive. The only limitation on speed is how quickly your machine's processor can read from the disk. This isn't a good indication of how quickly the site will load over a network.

First, Network transfer rates, even on a super-fast connection, can't begin to match the speed of a hard-disk read on a local machine. Also, when you load local files, you aren't sharing your CPU's processing power in the way a server does.

There are other issues, too. If your site uses CGIs, you must have a server running to activate the CGI program. The *only* way to make sure that a form is handled correctly is to test it on a server.

Using a test server enables your team members to evaluate the site privately. If you serve your site on its final server with a blatant typo on the home page, all your readers will see it. If you put your site on a test server first, you can limit access to your site's beta testers, who can ridicule you privately.

241

Testing Your Site

You can ask anyone with a Web browser and access to your pages to take a look at your site. Testers don't need to be Webmasters or veteran surfers—in fact, it's probably best if your group has a net.novice or two, especially if your intended audience does not comprise experts.

Consider giving your testing crew the following suggestions for testing purposes.

Checklist Items

If your site's testers haven't already used the preflight checklist included earlier in this chapter, email a copy to them and let them use it as a guide for proofreading your site.

Of course, not all the items on the checklist will make sense if the testers are looking at the site with a Web browser, rather than NetObjects Fusion. Still, the list has plenty of specific features to help structure the testing procedure.

Download Time

You'll want to see how quickly your site downloads in real-world conditions. This test is most realistic if the server is on a remote machine. If so, you can gauge your site's performance by loading it with a browser on your own machine. If the server is on your machine, or your machine's LAN, you should rely more on the information you get from your remote testers.

Download time is significantly influenced by the number of simultaneous users connected to the server and the server machine's hardware capability. A machine with a faster CPU and more memory can serve more files more quickly than a slower machine. Thus, your testing server cannot be a completely accurate measurement of how your server will stand up in the real world, unless the hardware is identical, and you're able to provide or simulate the amount of traffic that you expect to receive.

Browser, Platform, and Version

It may be interesting to try to load your site with an oddball browser other than Navigator or Internet Explorer. Of course, you can do this kind of check during the early stages of design, too, but it's worth seeing how these browsers interact with the site in the real world of the Net, and easier to try a wide range of tests with a group of friends to help.

I'm especially fond of Sun's HotJava browser, and I usually use it to take a look at pages at some point during the design process. If you or your testers have an America Online account, you might look at your site with AOL, if only for the rude shock (see Figure 8.9).

Otherwise, alternative browsers are a matter of personal taste. There are plenty of them already, and none has a compelling share of the browser market.

WARNING

Non-Italian Mac users—beware the Tiber Web browser from Video Online! When you install the software, it will reconfigure your MacTCP settings to dial up a PPP server in Italy, without warning, and without a chance to disable this option.

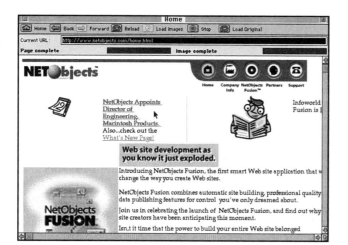

FIGURE 8.9

The NetObjects.com site, as seen through AOL's browser.

You can find Sun's Hot Java Browser for Windows 95 at http://www.javasoft.com/ java.sun.com/HotJava/CurrentRelease/. For a complete list of browsers that are available for download, take a look at http://browserwatch.iworld.com.

Ideally, at least one of your testers will look at your site using a browser on a platform other than the one that you used for development. Although Navigator and Internet Explorer are theoretically the same across platforms, the handling of plug-in material, Java and ActiveX, is not quite platform-transparent. Something that looks OK in Internet Explorer on your PC may not work in the Mac version of Internet Explorer.

While you're at it, you might look at the site in earlier versions of Navigator and Internet Explorer. There are quite a few users who haven't upgraded to the latest version of the software, and certain effects that you can create with NetObjects Fusion, such as tables with different background colors in each cell, aren't supported by fairly recent versions of the big two browsers.

Error Messages

One element you can't control is an error message that is built into the server software. No matter how carefully you build your site and check the links, if a reader enters the URL improperly, your server will send out an error.

243

Let's say that the Webmaster of another Web site has created a link to your home page and enters the link on his page as the following:

```
http://www.yoursite.com/hone.html
```

(Obviously, this bungler isn't using NetObjects Fusion, and didn't read Chapter 7 of the *NetObjects Fusion Handbook*.) Your server will send out an error message when it gets a request like this.

There may be nothing to do about this problem; it all depends on how the server software handles these errors, and how nitpicky you are about the look and feel of your site. If your server creates the error message on the fly, as FolkWeb does, you're stuck with the error message that it creates. If, like MacHTTP, your server software dishes up an HTML file called something like error.html, you can build this page yourself:

1. Create a new site by using the blank template.

2. Name the new site's home page error, or whatever filename your server software uses for its error messages.

3. Apply your full site's style to the new site.

4. Delete the banner and navigation bars from the new page (unless you want a banner and buttons that say "Error").

5. Create your kinder, gentler error message.

6. To link to your home page, create an external link to / + the name of your page (that is, /home.html).

7. Rename the error.html file that's already in the server's folder hierarchy (the one that you want to replace) as something like backup_error.html. If you're connecting via FTP, you may need to ask the server administrator to rename the file.

8. Publish the error site to the folder that contained the original error.html.

Figure 8.10 shows such an error page that is custom-made in NetObjects Fusion.

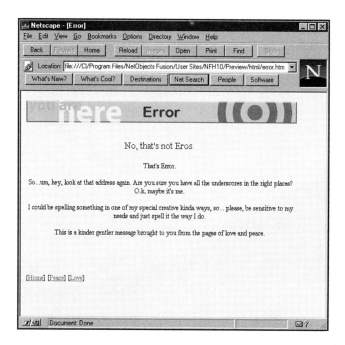

FIGURE 8.10

You can use NetObjects Fusion to tweak the server's error message file.

Publishing Your Site

After you and your team have had a chance to carefully examine your site on the staging server, and you have made any necessary revisions in NetObjects Fusion, you can publish your site.

Sending your site to the final server is just like sending it to the test server. Enter the appropriate address and filename preferences into the Publish panel of the Configure Publish dialog box and punch the truly enormous Publish button in the Publish window.

Remember, the transfer might take a while, especially if the site is large and the server is on a remote machine. As with the staging server upload, you may cancel the transfer at any time, but cancellation will not remove any files from the server.

After you have transferred the site with Fusion, you must transfer all the "invisible" files by hand, just as you did with the staging server. If you don't transfer all the support files, the special effects on your pages may not work properly.

If you want to add your own error message page, and your server uses HTML messages for error messages, use the techniques described in the previous section to create and publish the error message page.

After you've moved the support files to the permanent server, you will need to test the server again. You don't need to do exhaustive platform and browser testing, as your tests with the staging server will have revealed any such problems.

When the site has been tested, you can relax—at least until it's time to revise the site. May I suggest http://cigarworld.com?

Assessing the Site's Performance

Even if you're not the Webmaster of your site, it's your job to fret about how well your site is doing and to know how many readers visit your site each day, and from which exotic locations.

If you're not the Webmaster, you may have to ask for this data. However, if you have access to the files on the server, you may be able to find information on your own. At the least, you should arm yourself with the right questions.

If you are maintaining the server, or the test server, you will want to find more detailed information about how to assess your server's performance and how you can fine-tune the way that your server works.

Understanding Hit Counts

When you're assessing the amount of traffic on your server, the basic unit of measurement is the *hit count*. The site's hit count is the total number of Web transactions that take place between the server software and browsers asking for pages.

A server registers a hit for every file it sends out. Remember, every image on your page—every scan, every button, every custom rule—is a separate file, and thus a separate hit. Virtually every page created with Fusion consists of several images, and will show up as several hits in the server. Figure 8.11 shows the download of a single typical Fusion page, as seen in the server software's display window.

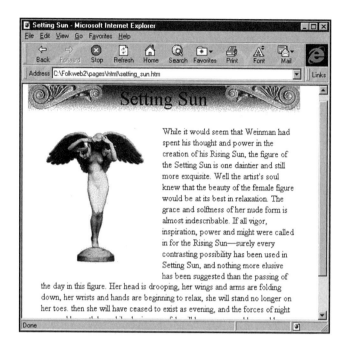

FIGURE 8.11

One page registers as several hits on the browser.

247

This means that the site's hit count is *not* an accurate measurement of the number of visitors to your site. Rather, it's a measurement of how hard your server is working. It's a useful number if you're thinking about buying a new computer, or upgrading your connection to the Net, but it isn't an accurate indication of how many people visit your site each day.

Understanding the Server Log

To determine the number of visitors to your site, you must examine the site's log. Every server package creates some sort of record of the server's activity: which files were served, who they were served to, when they were served, and so on. Server logs also keep track of errors, such as requests for files that the server didn't have, or failed attempts to log onto a site with a password.

Different servers create logs in different ways, but many servers on Windows 95 or Unix platforms use the common log format for recording server activity. This use of a standard format for log files has enabled the development of dedicated and powerful log analysis tools that can help you to profile your reader-base with great accuracy.

Some server packages, such as MacHTTP, don't use the common log format. In some cases, the server package itself provides some log analysis tools. In some cases (such as MacHTTP), third-party log analysis tools are available, even though the software uses a special log format. In some cases, you'll have to dig through the data yourself.

Looking at the Log File

Figure 8.12 shows a snippet of a log file generated by FolkWeb. This log file is in common log format. Notice that it shows the reader address, filename, transaction date, and more for every transaction.

FIGURE 8.12

A log file in common log format, produced by FolkWeb.

248

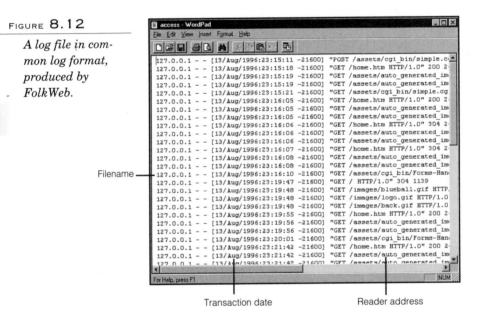

Filename

Transaction date   Reader address

Even a log file in nonstandard format, such as one produced by MacHTTP (see Figure 8.13), contains the same kind of basic information: who's on the site and what they're looking at.

Well, you may say, this seems simple enough...why do I need a log analysis program to read this? Isn't it fairly simple to read as it is?

Yes and no. Keep in mind that these are little snippets of log files. If your site is getting a fair amount of traffic, the log file can pile up hundreds or thousands of entries between readings. If nothing else, you want some sort of automation to help you make sense of this huge mass of data.

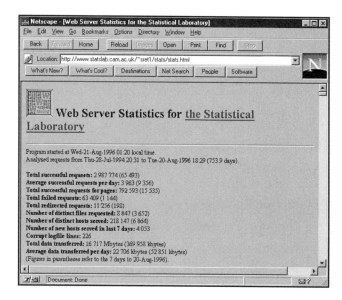

FIGURE 8.13

A nonstandard log, created by MacHTTP.

The idea is that you want to sort out the log file by address so that you count each group of downloads from a single address as a single user. Let's say a reader visits the site and looks at several pages. A few days later, the reader comes back to the site and looks at the home page again. Ideally, you want your records to show the following:

● Recognize that there is a single reader involved, even though the reader visited the site in two separate sessions.

● Add the reader to the tally of total number of readers only once.

● Recognize that a reader has looked at the site more than once and add the reader to the tally of return readers.

● Separate pages from hits and accurately tally the number of pages served.

There are probably a few points you need to know in your capacity as site designer:

● What browser are readers using to look at the site?

● What pages are readers looking at?

It's not that you can't determine these facts by looking at the log file—you can. You just don't have time to work through a giant log file and snoop out the details every day. This is where log analysis software comes in.

249

Choosing a Log Analysis Package

In this section, I've listed a few of the log analysis packages I've found, along with the URLs where you can find them. Some are commercial products, some are shareware or freeware.

Analog

Analog is free software that runs on a variety of platforms—Windows, Mac, and Unix—and handles both common log format files and MacHTTP files (see Figure 8.14). It provides fairly extensive information, albeit not quite as extensive (or graphical) as the output from net.Analysis. (It's what I use, but I'm cheap.)

FIGURE 8.14

The index of an Analog report.

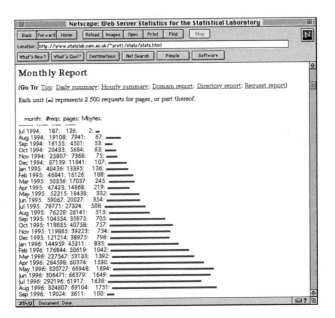

You can find Analog at `http://www.statslab.cam.ac.uk/~sret1/analog/`.

net.Analysis Desktop

The commercial product net.Analysis Desktop is definitely the high end of the log analysis package market. It runs on Windows 95 and handles anything in common log format.

net.Analysis provides the kinds of functionality you'd expect from commercial software. The information that net.Analysis can extract from a log file and display in graphical format is wide in scope. net.Analysis can be used to monitor multiple log files on multiple sites, and it automatically generates reports on each log file, according to the schedule that you set up.

You can download a trial copy of net.Analysis desktop from http://www.netgen.com/.

WebTrends

WebTrends is another Windows-based, high-end commercial application for analyzing log files in common log format.

WebTrends can handle multiple log files. It offers automatic report scheduling and report templates and also compiles a wide range of data about site use (see Figure 8.15).

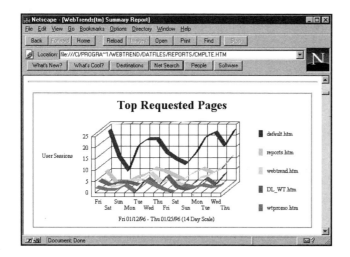

FIGURE 8.15

The commercial product WebTrends provides sophisticated reports.

251

You can download a trial version of WebTrends from http://www.webtrends.com.

wusage

The oddly named wusage is another commercial log analyzer for the Windows platform. Like net.Analysis, wusage creates a wide range of graphical reports from a common log format file, but it's not quite as versatile, and not nearly as expensive. (Universities and non-profits pay $25, all others pay $75.)

You can find demo version of wusage at http://www.boutell.com/wusage/.

getstats

getstats, the freeware formerly known as getsite, runs on Unix-based platforms. I mention it because it can handle MacHTTP log files, as well as common log format files, and because everyone should have a copy of Linux lying around.

The reports generated by getstats are a little sparse, and they lean toward technical, "is-the-server-handling-the-load" issues. It may be a little rough for Mac and Windows users to use, as the interface is straight-up Unix command line.

You can find getstats at http://www.eit.com/software/getstats/.

Gaining Access to the Log File

If the server is on your machine, or on your LAN, you shouldn't have any difficulty getting access to the server's log file. If the server is on a remote machine, you may need to use an FTP client to download the log file to your machine and process it with a log analyzer such as Analog.

> **TIP**
>
> If you're using the FTP approach, be sure to check with the site's Webmaster—just because you have permission to upload to the site, doesn't mean you can download the log file—and ask your Webmaster to check your permissions.

Alternatively, if your Webmaster is running some kind of log analysis, the analysis program can output a report in HTML, which can be served on the site. It won't look like the rest of your site, but it's not for public consumption, anyway. Ask your Webmaster for the report's URL, and you can check it anytime you like.

Finding Out More about Running a Server

By now, it's probably obvious that there's a lot going on under the hood of the Web server, and there's a lot of maintenance and fine-tuning to be done. If you find yourself responsible for running a server, you'll want something other than this book in your hand when the server crashes.

Even though it's simple enough to set up the server in the first place, there are plenty of issues to cover:

Is the server's hardware adequate? Is the server's network connection fast enough? How secure is your server? What will you do if the server crashes over the weekend? What will you do when the server crashes when you're vacationing in Japan?

Let me point you to a few resources that can help you find out more about the art and science of Webmastering. This is a quickly changing field, so you may find new resources that have become available after this book went to press.

Books

- *Web Server Construction Kit for Macintosh* (Stewart Buskirk, Hayden).

- *Webmaster Professional Reference* (New Riders Publishing).

- *Running a Perfect Web Site* (David Chandler, Que).

Usenet Newsgroups

Usenet newsgroups can be a rich source of information, or a complete waste of time. Start by looking for the group's FAQ, which should be posted on a regular basis. Spend a few weeks monitoring the group to see what type of questions are asked (and what kinds of questions are met with hostility) and then, when you've got a good idea, you can ask questions of your own. The main newsgroups that deal strictly with servers are:

- `comp.infosystems.www.servers.ms-windows`

- `comp.infosystems.www.servers.mac`

- `comp.infosystems.www.servers.misc`

You also may be interested in the following groups:

- `comp.infosystems.www.authoring.cgi`

- `comp.infosystems.www.authoring.html`

- `comp.infosystems.www.authoring.images`

- `comp.infosystems.www.authoring.misc`

And these:

- `comp.infosystems.www.browsers.ms-windows`

- `comp.infosystems.www. browsers.mac`

253

- `comp.infosystems.www. browsers.misc`

- `rec.music.bluenote`

(OK—I just slipped in that last one to encourage you to listen to jazz.)

> **TIP**
>
> You can load a Usenet newsgroup with Netscape Navigator by entering news: + the newsgroup's name (that is, news: `comp.infosystems.www.servers.misc`) in the location field.

Web Sites

There are zillions of Web sites that discuss Web site administration. Issues like site administration, page design, and instruction in basic HTML are often comingled in the same resources. I strongly recommend looking at a book first: the information will be more tightly focused on administration.

Once you've got a good idea what the issues are, you can find up-to-date information on the Web. A good place to start your search is at Yahoo's server directory, at `http://www.yahoo.com/computers_and_internet/internet/world_wide_web/servers`.

Summary

In this chapter, you learned how to serve your site, including the following issues:

- How to customize your site for the needs of special browsers.

- What to ask your Webmaster about the way that the server is set up.

- How to transfer your site to a staging server.

- What to look at when you're testing the staging server.

- How to transfer a site to a final server.

- How to assess a site's performance.

- Where to find more information about server administration.

In Part III of this book, "Getting Fancy," you'll learn how to add hip Web page elements such as applets and multimedia to your site. In Chapter 9, we'll start with clickable imagemaps.

URL Roundup

- Ws_ftp (Windows 95 ftp client):

  http://www.csra.net/junodj/ws-ftp.htm

- Anarchie, Fetch (Mac FTP clients):

  http://www.ots.utexas.edu/mac/internet-ftp.html

- HotJava (alternate browser for Windows 95):

  http://www.javasoft.com/java.sun.com/HotJava/
  CurrentRelease/

- Complete list of available browsers:

  http://browserwatch.iworld.com

- Where to go when your Web site is finished:

  http://cigarworld.com

- Analog (log analyzer):

  http://www.statslab.cam.ac.uk/~sret1/analog/

- getstats (log analyzer):

  http://www.eit.com/software/getstats/

- net.Analysis (log analyzer):

  http://www.netgen.com/

- wusage (log analyzer):

  http://www.boutell.com/wusage/

- WWWStat4Mac (log analyzer):

  http://www.ics.uci.edu/WebSoft/wwwstat/

- FTPWebLog:

  `http://www.netimages.com/~snowhare/utilities/ftpweblog/`

- Index of Web sites about server administration:

  `http://www.yahoo.com/computers_and_internet/internet/world_wide_web/servers`

PART

Getting Fancy

Creating Imagemaps

Imagemaps—images that contain clickable links to different URLs in different parts of the image—were one of the first signs that the Web was gonna be cool.

In very early Web browsers, like NCSA Mosaic 1.0, the only way to navigate was to click underlined text links or button-like images. Imagemaps, also called clickable maps, brought a new level of user-friendliness to Web pages and paved the way for things like navigation bars and clickable site maps. In my opinion, imagemaps can claim a great deal of the credit for making Web pages more like familiar Mac and Windows applications, and hence making the Web more intuitive for users.

What Is an Imagemap?

The way that an imagemap works is pretty intuitive—at least from the reader's point of view. An imagemap is simply a picture that contains one or more invisibly defined regions. Each region is associated with an URL—usually, but not always, another Web page—and when the reader clicks inside a region, the browser loads the URL that's associated with the region (see Figure 9.1).

FIGURE 9.1

Clicking one of the imagemap's defined regions loads the associated URL.

Active region ——

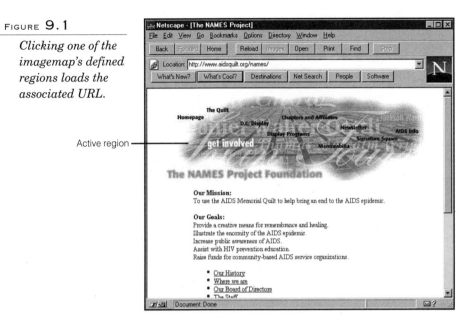

This technique has been adapted for many different effects. It's easy to apply the same kind of techniques to your NetObjects Fusion site.

Site Maps

One common use of clickable maps is to present the reader with a graphical guide to the site's organization. This can be very simple and functional—like a screen shot of the site's structure in NetObjects Fusion—or playful, like the Internet Underground Music Archive site map shown in Figure 9.2.

I've seen all kinds of variations on this approach: From maps that laid out the site as a cartoon map of a fairyland kingdom, where each territory and island represented a different part of the site; to an office, where each office supply represented a different part of the site (the filing cabinet represented archives, I think, and there was an address book sitting on the office's desk). Navigating this kind of page is a lot like playing Myst—if done well, it's intuitive, fun, and interesting.

Custom Navigation Bars

Imagemaps have long been used for creating navigation bars. Although you can easily create navigation bars with NetObjects Fusion, sometimes you might want to create a custom navigation bar that Fusion can't make for you automatically.

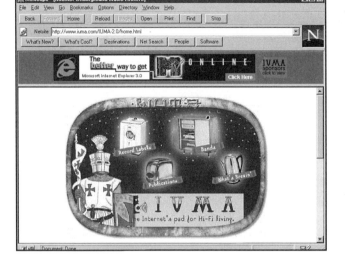

FIGURE 9.2

An imagemap used to map out the main areas of a site.

Perhaps you want to make a special navigation bar that runs vertically down the side of the page, like the one shown in Figure 9.3, or a bar with interlinking, irregular buttons like the one shown in Figure 9.4. NetObjects Fusion can't create this kind of navigation tool automatically (at least not yet). The best way to construct these kinds of navigation aids is by using an imagemap.

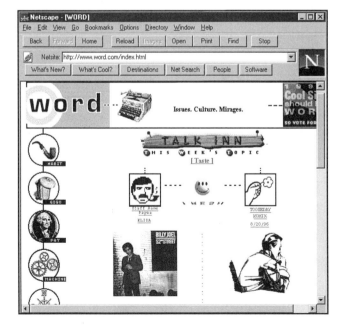

FIGURE 9.3

This vertical navigation bar can't be automatically generated; use an imagemap to build it.

FIGURE 9.4

Another kind of custom navigation bar best handled by an imagemap.

Geographical Maps

Sometimes, you may want to create a set of links to pages that are geographically or spatially related. One of the most elegant Web pages ever is one of the very first sites to feature an imagemap: Virtual Tourist's guide to all the sites in the world uses, quite naturally, a map of the world to organize the page (see Figure 9.5). Each area of this map goes to a submap, which in turn points to a list of Web servers at each map location.

FIGURE 9.5

Imagemaps can be used to organize geographical information.

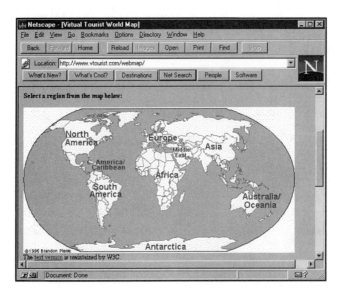

This is a great technique to use to represent, say, maps of cities, university or corporate campuses, or floor plans of buildings.

Close-Ups

Sometimes it's nice to be able to show an image at various levels of detail, and let the reader zoom in and out to look at various parts of the image. It's easy to create this kind of effect with an imagemap. The image shown in Figure 9.6 is a fantastic photograph of 50-some great jazz musicians gathered for this *Life* magazine photo shoot in 1957. (There's a great movie about this photo, by the way, called *A Great Day in Harlem*.)

FIGURE 9.6

Clickable maps are an easy way to provide "zoomable" images.

263

When you click the image, the browser loads a close-up view of the area. Figure 9.7 shows the close-up displayed when you click Thelonious Monk.

FIGURE 9.7

The results of zooming in on a part of the picture.

How Imagemaps Work

There are two different ways that an imagemap can be constructed: on the client-side and on the server-side. Originally, all imagemaps were on the server-side. Server-side imagemaps (the original imagemap format) require a CGI program on the Web server. Most browsers now support client-side imagemaps, which do not require the server software to run a CGI. (NetObjects Fusion creates client-side imagemaps, but with a little work you can build a server-side imagemap with Fusion.)

How Server-Side Maps Work

In a page that uses a server-side imagemap, the server does almost all the work of interpreting the reader's mouse click. Let's break down the process into stages, and see how the browser, server, and CGI each contribute to making the imagemap work.

What the Browser Does

When you're using a Web browser, there are a few key signs that will tell you that an image is a server-side imagemap. If you look at the source code of the page that contains the imagemap, you'll see a tag that looks something like this:

```
<a href = "navbar.map"><IMAGE ISMAP SRC="map.gif"></a>
```

This tag tells the browser that the image file (in this case, map.gif) is a server-side imagemap. If you're using Netscape Navigator, you'll notice that when you put the cursor inside the imagemap, the status bar at the bottom of the Navigator window shows the URL of the map, appended by a question mark and comma-separated coordinates, like this:

```
http://www.site-with-map/navbar.map?20,20
```

As you move the cursor around inside the map, the coordinates change to show the position of the cursor with respect to the top left corner of the image. (The distance is measured in pixels.) When you click the imagemap, the browser sends the URL, including the appended coordinates, to the server.

What the Server Does

Web servers aren't completely stupid. When the Web server sees a request for the URL, navbar.map, it recognizes that navbar.map is a map file, and a map-handling CGI will be needed to process the request. The server sends a message to the CGI program (launching it, if it hasn't already started) and includes the coordinates as part of the message.

265

What the CGI Does

When the map CGI program receives its orders and the coordinate information from the server program, it looks up the coordinates in a table that looks something like this:

```
ellipse http://site1.com 86,25 134,69
poly http://site2.com 46,97 90,60 119,106 88,100 74,123 50,100 46,97
rect http://site3 26,14 54,46
```

The bold is not part of the format. I added it so that it's easier for you to see that each line of the table contains an URL. The sets of numbers after each URL are a geometrical description of the shape of the polygon. (Aren't you glad that NetObjects Fusion takes care of all this stuff for you?)

The CGI takes the coordinates that the browser sent and looks through the table for an area that contains the coordinates. When it finds one, it sends the URL contained in the area's line back to the server. (For instance, if the CGI discovered that the coordinates were in the rectangle listed in the table above, it would send the URL http://site3.) The server sends the appropriate page back to the browser.

> **TIP**
>
> Imagemaps are so commonly used that some server packages, such as FolkWeb, have added imagemap support to the server. In other words, the CGI has been integrated into the server, and the server itself looks up the coordinates in the map table.

How Client-Side Maps Work

As you can see, there are some disadvantages to the server-side system: there are several files involved, and a lot of traffic between the browser, the server, and the CGI. This puts a strain on the server and sucks up bandwidth, which is a bad thing.

What the Browser Does

To solve this problem, client-side imagemaps were introduced. When you look at the source code of a page that contains a client-side imagemap, you'll see a tag that looks something like the following:

```
<IMG HEIGHT=200 WIDTH=200 SRC="map.gif" BORDER=0 USEMAP="#map1">
<MAP NAME="map1">
<AREA SHAPE="poly" ALT="poly" COORDS="16,178,17,96,34,83,53,95,57,162,48,
179,37,185" HREF="./html/c.htm">
<AREA SHAPE="circle" ALT="circle" COORDS="136,44,14" HREF="./html/b.htm">
<AREA SHAPE="rect" ALT="rect" COORDS="45,15,75,78" HREF="./html/a.htm">
</MAP></TD>
```

As you can see, the URLs and the coordinates are embedded in the HTML file itself. Thus, the browser doesn't need to send the cursor's coordinates to a CGI on the server machine to find out which area the cursor is in; the browser can figure it out for itself and load the appropriate URL.

What the Server Does

The server does nothing when the map is on the client-side. Everything is handled by the browser.

Server-Side versus Client-Side Imagemaps

This is a perfect example of the server-side versus client-side scripting that I talked about in Chapter 3. There are two good reasons why a client-side imagemap is preferable to a server-side imagemap:

- A server might be trying to respond to dozens of simultaneous requests. When the browser accesses a CGI to look up the address, traffic is routed through the server twice: once when the CGI is invoked, and once when the target page is loaded. If a client-side imagemap is used, the server only needs to handle the page, so the load on the server is cut in half.

- The CGI that handles the coordinates in a server-side system eats up processor power on the server machine (or network.) If the CGI can process more than one request at once, it uses processor power in proportion to the number of requests. If the CGI is handling dozens of lookups, everything will slow down. The client only has to worry about one lookup—its own.

There are still some server-side imagemaps out there, however. Some Webmasters use the server-side system because of the following reasons:

- That's what they've always done.

- Early versions of browser software, such as Netscape Navigator 1.0 and Internet Explorer 1.0 can't handle client-side maps.

- They want to conceal URLs from the user for find-the-hidden-link games. (One such Easter egg used to be on the About: Netscape page, but I'm not sure it's still there.)

Building an Imagemap with NetObjects Fusion

It's easy to build a client-side imagemap with NetObjects Fusion. Naturally, these imagemaps support standard Fusion links (Internal links, Smart links, and External links) and all of the coding is behind the scenes.

If you're not afraid of doing a little coding, you can make a server-side imagemap with Fusion, too. (Remember, this will increase the load on your server, so you should have a compelling reason to go server-side.)

Making a Client-Side Map

To make a client-side imagemap, start with a placed image. For this example, I'll use the NetObjects PhotoDiscObject6 image from the folder of PhotoDisc samples that's bundled with Fusion. You can practice with the site that I'm working on, called Imagemap, that you'll find in the Book/Sites folder on the *NetObjects Fusion Handbook* CD-ROM.

The tools that you use to create the imagemap's "hotspots" appear at the bottom of the Tools palette when the Picture tool is selected. From left to right on the Tools palette, the tools draw rectangular, oval, and polygonal hotspots, respectively (see Figure 9.8).

FIGURE 9.8

The hotspot tools.

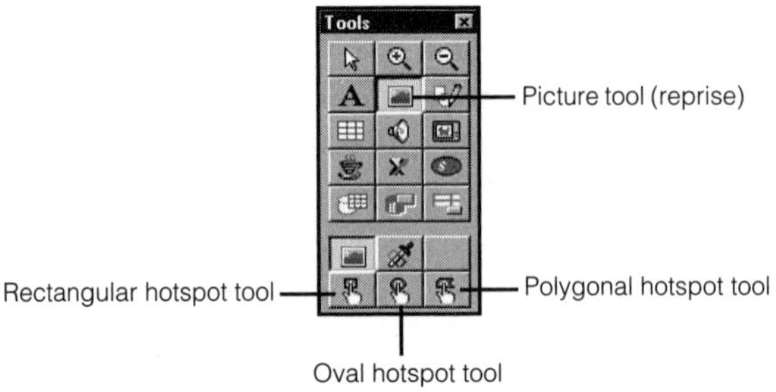

Picture tool (reprise)

Rectangular hotspot tool

Polygonal hotspot tool

Oval hotspot tool

Adding Hotspots

To create a clickable map, use the following steps:

1. Place the image in the layout. (If you're trying this with your own file, any file type is fine.)

2. Click the Picture tool in the Tools palette. The hotspot tools appear at the bottom of the palette.

3. Click the Rectangular hotspot tool. Use the cursor to draw a box around one of the radio tubes.

4. NetObjects Fusion presents its standard Links dialog box. Click the Page Link tab and enter a page name. I'll use page "a" of the example site.

5. Click the Oval hotspot tool and draw an oval around another one of the tubes. NetObjects Fusion presents another Links dialog box; use it to link to a different page.

6. Click the Polygonal hotspot tool and use it to trace the outline of one of the radio tubes. To put down a polygon vertex, click once; to close the polygon, double-click. When Fusion presents the Links dialog box, enter a third page.

You can see the results with the polygonal hotspot highlighted in Figure 9.9.

268

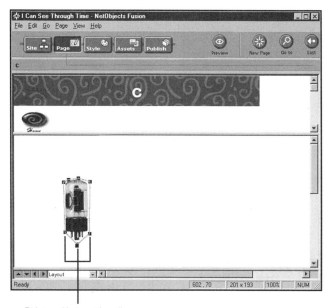

FIGURE 9.9

*An image with
hotspots added.*

Polygonal hotspot handles

269

WARNING

There's nothing to stop you from drawing one hotspot over another, and NetObjects Fusion doesn't mark the overlapping hotspots as it does with overlapping images. If hotspots overlap, the browser will load the first hotspot that it finds in the HTML file—not necessarily the top hotspot.

Editing Hotspots

Hotspots behave pretty much like the corresponding shapes that you'd create with the drawing tools. You can drag them around inside the image or change the hotspot's shape by dragging the handles around. (You can't change one kind of hotspot into another kind, or move a hotspot outside the image, however.) You can cut, copy, and paste hotspots with the standard Edit menu commands.

When a hotspot is selected, NetObjects Fusion creates a very minimalistic Hotspot tab in the Properties palette (see Figure 9.10). *Although you can enter a new link name in the link field, it won't take; the new link won't show up in the Assets window, and the hotspot will revert back to the original link.* To change the link, click the Link button at the bottom of the Hotspot palette. NetObjects Fusion will present the Links dialog box; use this to reassign the link.

FIGURE 9.10

There's not much to the Hot Spot palette.

Making a Server-Side Map

If you've decided that you absolutely must create a server-side map, you can do it. Here are the basic steps to follow:

1. Add a server-side map tag to the page with NetObjects Fusion.

2. Create a map look-up table.

3. Install a map CGI on the server, if necessary.

4. Transfer the support files to the server.

I'm going to use the same PhotoDisc image that I used in the client-side example, but I've renamed it tubes.jpg, to make the name easier to remember when I'm writing HTML.

> **WARNING**
>
> You must test a server-side map on a running server. If you test this by using the Preview button, it just won't work.

Adding the Code

First, let's add the map tag with NetObjects Fusion:

1. Add the map image to the page and design the rest of the page. Don't add any hotspots to the image; it's only there as a placeholder.

270

2. When you're done designing the page, draw a text box above the map image. Make the text box as wide as the image, but only a few pixels high. Leave the text box empty.

3. Select the text box and choose **Page→Element Script**. NetObjects Fusion presents the Script dialog box.

4. In the After Element field of the Script dialog box, enter the code:

   ```
   <a href = "tubes.map"><img ismap src = "tubes.jpg" border=0></a>
   ```

   (In general, the value for the <a href> tag is the name of the map file that you'll create in the next segment of these instructions, and the value for the <img> tag is the name of the map file.)

5. Delete the original map image. (If you don't, the map will appear twice on the page, but only the top one will work.)

Figure 9.11 shows what the Script dialog box should look like when you're done. After you've entered the code, click OK to dismiss the Script dialog box.

FIGURE 9.11

271

The Script dialog box.

Using a Map Utility

The easiest way to create a table that defines a map's hotspots is to use one of the freely available map utilities. (Actually, I have no idea how to do it by hand.)

TIP

You can find the freeware Windows 95 application Map This at `http://galadriel.ecaetc.ohio-state.edu/tc/mt/` and other major Windows shareware site. The shareware Mac application WebMap is available from `http://home.city.net/cnx/software/webmap.html`

Read the documentation for the utility that you choose. Map utilities all work in pretty much the same way—the basic procedure goes something like this:

1. Open an image file with the map utility program.

2. Use the program's drawing tools to create hotspots on the image.

3. Double-click each hotspot to edit the URLs associated with each hotspot.

4. Define a default URL for clicks that don't fall on a defined hotspot.

FIGURE 9.12

Using a map utility to create a map file.

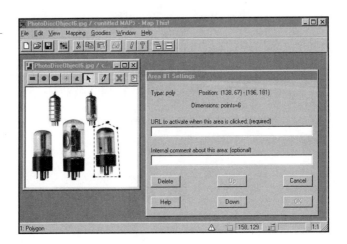

272

5. Save the image file, making sure that you give it the same name that you entered in Step 4 of the "Adding the Code" instructions earlier. (In this example, name it "tubes.map.")

Installing the CGI

Next, you'll need to install a map-handling CGI program. Each server package handles CGIs differently, and some servers even have an imagemap-handling CGI built into the server.

TIP

You can find the freeware MacOS CGI Mac-ImageMap at `http://weyl.zib-berlin.de/imagemap/mac-imagemap.html`. Windows users should consult their server software documentation for information about map handling; many Windows packages come bundled with an imagemap CGI in the cgi-bin folder, or have the CGI built into the application.

See your server's documentation about how to install imagemap handlers or CGIs.

Uploading the Files

Because you added the code for the server-side map yourself, NetObjects Fusion doesn't know about the image file or the map file. You'll need to transfer them to the server yourself.

The example code

```
<a href = "tubes.map"><img ismap src = "tubes.jpg" border=0></a>
```

that you entered in the Script dialog box assumes that both tubes.map and tubes.jpg are in the same folder as the page that contains the map. If it's the site's home page, these files should go in the folder that you specified when you published the site. If the map is on a page other than the home page, the files should go in the HTML folder on the site.

273

If you want, you can move these files to another folder, but if you do so, you must specify the URL correctly when you enter the map tag in the Script box. For example, if you want to put the tubes.jpg file in the Assets/images folder (a very sensible place for it), you'd enter

```
<a href = "tubes.map"><img ismap src = "./assets/images/tubes.jpg"
border=0></a>
```

if the map is on the home page, and you'd enter

```
<a href = "tubes.map"><img ismap src = "../assets/images/tubes.jpg"
border=0></a>
```

if the map is on a nonhome page.

(The difference, if you didn't notice, is the number of dots at the front of the address. A single dot signifies the current directory, and two dots signifies the parent directory.)

I told you it was complicated.

Summary

In this chapter, you learned about imagemaps, including:

- What an imagemap is.

- How imagemaps can be used for special effects.

- How imagemaps work.

- The difference between client-side and server-side imagemaps.

- How to create a client-side imagemap with NetObjects Fusion.

- How to create a server-side imagemap with NetObjects Fusion.

In Chapter 10, you'll look at multimedia (sounds, video, and Shockwave presentations) that can really add zing to your pages.

URL Roundup

- IUMA (Fancy site map):

    `http://www.iuma.com/IUMA-2.0/home.html`

- Vertical navigation bar:

    `http://www.word.com`

- Irregular, interlocking navigation buttons:

    `http://www.boutell.com`

- Virtual Tourist clickable world map:

    `http://www.vtourist.com/webmap/`

- Zoomable image:

    `http://www.actlab.utexas.edu/~horshak/greatday/page1.html`

- Map This (Windows imagemap utility):

    `http://galadriel.ecaetc.ohio-state.edu/tc/mt`

- WebMap(Mac imagemap utility):

    `http://home.city.net/cnx/software/webmap.html`

- Mac-ImageMap (Mac imagemap CGI):

    `http://weyl.zib-berlin.de/imagemap/mac-imagemap.html`

Multimedia: Sounds, Video, and Shockwave

Multimedia: you've heard about it, you've seen it, you've spent a lot of money on it. Multimedia is everywhere, and it's the next step in Web pages.

The rise of multimedia is closely related to the astonishing advances in desktop horsepower. In 1984, the jagged little black-and-white graphics and fonts on the original Mac seemed magical; nowadays, we complain that full-screen, full-motion video technology on the desktop isn't affordable yet. The multimedia revolution depends on cheap RAM and cheap hard disk space, which are now available in abundance. (The PowerBook that I'm writing on is fairly modest, and yet it has 16,000 times as much memory as my first computer did.)

There are now plenty of inexpensive tools that you can use to create your own sound and video files. There's also plenty of software, from freeware to professional-grade products, that you can use to edit, massage, and tweak your sound and video files until they're perfect.

For the really ambitious, there are multimedia presentation tools such as Macromedia Director and Adobe AfterEffects. These tools enable you to combine other multimedia elements—sound, video, and still images—into self-running presentations. You can even use Director's own scripting language, Lingo, to make your presentations interactively respond to user input. Macromedia has developed a special technology called Shockwave that enables you to embed Director Presentations right inside Web pages.

In this chapter, we'll look at ways that you can add sound, video, Shockwave, and other special files to your site, and speculate briefly on the future of multimedia.

Before You Add Multimedia to Your Pages

After you have created multimedia files in the correct format, it's very easy to add them to your NetObjects Fusion site—it's almost as simple as adding ordinary pictures.

Here's the problem: your readers may not be able to load or display the files as easily as you can add them to the pages. There are a few issues that you should fret about before you add multimedia elements to your pages.

Bandwidth

Even a very large GIF or JPEG image isn't *too* big—a page-sized image will usually load in two or three minutes, even over a modem.

A multimedia file, on the other hand, can get very large very quickly. Video files that are more than a few seconds long or larger than a postage stamp can quickly approach file sizes of a few megabytes. It's not uncommon to see 5MB video files out there. Downloading these files is always anticlimactic: the download lasts an hour and a half, and the video lasts 30 seconds.

Sound files are better, but they're still substantially larger than image files. For example, the IUMA site that we visited in Chapter 9 contains archives of songs by the musicians who are featured on the site. A complete three-minute song in stereo MPEG format is a whopping 4.5MB!

User-Savvy Requirements

Although Web browser technology has changed to make browsers even more user-friendly, most browsers will require some kind of technical action by the user, such as the installation of a plug-in or the installation of a helper application.

If you've made it this far through the book, dropping a plug-in into a folder doesn't seem like a very demanding task. However, this can be a real challenge for some users. No matter how simple you make it, there are obstacles to overcome. If the reader doesn't have some kind of decompression utility installed and configured as a helper application, downloading anything at all will be a problem. What if the browser dumps a file in a place where the user can't readily find it?

In short, the steps required to prepare a browser for multimedia can be frustrating to first-time users. Here's my rule of thumb for determining whether a multimedia addition requires too much reader-participation: can my parents figure it out without calling me? In other words, consider your audience's level of expertise with the Web and then serve for the lowest common denominator.

Platform Portability

There are two basic platform issues when you're looking at multimedia content.

Does it work at all? All of the basic sound, video, and Shockwave multimedia that I will discuss in this chapter should work on the PC and MacOS platforms, and almost all should work on most Unix-based platforms. However, some of the newer image file formats that I'll discuss at the end of this chapter may not be cross-platform. The MacOS usually gets the short end of the stick, compatibility-wise.

How well does it work on other platforms? Almost all of the formats that we'll look at were developed as single-platform formats. Although these formats may be supported on other platforms, the support can be limited.

Take MPEG audio, for example. Nowadays, most PCs have some sort of MPEG hardware that makes MPEG playback very slick indeed. Unfortunately, MPEG is a complete and utter zombie on the Mac platform. Although there are MacOS-based MPEG applications, they don't approach the success of MPEG on the PC.

Streaming

One of the biggest developments in Web technology is the concept of *streaming*. Streaming is all about playing multimedia applications in real(ish)-time, and it appears to be one of the cornerstones of the forthcoming Netscape Navigator 4.0

and 5.0 products. Streaming simply means that documents are displayed or played *as* they are downloaded, rather than *after* they're downloaded.

Before 1995 or so, to play audio or video files, browser software would download the file to disk and then launch an application to play the file. Thus, the reader had a complete copy of the file on disk to play back at will.

However, this system has serious limitations: the reader has to wait for minutes (or hours) for a short snippet of multimedia. Even if download time weren't an issue—and it certainly is—disk space issues become a problem. Something like an hour-long radio broadcast could easily use up an entire hard disk.

Streaming addresses this problem by piping the multimedia file straight to the screen and speakers without saving the file to disk. Modern desktop machines are fast enough to play the file as it comes in. Consequently, nothing needs to be saved to disk—which is still relatively slow, even on a fast machine—and no disk space is required.

Some plug-ins, such as MacZilla for the Macintosh, offer the best of both worlds; MacZilla can stream files to the screen and to the speakers even as it saves them to disk. Playback may be a little rougher than pure streaming offers, but readers have a copy of the file that they can play back whenever they wish.

Adding Sound

Adding sound to your NetObjects Fusion site is quite a bit like adding an image file. The hard part, if there is one, is choosing the appropriate sound file format.

Sound File Formats

I've listed some of the most common sound file formats here. Most of the shareware and commercial sound recording and editing software that's available enables you to save a sound file in more than one format; use this list as a guide to picking the format that's right for your site.

MPEG

MPEG stands for Motion Pictures Expert Group, and the MPEG is a compression technique that is used for both audio and video signals.

A digital audio file's quality is directly proportional to the sampling rate of the file. It's exactly like the resolution of a digital image: the more information you collect about a sound or a picture, the more accurate the representation. Use of the MPEG algorithm can substantially reduce the size of an audio file, especially high-quality files of large sizes.

Like it's cousin, JPEG, MPEG is a lossy compression algorithm. To make a sound file more compact, MPEG throws some of the information away. (Hence the term "lossy"—information is lost.) This makes the compression fairly efficient. MPEG throws away sound that the ear can't hear. (At least my ears can't hear the difference between an original and an MPEG file when it comes out of a pair of computer speakers.)

All of this compression and decompression is CPU-intensive—much more so than image compression algorithms such as JPEGs. Most MPEG packages require a 486-or-better PC or a 68040-or-better Mac. In fact, MPEG is so CPU-intensive that many newer PCs have on-board MPEG boards that handle the task of coding and decoding MPEG files. This kind of hardware approach is *substantially* faster than software solutions.

Unlike the other sound formats listed here, MPEG supports stereo sound. It's really the only choice when you want to deliver CD-quality sounds to readers.

279

Required plug-ins for MPEG follow:

- **MacOS.** The MacZilla plug-in works fine, and it can play the MPEG file as the file is downloading. You can find MacZilla at http://www.maczilla.com. You can also find the InterVu plug-in at http://www.InterVu.com.

- **Windows 95.** The InterVu player enables Windows 95 users to play MPEG audio (and video) files inline as the file is downloaded. You can find the InterVu plug-in at http://www.intervu.com.

AIFF

AIFF stands for Audio Interchange File Format, and it is probably the most widely used sound file format.

Until everyone on the Web has a machine with a150-MHz clock speed, AIFF will be a more universally useful file format. MPEG files just require too much horsepower, and most users with 386s and Mac IIs won't be able to play MPEG sounds at all. Even Amiga users (no offense meant) can play back AIFF files.

Furthermore, the latest versions of Netscape Navigator can play AIFF files inline without plug-ins and without launching any helper applications (see Figure

10.1). This makes putting AIFF files into Web pages far easier for users, who would normally need a plug-in to play MPEG sounds.

FIGURE 10.1

Netscape Navigator can play AIFF and other sound files without plug-ins or helper applications.

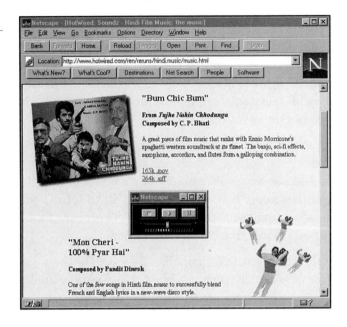

AU

AU is another fairly common audio file format. Originally developed for Unix platforms, u-laws files are reasonably small, of adequate quality, and supported on all platforms.

The AU format has quite a few different names (u-law, μ-law, Sun Audio), and a few different "flavors," that is, subtle variations in the file format. AU players can handle all AU flavors.

AU files are very much like AIFF in size and quality. Most sound-editing applications that support AU also support AIFF and vice-versa. Netscape Navigator can play AU files without any plug-ins or helper applications.

WAV and Mac Sounds

WAV and MacOS System 7 sounds are all platform specific sound formats. NetObjects Fusion recognizes each of these sound format files, and it's easy to place them on your site.

However, support for all these file formats is not built into Netscape Navigator on all platforms. Mac-based browsers seem to have a lot of trouble with WAV files, and it's nearly impossible to play a Mac System 7 sound on the Windows platform, no matter what tools you use.

For this reason, you should always convert WAV and Mac sound to AIFF or AU format. If you're using a sound-recording or sound-editing utility to create the sounds, you can probably just save the sound in AIFF or AU in the first place. Otherwise, you can use a sound-conversion utility such as the Windows shareware application Cool95 (a.k.a. Cool Edit for Windows 95, `http://www.syntrillium.com`) or the MacOS freeware application SoundApp (`http://wwwhost.ots.utexas.edu/mac/pub-mac-sound.html`).

MIDI

MIDI stands for Musical Instrument Digital Interface, and it's a little bit different from the previous kinds of sound files.

Sound files like MPEG, AIFF, and AU work by sampling sounds—recording the sound in segments that are a fraction of a second long and storing the value of each segment, or sample, as a numerical value. Sampling can store any kind of sound at all—music, speech, or the sound of two garbage can lids banging together.

281

MIDI is designed for recording and controlling the activities of musical instruments, especially synthesizers. As such, MIDI can only "record" the music played by musical instruments, and it plays the music back on a MIDI-controllable instrument, such as a synthesizer. MIDI can capture some very subtle data—how hard a keyboard player strikes a key, or the way a guitarist bends a string to change the pitch of a note—but it's not recording sound, per se. With the right equipment, you could use MIDI to record a clarinet and play back the MIDI data on an electric piano. (Alas, there are people who actually do this kind of stuff.)

Because MIDI doesn't use sampling, which uses thousands of samples for each second of recorded sounds, MIDI files are very compact compared to ordinary sound files. A two or three minute song might use less than 23K of bandwidth. MIDI isn't a recording of sound, only of musical instrument "keystrokes," and it can't capture any kind of sound, or all the nuances of a musical instrument.

If you're interested in MIDI, you can look at the MIDI archives at the Ultimate MIDI site (`http://www.angelfire.com/pg1/achtung/index.html`). Careful, there's a lot of cheesy classic rock from the Seventies and Eighties! If you want to add your own song-stylings to the Web, contact a musical instrument vendor about MIDI equipment and software.

RealAudio

RealAudio is another oddball case, but a very cool one. The RealAudio file format uses pure streaming—a RealAudio file is just a pointer to a RealAudio server on the Web. When a browser (or a RealAudio helper application) connects to the RealAudio server, the server sends an audio signal to the browser or client, which delivers the signal straight to the speakers.

As I mentioned in the section on streaming, this allows for some very long RealAudio broadcasts. You can find RealAudio archives of songs on IUMA and RealAudio reprises of NPR broadcasts like this example of Science Friday (see Figure 10.2).

FIGURE 10.2

The RealAudio plug-in can play large audio files in real time.

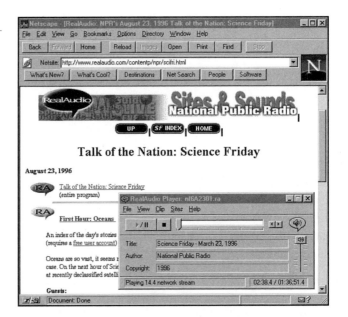

RealAudio doesn't use the usual TCP Internet protocol for transferring information. Rather, it uses a protocol called UDP. The UDP protocol isn't so fussy about whether all the data shows up or not, which enables the transfer to take place quickly. As a result, RealAudio can send sounds over a 28.8 modem (version 1 even supported 14.4 modems) in real time. The sound quality is kind of tinny, and sometimes drops out. To my ears, listening to a RealAudio broadcast is quite a bit like listening to the radio in a 1971 Chevy S-10 pickup. I loved my grandfather's S-10, so I love RealAudio. Your reaction may vary.

There aren't any freeware or shareware utilities to record RealAudio broadcasts: you must use the commercial products from RealAudio to create your RealAudio programs and serve them on the Web. See `http://www.realaudio.com` for more information.

The RealAudio plug-in comes bundled with the current release of Netscape Navigator, and is freely available to Internet Explorer users at the RealAudio Web site.

Choosing a Sound File Format

No sound file format is perfect for every situation. You need to look at the hardware and software you already have, the quality of sound you want to deliver, and the size of files your server can handle, then make a decision based on these factors. Table 10.1 summarizes the important attributes of each of these file formats.

TABLE 10.1

Sound File Formats Compared

File Format	Compression?	Compression Type	Machine Requirements	Quality Rating	Average Size
MPEG	Yes	Lossy compression	Fast PowerPC or Pentium	Excellent sound quality, stereo	Large
AIFF	Yes	Lossless compression	No machine requirements, but older machines may provide choppy playback	Good sound quality, no stereo	Medium-size
MIDI	No	N/A	No machine requirements	Good sound quality (if you like synthesizers)	Very small

continues

283

TABLE 10.1, CONTINUED

Sound File Formats Compared

File Format	Compression?	Compression Type	Machine Requirements	Quality Rating	Average Size
RealAudio	No/n/a		No CPU requirements, but requires a 28.8 modem	Fair to poor sound quality	N/A, file is streamed, rather than saved to disk

Using the Sound Tool

After you've settled on a sound format, you can add sound to your page. There are two basic approaches: you can add sound as a link or as in-line sound.

If you choose the link option, NetObjects Fusion adds a placeholder icon or button to the page. When the reader clicks the link, the browser loads the sound and plays it (see Figure 10.3).

FIGURE 10.3

Adding a sound as a link.

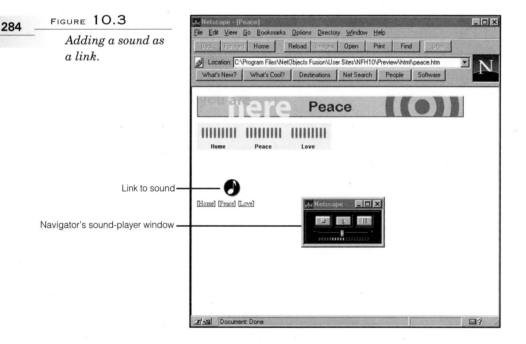

Link to sound

Navigator's sound-player window

If you choose the inline option, Netscape Navigator loads a stereo-deck style image so that the reader can control playback by using the deck's controls (see Figure 10.4). As of this writing, Internet Explorer handles this kind of inline sound by launching an external player.

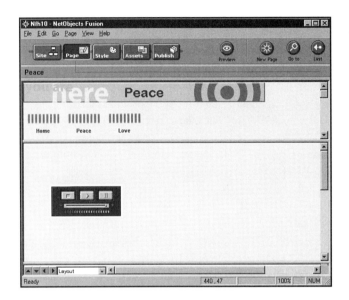

FIGURE 10.4

Adding a sound as an inline element.

285

Adding the Sound

Adding a sound file to a page with NetObjects Fusion is very much like adding an image file. For this example, use the AIFF file Nina.aiff, featuring my very good friend Nina Koroma saying, "Moo, moo, how are you doing?" You can find this sound in the Book/Sites folder on the *NetObjects Fusion Handbook* CD-ROM.

1. Choose the Sound tool from the Tools palette. (It's the second tool in the third row.)

2. Click in the layout where you want the link placeholder or sound deck to appear. You can draw a box, if you like.

3. NetObjects Fusion presents a standard file dialog box. Navigate to the sound file. Make sure that the Type of File pop-up menu is set to the sound format you're looking for. For this example, it should be set to AIFF files.

4. Fusion displays a basic sound icon in the Fusion layout (like the one shown in Figure 10.3). For now, let's leave the icon as it is because we'll see how to change the icon's appearance later.

5. Click the Preview button to launch the browser. Click the sound's icon in the browser window to play it.

TIP

You'll notice that Fusion doesn't include the MPEG format in the Type of File pop-up menu. You can add an MPEG sound file, anyway, by choosing All Files from the pop-up menu and selecting an MPEG file. NetObjects Fusion doesn't actually play sounds or convert sounds from one format to another, so it doesn't care what you enter here. (If you choose a non-sound file, expect some sort of error when you preview the site.)

Setting the Appearance

By default, NetObjects Fusion adds the rather lackluster musical-note icon shown in Figure 10.3. You can choose a different icon, substitute your own image, or create an inline sound deck by using the Sound panel in the Properties palette (see Figure 10.5).

FIGURE 10.5

The Sound panel of the Properties palette.

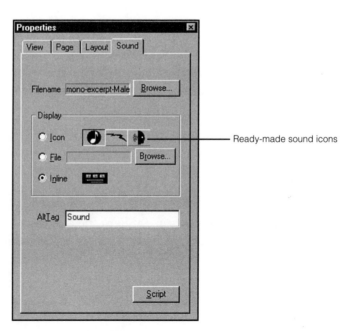

Ready-made sound icons

To use the ready-made lightning bolt icon or ear icon (which I think looks a little too much like a JFK assassination icon…), simply click the alternate icon in the Display group.

To substitute your own image, use the following steps:

1. Click the File radio button in the Display group.

2. Click the Browse button to get the standard Image dialog box.

3. Navigate to the image file that you want to use as a placeholder.

When you use an image as a sound placeholder, you can crop it with NetObjects Fusion, but that's about it. You can't resize the image, or tile it, or make it transparent.

TIP

If you do need to change the appearance of the placeholder image, make a copy of it and make your changes in an image-editing program. Click the Browse button in the Display group again and use the dialog box to navigate to the new version of the file.

To use an inline deck to represent your image for Netscape Navigator users, click the Inline button in the Display group.

Other Adjustments

You can relink a sound's placeholder to a different sound at any time by using the Sound panel of the Properties palette. Simply click the browse button next to the File field and use the resulting dialog box to navigate to a new sound file.

You can also specify an <alt> tag for the sound file. As you'll recall from Chapter 5, an <alt> tag is used as a text placeholder for missing images or images viewed by a browser with auto text-loading turned off.

A sound's <alt> tag *doesn't* refer to the sound's placeholder image. If, for some reason, the image doesn't load in the browser, the browser will simply display a missing image icon. A sound's <alt> tag is used when the sound is placed inline and the sound file is missing or otherwise unavailable.

Understanding Video and Multimedia

Let's start by defining some terms.

Video in this context is defined as digital versions of traditional videos or movies, excerpts from television shows or movies, or footage shot with a video camera.

Animation in this context is defined as movement created by manipulating separate image files. In some cases, this is as simple as moving one or more image files around on-screen, and in other cases, it means loading each file in succession to create a flipbook-style animation that's very much like a video.

TIP

Here's another way to define the difference between video and animation: in a video, all the frames are created and assembled by the video-digitizing device, and in an animation, the frames are created and combined by hand. This isn't always true, but it's usually the case.

Video and animation technology are still coming of age on the Web, and there are many different techniques that can be used to add motion to Web pages. We've already seen the simplest form of animation, animated GIFs, in Chapter 5. On the other end of the complexity spectrum are Java- and ActiveX-based animations. In this section, I'll inventory the animation and video techniques that are commonly used today. We'll look at video- and Shockwave-based solutions in detail later in this chapter and save programming-based solutions for Chapter 13.

Animated GIFs

As you saw in Chapter 5, an animated GIF is simply a group of pictures loaded in sequence. This is a simple, do-it-yourself style of animation that has become pervasive on Web sites.

Advantages of animated GIFs include the following:

- **They're easy to create.** Animated GIFs can be built with any image editor and a few freely available software tools.

- **They're small in size.** Animated GIFs are usually only a few dozen K in size—substantially smaller than other video formats.

- **They're widely supported.** Animated GIFs can be viewed inline by most browsers without helper applications or plug-ins.

Disadvantages of animated GIFs include the following:

- **Individual frame must be created by hand.** Even though it's easy to make an animated GIF once all the pieces are in place, it's tedious to create the individual frames.

- **Length of animation is almost always very brief.** Because each frame of an animated GIF is created by hand in almost all cases, animated GIFs are almost always short.

- **No sound track.** The animated GIF format does not support synchronized sound.

- **No interactivity or customization possible.** Animated GIFs just play themselves out, or loop endlessly. The reader can't pause the GIF, or repeat a section of it, or change the GIF's behavior by clicking different parts of the GIF.

Server Push/Client Pull

289

Server push and client pull were highlights of Netscape Navigator 1.1, when it was the only way to present moving images inline. These techniques rely on special capabilities of the Navigator browser and (usually) special CGIs on the server software.

The basic idea is this: the server sends an image file to the browser, and the image is updated periodically after it's loaded. In the case of server push, the file is specified as a special MIME type (multipart/x-gif-replace) and when the server sends a new image, it forces the browser to reload. In the case of client pull, the page that contains the image includes directions to the browser to reload the page periodically.

Now that it's possible to present video inline by other means, you don't see much server push/client pull these days, with the exception of cases where video is piped directly to a Web page from a camera or other video feed (see Figure 10.6). Take a look at http://www.earthcam.com for an extensive listing of video feeds on the Web. (Not all of these sites feature server push, however.) My favorite example of this approach remains Netscape's Incredible Fish Cam.

FIGURE 10.6

A live video feed, made possible by server push/client pull.

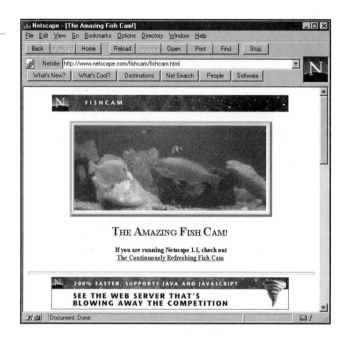

Because NetObjects Fusion isn't set up to handle this kind of animation without a lot of messing around, and server push/client pull techniques are best applied to very few situations, I will not cover this subject in detail. If you're interested in figuring out how to add this style of animation to your pages, you can get started with a look at `http://home.netscape.com/assist/net_sites/dynamic_docs.html`.

Advantages of server push/client pull animation include the following:

- **Live Video Feeds.** Server push/client pull animation can be used to feed self-updating video signals onto Web pages.

Disadvantages of server push/client pull animation include the following:

- **It's difficult to set up.** There are plenty of variables involved: the video hardware, video software, server hardware, and server software must all interact. Many setups will require some scripting or programming.

- **It creates a significant load on the server.** This kind of animation requires a more or less constant connection between the server and the client. This isn't really in the spirit of the HTTP protocol, and it limits the number of clients that the server can handle at one time.

- **No soundtrack.** Server push/client pull animation does not support a synchronized soundtrack.

- **Limited compatibility.** Server push/client pull animation is only supported on the Netscape Navigator browser.

Video Files

Video files are best suited for presenting movie trailers, snippets of television shows, and home movies. Due to the size of video files and the production cost of creating the video in the first place, it's not practical to use a video file to create the more complicated spinning icons or moving type, for example.

Advantages of video files include the following:

- **They're easy to create.** If you have the right hardware and software, a video file is easy to create. There's no need to assemble individual frames so a long video is as easy to produce as a short one.

- **Soundtrack support.** A video file can have a synchronized soundtrack.

291

- **(Limited) Support for Interactivity.** Readers can use the video file's control to control some aspects of playback: the video can be paused, sections of the video can be replayed, and so on.

Disadvantages of video files include the following:

- **Large file sizes.** Video files are usually much larger than other animation-based formats.

- **Production requires specialized hardware.** In order to digitize video, you need a video-savvy computer, or a special card, or other hardware add-ons.

- **Playback hardware requirements.** Smooth playback of video files requires a fairly fast CPU. (The InterVu plug-in, for instance, recommends a clock speed of at least 60 MHz.) Video will be very choppy on older machines.

Macromedia Presentations

The Macromedia Director application is meant to enable nonprogrammers, such as designers and production artists, to create animation and movement within presentations. You can use Director to create sophisticated animations by using a graphical editor, without doing a lick of programming, or you can use Director's built-in scripting language, Lingo, to make the presentations interactive.

(As you'll see later in this chapter, Shockwave isn't exclusively for animations or even Director presentations—there's quite a bit more that you can do with Shockwave technology.)

Advantages of Shockwave (as an animation tool) include the following:

- **Built-in animation tools.** You can create animations with Director without creating each individual frame by hand. Director provides a broad range of techniques for creating animations from a few components.

- **Multimedia within multimedia.** Shockwave presentations can contain other kinds of multimedia files. For example, you might create something like a video frame that bounces around inside a larger window.

- **Soundtrack support.** A Shockwave animation can contain a synchronized soundtrack.

Disadvantages of Shockwave include the following:

- **Requires the Shockwave plug-in.** Readers must download and install the Shockwave plug-in to view Shockwave animation.

- **Proprietary software.** There are no freeware or shareware tools that you can use to create Director presentations. You must use the commercial software from Macromedia, and it isn't cheap. (The Director to Shockwave converter is free, however.)

Application-Based Animation

Experienced programmers can create animation effects with general-purpose programming languages such as Java or C++. (C++ applications are delivered via Web pages by using ActiveX, which is not a programming language itself.) This is certainly the most flexible and the most complicated approach to creating animation on pages.

Advantages of application-based animation include the following:

- **Complete control over the animation.** When you're writing the code from scratch, you have complete control over the animation: you can control the frame rate and give the reader whatever kind of playback control you like.

Disadvantages of application-based animation include the following:

- **Complexity.** It's fairly easy to write a simple program, but nearly impossible to write a bug-free one. Even a simple animation can be time-consuming to create and maintain.

- **Security.** Although Java appears to be secure, some readers may have chosen to disable Java for security reasons. Likewise, readers always have the option to cancel the execution of an ActiveX component. Your animation will not appear if the user takes these security precautions.

- **Reusability.** It depends on how the application is written, but in general, application-based animations can be difficult to update or change. The labor that you put into building an application (or the labor you pay for) may be repeated for each animation.

Adding Video

Adding video components to your pages with NetObjects Fusion is very much like adding sound files. After you've got a video file in the appropriate format, you can add it to your page with a few clicks.

Video File Formats

There aren't many digital video file formats. By the time video appeared on the desktop scene, cross-platform compatibility between the MacOS, Windows, and Unix platforms was becoming the norm.

MPEG

The MPEG compression algorithm that you looked at in the Adding Sound section is also widely used for creating video files. (Remember, the format was created by the Motion Picture Experts Group.)

MPEG is widely used on the Windows and Unix platforms, and in the last year or so, it has gained both advocacy and technical support on the MacOS. MPEG offers the widest cross-platform compatibility (if you count Unix, and you probably should) and modest file sizes.

MPEG support isn't built into any of today's browsers: all browsers require plug-ins or helper applications to support MPEG (see Figure 10.7). There are quite a few competing plug-ins on the market today, all freely available to users. Most MPEG plug-ins support some sort of streaming (the display of the video even as it downloads).

FIGURE 10.7

An MPEG video clip displayed inline.

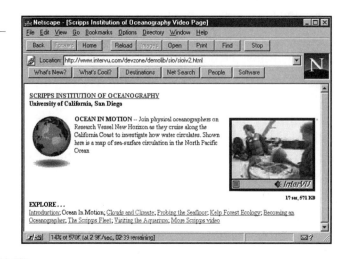

294

TIP

You can find a complete list of MPEG plug-ins with links to the vendor's pages at http://www.browserwatch.iworld.com/plug-in-mm.html.

Unfortunately, MPEG video is a problem on a slow machine, just as MPEG audio is, even with streaming. If you know that your audience is using spiffy new machines or dedicated MPEG cards—you might know this if you're designing for an intranet or creating the Rich Technophile home page—you can use MPEG video without guilt. If you must serve video to Unix users, you should grudgingly use MPEG. If you know you're serving video to readers on slow machines, you should think about using the QuickTime format.

QuickTime

QuickTime is video technology developed by Apple Computer for the Mac. QuickTime is supported (by Apple) on the Windows platform as well. The quality of QuickTime video is comparable to that of MPEG video, and QuickTime seems to fare better than MPEG on slower machines.

QuickTime also supports a very cool video format called QuickTime VR (the VR stands for Virtual Reality, by the way). The video clips created with QuickTime

VR technology don't resemble conventional videos. Rather than capturing motion, a QuickTime VR segment captures a still life in a way that lets the viewer explore the image in a very dynamic way.

Here's how it works: a QuickTime VR producer takes several pictures of a scene or an object and "stitches" them together into a QuickTime VR video. The reader can pan around the scene and zoom in and out on details by dragging the mouse. (If the image is an object, the viewer can rotate the object to view it from different angles, or zoom in and out.) Figures 10.8 and 10.9 show how this works with scenes and objects, respectively.

FIGURE 10.8

Four views of the same QuickTime VR scene (also called a panorama). A New York street on the lot of Twentieth Century Fox Studios.

295

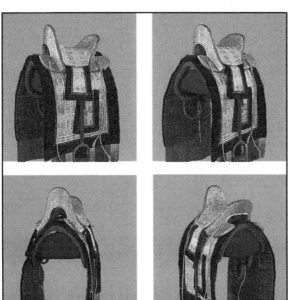

FIGURE 10.9

Four views of the same QuickTime VR object. A saddle for a high lama from the "Mongolia: Legacy of Genghis Khan" exhibit at the Asian Art Museum of San Francisco.

Refreshingly, QTVR is an open standard, and the software used to create this kind of VR object from still pictures is freely distributed by Apple and other sources. QuickTime VR is supported by the same plug-ins that support conventional QuickTime video on MacOS and Windows browsers.

You can find out more about QuickTime and the QuickTime plug-in from Apple's site at `http://quicktime.apple.com`, and more about QuickTime VR from `http://qtvr.quicktime.apple.com` and the excellent `http://w3.qtvr.com` site.

TIP

Mac users can convert QuickTime movies to MPEG format with the freeware application, Sparkle. Sparkle's documentation is terrible—it's huffy and incomplete—but at least the application works. You can find Sparkle at `ftp://sumex-aim.stanford.edu/info-mac/grf/util` and many other Mac sites.

AVI

AVI stands for Audio-Visual, and it's the video file format developed for the Windows platform.

AVI is supported on the Mac by the MacZilla plug-in. (If you haven't noticed by now, MacZilla supports just about every sound and video format on the Mac.) AVI support is built into Windows-based Web browsers. AVI is supported by helper applications, but not by plug-ins, on the Unix platform. (Plug-ins just aren't the Unix way, in any case.)

TIP

You can convert AVI movies to MPEG format with Microsoft VidEdit. (Of course, you can do quite a bit more besides.) VidEdit is freely distributed by Microsoft, and it is easily downloaded from `http://www.public.iastate.edu/~gregngng/download.html`.

Using the Video Tool

Adding a video clip to your site with NetObjects Fusion is the same kind of point-and-click operation that you used to add sounds to your site. (You already had a peek at the video procedure when we did our inventory of assets in Chapter 7.)

CD

If you don't have a movie handy, you can use the Klassy Karl.qt file that you'll find in the /Book/Multimedia folder on the *NetObjects Fusion Handbook* CD-ROM. (Again, that's my friend Carl Heino, co-star of the soon-to-be-international Minneapolis cable access hit "The Prima-Donnas," and yes, it's real lard.)

WARNING

> To preview any video clip with your Web browser, you must have the appropriate plug-in installed, or a helper application available. (You don't need to have the plug-in to actually add the clip—only to see it in the browser.) To view Klassy Karl.qt, you must have the QuickTime extension or the QuickTime player.

After you have created a video file in the appropriate format and installed the appropriate plug-ins or helper applications, you're ready to add the video to your page.

As was the case with sound files, video files can be added as external files that the viewer can load when the user clicks an icon or button, or as inline components of the page.

1. Choose the Video tool from the Tool palette. (It's the third icon in the third row.)

2. Use the Video tool to draw a box in the layout at the spot where you'd like the video or the video icon/button to appear.

3. NetObjects Fusion presents a dialog box. Make sure that the Files of Type pop-up menu is set to the appropriate file type. (To place Klassy Karl, make sure that QuickTime is selected.)

By default, NetObjects Fusion adds a movie camera icon as a link to the video. After the video file has been added to the page, you can change the Video's icon or button, or place the video inline, by using the Video panel in the Properties palette (see Figure 10.10).

To choose one of the alternative ready-made icons, simply click the icon in the Display group.

TIP

> Notice that the lightning bolt icon in the middle is identical to the lightning bolt icon available in the Sound panel. You might not want to use the same icons for both video and sound unless you warn the reader what they're getting with each download.

FIGURE 10.10

The Video panel of the Properties palette.

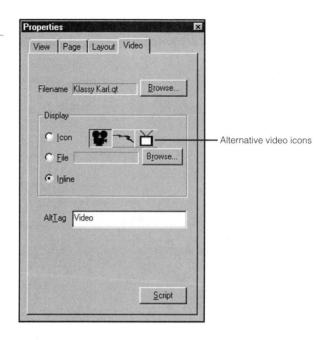

Alternative video icons

To substitute your own image for the standard icons, do the following:

1. Click the File button in the Display group.

2. Click the Browser button.

3. Use the resulting dialog box to navigate to the image file, making sure that the File of Type pop-up menu is set to the right flavor image file.

You can't change the size of the video placeholder image, tile the image, or make it transparent. To achieve this kind of effect, you need to alter the image in an image editing program before you place the image.

To make the video an inline component of your page, click the Inline button in the Display group. NetObjects Fusion will place a gray video placeholder in the layout (see Figure 10.11). The placeholder will be the same size as the default icon, that is, almost certainly too small. Grab one of the placeholder's control points and drag to enlarge the placeholder.

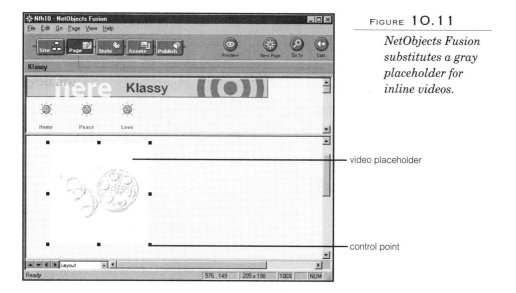

FIGURE 10.11

NetObjects Fusion substitutes a gray placeholder for inline videos.

video placeholder

control point

WARNING

If the placeholder isn't at least as large as the video's frame, the browser will crop the video in an unpredictable way when the page is displayed. In most cases, the video's playback controls will be cropped so that the reader has limited (if any) control over playback.

It's possible to change a video icon/button or video placeholder so that it links to a different video file. To do so, click the Browser button to the right of the File field in the Video panel, and use the resulting dialog box to link to the new file.

As with images and sounds, you may specify an <alt> tag for your video. The <alt> tag is a text message that appears when the browser can't load (or can't handle) the video file; the <alt> tag is not used if the icon or button happens to be unavailable. To enter an <alt> tag message, enter it into the <alt> tag field at the bottom of the Video panel of the Properties palette.

Shockwave

Shockwave is the technology that Macromedia has developed to deliver multimedia data developed with Macromedia tools through Web pages. Macromedia makes software to create all sorts of files—including sounds, vector-based drawings, and multimedia presentations. A single Shockwave plug-in acts as an inline player for all the different content that you can build with Macromedia products.

WARNING

Only the most recent releases of the Shockwave plug-in support *all* of these formats. Support for streamed audio, for instance, was added in the version of the plug-in released as this book was written. Be sure to provide your users with a link to the Macromedia home page so they can download the most recent plug-in.

Furthermore, content adapted for Web delivery ("shocked" content, in the company's parlance) is optimized for net.delivery. File sizes are compressed for quick downloads, audio is streamed, and new Web-wrangling commands are enabled in Macromedia's Lingo scripting language.

NetObjects Fusion won't create Shockwave content—you'll need to create (or find) your own. However, Fusion makes it simple to add finished Shockwave elements to your Web site.

TIP

One of the best things about using Shockwave is you only develop the Macromedia content *once*, and then adapt it for a variety of purposes. You can save the same Macromedia presentation in Shockwave format, or save it as a stand-alone presentation for MacOS or Windows.

What Can You Do with Shockwave?

Shockwave supports many different kinds of Web presentations. You can use Shockwave for tasks as simple as delivering audio, or as complex as creating games or mini-applications within the Web page. Let's look at some of the example sites featured in Macromedia's Epicenter Gallery (http:// www.macromedia.com/shockwave/epicenter/index.html) to see just what Shockwave can do.

WARNING

Before you look at any of the example sites or try any of the exercises in this section, you'll need to install the Shockwave plug-in on your machine. Point your browser at http://www.macromedia.com/shockwave/download to download a free copy of the plug-in.

Simple Audio

c|net's Web site presents an interesting audio-based Shockwave presentation on its Internet radio page (http://www.cnet.com/Content/Radio/Shockwave). The graphical front end of the presentation enables the reader to control the playback of an audio file (see Figure 10.12).

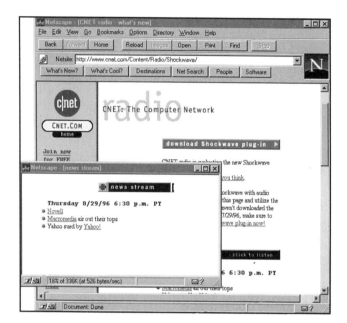

FIGURE 10.12

A sound-based Shockwave presentation without much visual content.

Informational Presentations

Many Shockwave presentations consist of a series of slide show-style pages, each of which contains animations, sounds, and hyperlink-style buttons. (The feel is often very much like a Web site within a Web site, with better typography and a soundtrack.)

A great demonstration of this approach can be found on the FedEx Canada site. (The site is constructed in a very baroque way: Almost every page is constructed on the fly, so there are no ordinary URLs as such. As a result, you can't go straight to the presentation page, but it's a perfect example of the kind of informational presentation that you can build with Shockwave.)

Go to http://www.fedex.ca, and click the demonstration button at the bottom of the page. Click the demo button on the new page, and your browser will load FedEx's Shockwave presentation, as shown in Figure 10.13.

FIGURE 10.13

An informational presentation created with Shockwave.

Games

Shockwave presentations can become so interactive that they become games. There are plenty of Shockwave-based games out there. My favorite so far is probably the Dilbert R & D lab game, a sort of real-world version of space invaders (see Figure 10.14). (You can find it at `http://www.unitedmedia.com/comics/dilbert/lab`.)

FIGURE 10.14

A game created with Shockwave.

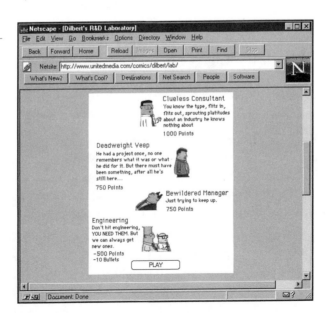

Creating a Shockwave Presentation

To create a Shockwave presentation, you'll need the following items:

- A Macromedia content-creator program that's compatible with Shockwave. As of this writing, this includes Macromedia Director and Authorware (used to create the presentations included previously), the vector-based illustration program FreeHand, and the sound-editing tool SoundEdit16 plus Deck II (which must be used together with Authorware to create sound streaming).

- The appropriate version of Afterburner, Macromedia's free tool for converting content documents into Shockwave content. Each content application uses its own version of Afterburner or other extensions to the applications, and these categories are further subdivided by platform and version number. As a result, there are quite a few software packages available, but you'll only need one or two. You can find all the appropriate files (on a very well-designed page) at http://www.macromedia.com/shockwave/devtools.html.

Consult the documentation included with the Afterburner package(s) for directions on installing and using Afterburner to convert your documents to Shockwave format.

If you're a complete newcomer to Macromedia Director, you might want to look at some of the books on Director and Shockwave from Hayden Books:

- *Macromedia Shockwave for Director*, by Jason Yeaman and Victoria Dawson.

- *Macromedia Director Lingo Workshop*, by John Thompson. (Separate MacOS and Windows versions are available in this title.)

- *Macromedia Director Design Guide*, by Lee Swearingen and Cathy Clark.

Using the Shockwave Tool

After you've got your Shockwave content in hand, you can easily add it to your Web site with NetObjects Fusion.

Just in case you don't have any of your own Shockwave content handy, I've included a 401(k)alculator Shockwave application on the *NetObjects Fusion Handbook* CD-ROM. It's the file called "401.dcr" in the Book/Multimedia folder. This application was created by my friend Joe Gallagher, chief luminary of Gallagher Design and Kalamazoo's king-o'-the-Mac. (You can also find a link to the calculator on the Gallagher Design home page at http://www.net-link.net/gdesign, which features a nifty Shockwave-based navigation bar.)

Let's add the 401(k)alculator to a NetObjects Fusion page.

1. Choose the Shockwave tool from the Tool palette. (It's the third icon in the fourth row.)

2. Use the Shockwave tool to draw a box for the Shockwave element. Try to make the box larger than the size of the Shockwave piece, but don't worry about it too much—you can adjust the box later if it's not quite right.

3. NetObjects Fusion presents a dialog box. Navigate to the Shockwave file (in this example, 401.dcr). Fusion adds a gray Shockwave placeholder, like the one shown in Figure 10.15.

FIGURE 10.15

NetObjects Fusion represents Shockwave files with a gray placeholder in the layout.

304

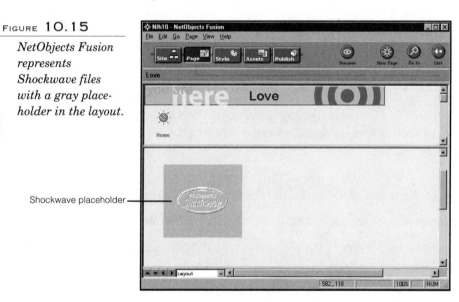

Shockwave placeholder —

4. Click the Preview button. (Remember, the Shockwave plug-in must be installed, or your browser won't display the Shockwave content.)

5. Make sure that all the edges of the Shockwave element are showing. If any of the edges appear to be cropped, go back to Page view and resize the placeholder by dragging its control points.

TIP

Strangely, you *can't* set the size of the Shockwave element's window in the Shockwave panel of the Properties palette. If you know the correct size of the element, set the grid size of the Fusion layout to the same size as the element in the View panel of the Properties palette. Joe's 401(k)alculator is about 500 pixels wide and 400 pixels high.

You may specify an <alt> tag, if you like, that will display if the Shockwave file is missing when the page is loaded by the browser. (If Netscape Navigator doesn't have the Shockwave plug-in installed, the page will contain the standard missing plug-in image and warn the reader that the page uses an uninstalled plug-in. Microsoft Internet Explorer will quietly leave a blank spot on the page.)

Portable Documents and Other Multimedia Formats

New multimedia file formats are developed every day. (I'm sure a few were announced in the time it took me to write this chapter.) Perhaps the most significant new *kind* of format—somewhat similar to Shockwave content—is designed to offer cross-platform portability of documents.

Here's the basic idea: when you move a document with a complicated layout, such as a QuarkXPress or PageMaker document from one machine to another, everything in the document tends to go wrong, even if they're on the same platform. The fonts may not display properly, the pictures, if they're linked externally, don't display properly, and so on.

305

To address this problem, several software developers have come up with portable documents that have the same appearance on every machine—no matter which platform they're on, no matter which fonts are installed, no matter what—the document has a consistent look everywhere. The most widely used portable format is Adobe's PDF (Portable Document Format). Common Ground and Envoy are similar solutions developed by No Hands Software and Tumbleweed Software, respectively.

There are also quite a few new formats that offer new forms of image compression and video-style animation. None of these formats has gained wide acceptance, and it's not clear which—if any—will become useful tools for multimedia delivery. None of these formats is directly supported by NetObjects Fusion.

Acrobat

Adobe is one of the largest vendors of software in the desktop publishing business, and for this reason, Adobe has a large stake in the development of new Web-based publishing tools. The Adobe Acrobat family is an entire suite of software applications that are used to create, manage, and view documents in Adobe's PDF format. Acrobat documents can be created from virtually any other application's documents.

Adobe Acrobat Reader, which can be used to view Acrobat documents in read-only mode, is freely distributed by Adobe. Many of the other Acrobat programs used to create and edit Acrobat documents, such as Acrobat Distiller and Acrobat Exchange, are bundled with popular products such as Adobe PageMaker, Illustrator, and Photoshop.

In the last few years, Adobe has done a great deal to make the Acrobat applications as Web-friendly as possible:

- Acrobat documents can be viewed as embedded elements in Web pages with the support of the Acrobat plug-in.

- Multipage Acrobat documents (such as a magazine or book) can be retrieved from Web servers on a page-by-page basis, rather than all at once.

- Acrobat documents can contain hypertext links to Internet URLs.

In fact, Adobe has repositioned the PDF format as an Internet tool so completely that the latest Acrobat product, which allows designers to create PDF documents from scratch using drawing tools, is called "Web Presenter," rather than Acrobat "Something-or-Other."

To find out more about the Acrobat product line and to download free versions of the Acrobat Reader, plug-in, and Web Presenter, point your browser to http://www.adobe.com/acrobat.

Special Image Formats

Some folks just aren't satisfied with the kinds of compromises necessary to make GIF and JPEG files small enough for zippy Web delivery. The race is on to create new, compact, high-quality image file formats to replace the current solutions.

There isn't a single new format that's taken the Web by storm. (In fact, I've never actually seen any of these file formats outside of the vendors' home pages, but I don't surf quite as broadly as I once did.) However... Java sat on the shelf for a few years (when it was called "Oak") before it really took off, and the same thing might happen with any of these products.

- **Fractal Image Format.** Viewed with the Fractal Viewer plug-in from Iterated Systems, Inc. (http://www.iterated.com/fracview/fv_home.htm),

Fractal Image Format files offer supercompression of images without loss of quality.

- **Lightning Strike.** Viewed with the Lightning Strike plug-in, Lightning Strike is another supercompressed format, developed by Infinop, Inc. (`http://www.infinop.com`). Lightning Strike images are about the same size as maximum-compression JPEG images, but of much better image quality.

- **CGM.** CGM stands for Computer Graphics Metafile, and CGM files can contain bitmaps, compact and easily-scalable vector images (such as Adobe Illustrator or Corel CMX files), and other special components. There are several different flavors and variations on CGM, and several plug-ins from several vendors, such as FIGLeaf Inline from Carberry Technology (`http://www.ct.ebt.com/figinline`) and the InterCAP plug-in from InterCAP Graphics system (`http://www.intercap.com/icap.activCGM.html`).

These are just a *few* examples that I looked at when this kind of plug-in started to appear shortly after the release of Netscape Navigator 2.0. There are dozens of specialized graphics formats and plug-ins that support them. For an up-to-date list, take a look at `http://browserwatch.iworld.com/plug-in-gr.htm`.

307

Adding Special Files to Your Pages

In general, you can add files in special new formats to your NetObjects Fusion pages, but you won't be able to view them in your layout—at least not in version 1.0 of Fusion.

WARNING

Don't just type in the sample code from the example! Different file formats will require different HTML tags. If you've got a package that creates files in one of these special formats, consult the package's documentation to see which HTML tags the format uses.

Most of the special image format files discussed are added to Web pages using HTML's basic <embed> tag, such as:

```
<embed src = " your-filename-here " width = X height = Y>
```

Each format might add its own modifiers (like type or palette) to the basic tag.

To add this code to your page, do the following:

1. Create an empty text box. Make it as wide as the image, but only a few pixels high.

2. Select the element and choose **Page→Element Script.**

3. Type the tag into the After Element field.

4. Delete the empty text box.

Remember, this won't show up in the NetObjects Fusion layout. Click the Preview button to test the image.

Summary

In this chapter, you looked at some basic forms of multimedia: sound, video, and Shockwave presentations, and you learned how to add these elements to your pages with NetObjects Fusion. Specifically, you learned the following:

- Some of the special pitfalls of multimedia.
- What streaming is.
- The various sound file formats commonly used.
- How to add sounds to your pages.
- The basic forms of video and animation.
- The video file formats commonly used.
- How to add video to your pages with Fusion.
- What Shockwave is, and what it can do.
- How to add Shockwave to your pages.
- What portable documents are.
- What special image file formats are.
- How to add special files to your pages.

URL Roundup

- MacZilla ((almost) Universal sound plug-in for Mac):

  http://www.maczilla.com

- InterVu (MPEG audio and video plug-in for Windows and Mac):

  http://www.InterVu.com

- MIDI repository:

  http://www.angelfire.com/pg1/achtung/index.html

- RealAudio home page:

  http://www.realaudio.com

- Video feeds on the Web:

  http://www.earthcam.com

- Netscape's documentation on server push/client pull animation:

  http://home.netscape.com/assist/net_sites/
  dynamic_docs.html

- Cool95 (sound editor/converter for Windows 95):

  http://www.syntrillium.com

- SoundApp Cool95 (sound editor/converter for MacOS):

  http://wwwhost.ots.utexas.edu/mac/pub-mac-sound.html

- QuickTime and the QuickTime plug-in:

  http://quicktime.apple.com

- QuickTime VR:
  http://qtvr.quicktime.apple.com, or
  http://w3.qtvr.com site. New York scene:
  http://view360.com/showroom/media/nyst.mov
  and the Mongolian saddle:
  http//sfasian.apple.com/Mongolia/Tour/catalog/
  cat002.htm

- Sparkle (QuickTime to MPEG converter):

  ftp://sumex-aim.stanford.edu/infomac_
  Graphic_%26_Sound_Tool/_Movie/

- Shockwave plug-in:

  http://www.macromedia.com/shockwave/download

- Vanguard Gallery:

  http://www.macromedia.com/shockwave/new/vanguard/
  index.html

- Gallagher Design home page:

  http://www.net-link.net/gdesign

CHAPTER · *11*

Forms and Form Processing

Forms are a common sight on Web pages—they're an essential tool for passing information from the reader back to the site. Back in 1994, forms were major innovations in the way that the Web worked: they were the first, simple step toward creating interactivity on the Web.

Originally, forms were developed as a simple means of gathering feedback from readers. As is the case with most Web page elements, innovative page designers and Webmasters began to reinvent the form for other purposes. Today, you'll see forms that serve as navigational aids, application interfaces, and as purely decorative elements.

As you learned in Chapter 3, there are two basic steps involved in setting up a form on your site:

- **Creating the form.** Basic form components such as text entry fields and buttons are added to pages with the <form> HTML tag. It's easy to build a form interface with the tools provided by NetObjects Fusion.

- **Processing the form.** After the form has been submitted by the reader, the form must be handled by a CGI on the server machine. Creating a CGI program isn't simple, but fortunately, there are some ready-made commercial, shareware, and freeware CGIs that may suit your purposes. A basic form-handling CGI is included with NetObjects Fusion.

In this chapter, you'll learn how to create a form on your page and how to set up a ready-made CGI program. I won't teach you how to write your own CGI—that's a subject big enough for another book—but I will give a few pointers to adventurous readers.

> **WARNING**
>
> Remember, you can't test a form with NetObjects Fusion's Preview button; the CGI program must be on a running server for everything to work properly. If you must, you *can* run a server and a client on the same machine by using the loopback techniques that I describe in the sections on setting up servers for Windows and MacOS Appendix B, but it's much easier to test forms with a staging server on another machine.

What Are Forms For?

Forms are very flexible, and can be used in many different ways to collect information from readers, or to give readers a means of interacting with the site. Let's look at some of the ways that forms have been used on Web pages, including some very functional and innovative techniques.

Compiling Information

The most basic purpose of the form is to allow readers to upload data to the server. This might be information about the reader, feedback about the site, or other special information.

In the download registration and guestbook examples, the look of the form and the basic kind of information collected is very similar in each case. What's different is the way that the form data is processed on the server end.

Download Registration Form

If you've downloaded much free or demo software from commercial sites, chances are that you filled out some kind of download registration form. (The form that must be filled out to download the trial beta version of NetObjects Fusion is shown in Figure 11.1.)

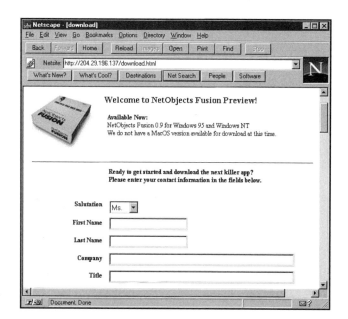

FIGURE 11.1

A download registration form at the NetObjects Fusion site.

313

Vendors usually use the data collected from this kind of form for marketing and making decisions about product development. There are some other advantages to using a form in this context: it will discourage casual and robotic downloads, and force the reader to pause long enough for you to impart some vital information ("may cause your CPU to melt") before the reader loads the page.

Typically, the CGI that handles this kind of form will take the data and stick it into a database application.

Guestbooks

There are many guestbooks all over the Web. (My last Infoseek search yielded more than 13,000 hits!) The kind of information collected for guestbooks varies from site to site, but it's not too different from the kind of information collected in download forms (see Figure 11.2).

FIGURE 11.2

A guestbook entry form.

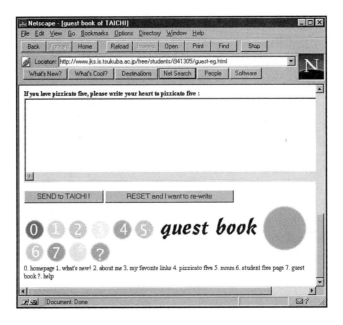

The main difference between a guestbook and a download registration form is the CGI on the other end. A guestbook's CGI pipes the form's data back onto a Web page rather than storing it in a database. This allows other visitors to the site to read other guestbook entries (see Figure 11.3).

FIGURE 11.3

The resulting guestbook from Figure 11.2.

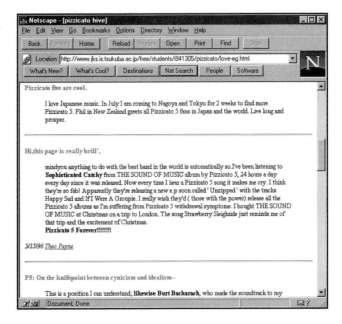

Navigation and Search Engines

Forms are often used as a navigational aid on a very large site. Some site-search engines use a simple form as a front end; very often, the form is nothing more than a text entry box and a "search" button. Some searches, such as the Netscape application locator form (see Figure 11.4), enable the reader to enter several search criteria, and they deliver the reader to the appropriate software download page after the form is submitted.

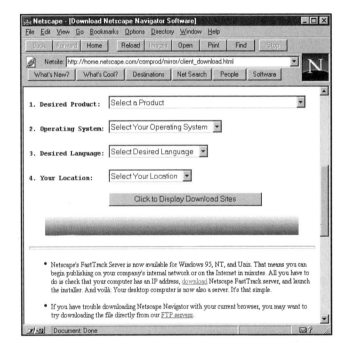

FIGURE 11.4

This form is used to enable readers to search the Netscape site for the appropriate download page.

315

Another common application of forms as a navigation aid is a simple pop-up menu with a "go to" button (see Figure 11.5). This is an elegant reinvention of the way that forms work: it's not really what the form-gods had in mind (judging by the absence of entry boxes), but it's a perfectly legal use of form technology to provide an intuitive navigational tool.

Form pop-up menu

FIGURE 11.5

*Another use of
forms as a naviga-
tional aid.*

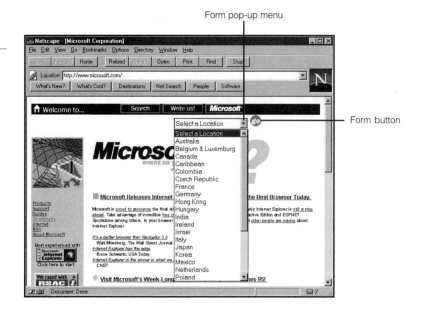

Form button

316

Application Front-Ends

Before the arrival of Java and other executable code in Web pages, forms were
the only way that a running program could interact with a user. In this kind of
setup, the application runs on the server as a special kind of CGI. The form is
used as a way for the user to control the application remotely, and the application communicates with the reader via the Web page. (This use of forms has
been somewhat supplanted by Java and ActiveX, which can run right in the
browser window, but there are still plenty of forms out there.)

Sometimes, the application can be very simple, like the Kiersey Temperament
Sorter page at http://sunsite.unc.edu/personality/keirsey.html (see Figure
11.6). This application enables readers to take a simple personality test, and
displays the results in a graphical way. Unlike a CGI that stores form answers
in a database or posts the results in a guestbook, the CGI that processes this
form provides customized feedback to the reader based on the form entries.

This can get ambitious. One of the most interesting uses of a form is as a means
of remotely controlling a camera or other device wired to the Web, such as the
remotely controlled telescope at http://www.deepspace.ucsb.edu/ir.htm (see
Figure 11.7).

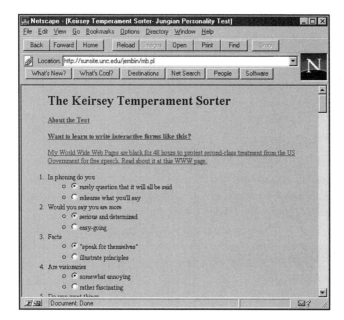

FIGURE 11.6

A form used as a simple application front end.

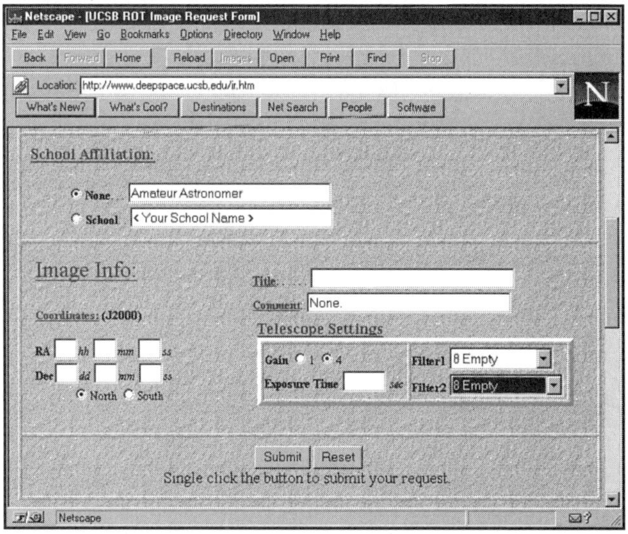

FIGURE 11.7

A form used to control a telescope at the University of California–Santa Barbara.

Obviously, using forms this way will require some custom programming. The program is really the whole point of the form. Even so, the form itself is fairly simple to create.

Form Parameters

The HTML code that creates a form on a Web page includes both a description of the components that make up the form—the text entry boxes, buttons, and so on—as well as instructions to the browser about how the form data should be handled. Let's look at each of the different kinds of components.

TIP

It's important to understand that the NetObjects Fusion form tool doesn't really add forms to the page—it adds form components. Every form component on the same NetObjects Fusion page is added to a single form for the page.

Each of the form components that you'll look at in the next section has some sort of "value." The value can be a number, or a text string, and it can be assigned to the component in different ways, according to the kind of component. In every case, the value of the component is unique—a component can only have one value at any time—and values are changed when the reader interacts with the form. For example, if I type "Bubbles" into a text entry field, it changes the value of the field to the character string *Bubbles*.

Let's say a form has two basic components, called *component1* and *component 2*. When the browser submits the form's data to the server, it sends each component's name paired with the component's value, like this:

```
component1="Michael"&component2=bubbles
```

The form-level instructions tell the browser:

- Where to send this information

- How to send the information

- How to encode the information

These instructions are entered via the Form group at the bottom of each of the form components' tabs in the Properties tab. Each kind of component has a different style of tab in the Properties palette, but all the tabs share a common Form group at the bottom of the tab. (Figure 11.8 shows the Form group at the bottom of a Radio Button tab.)

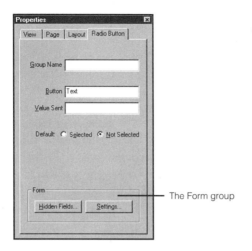

FIGURE 11.8

*All form component
tabs share the same
Form group at the
bottom of the tab.*

The Form group

To enter the form-level instructions for a component, click the Settings button in
the Form group. NetObjects Fusion presents the Form Settings dialog box shown
in Figure 11.9.

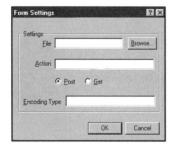

FIGURE 11.9

*The Form Settings
dialog box.*

Here's where you tell the form how to handle the data.

File/Action Fields

The File button and the Action field in the Form Settings box are both used to
specify the location of the CGI that will handle the form. The File button is used
to specify files on your local machine that are to be transferred to the server with
the rest of the site; the Action field is used to specify a CGI application that's
already installed on the server.

Let's say that you're working with the Form Handler CGI that comes bundled
with the Fusion package, which you can find in the NetObjects Fusion/Parts/
Smart Parts/CGI folder. To specify this CGI, click the file button and navigate to
the Forms-Handler.cgi application.

WARNING

MAC
WINDOWS

If you're a MacOS user, consult the NetObjects Fusion documentation about the Forms-Handler.cgi application. It's designed for use on a Unix or Windows server, and may not work with a Mac server. (Maybe it does…I haven't seen the Mac Fusion distribution at the time of this writing.) If you can't use it, or you're not sure, use one of the ready-made MacOS CGIs described in the Forms-processing section at the end of this chapter, or use the book.cgi CGI, written by your old Uncle Tim, in the Book/cgi folder in the NetObjects Fusion Handbook folder.

If you're using a CGI that you or your Webmaster has installed on the server already, you should specify the address of the CGI in the Action field. (You can also install the CGI after the site is published, if you want.) For example, if you've installed the CGI in the Assets/cgi_bin folder, you should specify the path /assets/cgi_bin/*name-of the-cgi-program*. If you put the CGI in the server's own cgi-bin folder, you would specify the path /cgi-bin. (Ask your Webmaster for details, or consult your server software's documentation.)

TIP

The CGI program doesn't necessarily need to be on the Server machine. You can specify any URL you like in the Action field. However, the URL has to be a CGI that can handle the form data, and you had better have the permission of another site's Webmaster before you send data to a CGI on the other site.

Method Used to Send Data

The (unlabelled) Post and Get radio buttons specify how the form data is sent to the CGI for processing. You'll need to look at the CGI's documentation to know which method to use: some CGIs accept data sent via the Get method, some accept data via Post, and some take it both ways.

GET Method

When the browser sends data to the server via the GET method, the data is appended to the CGI's URL. You've probably seen URLs with this format in your browser's location window if you've used the Infoseek search service. The browser adds a question mark to separate the URL from the data, like this:

```
http://www.imaginary-site.com?component-value=100
```

If the form sends more than one data pair, the data pairs are joined by ampersands, like so:

```
component1=apple&component2=banana
```

Special characters such as spaces are replaced by the hexadecimal notation of their ASCII value. For example, spaces are replaced by %20, hex notation for 32, like this:

```
component=two%20words
```

Figure 11.10 shows how this appears in a real-word form—you can see the data from an Infoseek query in the browser's location box.

Data attached to URL

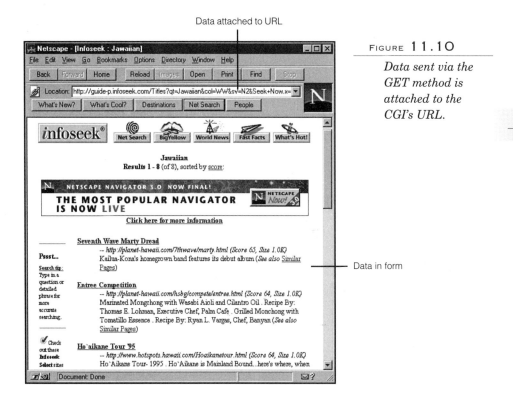

FIGURE 11.10

Data sent via the GET method is attached to the CGI's URL.

321

Data in form

After the URL/data string is constructed, the browser sends it to the server specified in the URL portion of the string. The server recognizes that the URL has data attached (thanks to the question mark), splits apart the URL and data, and sends the data to the CGI specified by the URL.

There is a significant disadvantage to the GET method: the entire URL string has an absolute limit of 1024 characters, so the browser may lose information set via GET from a large form or a long text block entry.

POST Method

When form information is sent via POST, the data is encoded in the same way as the GET method—with ampersands between data pairs and hex notation for special characters. However, the information isn't attached to a URL—it's simply sent to the CGI specified in the action field.

Because there's no limit on the size of the data sent via POST, you should almost always use POST rather than GET. Some CGIs and servers, however, support only the GET protocol. Check the server and CGI documentation to be sure.

Encoding Field

The encoding field is used to specify how the browser and server chop up and reconstitute data sent via POST. As such, it doesn't affect forms that use the GET method.

As of this writing, there's still only one method for encoding forms, application/x-www-form-urlencoded. You can enter this in the Encoding field, but don't—if you leave the field blank, it will be entered as a default, and if you mistype, you risk messing up your form.

WARNING

Leave the encoding field blank unless your server software documentation tells you otherwise.

Hidden Fields

Sometimes, you'll want to send data to a CGI, but you don't want the data to show up in the form where the reader can see it. When you store data in a hidden field, the data is sent to the CGI with the rest of the form when the form is submitted.

For example, the Form-Handler CGI that is bundled with NetObjects Fusion enables you to specify the name of the file that the CGI uses to store the data sent by the form. Thus, if you have two different forms on two different pages, each form can use the Form Handler CGI to write data to its own file.

To enter data in a hidden field, use the following steps:

1. Click the Hidden Fields button in the Form group. NetObjects Fusion presents the Hidden Fields dialog box (see Figure 11.11).

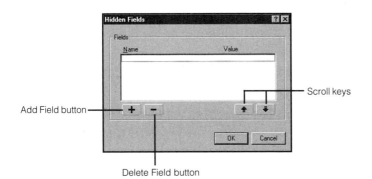

FIGURE 11.11

The Hidden Fields dialog box.

2. Click the Add Field button (the big plus sign). Fusion presents the Enter Value dialog box shown in Figure 11.12.

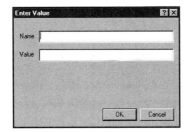

FIGURE 11.12

The Enter Value dialog box.

3. Enter a name and value pair in the Enter Value dialog box. Be careful to enter the name and value (especially the name) *exactly* as specified in the CGI's documentation. Some CGIs may be case-sensitive, so pay careful attention to capitalization.

4. To delete a field, select its name in the Fields group of the Hidden Field dialog box and click the Delete field button (the big minus sign). You can't undo this kind of deletion, so be careful!

Anatomy of a Form Component

There are several basic kinds of form components, each with its own special attributes, but *all* components have name and value attributes.

Name Field Component

Every individual component has its own name, and this is the name that's sent to the CGI as part of the name/value pair.

You can leave the name field for a component blank, in which case NetObjects Fusion names the component with a null string, that is, it enters:

```
NAME = " "
```

in the form's HTML tag. This is technically legal HTML, but it's bound to confuse your CGI. Likewise, you can assign the same name to more than one form component. The browser will encode the name into the form data as many times as it appears, like this:

```
a=1&a=2&a=3
```

rather than picking a single component as "the real a." Perhaps your CGI can make sense of this, but most CGIs will have trouble with this kind of ambiguity.

Value Field Component

Every form component has a value that is submitted to the CGI as part of the component's name/value pair. Each kind of component's value is determined in a different way—a text field's value is the string entered in the field, a check box's value is "checked" or "unchecked," and so on—but each component has some sort of value, if only a default. (See the following section for information about each kind of component's value and default.)

It's not so unusual for two components to have the same value: if you're filling out a form to download pictures of new cars, for example, it wouldn't be strange at all to see something like this:

```
paint_color=red&interior=red
```

It's confusing only if components share names, not values.

The Form Component Lineup

Form components are added to a NetObjects Fusion with the Form tool. When the Form tool is selected, a set of six component tools appear in the Secondary tool palette (see Figure 11.13).

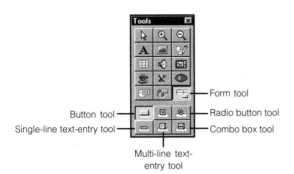

FIGURE 11.13

The Form tool.

Let's run down the list of basic form components and review each component's default values and special features.

Buttons

Basic form buttons are used for two basic functions: to submit the form's data to the server and to reset all the form's components to their default values. Figure 11.14 shows several ways that buttons can be implemented.

325

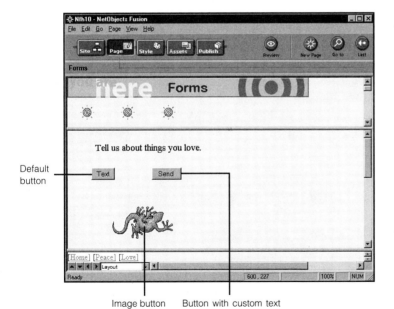

FIGURE 11.14

An assortment pack o' buttons.

TIP

You may have seen form buttons that do something else, like perform arithmetic operations, when they're clicked. These kinds of effects are made possible with JavaScript scripts, which we'll look at in Chapter 13.

To add a button to your page, follow these steps:

1. Click with the Button tool in the layout. You can draw a box, if you like, but the button will always be about 50 pixels wide and 25 pixels high.
2. Enter a name in the Name field. This is the name submitted to the CGI, and it will not appear in the form or on the Web page.
3. If you want the button to have a text label, leave the Text group radio button checked. Enter a text label of any size in the Text field. Notice that the text label appears in the button, which widens to accommodate the width of the label.
4. To make the button function as a Submit button, click the Submit radio button in the Text group of the Button tab (in the Properties Palette). To make the button a Reset button, simply click the Reset radio button.
5. If you want the button to represent an image, click the radio button at the top of the image group. Click the Browse button and use the text box to navigate to the desired image file.

If the button is a submit button, the value of the button in the name/value pair is the button's label. Let's say that your button's name is button1, and the button's label is "Click me." When the form is submitted, the browser sends

`button1=click%20me`

to the browser.

If the button is a reset button, the browser sends a null string to the browser for the button's name and the button's value—no matter what name or label you may have entered for the button.

If the button is an image button, the browser sends the mouse's coordinates to the server as soon as the button is clicked. These coordinates are measured in pixels from the top left corner of the image. The names of the coordinates are attached to the button's name, like so:

`button1.x=25&button1.y=30`

As you can see, an image button behaves very much like an imagemap, but the coordinates are submitted in a different format. (Don't send an image form's data to an imagemap CGI!)

Text Fields

Single-line text entry fields and text entry areas are used to accept typed reader input. Although they look very similar, text fields and text areas are handled with separate form tools, and have different Properties tab palettes, so I cover them individually.

To add a text field to your page, follow these steps:

1. Select the single-line text entry tool from the Tool palette and click in the layout where you'd like the text field to appear. You can draw a box if you like, but the text field will always be about 50 pixels wide and 20 pixels high when it first appears.

2. Give the text field a name in the Name field of the Single Line tab in the Properties palette. This name is the name used in the name value pair, and will not appear anywhere in the layout.

327

3. If you like, enter some default text in the Text field in the Properties palette. (Not in the actual text field in the layout...it won't work, anyway.) Any text you enter here will appear in the field as a default when the browser loads the form (see Figure 11.15).

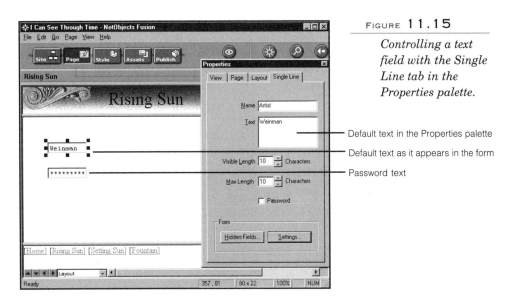

FIGURE 11.15

Controlling a text field with the Single Line tab in the Properties palette.

Default text in the Properties palette

Default text as it appears in the form

Password text

4. If you want to make the text field wider or shorter, enter a new value in the Visible Length field in the Properties palette. The length is measured in text characters—each character is about eight pixels wide.

5. Enter a maximum length for text strings that the field will accept in the Max Length field in the Properties palette. If the reader tries to enter a string that's longer than this maximum, the browser's host machine will beep, and anything the user types will be sent to keyboard limbo.

It's OK to make the maximum length greater than the visible length from step 4. If you do, the text will scroll left as soon as it reaches the right edge of the field. (You've probably seen this scrolling many times.)

WARNING

You can make the default text (from step 2) longer than the maximum length specified in the Max Length field. If you do, all the text will display and be sent to the CGI without a problem. If your CGI imposes a maximum length on the string (which is probably why you set the maximum length in the first place), you may be in for a problem. Default strings that are longer than the maximum length are probably confusing to the reader, too.

6. If you want the browser to hide what the user types as it's entered into the field, click the password check box. The browser will show a bullet for each of the characters entered into the text field (see Figure 11.15).

WARNING

Using the password feature merely prevents evil-doers from shoulder-surfing the password from the reader's screen: it doesn't encrypt the password when the form is sent over the net or provide any other kind of security.

When the form is submitted, whatever the reader has typed into the text field is sent as the field's value in the name/value pair. If the field is empty, the browser sends the null string. If the reader left any default text in the box, the default text will be used as the field's value.

> **TIP**
>
> It's hard to line up a line text with a text field when you're building a form. (And there's almost always instructions like "Enter your phone number here" to align with a text field.) For best results, choose **Edit→Preferences**, click on the Layout Preferences tab, and check Snap to Grid.

Text Areas

A text area is just a text box with more than one line. However, NetObjects Fusion uses a separate tool and a separate Properties palette tab to handle them—probably because they're handled with different tags in HTML.

To add a text area to your page, follow these steps:

1. Choose the Multi-line text entry tool and click in the layout where you'd like the top left corner of the text area to appear. You can draw a box, if you like, but the text area will always appear at the default size of 175 pixels high by 100 pixels wide (see Figure 11.16).

2. Enter a name in the Name field in the Properties palette. This is the name used in the name/value pair, and it won't appear anywhere on the page.

3. Enter any default text you like into the Text field in the Multi-Line tab in the Properties palette—not in the text area itself.

4. If you want to widen or narrow the text area, type a new value on the Visible Length field in the Properties palette. This value is measured in characters—each character is about eight pixels wide.

5. If you want to change the height of the text area, enter a new value into the Visible Height field of the Properties value. This value is measured in characters. It's not *quite* the number of lines that show in the text area—usually, the number of lines that actually appear is the Visible height value + 1, that is, if you specify a value of one in the Visible Height field, two lines will appear.

When the form is submitted to the server, the contents of the text area are sent as the text area's value in the name/value pair. If the form is blank, the browser will send a null string. If the reader leaves any default text untouched, the default text will be sent as the text area's value.

Check Boxes

Check boxes, like the ones shown in Figure 11.16, enable the reader to submit true/false information. To add a check box to your form, do the following:

1. Choose the Check box tool and click in the layout where you'd like the check box to appear. You can draw a box with the Check box tool, but the check box will always appear at the default size of 50 pixels wide and about 20 pixels high.

FIGURE 11.16

*Check boxes enable
readers to submit
true/false values to
the server.*

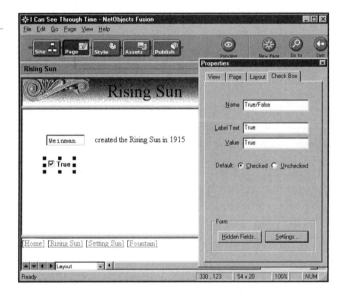

330

2. Give the check box a name in the Name field of the Properties palette. This will be the check box's name in the name/value pair, and will not appear anywhere in the layout.

3. Change the text's label by entering your own message into the Label Text field of the Properties palette. Notice that the check box object widens (or narrows) to fit the new label.

4. Enter a value in the Value field of the Properties palette. This is the value that will be set to the server for the check box in the name/value pair, *if* the check box is checked when the form is submitted. If the check box is unchecked when the form is submitted, the browser will send null strings for both the check box's name and its value, that is, the data string might look like the following:

```
http://www.imaginary-site.com?=&submit_button=send
```

That first "=" (between the question mark and ampersand) is the remnant of the unchecked check box (submit_button doesn't have anything to do with the checkbox—it's the name of the submit button that's used to submit the form. You form's submit button will *always* be included in the form's data string.).

5. Enter a default value of Checked or Unchecked.

Radio Buttons

You've certainly used radio buttons before—they're all over the place in NetObjects Fusion's tabs. In a set of radio buttons, only one button can be checked at any time: when a button is selected, all of its group mates are not selected.

Radio buttons aren't really individual components in themselves—they're added in groups, and the whole group shares a common name and value. It's possible to add a single radio button, of course, but there's no reason to do so.

To add a set of radio buttons to your page, follow these steps:

1. Select the Radio Button tool from the tool palette and click in the layout where you'd like the button to appear. You can draw a box if you like, but the radio button will always appear at a default size of about 50 pixels wide by 20 pixels high.

2. Give the radio button a name in the Group Name field of the Properties palette. The radio button will share this name with its peers, and the group of buttons will use the Group Name as its name in the name/value pair when the form is submitted.

3. Add a text label for the button in the Button field of the Properties palette. The button will change sizes to accommodate the new label.

4. Enter a value for the individual button in the Value Sent field. This is the value that will be sent if this particular text box is selected when the form is submitted.

5. Click the Not Selected button in the Radio Button Properties palette. (Do it for now, even if this is the button you want as a default.)

6. Select the new radio button. Choose **Edit→Copy** and then **Edit→Paste** to create a copy of the button.

TIP

You could also create a new radio button from scratch with the Form tool, but if you mistype the Group Name for the new button, it will not be part of the first button's group. Copying and pasting assures that both buttons are part of the same group.

7. Select the new button. Enter a new label in the Button field of the Properties palette, and a new value in the Value sent field.

8. Repeat steps 6 and 7 as necessary to complete the group of buttons.

9. Select the button that you want to use as the Default selected button. Click the Default selected radio button in the Radio Button tab of the Properties palette. The NetObjects Fusion layout will show the current radio button as selected, and the other radio buttons in the group as unselected.

WARNING

Sometimes, if you accidentally set more than one radio button in a group to Selected, they will both be selected in the NetObjects Fusion layout and in the browser window (see Figure 11.17). As soon as the reader clicks an unselected button, the group will revert to normal, assuming that there's an unselected button to click. If not, the buttons will be locked in the selected position. This is a bad thing, so double-check to make sure that only one button is selected.

FIGURE 11.17

Avoid setting more than one radio button in a group to the default button.

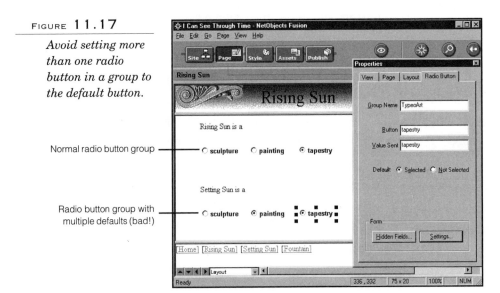

Normal radio button group ——

Radio button group with multiple defaults (bad!) ——

List Boxes and Drop-Down Menus

List boxes and drop-down (a.k.a. pop-up) menus both provide the reader with a list of several items to pick from. Both are handled with the Combo Box tool and the Combo Box tab in the Properties palette (see Figure 11.18).

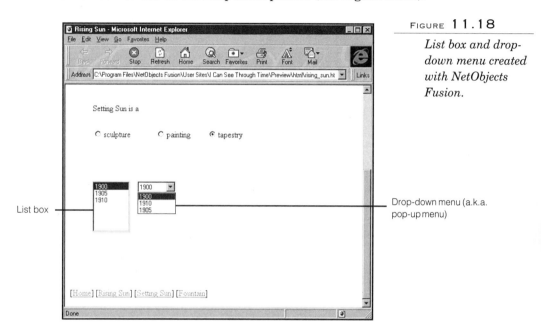

FIGURE 11.18

List box and drop-down menu created with NetObjects Fusion.

List box

Drop-down menu (a.k.a. pop-up menu)

333

A list box displays more than one of its entries at once, although it doesn't necessarily display the complete list. One of the list members can be selected as a default, or the list may have no default value. Hence, it's possible that when the reader submits the form to the server, the list box has no list items selected.

A pop-up menu also contains a list of items, but only one item appears while the menu is inactive. The pop-up menu must always show a value. If you don't specify a default for a pop-up menu, the first list item is displayed and used to determine the menu's value when the form is submitted.

TIP

Combo boxes and drop-down menus have the same attributes and use the same tab in the Properties palette. You can always change a list box into a drop-down menu, or a drop-down menu into a list box, by clicking the appropriate Option radio button in the Combo Box tab of the Properties palette.

To add a list box or drop-down menu to your page, follow these steps:

1. Choose the Combo Box tool and use it to click in the layout where you'd like the element to appear. You can draw a box if you like, but the element will always appear as a list box about 25 pixels wide and 50 pixels high.

2. Enter a name for the element in the Name field of the Combo Box tab of the Properties palette. This is the name that will be used in the name/value pair, and it will not appear anywhere in the layout.

3. Decide whether you want a pop-up menu (called a Dropdown list in the tab, but nowhere else) or a list box, and click the appropriate radio button in the Properties palette. Remember, you can always change your mind later.

4. If the element is a list box, enter a height for the element. The height is measured in characters, and the number of characters is the number of items that the box will display. (Notice that this is different, and more intuitive, than the way that text areas work.) If the element is a pop-up menu, this field will be inactive.

5. Click the add element button (the big plus sign) in the Elements group of the Properties palette. NetObjects Fusion presents the Enter Value dialog box. (This is the same dialog box that you saw in Figure 11.12, when we were entering hidden fields.)

6. Type a label into the Name field of the Enter Value dialog box. This is *not* the name of the component—it's the text label that will appear as a list item in the browser window.

7. Enter a value into the Value field of the Enter Value dialog box. This is the value that will be sent to the server if the text label entered in step 6 is chosen by the reader.

8. If you like, click the Selected by Default check box. If you're using a list box, you can select more than one item as a default; if you're using a pop-up menu, you can select more than one default, but only the first item will be displayed.

9. Repeat steps 5–9 to continue to add items to the list.

TIP

You can't directly set or affect the width of either a list box or a drop-down menu. In both cases, the menu will be a little wider than the widest item on the list.

The way that name/value pairs work with these kinds of elements is a little confusing—at least to me. In the case of buttons and fields, the text that appears on-screen is the value that's sent to the browser. In the case of list boxes and pop-ups, the values are hidden in the Properties palette.

Form-Processing

Your finished form is of no use without some kind of CGI software on the server. Adding a CGI can be as simple as installing a ready-made application or script, or as complex as writing your own code.

As you'll recall from our discussion of CGIs in Chapter 3, there are many practical consequences to running a CGI on your server. Perhaps most significantly, the CGI will consume server resources: memory, CPU time, and possibly storage space. You should not plan to install or use any CGI on the server machine without consulting with your site's Webmaster!

CGIs are far more platform-dependent and individualistic than much of the Web technology that we've discussed in this book. Sure, there are separate Windows and MacOS versions of browsers and plug-ins, but each platform's version of these kinds of applications run in pretty much the same way and share the same basic interface. There aren't any standard CGIs that run on all platforms in the same way—more than any other kind of software, CGIs are largely home-brewed.

335

Test Sites

If you've got your form ready, but your CGI still isn't in place, you can use one of the "public CGIs" provided by the fine folks at NSCA to see how your form works in the real world. These CGIs will simply look at the name value pairs submitted by your form and return them as pairs on a Web page like the one shown in Figure 11.19.

Here's how to test your form using NCSA's CGIs:

1. Click one of any of the form's elements to bring up its tab in the Properties palette.

2. Click the Settings button in the Form group at the bottom of the tab. NetObjects Fusion presents the Forms Settings dialog box.

3. To test a form submitted via POST, enter `http://hoohoo.ncsa.uiuc.edu/cgi-bin/post-query` in the Action field of the Form Settings dialog box and click the Post radio button.

To test a form submitted via GET, enter `http://hoohoo.ncsa.uiuc.edu/cgi-bin/` query in the Action field of the Forms Settings dialog box and click the Get radio button.

4. Click the Preview button. The browser loads your form.

5. Fill out your form and click the submit button (or an image button). You did add one of these, didn't you?

6. The browser sends your form's data to NSCA and returns your data in the following format:

```
name1 = value1
name2 = value2
name3 = value3
etc.
```

(If a name is a null string, nothing will appear on the left side of the equals sign. If a value is a null string, nothing will appear on the right side of the equals sign.)

FIGURE 11.19

Results of sending a test form to a public CGI at NSCA's site.

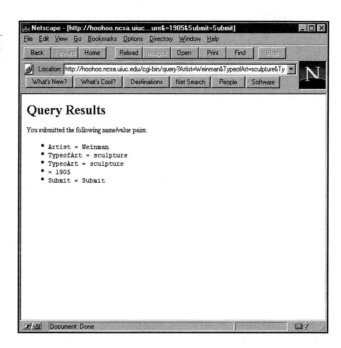

Netscape - [http://hoohoo.ncsa.uiuc...ure&=1905&Submit=Submit]

File Edit View Go Bookmarks Options Directory Window Help

Back | Forward | Home | Reload | Images | Open | Print | Find | Stop

Location: http://hoohoo.ncsa.uiuc.edu/cgi-bin/query?Artist=Weinman&TypeofArt=sculpture&Ty

What's New? | What's Cool? | Destinations | Net Search | People | Software

Query Results

You submitted the following name/value pairs:

* Artist = Weinman
* TypeofArt = sculpture
* TypeoArt = sculpture
* = 1905
* Submit = Submit

Document: Done

Canned CGIs for Macintosh

There are a number of ready-made CGIs available for the MacOS that handle forms. I've included one that I wrote myself, called book.cgi, on the *NetObjects Fusion Handbook* CD-ROM in the Book/Forms/CGI folder. (Remember, I'm a production artist and a writer by profession, not a programmer, and my CGI is not meant for industrial grade applications. See the Read Me file on the CGI for details on installing and using the CGI.)

NetForms is a commercial CGI application from Maxum Development that handles forms. NetForms puts form data into HTML format, so it's especially good at guestbook-style applications. Maxum is one of the earliest developers of CGI software for the Mac, and they make excellent products. You can find more information at http://www.maxum.com/netforms/.

FormSaver is a commercial CGI application that takes form data and saves it on disk on the server machine. (It's a commercial grade, industrial-strength version of my own book.cgi.) You can find out more about FormSaver at http://ns.iliad.com/formsaver.

337

Forms.acgi is a freeware CGI that takes form data and mails it to an email address specified in a hidden field in the form. (It's a good product, and very widely used.) For more information, take a look at http://web77.biola.edu/~steve/cgi/forms.
Flexmail is a commercial CGI that emails form data. It's also very popular. You can find more information and a demo version at http://www.netdreams.com/net.dreams/software.

There are a number of Database CGIs for the Mac, both commercial and shareware, that allow you to add form data to databases (and query databases with forms). Each database needs its own CGI—there aren't any universal CGI applications that work with all databases. See http://www.comvista.com/net/www/cgidata.html for a pretty good list of database CGIs.

Canned CGIs for Windows

The Windows platform is seriously under-represented in the ready-made CGI market. There are plenty of precompiled CGI applications for Unix servers and CGI applications for the MacOS, but there aren't many Windows 95 CGIs that are ready to run out of the box.

As a result (or maybe this is the cause), server packages are more likely to come bundled with some sort of basic CGI that will handle forms. Consult your server's documentation for more information.

Your server may also offer support for automatically running scripts written in the Perl language. Perl isn't compiled—not in the same way that C is compiled, anyway—and so Perl programs developed for other platforms don't need to be compiled into executable .dll or .exe files. This doesn't mean that any Perl script that you find on the Web will run without modification on a Windows server, but fortunately, CGI scripts written in Perl are *fairly* portable to the Windows environment.

Forms Handler is the CGI application that comes bundled with NetObjects Fusion. Forms handler takes the data submitted by the form and dumps it into a file on the server's hard drive. To find out more about how to install and use Form Hander, read the documentation in the NetObjects Fusion/Parts/Smart Parts/CGI folder.

Home-Brewing Your Own CGIs

The time may come when you decide that you want to write your own CGIs. Perhaps the ready-made CGIs that are available on your platform don't do exactly what you'd like with the form data, or perhaps you want to use a form as an interface for an application that you've written.

I'm not going to teach you how to write CGI scripts. There's too much turf to cover in a book about NetObjects Fusion, and there are plenty of training resources available.

You can write CGIs in just about any programming language you like. (OK, maybe not COBOL.) Remember, CGI isn't a language, or even a type of language. It's a protocol that specifies how information is passed back and forth between a Web server and an application that "helps" the server.

However, let me strongly suggest that you write your CGIs by using the Perl language. There are plenty of good reasons to use Perl, even if you have experience with another language:

● **Everybody else does.** Many to most of the CGIs out there are written in Perl. As a result, there are plenty of resources on the particulars of CGI programming, using Perl as an example.

- **Text Handling.** Perl has sophisticated text-handling functions built right into the language. Everything you send to a CGI is a string of characters, right? So you might as well have great text-wrangling tools at your disposal when you're handling this data.

- **Fun.** I've programmed in many languages, and Perl is the only language I would describe as fun. You can be as sloppy or as formal as you want to be when you're writing Perl, and most of the time Perl magically fills in the blanks for you.

- **Support.** You can find answers to questions on many Usenet newsgroups, but `comp.lang.perl.misc` is justly famous as a great place to find quick answers to questions. (They're also famous for reminding you to check the documentation before you ask a question, so read the FAQ!)

Finding the Basic Tools

To get started, you'll need a few tools. All the software that you need is freely available on the Net.

339

Tools for MacOS Users

Yes, there's a port of Perl to the Mac, and it's pretty swell. (In fact, I used MacPerl to create the book.cgi application.) You'll need the basic MacPerl distribution, which I have included on the CD-ROM.

You can find the most recent version of MacPerl, and boatloads of MacPerl information at the MacPerl home page (`http://www.iis.ee.ethz.ch/~neeri/macintosh/perl.html`). This page is maintained by Matthias Neerachers, who ported Perl to the Mac.

You will also need the MacCGI script extension, which will let you save your Perl scripts as WebSTAR/MacHTTP-savvy CGI applications. You can find this extension at `ftp://err.ethz.ch/pub/neeri/MacPerlBeta/PCGI`.

Tools for Windows 95 Users

Perl has been ported to the Windows 95 platform by hip communications inc. You can find the latest version at `http://www.perl.hip.com`.

If your Web server software doesn't directly support the execution of Perl scripts, you can use hip's hip Web Kit to add your scripts to your server. For more information, see http://www.perl.hip.com/webkit.htm.

Books and Other Sources

Alas, there are no Mac-specific books about CGI programming, but you should be able to use The Other People's books to figure out the basics of Perl. (After all, you were smart enough to buy a Mac.)

Caveats for New Programmers

Before you start climbing that learning curve, there are a few complications that you should know about. Writing your own CGIs can give you a great deal of control over the way that your site works, but it can also create new headaches.

Security

340

All server packages have some sort of security features built in—usually, these features limit the server's access to a particular folder or particular files on the machine. When a CGI is involved, however, these restrictions do not apply to the CGI.

In other words, unless you build restrictions into the CGI, it can read from anywhere on the server's machine, or even the server's LAN. Depending on the CGI, it may not be possible for a hacker to coerce the CGI into returning or damaging any of the files outside of the server folder, but, in general, a CGI without some kind of security features is a security hole. Be careful about the directories where your CGI can read and write.

Bugs

Server applications are simple enough that they don't usually crash—at least under an ordinary load. If you're an experienced professional programmer who has lead an exemplary life, your CGIs may be bug-free. However, in general, your CGIs are the weak link in the robustness of your site, and they may act strangely, or even bring your whole site down.

If you're working with Perl, this might not be *too* much of a problem. Your CGIs may return strange results to the reader, or lose data, but it's unlikely that the whole machine will bomb. A Perl program doesn't access the computer's memory directly, so it can't do anything *too dangerous*.

If you're writing in something like C++, however, you run the risk of crashing the machine that hosts the CGI application. (You know what I mean—a System error on the MacOS, or a General Protection Fault on Windows 95.) If the server is on the same machine as the CGI—and it usually is— when the CGI goes down, the server goes down with it. This will cause your site to disappear until the server is restarted. (It's not uncommon to see sites that are down over the weekend because of crashes.)

Threading

An application that executes more than one set of instructions at once is said to be *multithreaded*. It's fairly simple to create a CGI that handles one request at a time, and quite another thing to write an application that can sensibly manage a hundred simultaneous requests. Even if you have the hardware to handle all those hits, the programming may be more difficult. If you're writing to a file or to a database, you can only write one set of data at a time, and this is a tremendous bottleneck. It's possible to get around this kind of problem, but it requires a more extensive knowledge of programming and the way that your system works than a casual or amateur program may have. Know when to use a commercial CGI or hand off programming to a professional programmer!

341

Summary

In this chapter, you learned about forms and how to use them on your site. Specifically, you learned the following information:

- What forms are and how they're used.

- How to set a form's global parameters.

- What a name/value pair is.

- How to add form components to your layout.

- What must be installed on your server to handle the form.

- What you'll need, and what to consider, when writing your own form-handling CGIs.

In Chapter 12, we'll learn how to use NetObjects Fusion to publish a database as part of your Fusion site.

URL Roundup

- The Keirsey Temperament Sorter:
  `http://sunsite.unc.edu/personality/keirsey.html`

- An interesting use of forms to remotely control a telescope at the University of California—Santa Barbara:
  `http://www.deepspace.ucsb.edu/ir.htm`

- To test your form submitted via POST, enter this URL in the Action field of the Form Settings dialog box and click the Post radio button:
  `http://hoohoo.ncsa.uiuc.edu/cgi-bin/post-query`

- To test your form submitted via GET, enter this URL in the Action field of the Form Settings dialog box and click the Get radio button:
  `http://hoohoo.ncsa.uiuc.edu/cgi-bin/ query`

- NetForms from Maxum Development, a commercial CGI application:
  `http://www.maxum.com/netforms/`

- FormSaver, another commercial CGI application that takes form data and saves it on disk on the server machine:
  `http://ns.iliad.com/formsaver`

- Forms.acgi, a freeware CGI:
  `http://web77.biola.edu/~steve/cgi/forms`

- Flexmail, a commercial CGI that emails form data:
  `http://www.netdreams.com/net.dreams/software`

- A pretty good list of database CGIs:
  `http://www.comvista.com/net/www/cgidata.html`

- MacPerl home page:
  `http://www.iis.ee.ethz.ch/~neeri/macintosh/perl.html`

- MacCGI script extension:
  `ftp:///err.ethz.ch/pub/neeri/MacPerlBeta/PCGI`

- hip communications' PowerPC version and Windows 95 platform of Perl:
  `http://www.perl.hip.com`

- hip Web Kit:
  `http://www.perl.hip.com/webkit.htm`

Data Objects and Data Lists

Publishing databases on the Web has become a very hot topic in Web-mastering and software development circles. Here's the basic notion: if you've got a database, you've already got a boatload of information that's available in digital form. Why go through the laborious process of adding this data to Web pages by hand, even if you're using tools as simple and intuitive as NetObjects Fusion's database tools? A database can have dozens or even hundreds of records, each with a few fields of its own. Even a small database requires hours of cutting and pasting by hand to create a site by using simple page tools.

Fortunately, NetObjects Fusion enables you to import a database and format each record as a separate page, using a template that you design with NetObjects Fusion's page layout tools. Each page created from the database is indexed on a master page, making it easy for readers to navigate through the database's information.

Using a database can help you manage large sites that use content developed by a large, wide-spread team. NetObjects Fusion *isn't* a multi-user application— only one person can work on a site at any time—but most database applications are groupware. Many users can access and modify a database at the same time.

When you use NetObjects Fusion to publish a database, you can consolidate everyone's work into your site with a few clicks.

In fact, you can create your own database *inside* NetObjects Fusion. When you create a Fusion database, you ensure that a group of similar pages has a consistent layout and that the pages are all indexed automatically.

Introduction to Database Publishing

If you look around on the Web, you'll discover that there are approaches to combining Web and database technology other than Fusion's model. Some databases *are* Web servers, and they answer browser requests by serving up database records that have been dressed up with a little HTML formatting. Some Web servers (or CGIs) can query databases on the fly and create pages based on the contents of the database.

These kinds of solutions are *dynamic:* the reader has, in effect, a direct pipeline into the database. The site never needs to be updated to reflect changes in the database because each page is built from the most current database information. In a sense, the site (or at least part of it) *is* the database.

There are certainly advantages to this approach, but it's *not* the way that NetObjects Fusion works. Rather, Fusion takes a snapshot of the database, formats it according to the template that you've created, and stores the data in HTML format on the Web server.

Using a snapshot of the database means that automatic updates are not possible; any changes to the database will not be reflected in the site until the site is updated. The advantage that is lost in the area of automatic updates is regained in the sophistication of the page design. By storing the database information as part of your site, you can use NetObjects Fusion's automatic navigation tools and site-wide styles to make your database pages look just as good as your home page.

TIP

Remember, updating your site is as simple as clicking the Publish button in Publish view. You can update your site every 15 minutes, if you like. (Hint to academic users: this is the kind of job that work-study students were born to do!)

Real-World Examples of Database Publishing

Let's take a look at a few sites on the Web that use database publishing to create a large, cohesive site using information stored in a database. These examples weren't all created with NetObjects Fusion—this book was written at the dawn of the Fusion era, and Fusion-based sites are still a little hard to find. (By the time you read this, you'll probably be able to find quite a few sites, including database sites, created with Fusion.)

Day in the Life

Rick Smolan's *Day in the Life of Cyberspace* site (http://www.1010.org/ bitsoflife/top.html) uses database technology and an early prototype of NetObjects Fusion to build a truly gigantic site in the space of 24 hours. Smolan's collaborators created content for the site and put it in an Illustra database, and Smolan used Fusion to organize and publish the various database elements into a coherent site (see Figure 12.1).

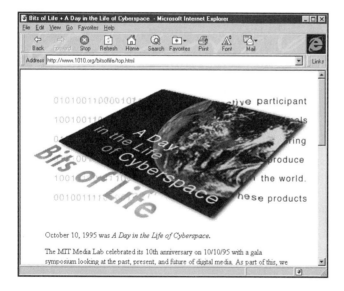

FIGURE 12.1

A Day in the Life of Cyberspace, created with NetObjects Fusion and an Illustra database.

Catalogs

Online order catalogs are another common application for database publishing on the Web. Catalogs use the same basic information for each item (a picture, description, price, and so on), and individual items must be routinely added and removed from the catalog.

One such site (not built with Fusion) is L.L. Bean's online product list, which you can find at http://www.llbean.com/products. This site would take months to create by hand. By using a database publishing solution, L.L. Bean's Web designers were able to assemble dozens of products into an organized and well-indexed site.

Understanding NetObjects Fusion Database Basics

Before you get into the particulars of each step of publishing a database with NetObjects Fusion, take a look at each of the different parts that you'll use and how they work together.

Data Objects

A Data Object is the basic building block of database publishing with Fusion. Data Objects are templates for each record in a particular database—basically a list of each of the fields in the database and the kind of information that each record contains.

For example, if you're working with a product catalog, your Data Object fields might be "Product Name" (of type text), "Price" (of type number), and "Picture" (of type picture). Figure 12.2 shows a Data Object that uses these categories as fields.

FIGURE 12.2

A Data Object is a list of the fields in each record of an internal or external database.

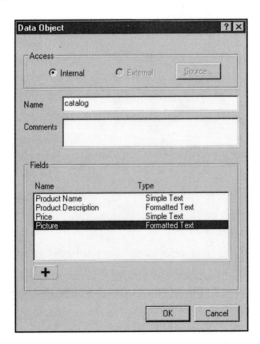

If you're creating your own database, you must create the fields you need and add them to the Data Objects. If you're linking to an external database, Fusion automatically creates a Data Object based on the database's native fields.

Data Lists

A Data List is a special kind of table that indexes each record in a database. You might think of it as the database's table of contents, which the reader can use to quickly scan the records in the database and navigate to an individual record. (You took a quick look at Data Lists in Chapter 6, when you were building Data List icons on Site view.)

Each horizontal row of the Data List represents a single record in the database, and each column is one of the record's fields. You can pick the fields to be displayed in the Data List; ordinarily, not all the fields are displayed in the index. In our product catalog example, for instance, you would probably put the product's name in the Data List, but not a large picture of the product (see Figure 12.3).

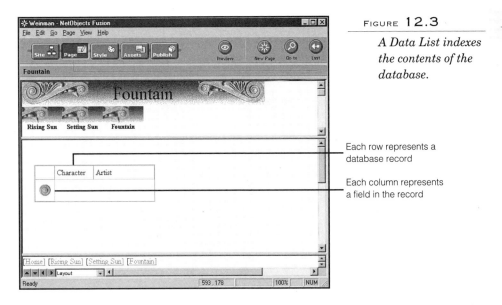

FIGURE 12.3

A Data List indexes the contents of the database.

Each row represents a database record

Each column represents a field in the record

347

Data Pages

NetObjects Fusion stores each record of the database on a separate page of the site, using special Data Pages. (NetObjects Fusion also calls Data Pages "stacked pages.") You had a peek at the way stacked pages worked in Chapter 4, when you looked at Site view.

When you add a Data List to a page on your site, NetObjects Fusion automatically adds a set of Data Pages. If you're creating your own internal database, you can add records to your database by adding pages to the stack and entering values to each field. If you are linking to an external database, Fusion automatically creates one page in the stack for every record in the database.

Data Fields

NetObjects Fusion doesn't automatically display the data in each record on the record's Data Pages—you must specify where each field goes by creating a Data Field box (exactly like a text box or image box) and linking the Data Field to a field in the Data Object. (See Figure 12.4.)

Data Pages act as templates: when you add or modify a Data Field on any of the Data Pages in a stack, the same Data Field is added or changed in *all* the Data Pages in the stack.

FIGURE 12.4

A Data Field displays the contents of one field from one record in the database.

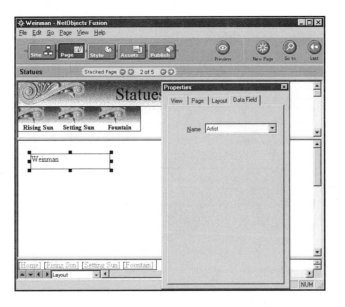

Creating an Internal Database

The procedure for creating an internal database within NetObjects Fusion is very similar to the techniques for linking to an external database. First, you can see how databases are created from scratch, and then you'll apply these techniques to working with databases such as Microsoft Access and Claris FileMaker Pro.

Creating the Data Object

To create a Data Object, use the following steps:

1. Choose the Data List tool (the first icon in the fifth row of the Tool palette) and click in the layout where you'd like the DataObject's Data List to appear. NetObjects Fusion presents the Data List dialog box.

2. Click the New button to the right of the DataObject field. NetObjects Fusion presents the Data Object dialog box shown in Figure 12.5.

FIGURE 12.5

The Data Object dialog box.

349

3. Make sure that the Internal radio button in the Access group is selected. (It should be—this is the default.)

4. Give the DataObject a name in the Name field and add an annotation in the comments field.

5. Click the Add Field button (the big plus sign) in the Fields group. NetObjects Fusion presents the Data Field dialog box shown in Figure 12.6.

6. Give the field a name in the Name field.

7. Choose one of the options from the Type group. Formatted text means text with styles added, such as bolding or color; Simple text is plain black text with no styles added (such as a text-only document).

FIGURE 12.6

The Data Field
dialog box.

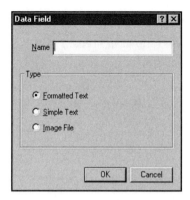

WARNING

Choose carefully when creating your data type—after you click the OK button, you can't change the data type of a data field, and you can't delete the field from the DataObject. Double-check your entry before you exit the field.

350

8. Repeat steps 5-7 to continue to add fields to the DataObject. You can always add new fields later, but you can't delete fields from the DataObject.

To edit a DataObject after the Data Object dialog box has been dismissed, use these steps:

1. Click the Assets view button.

2. Click the DataObject button in the Secondary control bar.

3. Double-click the DataObject's name in the Assets window. NetObjects Fusion will present the Data Object dialog box.

4. Edit the DataObject, using steps 5–7 of the set of instructions, above.

TIP

You can also create a DataObject without linking it to a specific Data List. Go to Assets view, click the DataObject button in the Secondary control bar, and choose **Edit→New DataObject**. There's no special reason why you'd want to do this—to use the DataObject, you'll need to link it to a Data List sooner or later.

You'll learn how to add data to your new DataObject in the section on Data Pages later in this chapter.

Linking to an External Database

Linking to an external database creates the same end product—a DataObject with a list of fields, each with its own data type—but the data fields are the fields or table columns used in the external database.

NetObjects Fusion offers support for several database file formats, including Microsoft Access, dBASE, Microsoft FoxPro, Paradox, Microsoft Excel (OK, it's a spreadsheet, not a database), Lotus 1-2-3, and plain old tab-delineated text files. As of this writing, it's likely that NetObjects Fusion will support FileMaker Pro on the Mac, but I have not seen it with my own eyes.

ODBC, which stands for Open Database Conductivity, is Microsoft's implementation of a Call Level Interface specification defined by the SQL Access Group. It enables a client application (a Windows program) to connect to a variety of data sources by using SQL as the standard data access language. ODBC connections require that you have the necessary ODBC compliant drivers. You should define and test your ODBC data sources before attempting to incorporate them within NetObjects Fusion.

351

> **TIP**
>
> In a pinch, you can export your database from your database application as a tab-delimited text file and open the text file with Fusion. This will require an export every time you want to update your site. It's not a very elegant workaround, but it will work with just about any database package on any platform.

To link to an external database, follow these steps:

1. Choose the Data List tool (the first icon in the fifth row of the Tool palette) and click in the layout where you'd like the Data List to appear. NetObjects Fusion presents the Data List dialog box.

2. Click the New button to the right of the DataObject field. NetObjects Fusion presents the DataObject dialog box.

3. Click the External radio button in the Access group. When the Source button becomes active, click it. NetObjects Fusion presents the Data Source Type dialog box (see Figure 12.7).

FIGURE 12.7

*The Data Source
Type dialog box.*

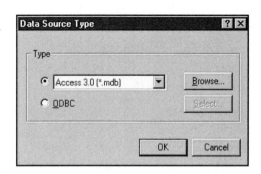

4. To link to a database file:

   a. Click the top radio button.

   b. Choose the appropriate database format from the pop-up menu.

   c. Click the Browse button and navigate to the database file.

5. To link to an ODBC server:

   a. Click the ODBC radio button and click the Select button.

   b. If the server appears in the SQL data sources list, select the server's name in the SQL Data Sources dialog box.

   c. If the server's name doesn't appear, click the New button. Choose your database's ODBC driver from the Add Data source dialog box. The dialog box that appears depends on which ODBC driver you have installed. Consult your database program's documentation for guidance.

6. After you've linked to a file or a server, NetObjects Fusion presents a Select dialog box, like the one shown in Figure 12.8.

   This is a list of all the tables or views that Fusion could find in the database. (If you're linking to a spreadsheet, like Excel, this is a list of the "pages"—the individual spreadsheets within the document file.)

7. After you pick a table or view from the Select menu, NetObjects Fusion adds all the selected item's columns to the DataObject's list of fields.

TIP

If you've linked to an external database, you can review the DataObject dialog box via Assets view, but you can't change anything in the dialog box, except for the Comments field.

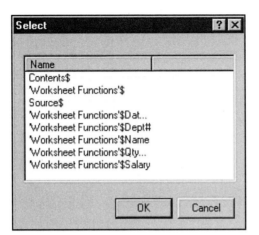

FIGURE 12.8

The Select dialog box shows a list of all the tables contained in the database.

Using the Data List Tool

After you've built your DataObject, you can index it with a Data List. You've already used the Data List tool to create your DataObject. Now you can use the Data List control panel and the Data List palette of the Properties tab to refine the way that the Data List is presented.

353

Let's assume that you have just completed one of the "Creating an Internal Database" or "Linking to an External Database" sections, and you still have the Data List dialog box open. (If it's not open, click the Define button next to the List Name field in the Data List tab of the Properties palette.)

TIP

Double-clicking a Data List in Page Layout view brings up the Data List dialog box.

When you create a Data List, you have the option of naming it. This is a good idea—it enables you to save more than one style of index to a particular object. When you give the Data List a name, the name is added to the List Name pop-up menu in the Data List tab of the Properties palette.

Sorting the Data

You can control the way that the database records are organized in the Data List. By default, the items displayed in the Data List are sorted by the first field in the DataObject (this is the first field listed in the Fields window of the Data Object dialog box).

If you're working with an external database, you can select any field in the DataObject as the field used to sort the record. Simply click the Sort By pop-up menu in the Data List dialog box and choose the field you want to use for sorting. (You don't have this option when you're working with an Internal database because the Sort By pop-up menu will be inactive.)

Both internal and external databases enable you to sort the order in which the fields are displayed within each row of the Data List. The fields are displayed in the same order as the fields are listed in the Data List Fields window of the Data List dialog box.

To juggle the order of the fields in the list, click a field's name and use the up and down arrows to move, promote, or demote the item in the list's order (see Figure 12.9).

FIGURE 12.9

You can alter the order of fields in the Data List.

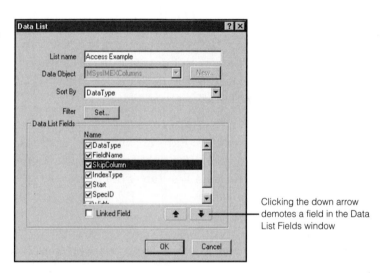

Clicking the down arrow demotes a field in the Data List Fields window

TIP

You can sort the records displayed in the Data List by any of the Data Objects fields, even if the field isn't displayed in the Data List. In fact, if you have a special order in mind, you might want to think about creating a new "sort" field in your external database and numbering these fields in the desired display order.

Filtering the Data

You may not want to display all the records that a database contains. NetObjects Fusion enables you to "filter" the database so that only records that meet a certain criteria are displayed.

Let's say that your database contains a record for each of the employees in a large corporation, and one of the fields in the DataObject is the employee's department. Suppose that you want to create pages for only those employees in the marketing department. Here's how you'd filter the information in the database:

1. Click the Filter button in the Data List dialog box. NetObjects Fusion presents the Query dialog box shown in Figure 12.10.

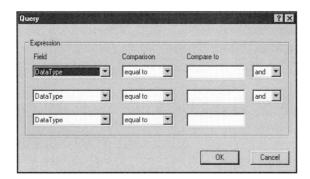

FIGURE 12.10

The Query dialog box.

355

2. In the first column of the first row of the Query dialog box, choose the Field that you want to limit. In the example above, you'd pick the "Department" field.

3. In the first row of the Comparison column, choose the kind of test you want to perform. The contents of this pop-up menu will vary according to the data type of the field on the first column. (If the data type is text, the menu will let you match strings at the beginning or end of the field's data. If the field contains a number, you can choose from greater-than, less-than, or equal-to comparisons.) In the current example, I chose "begins with."

4. In the first row of the Compare to column, enter the value that you want to use as your "yardstick." For example, if you want to find members of the marketing department, you'd enter "marketing" in this field. (Assuming that "marketing" is the entry used to designate the marketing department in the database.)

5. If this is the only test you want to perform, choose End from the pop-up menu in the fourth column. (In this case, it is.)

If you want to perform an additional test to refine or expand the output of the test, you can choose the "And" or "Or" operators from the pop-up menu in the fourth column to add a second (and third, if you want) condition to the search string.

The "Or" operator makes the search more inclusive. When "Or" is selected in the third column, NetObjects Fusion will include all the records that match either the condition in line one or the condition in line two. Suppose that you want to find employees from the marketing and the engineering department. You would use this information:

```
department contains marketing or department contains engineering
```

to find all the records that match one of the two lines.

The "And" operator refines the search. When "And" is selected in the third column, Fusion will include only those records that match *both* the condition in line one and the condition in line two. If you were to enter this information:

```
department contains marketing and department contains engineering
```

Fusion would display *no* entries because no records have both "marketing" and "engineering" in the department field.

Let's say that you want to find all the employees in the marketing department whose names start with the letter "A." You'd use the "And" operator to construct your query, like this:

```
department contains marketing and last name starts with A
```

An employee in the marketing department whose last name falls within B-Z fails the second test. Because the "And" operator requires that a record pass both tests, these employees are filtered out of the Data List.

TIP

Filtering the DataObject in the Data List dialog box doesn't just filter the Data List—records that don't pass the filter test are not imported into the NetObjects Fusion site as Data Pages.

Picking the Fields

You can choose which fields appear in your Data List. In most cases, you'll want to limit the number of items in each row—after all, the Data List is supposed to be an index, not a table that contains the entire database.

WARNING

The Data List is no wider than the page that contains it. (By default, pages are 600 pixels wide.) If a Data List has too many fields in each row—say 10 or so—the entries in each field will be seriously pinched.

To remove a field from the Data List display, click the check box to the left of its name in the Data List fields window to deselect the field. Only those fields with selected check boxes appear in the Data List.

Removing a field from the Data List doesn't remove it from the DataObject by any means, and you can use the field for filtering (and with external databases) and sorting the database.

Suppose that your database contains a field that contains a code for the employee's status: say 1 represents an active employee, 2 represents retired employees, and 3 represents former employees. Even if the status field doesn't appear in the Data List, you can use the test:

```
status equals 1
```

as a filter to limit the list to active employees.

357

Linking Fields to Pages

Fields in the Data List can contain links to Data Pages. Both text and image fields can contain links (see Figure 12.11).

FIGURE 12.11

Data List entries can contain links to their data pages.

All of the links in any particular row of the Data List link to the same location—the Data Page that contains the row's records. (As a result, you probably shouldn't link more than one or two fields to the Data Pages—it's redundant, misleading, and it looks funny.) Of course, the Data List icon at the left of each row is already in place, and points to the same page, but a text link may be an appropriate way to highlight the connection between a particular field and its Data Page.

Fine-Tuning the Data List

You can further alter the appearance of the Data List with the Data List tab in the Properties palette (see Figure 12.12). You can change the look of the Data List icons, or change the look of the entire table.

FIGURE 12.12

The Data List tab in the Properties palette.

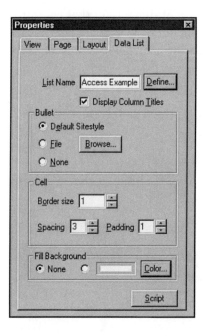

By default, NetObjects Fusion uses the Data List icon defined in the SiteStyle as the bullet for each row of the Data List table. If you want, you can substitute your own image by clicking the File radio button in the Bullet group of the Data List tab. (Click the browse button and navigate to the desired image with the resulting dialog box.) You may also choose to remove the Data List icon from the Data List.

You can change the width of the Data List. Simply click on one of the Data List's handles in the layout and drag. (Changes in the height of the Data List will *not* be implemented—the height of each cell is determined by its contents.) To change the width of Data List columns, simply drag the column dividers to the desired position.

You may further alter the appearance of the Data List with the controls in the Cell group of the Data List tab. All values in this group are measured in pixels:

Border Size reflects only the thickness of the border of the whole Data List table—not the thickness of the crossbars between cells. A value of zero removes the border entirely. (A value of zero *does* remove the crossbars.) To my taste, these kinds of borders are really, really ugly—especially at sizes larger than two or three (see Figure 12.13). These examples are from the pages of the Prima-Donns' site, the Minneapolis cable access show that you saw in Chapters 7 and 10. The database contains lists of the favorite kings and presidents of the Klassy Karl character. (I just wanted to make it clear that I do not think John Adams was misunderstood.)

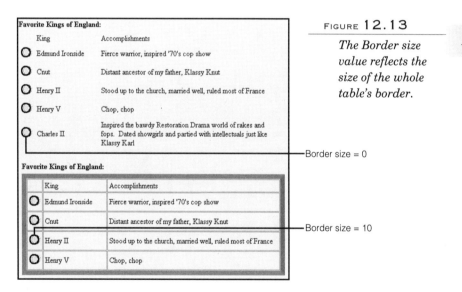

FIGURE 12.13

The Border size value reflects the size of the whole table's border.

Spacing reflects the amount of added space between a cell entry and the edges of the cell. When the value of spacing is zero, the cell entry butts up against the edge of the cell (see Figure 12.14).

FIGURE 12.14

Spacing reflects the distance between the cell's edge and the cell's entry.

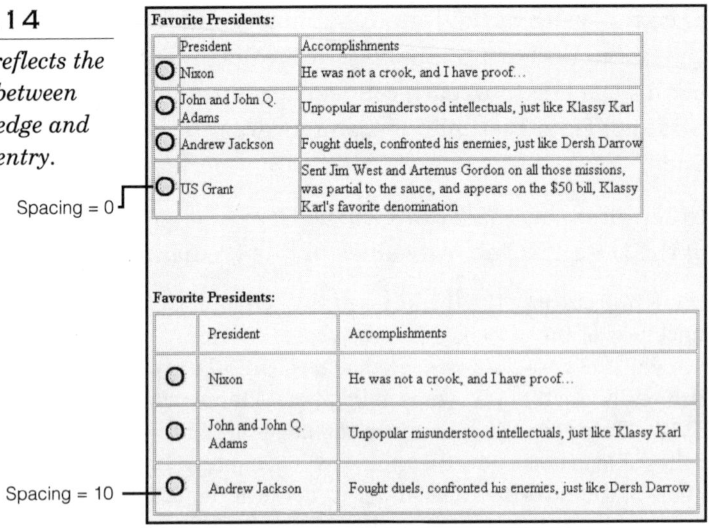

Padding reflects the gap between columns and rows of the chart (see Figure 12.15). When the value of Padding is zero, the cells touch each other. (This isn't necessarily a problem, unless the value of spacing is also zero.)

FIGURE 12.15

Padding reflects the gap between columns and rows of the chart.

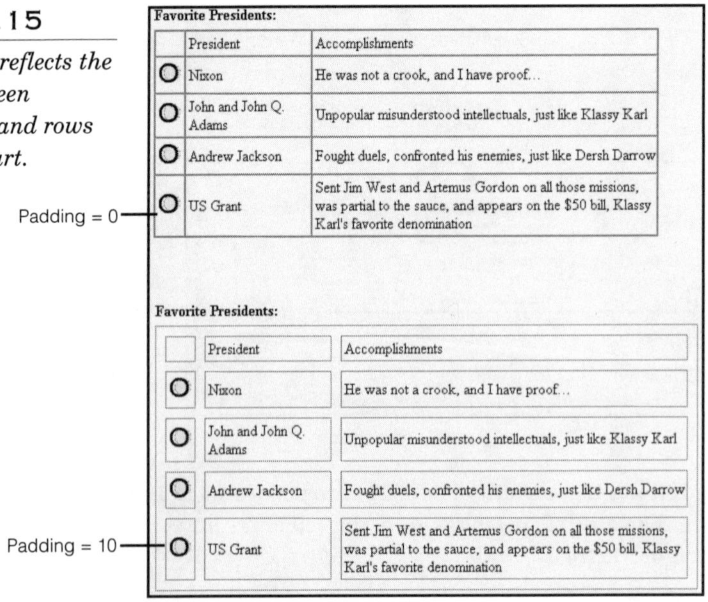

You can add color to the Data List by selecting the radio button next to the color swatch in the Fill Background group and clicking the Color button to invoke the standard color picker. Color added to the chart is added to the column heads and each of the cells, but not to the space between the cells.

WARNING

If you add color to a Data List, make sure that the Data List icon is transparent and remove the icon, or be prepared to grit your teeth whenever you look at the Data List. You can't make the Data List transparent in NetObjects Fusion: you'll need to edit the source image file for the icon with a GIF89-friendly image editor. See Chapter 6 for details about editing components of the site's style.

Using the Data Field Tool

After you've customized your Data List, it's time to design your Data Pages. Remember, each Data Page represents a record in the database. When you work on a Data Page, you're editing a template for *all* the Data Pages, rather than designing an individual page.

Data Pages are added to the layout automatically when you create a Data List. In Site view, Data Pages are represented by the Stacked Page icon, and they appear as a child of the page that contains the Data List (see Figure 12.16). As you saw in Chapter 4, the Data Pages don't need to stay directly underneath the Data List page—you can move them anywhere you like, and they will remain linked to the Data List.

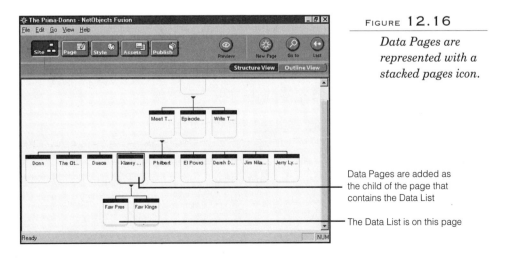

FIGURE 12.16

Data Pages are represented with a stacked pages icon.

Data Pages are added as the child of the page that contains the Data List

The Data List is on this page

Let's look at an individual Data Page. You can look at a Data Page in Site view, just as if it were an ordinary page. Data Pages have a special set of controls in the Secondary control bar. These controls, shown in Figure 12.17, enable you to add and delete pages from an internal database, display the current number of pages in the stack, and navigate through the stack.

FIGURE 12.17

Data Pages have a special set of controls in the Secondary control bar.

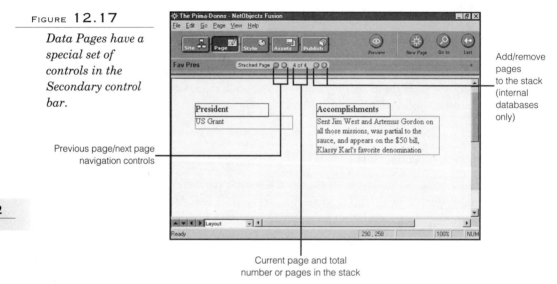

Add/remove pages to the stack (internal databases only)

Previous page/next page navigation controls

Current page and total number or pages in the stack

If you're building an internal database, NetObjects Fusion puts a single Data Page in the stack to start you off. If you're linking to an external database, Fusion creates one page in the stack for each record in the database. You can add pages to an internal database with the Secondary control bar controls—in fact, it's the only way you *can* add records to the database. However, external databases are read-only, which means that you can't add any pages to their stack. Likewise, an individual Data Page can't be removed from a stack created from an external database.

Adding a Data Field to a Data Page

You can add any ordinary element you like to a Data Page—text, images, multi-media, applets, whatever—but keep in mind: *anything that you add to any Data Page appears on every Data Page in the stack.* If you add a 900 K movie to one Data Page, the same movie will appear on every Data Page in the same position. The only components that change from page to page in a stack of Data Pages are the contents of DataFields.

A Data Field is a kind of window into the database record that the Data Page represents. When you add a Data Field to a page, the DataField's *frame* appears on all the pages in the stack in the same position, but the DataField's *contents* reflect a field in the database record that is represented by the current page.

DataFields are added to Data Pages with the Data Field tool. The Data Field tool is that mysterious second icon in the fifth row of the Tool palette (it's ordinarily grayed out), and it is active only when you're looking at a Data Page in Page view.

To add a Data Field to a Data Page, follow these steps:

1. Select the Data Field tool from the Tool palette.

2. Use the Data Field tool to draw a box for the Data Field. You don't need to be too exact because you can always adjust the size later.

3. NetObjects Fusion presents the Data Field dialog box. Click the name pop-up menu to view a list of all the fields in the current DataObject. Select the desired field.

4. Notice that the Data Field's box in the NetObjects Fusion is red, rather than black. (This use of color simply helps you recognize the Data List items when you're scanning Data Pages.)

5. If you're working with an internal database, the contents of the Data Field will be blank. You can add them yourself. If you're working with an external database, the Data Field will be filled with the field's value in the current database record.

6. If the Data Field contains text, apply whatever style (bolding, color, paragraph styling, and so on) you like to the text. You can't apply character styles to individual characters in a Data List box that contains text; any styling you add will be applied to all the characters in the text box. (After all, you don't know what will be in the same Data Field box on a different Data Page.)

DataFields that contain text grow vertically according to the length of the DataField's content. DataFields that contain images grow both vertically and horizontally to accommodate the image. When you're sizing and positioning a Data Field, always look at the Data Page with the longest text, or the biggest picture, for the Data Field.

Let's say that you're working with a database that contains images, and the images vary greatly in size. You've set up an image Data Field in the top left corner of the layout and put a text Data Field that contains the image's caption next to the image (see Figure 12.18).

FIGURE **12.18**

These DataFields look fine on this Data Page.

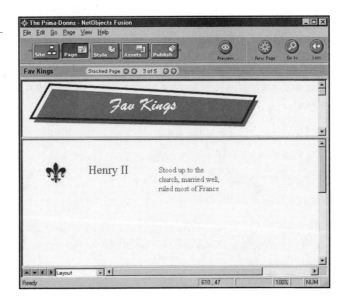

Figure 12.18 looks fine because there's plenty of space between the two DataFields. Suppose, however, that another image in the database is substantially wider than the image of the fleur de lis. The image Data Field will grow to accommodate the larger image, and the two DataFields will collide, as shown in Figure 12.19.

FIGURE **12.19**

The DataFields from Figure 12.18 collide on a different Data Page in the same stack.

WARNING

If you're building an internal database, you'll probably catch colliding-Data Field problems when you're adding images to the database, *but be careful when you're repositioning images.* Always double-check by looking at the page with the biggest picture and the longest text entries for the Data Field that you move. If you're linking to an external database, you'll probably want to look at each of the Data Pages to see where the problem pages are.

Fine-Tuning the Data Pages

After you double-check the placement of DataFields to make sure that they don't collide with each other or other page elements, you can add the final touches to the Data Pages. (For the most part, you'll need to worry about navigation issues.) The following sections give you some issues to consider when you're finishing your Data Pages.

The Banner

By default, Data Pages uses the same header and footer as regular pages, and the banner reads "Untitled Stacked Page." This is not very polished-looking. At the very least, you'll need to give the stacked pages some sort of generic title that works for all the pages in the stack. (You might use "tools" for the stack that contains Figures 12.17 and 12.18, for example.)

To alter this banner entry, simply enter the new title in the stack's icon in Site view—just as if you were renaming an ordinary page.

Headers and Footers

You might want to think about deleting the header for the Data Pages altogether. Remember, all the non-Data Field elements on the Data Pages are repeated on all the pages, anyway, and it may suit your design to put a descriptive Data Field rather than a banner at the top of the page. (See Chapter 4 for details about handling headers and footers.)

Navigation Tools

One of the great things about Data Pages is that you can use navigation bars, which are normally confined to the top or bottom of a page, to any position on the Data Page. You can grab a navigation bar from any header on the site (with

Edit→Copy) and paste it anywhere you like on the Data Page. Because the navigation bar isn't a Data Field, it appears in exactly the same way on all the Data Pages.

Similarly, you can use Smart Links anywhere you like on the Data Page—you don't need to stick them into the DataPage's header. (As you'll recall from Chapter 4, Smart Links are links to pages that have a certain relationship to the current page, rather than links to a specific, named page.) There's a special pair of Smart Links, "Previous Stacked Page" and "Next Stacked Page," which enable the reader to navigate between stacked pages exactly as you navigate by using the controls in the Secondary control palette.

Summary

In this chapter, you learned how to publish databases with NetObjects Fusion. In particular you learned the following information:

- Why you might want to publish a database.

- How Fusion handles database publishing differently from other Web/ database tools.

- How to create an internal database with Fusion.

- How to link to an external database.

- How to index the database with a Data List.

- How to fine-tune the DataList's appearance.

- How to display the database's data on Data Pages.

In Chapter 13, you'll learn about executable code—programs that run *inside* your Web pages—and how to add them to your site with NetObjects Fusion.

URL Roundup

- Rick Smolan's *Day in the Life of Cyberspace* site uses an Illustra database and an early prototype of NetObjects Fusion:
  http://www.1010.org/bitsoflife/top.html

- L.L. Bean's online product list:
  http://www.llbean.com/products

Executable Code: Java, JavaScript, and ActiveX

OK now, mateys—if you've sailed this far, you're at the cutting edge of what you can do on a Web site. Nowadays, developers are focusing on technologies to deliver executable code via Web pages.

As you learned in Chapter 3, the two major vendors of Web browsers, Netscape and Microsoft, are quietly removing the distinction between Web browsers and operating systems. Each company is taking a slightly different approach to this problem. Netscape is turning Navigator into a second operating system that runs "on top of" other operating systems the way that Windows 3.x and its predecessors ran on top of DOS. Microsoft is simply building Internet Explorer's functionality into the basic Windows 95/NT operating systems.

What this means is that browsers will run programs, in exactly the same way that operating systems run programs now. The browser window becomes, in effect, the desktop of the new Internet-based operating system.

As OS/2 users know, a new operating system needs applications to be successful. The languages and tools that are covered in this chapter—the Java and JavaScript languages, and ActiveX technology—are among the first tools available for building the applications that are native to the Internet.

Executable code that runs on the Internet can range from novelties—like video games that run in Web pages—to a rethinking of the way that desktop computers work. The real Internet operating system radicals, like the folks at Netscape, Sun, and Oracle, suggest that in the future, applications won't reside on machines at all—they'll be downloaded, run, and discarded as needed.

Furthermore, the model for future applications is strongly component-based; rather than downloading a word processor, for instance, you might download a text-handling component. When you want to check the spelling, you'll download a spell checker. (The application-component idea is what Microsoft's OLE and Apple & IBM's OpenDoc systems are all about.)

Network-based application components are the real agenda behind Java, ActiveX, and some of the emerging technologies such as Tcl/Tk. For now, much of this vision remains science fiction, but it is the blueprint for the development of the Web over the next few years. The kinds of Java and ActiveX stuff that you see in your Net.travels now, and the kinds of things that you can add to your pages, are really just a dog-and-pony show to sell the technology. (They're cool anyway—who doesn't like dogs and ponies?)

I'm not going to teach you to program in any of the languages that I'll talk about in this chapter. There isn't enough room in a single chapter, or a single book, to cover all the bases. You could build a house out of the books written about Java and JavaScript, and there will be plenty of ActiveX books soon enough. Rather, I'll show you how to add finished programs to Web pages.

TIP

Strictly speaking, "executable code" refers only to machine-readable applications, or bytecodes that are run by a virtual machine—not scripts that are run by interpreters, such as JavaScripts or Visual Basic scripts. It's a subtle distinction, and we'll call everything executable code, just to make it simple.

Java

As mentioned in Chapter 3, Java was developed by Sun Microsystems to be a simple, secure, cross-platform tool for application development. Java makes it easy for experienced programmers to develop applications that are bug-free, virus-free, and that can run on a variety of systems, including the emerging Internet-based platforms from Netscape and Microsoft.

Understanding Java

A Java applet that runs inside a Web page begins as source code written in the Java language. Java source code looks quite a bit like C source, and supports many of the basic constructs, loops, conditional tests, variables, and arrays of variables that are found in most basic programming languages. (Java doesn't have pointers, the much-loved and much-misused feature of languages such as C and Pascal.)

Here's the famous Hello, World program (a simple demonstration of what a language's source code looks like) rendered in Java:

```
import java.applet.*;
import java.awt.*;

public class HelloWorld extends Applet {
public void paint(Graphics g) {
g.drawString("Hello, World",100,100);
    }
}
```

After the Java source code is written, it's compiled, or translated, into "bytecodes." (The bytecode version of the program is stored in a file with the extension .class, and Java executables are commonly referred to as .class—or just "class"—files.) Bytecodes are similar to the machine-readable executable code found in application files, but unlike true executable code, which can be read and run by a computer's CPU, Java bytecodes are read and run by a "soft" CPU.

A soft CPU is an application that thinks it's a CPU and runs Java bytecodes as if they were executable code. Figure 13.1 shows the raw Java bytecodes created from the Hello, World application, along with the machine-level instructions that each bytecodes represents.

Why all this indirection? Ordinary executable code is platform specific. Each "line" of executable code corresponds to a particular operation in the CPU's instruction set. Java's bytecodes aren't specific to any particular hardware machine, so they can be executed on any machine that supports Java's soft CPU, called the "Java Virtual Machine."

As a result, any Java application written on any platform runs in exactly the same way anywhere the Java Virtual Machine is present. And the Java machine is everywhere—it's built into Navigator and Internet Explorer, and it's available on almost every platform. Soon the Java Virtual Machine will be built into MacOS at a very fundamental level.

FIGURE 13.1

A compiler turns Java source code into bytecodes, similar to the program shown here.

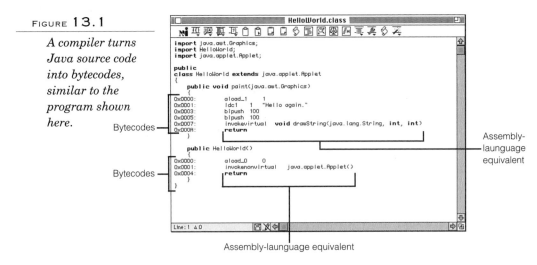

Bytecodes

Bytecodes

Assembly-launguage equivalent

Assembly-launguage equivalent

(I lied when I said that Java bytecodes aren't specific to any machine: after the virtual machine specification was already developed, Sun created a line of chips that implement the Java Virtual Machine in hardware. In a few years, your electric toothbrush will sport a Java Virtual Machine.)

When you place a Java applet in a Web page, you are instructing the browser to run the executable code in the Java program by using the browser's built-in virtual machine. (Later implementations of browsers may borrow the system's virtual machine for the task.) The Java Virtual Machine uses the applet's portion of the Web page as a tiny monitor, and displays its results inside the page (see Figure 13.2).

FIGURE 13.2

The Hello World application running inside the browser.

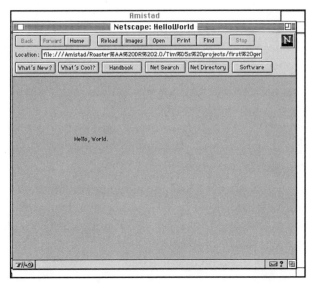

Just as applications can communicate with each other and with the operating system under MacOS and Windows 95, Java applets can communicate with each other and with the browser when they're running inside the browser window. A full-blown Java system might use a whole bevy of Java .class files that work together as a team—a Java applet does not need to restrict itself to a single class file. Furthermore, Java applets can communicate with Java applications that are running on the server machine, or cause the browser to load another Web page, which may, in turn, contain a set of new applets.

I hope you're beginning to see what you're getting into with Java. It's fairly easy to learn how to write a simple applet that bounces around on your page, but this is only a small part of what Java can do. We'll confine ourselves to dealing with fairly simple stand-alone applets.

Example Applets

If you'd like to see the full range of the kinds of things that Java can do, from PacMan to interactive chat systems, the most exhaustive archive of Java applications can be found at the Gamelan site, at `http://www.gamelan.com`.

371

TIP

Make sure that you have a Java-savvy browser, such as the latest versions of Navigator and Explorer, before you visit Gamelan or any of the sites mentioned in this chapter.

Let's take a look at some specific examples of Java applets that can add some sophistication to your site:

SiteMapper. NetObjects features the SiteMapper applet (which comes bundled with Fusion) on the NetObjects home page (`http://www.netobjects.com`). The SiteMapper applet examines a Fusion-based host site and draws a clickable site map for the user (see Figure 13.3).

You can find the Sitemapper applet and instructions for installing it in the NetObjects Fusion/Parts/SmartObjects/Sitemapper folder on the CD.

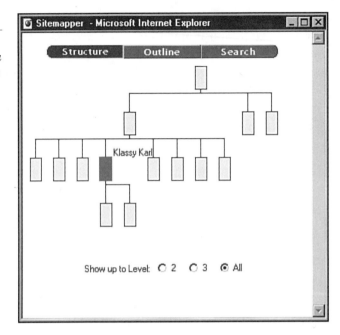

FIGURE 13.3

Sitemapper, a Java applet that creates a clickable map of the host site on the fly.

372

Games. Just to show that Applets can do anything that conventional applications can (and just in case every desktop machine in the world doesn't have a copy of solitaire already installed) take a look at the solitaire game at `http://w3.gwis.com/~thorn/Solitaire.html` (shown in Figure 13.4).

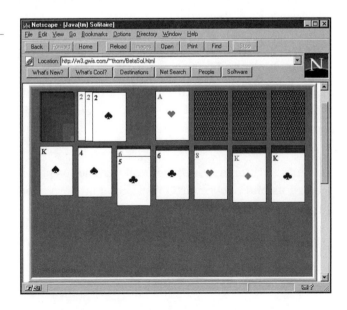

FIGURE 13.4

A solitaire game written in Java.

Text Effects. Some of the easiest applets to write can add special effects to the text on your pages: scrolling it across the screen, bouncing it around, or causing it to change. I'm especially fond of the magnetic letters/magnetic poetry genre. See Figure 13.5, which you can find at `http://www.codepilot.com/~kbenell/letters/letterboard.html` for an example of this kind of effect.

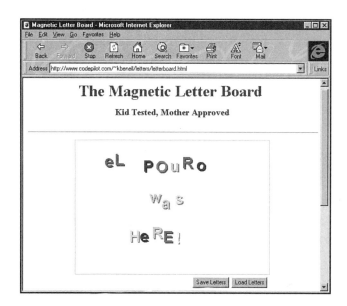

FIGURE 13.5

A text special effect created with Java.

373

Sources for Applets

Naturally, you can learn Java and write your own applets. Fortunately, there are sources for applets, which are a good place to start:

- Gamelan is probably the biggest directory of applets on the Web. Many of the applets that are featured on the Gamelan site are freely available or may be licensed from the authors. You can visit the commercial side of the Gamelan site at `http://direct.gamelan.com/index.shtml`. The Gamelan Direct site includes an index of commercially available applets and other Java-based tools.

- The basic Java Development Kit (JDK), distributed freely by Sun, contains a selection of basic Java applets that you may use as you wish. All Java tools must include the complete JDK as part of the Java licensing agreement. You can also download the basic JDK from Sun's `http://www.javasoft.com` site.

Using the Java Tool

After you have an applet ready to place, it's easy to add it to your site with NetObjects Fusion. If you don't have an applet of your own, you can find the Nervous Text applet (which I stole from the Java Development Kit) in the NetObjects Fusion/Book/Executable folder on the CD-ROM. NervousText takes any text string that you give it as a parameter and animates it, jiggling around each of the letters with its own random motion.

To add the applet to your page, do the following:

1. Set the background of the page to plain old browser gray by using the Background group in the Layout tab of the Properties palette. (This isn't strictly necessary, but it matches your page to NervousText's background. Browser gray is the third swatch from the right edge of the bottom row of the Color dialog box.)

2. Choose the Java tool from the Tool palette (it's the first icon in the fourth row) and use it to draw a box for the applet. For the NervousText applet, make the box about as wide as the page's banner. NetObjects Fusion adds a Java placeholder box to the layout (see Figure 13.6).

FIGURE 13.6

NetObjects Fusion represents a Java applet with a white placeholder box in the layout.

3. Consult your Java applet's documentation to see which parameter(s) the applet uses. For instance, the NervousText applet uses one parameter, named "text." NervousText uses the text parameter as the text string that it displays. Parameters are case-sensitive, so make sure that you have the parameters' names exactly as listed in the documentation.

4. Click the add parameter button (the big plus sign in the Parameter group). NetObjects Fusion presents the Enter Value dialog box.

5. Enter a parameter's name in the name field, exactly as the parameter appears in the applet's documentation.

6. Enter a value for the parameter. NervousText looks better if you put spaces between the letters in your message.

7. The Java Applet tab in the Properties palette displays the parameter and its value in the Parameter group Java Applet tab (see Figure 13.7).

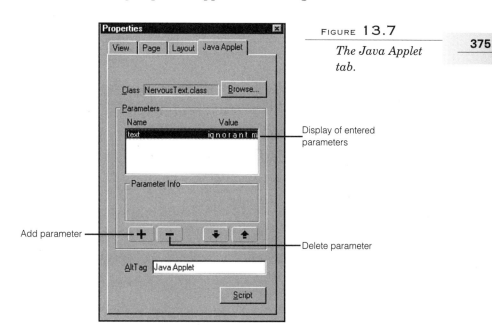

FIGURE 13.7

The Java Applet tab.

375

8. If you're using an Applet other than NervousText that uses more than one parameter, repeat steps 4–6 to add the additional parameters.

9. Click the Preview button to preview your applet in the browser window (see Figure 13.8).

FIGURE 13.8

The NervousText applet.

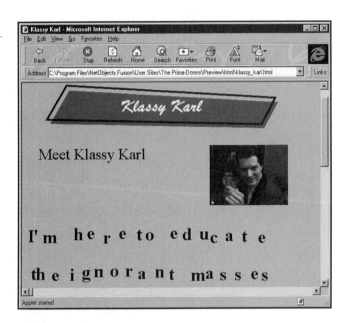

Where to Find More Information

There are *way* too many Java books on the market. Naturally, the authoritative book for Mac developers is:

- *Teach Yourself Java in 21 Days for Macintosh* (by Laura LeMay, Charles Perkins, and Timothy Webster, Hayden Books.) Make sure that you get the second edition with the DR2 version of the Roaster software.

Windows 95 developers might start with either of the following:

- *Teach Yourself Java in 21 Days* (by Laura Lemay and Charles Perkins, Sams Publishing).

- *Programming with Java!* (by Tim Ritchey, New Riders Publishing).

JavaScript

JavaScript is a scripting language developed by the folks at Netscape. Originally called LiveScript, JavaScript isn't anything like Java, and the two have very little in common.

As you learned in Chapter 3, JavaScript was developed as a tool to perform simple, nongraphical tasks on Netscape Navigator pages. For example, a JavaScript might check to make sure that a text entry field that's supposed to contain a credit card number contains 16 digits when the form is submitted. JavaScripts can do some useful things, like open new browser windows, but they can't do much in the way of animation or fancy number-crunching.

JavaScript is certainly simpler than Java. Personally, I think it's very easy to learn if you have an understanding of basic object-oriented programming concepts like methods and object hierarchies. If you haven't worked with something like Java or C++ before, or you haven't programmed at all, you'll still need to learn some basic object-oriented programming ideas, and this will take some time, even if you're working with a simple language.

377

What Is a JavaScript, and the Java versus JavaScript Sermon

As you saw in the previous section, Java programs are created as source code and compiled into .class files of pseudo-machine code. The Java .class file is added to the document in much the same way that an image or a Shockwave presentation is added—the applet and the HTML code that links to the applet are separate entities.

A JavaScript is quite a bit more tangled up in the HTML code. JavaScripts are *not* compiled. The JavaScript source is added directly to the HTML code, and the browser (either Navigator or Explorer) interprets the JavaScript source directly.

(As a result, there's no need for a JavaScript virtual machine because there are no JavaScript bytecodes. However, this also means that the JavaScript can't run on any platform or system that contains a Java Virtual Machine—JavaScripts can *only* run inside JavaScript-savvy browser windows.)

Because of JavaScript's special relationship with HTML, a JavaScript can be spread throughout an HTML file, or a single line or two of JavaScript code can be attached to an HTML element. For example, here are a few lines of JavaScript attached to a text link:

```
<a href = "magic.html" OnMouseOver = "self.status = 'hello, world!'; return
true"> The Magic Page </a>
```

It's not immediately obvious where the HTML ends and the JavaScript begins, is it? In fact, the JavaScript section is:

```
OnMouseOver = "self.status = 'hello, world!'; return true"
```

which is invoked when the mouse passes over the link to magic.html. (The script simply puts the "hello, world!" message in the browser's status bar. See Figure 13.9.)

FIGURE 13.9

One possible "Hello, World" JavaScript in action.

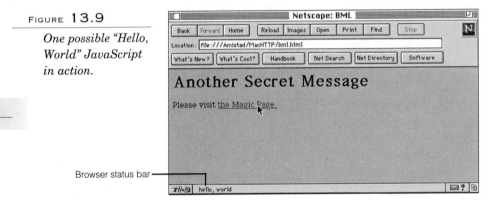

JavaScripts can also be associated with the whole page, rather than a particular element. Such scripts are placed in the page's <HEAD> section, and are executed immediately when the page loads. Very often, these page scripts are function definitions that are called by JavaScript snippets attached to page elements, something like this:

```
<head>
<script language = "JavaScript"
function do_something(){
do something marvelous
}
!—end script>
</head>
<body>
<a href OnMouseOver = "do_something()"> link text </a>
<body>
```

This example has a page-level JavaScript (lines 2–6) and a JavaScript snippet attached to a text link (line 9). The JavaScript in line 8 calls the page-level JavaScript. This kind of approach is often used so that several elements on the page can share the same core routine.

> **WARNING**
>
> The example of the do_something() JavaScript function is pseudo-code. Don't type it into any of NetObjects Fusion's dialog boxes or try to load it into a browser. As you probably guessed, "do something marvelous" is not valid JavaScript syntax.

Sample JavaScripts from the Web

One of the best sources for sample JavaScripts is the Gamelan site that you looked at in the section on Java. JavaScript isn't Java (as I've said many times), but Gamelan keeps a good-sized collection of JavaScripts, anyway.

Because JavaScript is so tightly integrated with the HTML that contains it, and in many cases, invisible (or at least, unobtrusive), the kinds of example JavaScripts that you'll find at Gamelan or other Internet repositories tend toward flashy, rather than functional examples.

Adding JavaScripts to NetObjects Fusion Pages

You can add JavaScripts to a NetObjects Fusion layout in the layout's <HEAD> section, or you can attach JavaScripts to individual elements. Let's add a few scripts to a page. You can type the scripts as shown, or for the truly lazy, use the text file that you'll find in the Book/Executables folder on the *NetObjects Fusion Handbook* CD-ROM.

First, let's add a script for the whole page. This script defines a function that you will be invoking with a JavaScript attached to a form element.

1. Start with a new Fusion page.

2. Choose the **Page→Layout Script** menu command. NetObjects Fusion presents the Script dialog box.

3. To enter the script by hand (a good idea, if you plan to learn how scripts work), enter the following in the Before Element field, exactly as it appears:

```
<script language = "JavaScript">
<!--
function doublecheck() {
flag = confirm("Checking this box will bring a torrent of junkmail to your
door. Do you still want to subscribe?");
if (!flag) {
document.forms[0].junkmail.click(0);
    }
}
// -->
</script>
```

379

4. To add the script automatically, click the Insert button at the bottom of the Script dialog box and navigate to the text file that contains the script. (The name of the file on the CD-ROM example is "doublecheck.txt.")

Whether you insert the script manually or automatically, the Script dialog box should look like Figure 13.10 when you're done.

Figure **13.10**

A JavaScript entered in the Script dialog box.

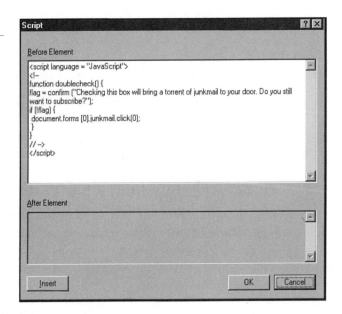

TIP

You can customize the "Checking this box" message, of course, but make sure that double-quotes appear on each end, and your new message doesn't contain any single or double quotes (unless you know how to do JavaScript substitutions).

The doublecheck script doesn't work on its own—it must be invoked by another JavaScript in the page that calls the `doublecheck()` function. Let's add such a script:

1. Create a check box with the Form tool.

2. In the Check box tab of the Properties palette, give the check box the name "junkmail" in the Name field and enter something like "Would you like to be on our mailing list?" in the Label Text field.

3. Choose the **Page→Element Script** menu command. (The check box must be highlighted or the command will be inactive in the menu.) NetObjects Fusion presents the Script dialog box.

4. Enter the following text into the Inside Element field, exactly as it appears here:

```
onClick = "doublecheck()"
```

5. Click the Preview button.

After the browser loads the page, click the check box. The browser should bring up a confirmation box, like the one shown in Figure 13.11. If you click OK in the dialog box, the check box on the page will remain checked—if you cancel out of the dialog box, the check box on the page will automatically uncheck itself.

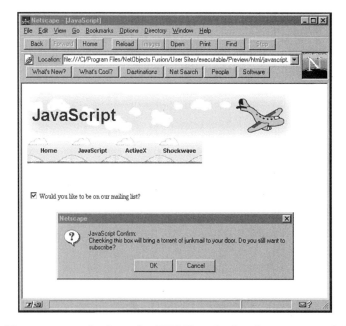

FIGURE 13.11

A JavaScript in action.

381

If you were to look at the HTML code for this page (with **View→Document Source**), you'd see that the HTML/JavaScript for the check box looks something like this:

```
<input type = "checkbox" name = "junkmail" value = "yes" onclick =
"doublecheck()">
```

Sometimes, however, you want to wrap JavaScript around both sides of an element. For instance, NetObjects Fusion does not recognize that a JavaScript might go inside the <href> tags that are used to create links to other pages. If you want to add or create a readout in the browser's status bar, as in the "hello, world" JavaScript pictured in Figure 13.9, you must create the entire link tag by hand:

1. Create a text box or image box in the layout.

2. Click the Script button in the Text or Image tab of the Properties palette or choose **Page→Element Script**.

3. In the Before Element field, enter the HTML code for the link and the JavaScript that contains the message. To link to the NetObjects home page, for example, you enter:

   ```
   <a href = "http://www.netobjects.com" onMouseOver = "self.status='Home
   of Fusion'; return true")
   ```

4. In the After Element field, enter:

   ```
   </a>
   ```

to close the tag. Notice that the link doesn't appear in the NetObjects Fusion layout or in the Assets window. You'll need to test this kind of link by hand.

Where to Find More Information

Because JavaScript is run by a browser, rather than executed directly by a machine's CPU, JavaScript is completely cross-platform. You may see books "for Windows" or "for Macintosh," but the tools that you need to develop a JavaScript—NetObjects Fusion, your native wits, and some spare time—are the same on any platform.

I really liked this book:

- *JavaScript for Macintosh* (by Shohe and Ritchey, Hayden Books).

Windows users will find the Mac book perfectly useful, but if you must have a book that doesn't have Macintosh in the title, try this one:

- *Web Page Scripting Techniques* (Bloomberg, Kawski, and Treffers, Hayden Books).

You may also be interested in the comp.lang.javascript newsgroup. I think that most programming newsgroups aren't worth the time it takes to read through hundreds (or thousands!) of daily postings, but the traffic on comp.lang.javascript is usually pretty sane.

ActiveX Controls

ActiveX isn't a language in the same way that Java or JavaScript are languages. Rather, ActiveX is a technology for delivering applications created with Microsoft's development tools, such as Visual C++, via Web pages. In many ways, the end result—an application that runs inside a browser window—is the same, but the architecture and the philosophy behind ActiveX is quite a bit different from Java technology.

What Is ActiveX?

ActiveX is an outgrowth (some would say a rechristening) of Microsoft's OLE custom control technology. In the world of Microsoft development technology, "controls" are encapsulated bits of program functionality that can be added to applications.

For example, the slider control shown in Figure 13.12 is a typical ActiveX control. The slider isn't just a picture of a slider: it's a functioning interface element.

383

Using a development tool like Visual Basic, you can paste the slider into an application, and the user can move the slider's knob up and down to change the slider's value. Writing this kind of interface widget from scratch is fairly complicated, but with OLE/ActiveX technology, all the details of the control's implementation are hidden away. From the developer's point of view, the slider is just a slider that has certain attributes, such as height, width, and knob position.

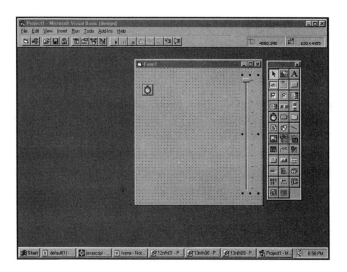

FIGURE 13.12

An OLE control, as seen in the Visual Basic development environment.

An OLE control doesn't need to be as simple as a little slider widget; it can be as complex and multifunctional as the programmer wants to make it. (In fact, on the Windows platform, Internet Explorer is a giant ActiveX control.) In general, any application or application functionality can be saved in OLE format.

OLE controls don't necessarily need to be included in an application program when the program is written—a running application can also load and run an OLE control that's stored in an external file. (And here's where ActiveX enters the picture.)

An ActiveX control is simply an OLE control that has been optimized for delivery over the Internet. ActiveX controls are (usually) a little smaller than the OLE equivalent, and they use a slightly different system for registering themselves with the Windows 95 operating system, but ActiveX controls are, functionally speaking, OLE controls. When the Internet Explorer browser finds an ActiveX component embedded in a Web page, it downloads the component, stores it in an external file, and then adds the control's functionality to its own.

After the control is downloaded, any subsequent content that Explorer finds that uses the code can be handled by the control that's already on the machine. For example, Adobe has released a beta version of the Adobe Acrobat Reader program in ActiveX control format. Users don't want to download the 900K-ish Acrobat control every time they look at a 50K Acrobat document, right? When Explorer finds content that uses the Acrobat control, it checks to see whether the control is already installed. If so, it downloads the content, rather than the control. (In this context, you might think of an ActiveX control as a self-installing plug-in.)

TIP

To look at any of the ActiveX example sites or do any of the experiments in this section, you'll need to be running Windows 95 (sorry, my Mac compadres) with Internet Explorer 3.0 (the final version, not a beta).

Examples of ActiveX

The range of applications that are possible with ActiveX are as wide as the possibilities with Java applications. Before you look at these pages, let's set up Internet Explorer's security to view the ActiveX controls:

1. Choose **View→Option** from the Internet Explorer menu bar.

2. Click the Security tab of the Options dialog box. Check all the check boxes in the Active content group and click the Safety Level button. Click the Medium button in the Active content security group (see Figure 13.13).

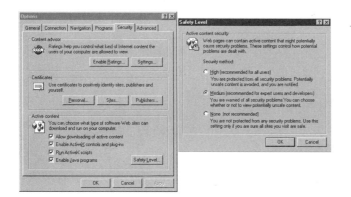

FIGURE 13.13

The correct Internet Explorer security settings for the following exercise.

Games

385

The ActiveX implementation of the game of Go from Brilliance Labs, Inc. (see Figure 13.14) is especially exciting; not only is it a colorful, well-executed application that runs in a browser window—it's also an Internet-based client application. Using this CyberGO software, you can play live games of Go against other users on the Web. You can find the CyberGO control at `http://www.brlabs.com`.

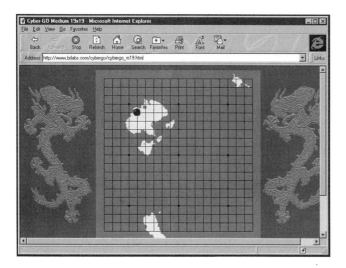

FIGURE 13.14

A game / Internet client written in ActiveX.

Multimedia Plug-Ins

As I mentioned in the introduction to this section, ActiveX can function very much like a multimedia plug-in. One such ActiveX control is available from Vivo Software, Inc. The VivoActive player can handle a stream of digital video information, just like the Intervu and MacZilla plug-ins that you looked at in Chapter 10 (see Figure 13.15). See `http://www.vivo.com` for more information.

FIGURE 13.15

ActiveX can provide a plug-in type of functionality.

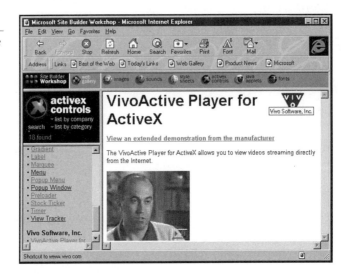

Special Page Effects

You can use little ActiveX controls to add animation-style effects to your pages, along the lines of the NervousText applet that you looked at in the Java section. In fact, it's a little simpler to create these kinds of effects yourself with Microsoft's development tools.

One of the basic ActiveX controls provided by Microsoft is the Stock Ticker control shown in Figure 13.16. The Stock Ticker control takes information from a text file at any Internet URL, or another ActiveX component, and scrolls it across the control's area. You can find this control at `http://www.microsoft.com/activex/gallery/default.htm`. (We'll download more stuff from this site in the next few pages.)

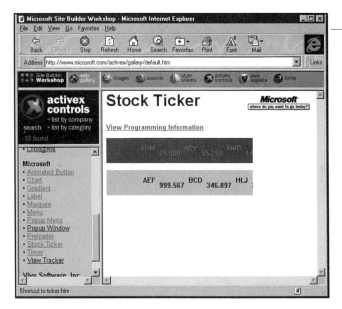

FIGURE 13.16

Special page effects created with ActiveX.

The Gamelan site (which you've visited twice in this chapter already) contains a growing collection of ActiveX controls and links to other ActiveX collections. Point your browser to `http://www.gamelan.com` (if you haven't made a bookmark for it already!). You might also want to take a look at our old friend Browserwatch's collection of controls at `http://browserwatch.iworld.com/activex.html`.

Adding ActiveX Controls to Web Pages

OK, let's add an ActiveX control to a page. First, you'll grab a control from Microsoft's developer's site by using the following steps:

1. Point Explorer to `http://browserwatch.iworld.com/activex/gallery/`. In the bottom left-hand frame, click the `Label` link under the Microsoft heading.

2. When the Label frame loads in the page's main frame, click the Download and Run a Working Sample link.

3. Explorer presents a security dialog box that asks if you want to install and load the control. Examine the certificate, if you like, and then click Yes. It will take a few seconds for Explorer to download the control.

387

When you download the control and play it, the control is added to your Windows' registry. NetObjects Fusion can only find ActiveX components that are in the registry, so it's important that the control be installed. Now let's put the control in the layout.

1. Choose the ActiveX tool (the middle tool in the fourth row of the Tool palette) and draw a box in the layout. NetObjects Fusion presents the Insert ActiveX Control dialog box (see Figure 13.17).

FIGURE 13.17

The Insert ActiveX Control dialog box.

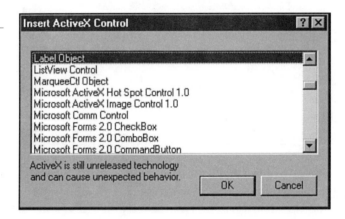

388

2. The Insert ActiveX Control dialog box contains a list of all of the OLE and ActiveX controls that NetObjects Fusion could find in your registry. (As a result, your dialog box may differ slightly from Figure 13.17.) Pick the Label Object from the list of controls and click OK.

3. Fusion previews the label control in the layout. The control should look something like Figure 13.18, when it's been placed. (Give the text plenty of room because it's going to swing around!)

4. Now, let's give the control some flavor. The Label Object window in the ActiveX tab of the Properties palette contains a list of the control's properties (see Figure 13.19). Locate the ID properties and double-click its name. Fusion presents the Edit Property dialog box.

5. Enter "myLabel" (without the quotes) in the Edit Property box.

6. Double-click the Caption property in the Label Object window. Enter "Click me!" (or your own little witticism) as the Caption Property.

7. Enter 1 as the FontBold Property.

FIGURE 13.18

The ActiveX control immediately after placement.

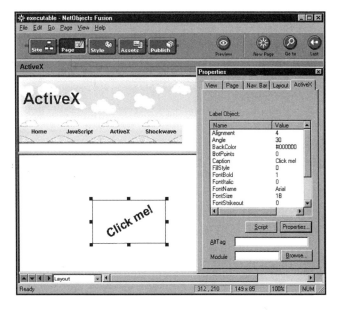

FIGURE 13.19

The ActiveX control after the properties have been altered.

8. Enter 18 for the FontSize property.

9. Enter 30 for the Angle Property. (This is really the first interesting thing that's happened, isn't it?) At this point, your control should look like Figure 13.19.

You can find complete documentation about each of the Label properties of the Label component on the page where you found the component.

Some ActiveX controls also support preference-style dialog boxes to set the control properties in the Fusion layout. (The Label control does not support this feature.) To edit the control with these developer-friendly dialog boxes, click the Properties button in the ActiveX tab of the Properties palette. If property pages are supported, Fusion (actually, the control itself) will present a dialog box like the one shown in Figure 13.20.

FIGURE 13.20

Some ActiveX controls offer preference box style editing of the control's properties.

390

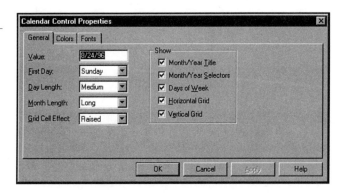

OK, our layout is still pretty lame. To make the control move, you'll need to link it to what's happening in the browser window. To do this, you'll use a VBScript. VBScript is a scripting language based on Visual Basic. It's still under development, so I haven't given it a section of its own, but it will do for this particular task.

1. Select the Label object and choose **Page→Element Script**.

2. Enter the following script into the After Element field:

```
<script language = "vbscript">
sub myLabel_click
myLabel.Angle = (myLabel.Angle + 45) mod 360
end sub
</script>
```

3. Click the Preview button, making sure that your preferences are such that Internet Explorer is the default browser. Click the label a few times to see what happens.

The example script handles mouse clicks inside the ActiveX object. When the script "hears" a click, it changes the label's Angle value, just as if you had changed the value of the Angle property in the Properties palette.

Where to Find More Information

For more information about scripting with VBScript, see Microsoft's VBScript home page at `http://www.microsoft.com/vbscript`. The previously mentioned book, *Web Page Scripting Techniques*, has an entire section on VBScripts as well.

How Is ActiveX Different from Java?

If you've heard much about ActiveX, you've probably heard it compared to Java. Although the Java Virtual Machine and ActiveX are both systems for delivering executable code inside the browser window, they take radically different approaches to delivering the goods.

There are advantages and disadvantages to each system. There's no reason why you can't use both technologies to construct your pages if you have the resources, but you should pick the right tool for the job. Here are some of the critical differences between the two systems.

Cross-Platform Portability

Java is the clear winner in this category. The current implementation of ActiveX is heavily dependent on the Windows operating system's Windows Registry, and as such, ActiveX controls will only run on Windows machines, no matter what browser is used.

This could change, of course, but it's not likely to change soon. There's no official schedule for the appearance of ActiveX technology on the MacOS or Unix platforms, but it's a fairly safe bet that it won't arrive for MacOS in the next year, and it may never be implemented on Unix.

As you learned in the section on Java, Java can run wherever the Java Virtual Machine is present, and it runs in much the same way wherever the Virtual machine may be. The Java Virtual machine runs on all the Windows-, MacOS-, and Unix-based systems, and a few more besides.

Cross-Browser Portability

Technically, it's certainly possible to build in support for ActiveX in the Netscape Navigator browser, at least on the Windows platform. Politically, it's nearly impossible. The folks at Netscape have made it clear that they do not intend to support ActiveX as an integral part of Navigator, and there's no sign (at an admittedly early stage) that anyone is wavering about this decision.

As it turns out, the Canadian software company Ncompass Labs, Inc. has, for now, defused the situation by offering an ActiveX player plug-in for Netscape Navigator. When the ScriptActive plug-in is installed, Navigator users can load and run ActiveX components.

Cross-Application Portability

ActiveX is the clear winner here. Any kind of OLE custom controls that developers have created for desktop applications can be converted (with a little work) into ActiveX controls. Furthermore, ActiveX controls are, by definition, OLE controls, and as such may be used by other applications.

For example, you can take the Internet Explorer label ActiveX control that you downloaded in the ActiveX section and paste it into a Visual Basic application, applying exactly the same kind of attributes that you used in NetObjects Fusion. The ActiveX object is completely encapsulated, and doesn't care if it's in a browser window or a stand-alone application.

This is theoretically possible to do in Java—in fact, one day Java might be able to handle this kind of task more gracefully than ActiveX—but now, in 1996, there are no tools in place to handle Java-based objects with simple cut-and-paste.

Persistence

Java applets are fleeting things—as soon as you move along to a new page, any applets that you have loaded in your browser window disappear and must be reloaded when you want to run the applet again. Neither major browser caches applets in the way that images and HTML pages are cached—the page is simply deleted.

Furthermore, under the current implementation of the major browsers, Java applets can't store any kind of information on the browser's machine. (See the discussion of security for an explanation.) As a result, a Java applet can't "remember" anything between sessions, unless the applet stores information about the browser's owner on the server machine. This kind of storage is tricky—the browser only knows so much about the user in the first place—and might possibly require the server to store information for hundreds or thousands of applet users. This might be practical for Intranet servers with terabyte-sized storage drives, but it is impractical for many server setups.

ActiveX, however, has no such restrictions on what it can do with the reader's hard drive. An ActiveX control can store itself, and any information it likes, on the reader's hard drive. In fact, ActiveX controls are automatically stored away in the Windows registry, and it's not easy to remove them from a machine after they're installed.

Security

Java and ActiveX use radically different security models.

The Java Virtual Machine runs in its own territory on the host machine. The Java applet only knows about the Java Virtual Machine, and it has no access to the "real" machine that it's running on.

393

As a result, the user can have complete control over what the Java program can and cannot do. By default, a Java applet can't read or write to the user's disk or gain access to sensitive system information. In future versions of Navigator (and presumably, Internet Explorer), the reader will be able to give the applet disk access at various levels of freedom. As of this writing, however, Navigator is still fairly paranoid, and applets can run in only high-security, no-disk-access mode, or not at all.

ActiveX uses a system of digital signatures to provide security. Before Internet Explorer loads an ActiveX control, it reads the digital certificate embedded in the component. If Explorer recognizes the originator of the certificate as a member of the reader's "approved" list, Explorer loads the control. If the signature isn't recognized, Explorer may prompt the user to make a decision or simply not load the control, depending on the way Explorer's preferences are set.

After the ActiveX passes the certificate test and is loaded on the browser's machine, it can do whatever it likes: read and write to the disk, communicate with the operating system, delete preference files of rival online services' applications—whatever. The official ActiveX security policy boils down to this: if you trust the vendor, you trust the vendor's software.

There's little doubt that certificates can't be forged. Furthermore, the encryption used to sign an ActiveX component guarantees that the signed component is in the same form as it was when it was created—in other words, bad guys can't download a Microsoft control, cook up the control by editing its machine code directly, and serve it up as a harmless Microsoft product.

Open Standards

This is really a political issue more than a technical question. Java is an open standard—Sun has freely distributed the Java standard, and anyone can create a Java Virtual Machine, Java compilers, or other Java development tools. Sun certainly retains a great deal of control over Java, but it's free, like butterflies, and the best things in life.

According to a July 1996 Microsoft press release, ActiveX is undergoing a transition to open standards. The VBScript specification is already freely available. Many net.denizens are suspicious or paranoid about Microsoft's business practices, but ActiveX and VBScript appear to be open standards.

Summary

In this chapter, you learned about executable code, and how to add it to your pages. Specifically, you learned the following information:

- What Java is and how it works.

- How to add Java applets to your pages.

- What JavaScripts are and how they're different from Java.

- How to add JavaScripts to your pages.

- What ActiveX controls are and how they work.

- How to add ActiveX components to your pages.

- How Java and ActiveX are different approaches to the delivery of executable code.

Goodbye

In the last 13 chapters, you've learned how to create a site with NetObjects Fusion: design the site's architecture, apply a consistent site-wide style, implement pages, and send the site to a Web server.

You've also learned a bit about some of the special content that you can add to your site with NetObjects Fusion: imagemaps, multimedia content, forms, database information, and even executable code.

Appendix A contains a round-up of the basic tools and property tabs that you've looked at throughout the book, sort of like the URL round-up at the end of each chapter. Appendix B contains a glossary of basic Fusion and Internet terms.

Be sure to stop in at `http://www.netobjects.com` and `http://www.hayden.com/internet/fusion.html` for late-breaking news. I'm sure that *NetObjects Fusion Handbook* will make you more productive in your Web-building endeavors and give you the chance to use your energy on design, rather than implementation. In fact, I suspect that you'll find that working with Fusion is a lot of fun.

URL Roundup

- Most exhaustive archive of Java applications can be found at the Gamelan site:
  `http://www.gamelan.com`

- JavaScript solitaire game:
  `http://w3.gwis.com/~thorn/Solitaire.html`

- Magnetic letters applet:
  `http://www.codepilot.com/~kbenell/letters/letterboard.html`

- The basic Java Development Kit (JDK) distributed freely by Sun:
  `http://www.javasoft.com site`

- CyberGO control:
  `http://www.brlabs.com`

- The VivoActive player from Vivo Software:
  `http://www.vivo.com`

- The ActiveX StockTicker control:
  `http://www.microsoft.com/activex/gallery/default.htm`

- A source for ActiveX controls:
  `http://browserwatch.iworld.com/activex.html`

- Microsoft's VBScript home page:
  `http://www.microsoft.com/vbscript`

PART **IV**

References

APPENDIX

A

NetObjects Fusion Object Roundup

In this appendix, I'll review all the basic objects that you will work with in
NetObjects Fusion:

- The object's name

- A basic description

- Any special features of the object

- The object's tab in the Properties palette

The Selection Tool

The selection tool doesn't have any particular objects associated with it; rather,
it's used to move or resize existing objects.

TIP

Windows users have probably noticed that they can invoke a contextual menu by
right-clicking an object with the selection tool. (In the interest of cross-platform
courtesy to Mac users, I've avoided rubbing this in throughout the book.)

Text Objects

A text box is used to contain type. It's created with the text tool, the first tool in the second row of the tool palette (see Figure A.1). A text box can be placed anywhere in the layout, and moved and resized as desired. See Chapter 5 for more information about text objects.

A text box and the Text Properties palette.

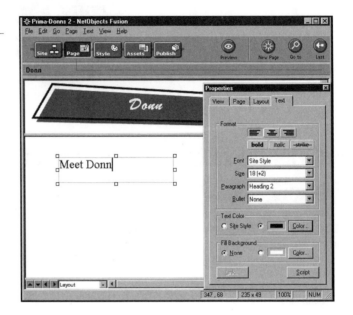

400

The Format Group

The Format Group consists of the following items:

- **Alignment buttons** apply left-justification, centering, or right-justification to the selected paragraph.

- **The Character Style buttons** apply bold, italic, and strikethrough styles to selected characters.

- **The Font pop-up menu** applies a particular typeface to selected characters.

- **The Size pop-up menu** sets the size of the selected characters.

- **The Paragraph pop-up menu** applies predefined or user-defined styles to the current paragraph.

- **The Bullet pop-up menu** indents the selected paragraph and adds a number, character, or bullet in the paragraph's left margin.

The Text Color Group

The Text Color group enables the user to change the color of the selected text. By default, all text is the text color that is defined in the site's SiteStyle. Clicking the radio button next to the color swatch overrides this default. Clicking the Color button brings up the standard NetObjects Fusion color picker.

The Fill Background Group

The Fill Background group changes the color of the selected text box. By default, a text box is transparent; clicking the radio button next to the color swatch overrides this default. Clicking the Color button overrides this default.

The Link Button

The Link button invokes the standard Link dialog box. The selected text (not the box itself) may be linked to a page in the NetObjects Fusion site or to an external URL.

The Script Button

The Script button invokes the standard script dialog box. JavaScripts, VBScripts, or standard HTML may be added before or after the text box in the page's HTML. The inserted material appears *outside* any link tags contained in the text.

Picture Objects

Picture objects contain digital images. NetObjects Fusion supports a wide variety of image formats, but converts all images to either GIF or JPEG format when they are placed in the Fusion layout. Picture boxes are created with the Picture tool, the second tool in the second row of the Tool palette (see Figure A.2). See Chapter 5 for more information about picture objects.

FIGURE A.2

A Picture box and the Picture Properties palette.

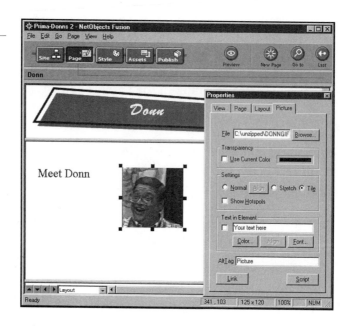

The File Pop-Up Menu

The File pop-up menu displays the file path of the image in the selected Picture box. The Browse button invokes the Standard OpenPicture dialog box. You may replace the image in the selected image box at any time by using the Browse button to navigate to a new image file.

The Transparency Check Box

Checking the Transparency check box converts the current image to GIF89 format. All colors in the image that match the color in the color swatch are rendered transparent. (Use the eyedropper tool, which appears in the Secondary control palette when the Picture tool is active, to sample new colors from the image and add them to the color swatch.)

The Settings Group

The Settings Group consists of the following items:

- **The Align button** positions the image within its image box. By default, images are aligned with the top left corner of the Picture box.

- **The Stretch button** resizes the image so that it is the same size as its Picture box.

- **The Tile button** repeats the image within the Picture box by filling the Picture box completely.

- **The Show Hotspots button** toggles the display of imagemap areas that the user has added to the image.

The Text in Element Group

The Text in Element Group adds a caption to the current image. By default, images don't have captions; clicking the check box next to the text field overrides the default and adds the contents of the text field as the image's caption.

- **The Color button** invokes the standard color palette and applies the selected color to the entire label.

- **The Align button** positions the label within the image (not within the Picture box).

- **The Font button** invokes the standard Font dialog box and applies the selected type attributes to the entire label.

The AltTag Field

The AltTag field specifies a text message to be displayed in the picture's place in the layout if the browser is unable to load the selected picture.

The Link Button

Clicking the Link button invokes the standard NetObjects Fusion Links dialog box. An image may be linked to an internal page or to an external URL. Linked images do *not* display a border, unlike the HTML default.

The Script Button

Clicking the Script button invokes the standard Script dialog box. A JavaScript, VBScript, or standard HTML may be added to the page before or after the Picture object. The script will be placed *outside* the picture's <img> tag.

Rectangle Objects

Rectangles are created by the Rectangle tool. The Rectangle tool appears in the Secondary tool palette when the Drawing tool, the third tool in the second row of the tool palette, is selected (see Figure A.3). In the NetObjects Fusion layout, rectangles act like they would in a drawing program—style objects with movable control points; however, when the page is converted to HTML, the rectangle is rendered as a GIF. See Chapter 5 for more information about rectangles.

FIGURE **A.3**

A rectangle and the Rectangle Properties palette.

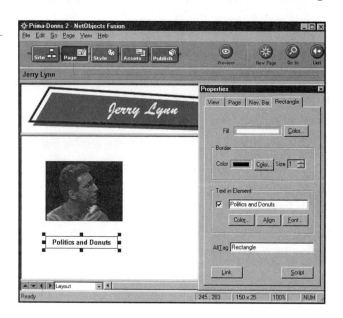

The Fill Swatch

The fill swatch displays the fill color of the selected rectangle. To change the rectangle's color, click the Color button, which invokes the standard Color Picker.

The Border Group

The Border group consists of the following items:

- The **Color Swatch** displays the color of the border of the currently selected rectangle. The Color button invokes the Standard Color Picker.

- The **Size field** displays the line weight in pixels of the rectangle's border. A value of 0 removes the border.

The Text in Element Group

The Text in Element Group adds a caption to the current rectangle. By default, rectangles don't have captions; clicking the check box next to the text field overrides the default and adds the contents of the text field as the image's caption.

- **The Color button** invokes the standard color palette and applies the selected color to the entire label.

- **The Align button** positions the label within the image (not within the picture box).

- **The Font button** invokes the standard Font dialog box and applies the selected type attributes to the entire label.

The AltTag Field

The AltTag field specifies a text message to be displayed in the picture's place in the layout if the browser is unable to load the GIF rendering of the rectangle.

The Link Button

Clicking the Link button invokes the standard NetObjects Fusion Links dialog box. A rectangle may be linked to an internal page or an external URL.

The Script Button

Clicking the Script button invokes the standard Script dialog box. A JavaScript, VBScript, or standard HTML may be added to the page before or after the rectangle object. The script will be placed *outside* the rectangle's <img> tag.

Rounded Rectangle Objects

Rounded Rectangle objects are created with the Rounded Rectangle tool. The tool is visible in the Secondary tool palette when the Drawing tool (the third tool in the second row of the Tool palette) is active.

Rounded rectangles are like ordinary rectangles, but contain an extra control point that may be used to give the rectangle convex edges on its top and bottom or sides. The Rounded Rectangle tab in the Properties palette is identical in every way to the Rectangle tab. See the previous section on rectangles for details on the Properties palette and Chapter 5 for more information about Rounded Rectangles.

Oval Objects

Oval objects are created with the Oval Rectangle tool. The Oval tool is visible in the Secondary tool palette when the Drawing tool (the third tool in the second row of the Tool palette) is active.

Ovals appear in the layout as drawing program-style objects, and may be resized or reshaped as desired. Ovals are rendered into GIF images when the layout is converted to HTML.

The Oval Tab in the Properties palette is identical in every way to the Rectangle tab. See the rectangle section for details on the Properties palette and Chapter 5 for more information about Ovals.

Polygon Objects

Polygon objects are created with the Polygon Rectangle tool. The Polygon tool is visible in the Secondary tool palette when the Drawing tool (the third tool in the second row of the Tool palette) is active.

Polygons appear in the layout as a series of connected control points. Any of the polygon's vertices may be moved as desired to reshape the polygon, but vertices may not be added or removed once the polygon is closed. Polygons are rendered into GIF images when the layout is converted to HTML.

The Polygon Tab in the Properties palette is identical in every way to the Rectangle tab. See the Rectangle section above for details on the Properties palette and Chapter 5 for more information about Polygons.

Line Objects

Line objects are created with the Line tool (see Figure A.4). The Line tool is visible in the Secondary tool palette when the Drawing tool (the third tool in the second row of the Tool palette) is active.

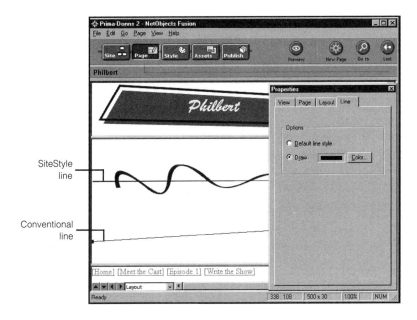

SiteStyle
line

Conventional
line

FIGURE **A.4**

*Two kinds of line
objects and the Line
Properties palette.*

407

The Options Group

A line object can take two different forms: the line defined in the current
SiteStyle, or a simple, one pixel-wide line. By default, the line is the SiteStyle
line: this is a user-supplied (or ready-made) image file, and will be horizontal, no
matter how the line is drawn.

Clicking the Draw radio button will turn the line into a simple line with two
control points. Both control points may be moved as desired.

Clicking the Color button brings up the standard color picker. The selected color
will be applied to the current line.

For more information about Lines, see Chapter 5. For more information about
SiteStyles, see Chapter 6.

Table Objects

Table Objects are created with the Table tool, the first tool in the third row of the
Tool palette.

The table cell attributes discussed next are accessible only via right-clicking the table cell and choosing the appropriate attribute from the contextual menu; that is, there is no mechanism under MacOS to alter table cells (see Figure A.5)! (Surely some sort of access will be implemented, but the Mac version of the software was unavailable as this book went to press.)

FIGURE A.5

A table object and the Table Properties palette.

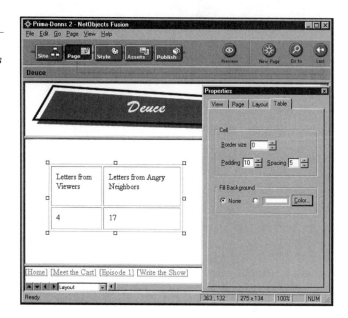

The Cell Group

The Cell Group consists of the following items:

- **The Border Size field** affects the size of the picture frame border that appears around the entire table. The table's crossbars are affected by the border size *only* if the border size is zero, in which case, both the border and the crossbar do not appear. Otherwise, the border size value does not affect the size or appearance of the table's crossbars.

- **The Padding field** measures the space between table cells in pixels.

- **The Spacing field** measures the space between a cell entry and the edge of the cell.

The Fill Background Group

The Fill Background controls affect the background color of the currently selected table cell, *not* the entire table. By default, table cells are transparent. To change this default, click the radio button next to the color swatch and click the Color swatch to bring up the color palette.

Table Cell Type

An individual Table Cell may contain picture box content or text box content, but not both. You may invoke the Cell Type dialog box by right-clicking the cell and choosing Cell Type from the contextual menu.

Table Height

The height of the table in rows can't be entered directly. Rather, rows must be added and removed individually. To add a row, right-click a table cell and choose Add Row from the contextual menu. The new row will be added directly underneath the selected row. To remove a row, right-click one of its cells and choose Remove Row from the contextual menu.

Table Width

Likewise, the number of columns in a table can't be entered directly: columns must be added and removed individually. To add a column, right-click a table cell and choose Add Column from the contextual menu. The new column will be added to the right of the selected column. To remove a column, right-click one of its cells and choose Remove Column from the contextual menu.

Sound Objects

Sound objects are added with the Sound tool, the second tool in the third row of the Tool palette (see Figure A.6). A sound object may appear in the browser window as a clickable link, which, when pressed, plays a sound, or as an in-line sound deck. See Chapter 10 for more information about sound objects.

FIGURE A.6

*The Sound
Properties palette.*

NetObjects Fusion supports a variety of common sound formats. Fusion does not *play* any sound format itself; it merely creates the appropriate HTML tags for the browser to recognize and play the sound correctly.

The File Field

The File field displays the location of the current sound field. The current sound file can be replaced at any time by clicking the Browser button and navigating to a new sound file.

The Display Group

The Display group contains the following items:

- **The Icon radio button** uses the selected icon to represent the link to the sound in the layout. By default, this radio button is selected.

- **The File radio button** uses a user-provided image as the link to the sound in the layout. The Browse button invokes the standard Add Image dialog box, which can be used to navigate to the desired image.

- **The Inline radio button** adds an inline sound deck to the layout. Readers with the appropriate plug-ins can play the sound by using the sound deck controls.

The AltTag Field

The AltTag group contains a text message that is displayed in the layout when the browser can't load the sound file.

The Video Tool

Video objects are added with the Video tool, the third tool in the third row of the Tool palette. A video object may appear in the browser window as a clickable link. When the link is pressed, it plays a video in a separate window. Alternatively, the video may be used as an integral part of the page's layout. See Chapter 10 for more information about video objects.

The Video tab in the Properties palette is identical to the Sound tab. See the section on Sound Objects for more information about the Tab's controls.

Java Applets

Java Applets are added to the layout by using the Applet tool, the first tool in the fourth row of the Tool palette (see Figure A.7).

FIGURE A.7

The Java Properties palette.

411

The Class Field

The Class field displays the location of the Java applet's .class file that contains the applet's executable code. (Java source files, which use the extension .java, are not executable and should not appear in this window.)

The Java applet may be replaced by another applet by clicking the Browser button to the right of the Class field.

The Parameters Group

The parameters group contains the following items:

- **The Parameters List window** displays the names and values of the parameters (if any) passed to the applet by the Web page. To edit a parameter, double-click its name in the window.

- **The Parameter Info window** is inactive in the current version of NetObjects Fusion.

- **The Add/Remove Parameter** buttons (see Figure A.7) are used to add parameter/value pairs to the Parameter List window.

- **The Promote/Demote Parameter** buttons (see Figure A.7) change the ordering of the parameters in the Parameter List window. Clicking the Promote button moves the selected item up in the list (for example, the second entry would become the first entry, and the first would move to second place); clicking the Demote button moves the item down in the list (for example, the second item would become the third item, and the third would move to second place).

The AltTag Field

The AltTag field contains a text message to be displayed in the layout when the browser can't load the Java applet.

The Script Button

Clicking the Script button invokes the standard Script dialog box. A JavaScript, VBScript, or standard HTML may be added to the page before or after the Java object.

ActiveX Controls

ActiveX controls are added with the ActiveX tool, the second tool in the fourth row of the Tool palette (see Figure A.8).

 ActiveX is, for the foreseeable future, Windows-only technology. The ActiveX tool does not appear in the Mac version of NetObjects Fusion.

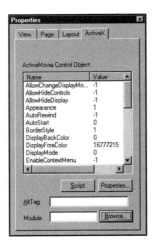

FIGURE A.8

The ActiveX Properties palette.

The Control Properties List Window

Each ActiveX control has a set of properties built into the control. The control's name appears as the caption of the Properties list window. To edit a property, click its name in the window to invoke the Edit Property dialog box.

413

The Script Button

Clicking the Script button invokes the standard Script dialog box. A JavaScript, VBScript, or standard HTML may be added to the page before or after the ActiveX. The script will be added *outside* the ActiveX control's <object></object> tags.

The Properties Buttons

Some ActiveX controls contain their own built-in property tabs. (Some don't.) To bring up any such tab, click the Properties button.

The AltTag Field

The AltTag field contains a text message to be displayed in the layout when the browser can't load the ActiveX control.

Module

The module button is used to link the current ActiveX box to a different ActiveX control. It does not look for controls in the Windows registry; rather, it looks for .ocx format files (and .cab files, which can also store ActiveX controls) on disk.

Shockwave Objects

Shockwave objects are added with the Shockwave tool, the third tool in the fourth row of the Tools palette (see Figure A.9). NetObjects Fusion doesn't "play" Shockwave content—it merely creates a placeholder in the layout. For more information about Shockwave, see Chapter 10.

FIGURE A.9

The Shockwave Properties palette.

The File Field

The File field displays the current location of the selected Shockwave file. The selected file may be replaced by clicking the Browse button and using the standard file dialog box to navigate to a new Director (.dcr) file.

The AltTag Field

The AltTag field contains a text message to be displayed in the layout when the browser can't load the Shockwave content file.

Data Objects

A Data Object is NetObjects Fusion's representation of a database. The Data Object is not the database itself; rather, the Data Object documents the names and data types in an external or internal database. Data Objects are not directly displayed in a NetObjects Fusion layout; they are created when a database is created or imported with the Data List tool, or created with the **Edit→Create Data Object** menu command when Fusion is in Assets view and the Data

Objects mode is selected (see Figure A.10). For more information about Data Objects, see Chapter 12.

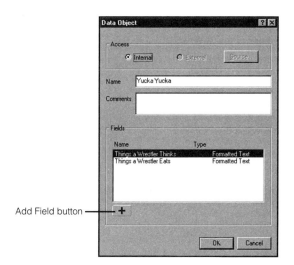

FIGURE A.10

The Data Object dialog box.

415

The Access Group

The controls in the Access group determine the source of the database associated with the Data Object:

- **The Internal radio button** is used to create an internal database within NetObjects Fusion. All internal database data is stored in the pages of the Fusion site.

- **The External radio button** links the Data Object to an external database, tab-delimited text file, or ODBC-compliant data source. Clicking the Source button invokes the Data Source dialog box, which allows users to specify the external database or source.

The Name Field

The Name Field displays the name of the Data Object. In the case of an internal database, the name is set by the user and may be edited as desired. In the case of an imported external database, the name of the Data Object is the name of the imported database table, and this name may not be edited.

The Comments Field

The Comments field contains any comments that the user cares to enter. Comments do not appear in the site's layout, the site's HTML, or anywhere but this comment field.

The Fields Group

The Fields group contains information about the fields (a.k.a. columns or attributes) in the current Data Object:

- **The Field names window** contains a list of all fields in the current database and the data type of each field. To edit the field name or field type of an internal database, double-click the field's name in the window. Field names and data types of imported external databases are read-only and cannot be edited.

- **The Add Field button** adds a new field to internal databases. The Add Field button appears, but is inactive, when an external database is displayed in the Data Object Tab.

Data List Objects

Data List Objects are created with the Data List tool, the first tool in the fifth row of the Tool palette. Data Lists are essentially tables that index the content of an internal or external database. For more information about Data Lists, see Chapter 12.

A Data List in the NetObjects Fusion consists of a single row of empty cells; each cell represents a field of the associated Data Object. When the Data List is displayed in the browser window, it has one row for every record in the associated database (see Figure A.11).

The appearance and behavior of the Data List is controlled by *both* the Data List dialog box and the Data List tab in the Properties palette. To access the Data List dialog box once the Data List has been placed, double-click the Data List in the layout.

FIGURE A.11

*The Data List
dialog box.*

List Name Field (Dialog Box)

The List Name field contains a user-defined name for the selected Data List format. Users may define as many Data List formats as needed.

417

The Data Object Field (Dialog Box)

The Data List field contains the name Data Object associated with the current Data List. The Data Object may be freely chosen when the Data List is created; however, after the Data List is placed in the layout, the Data List is forever bound to the displayed Data Object.

The Sort By Pop-Up Menu (Dialog Box)

The Sort By pop-up menu enables the user to choose which field of an imported external database is used as a key to sort the records in the database. Only external databases can be sorted by an arbitrary field; this menu is inactive when an internal database is associated with the Data List.

The Filter Button (Dialog Box)

The filter button is used to invoke the Filter dialog box. Using the Filter dialog box, users can set up simply SQL-like queries that limit the data imported from an external database. Only those records that match the terms of the query are imported into the database. The Filter button is active only when the current Data List is associated with an external database.

The Data List Fields Group (Dialog Box)

The Data List Fields group contains information about the Data Object fields that appear in the Data List (see Figure A.12).

- **The Names window** contains a list of all the fields in the Data Object associated with the Data List. Only those fields marked with a check will appear in the Data List.

- When the **Linked Field check box** is checked, the items in the selected field will contain links to each item's Data Page.

- The **Promote Item/Demote Item** buttons change the ranking of the selected item in the Names window. For example, clicking the Promote Item button will move the second item in the list to the first position, and move the first item to second position. Clicking the Demote button will move the second item to the third position, and the third item to second position.

418 FIGURE A.12

The Data List Properties palette.

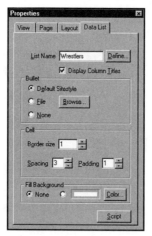

The List Name Pop-Up Menu (Tab)

The List Name pop-up menu enables the user to specify user-defined Data Lists. The menu displays a list of all Data List formats that the user has named with the Name field in the Data List dialog box. The Define button invokes the Data List dialog box.

The Display Column Titles check box (which just didn't seem to warrant its own section head) toggles the display of field names at the top of each Data List column.

The Bullet Group (Tab)

The bullet Group controls the appearance of the icon at the far left of each row of the Data List:

- When the **Default SiteStyle radio button** is selected, the Data List uses the Data List icon defined in the site's Style window as a bullet. (See Chapter 6 for more information about SiteStyles.)

- When the **File radio button** is selected, the Data List displays a user-selected image as the Data List's bullet. Clicking the Browse button invokes the standard Open Image dialog box.

- When the **None radio button** is selected, no bullet is displayed in any row.

The Cell Group (Tab)

419

The controls in the Cell group affect the appearance of the table that contains the Data List:

- **The Border Size Field** affects the size of the picture frame-like border around the entire table. The table's crossbars are affected by the border size *only* if the border size is zero, in which case, both the border and the crossbar do not appear. Otherwise, the border size value does not affect the size or appearance of the table's crossbars.

- **The Padding Field** measures the space between table cells in pixels.

- **The Spacing Field** measures the space between a cell entry and the edge of the cell.

The Fill Background Group (Tab)

The Fill Background group controls the color of the Data List. All of the Data List cells, including the column heads, are affected.

The Script Button

Clicking the Script button invokes the standard Script dialog box. A JavaScript, VBScript, or standard HTML may be added to the page before or after the ActiveX.

Data Field Objects

Data Fields are added to the NetObjects Fusion layout with the Data Field tool, the second tool in the fifth row of the Tool palette. The Data Field tool is active only when viewing a Data Page in Page View mode (see Figure A.13). For more information about Data Fields and Data Objects, see Chapter 12.

Data Fields display the values of individual fields in a Data Object. Data Fields can contain either text or image data, depending on the data type of the associated data field.

FIGURE A.13

The Data Field Properties palette.

420

The Name Field

The Name Field contains the name of the Data Object field that is associated with the Data Field. Each page of a set of stacked pages displays the same Data Field in the same position in the layout, but each page displays a different value inside the Data Field (for example, the value of the Data Object field for the record associated with that Data Page).

Additional Tabs

Each Data Field also has a Text tab or Image tab associated with it in the Properties palette. (The kind of tab depends on the kind of content in the Data Field.) Such Text and Image tabs are identical to the ordinary Text and Image tabs discussed earlier in this chapter.

Form Objects

Forms aren't explicitly added to NetObjects Fusion layouts; rather, all the individual form component objects added to a page are considered to be a single form. Form-level attributes are available via the Form Settings button at the bottom of each of the individual Form component's tabs in the Properties palette.

The Hidden Fields Dialog Box

The Hidden Fields dialog box adds hidden fields to the page's form. Hidden fields are a form-level attribute, and are not associated with any particular form component (see Figure A.14).

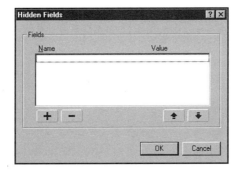

FIGURE A.14

The Hidden Fields dialog box.

421

- **The Name/Value window** contains the name/value pairs of all the hidden fields in the form. To edit an entry, double-click its name.

- **The Add field/Delete field buttons** add and remove fields from the list in the Name/Value window.

- The **Promote Item/Demote Item** buttons change the ranking of the selected item in the Name/Value window. For example, clicking the Promote Item button will move the second item in the list to the first position, and move the first item to second position. Clicking the Demote button will move the second item to the third position, and the third item to second position.

The Settings Dialog Box

Figure A.15 shows the Settings dialog box.

FIGURE A.15

The Form Settings dialog box.

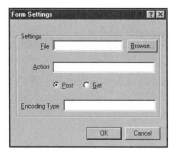

- **The File field** displays the name of the CGI script or application that resides on the local machine or network. The local file may be replaced at any time by clicking the Browser button and navigating to the new CGI file.

- **The Action field** is used to specify the URL of a CGI on the server machine (or any machine that hosts a CGI usable by the form.)

- **The Post radio button** specifies that the form data be sent to the server via POST, that is, as an independent package of data.

- **The Get radio button** specifies that the form data be sent to the server via GET, that is, attached to server's URL.

- **The Encoding Type field** specifies how the form data is encoded. *Leave it blank!*

Button Objects

Button Objects are added with the Button tool. The Button tool appears in the Secondary tool palette when the Form tool is active. Figure A.16 shows the Button property tab. For more information about forms, see Chapter 12.

The Name Field

The Name Field contains the button's name in the name/value pair. The button's name does not appear in the layout.

The Text Group

The text group's controls are active when the radio button next to the group's label is selected.

*The Button
Properties palette.*

- The **Text field** is used as the button's label in the layout, and is sent to the server as the value in the component's name/value pair.

- When the **Submit radio button** is checked, the button will send all the form's data to the server when clicked by the reader.

- When the **Reset radio button** is checked, the button will reset all the form's fields to their default values.

The Image Group

The Image group is active when the radio button next to the group's label is selected. If the Image group is active, a user-defined image file is used to represent the button. The button will have no label, and will act as a submit button, sending the form's data to the server when clicked.

The field in the image group displays the location of the image file used as the button. The image may be replaced at any time by clicking the Browse button, which invokes the standard Open Image dialog box.

Check Box Objects

Check box objects are added with the Check box tool. The Check box tool appears in the Secondary tool palette when the Form tool is active. Figure A.16 shows the Check box Properties palette. For more information about forms, see Chapter 12.

423

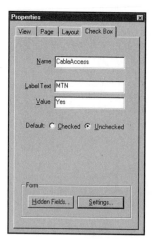

FIGURE **A.17**

The Check Box Properties palette.

The Name Field

The Name Field contains the name sent to the server in the component's name/value pair. It does not appear anywhere in the layout.

The Label Text Field

The Label Text field contains the label that appears in the layout to the right of the check box.

The Value Field

The Value field contains the value sent to the server in the component's name/value pair. It does not appear in the layout.

The Default Radio Buttons

When the **Checked radio button** is selected, the check box will be checked when first loaded in the reader's browser window. By default, the **Unchecked radio button** is selected, and the check box will be unchecked in the browser window.

Radio Button Objects

Radio button objects are added with the Radio Button tool. The tool appears in the Secondary tool palette when the Form tool is active. Figure A.16 shows the Radio button properties palette. For more information about forms, see Chapter 12.

FIGURE A.18

The Radio Button Properties palette.

The Group Name Field

The Group Name field is used to specify the set of radio buttons to which the current radio button belongs. Only one radio button in a group can be selected at any time. The Group Name is sent as the component's name in the name/value pair (once, for the whole set of buttons). It does not appear in the layout.

425

The Button Field

The contents of the Button field are used as the radio button's label in the layout. It is not part of the radio button group's name/value pair.

The Value Sent Field

If the current radio button is selected when the form is submitted by the reader, the contents of the Button field are sent as the value in the name/value pair. The contents of the Value Sent field do not appear in the layout.

Single-Line Text Entry Field Objects

Single-Line Text Entry field objects are added with the Forms Edit tool (see Figure A.19). The Forms Edit tool appears in the Secondary tool palette when the Form tool is active. For more information about forms, see Chapter 12.

FIGURE A.19

*The Single Line
Properties palette.*

The Name Field

The contents of the Name field are sent to the server as the name in the component's name/value pair. The entry box's name does not appear in the layout.

The Text Field

The contents of the Text field will appear in the text field as a default entry when the reader loads the form in her browser.

The Visible Length and Max Length Fields

The contents of the **Visible Length field** determine the width of the Text entry field, as measured in characters. By default, the field is ten characters wide.

The contents of the **Max Length field** determine the maximum number of characters the reader may enter into the Text entry field. By default, the maximum entry is ten characters long.

The Password Check Box

When the Password check box is checked, all text entered in the text entry form by the user will be rendered on-screen with bullet characters, rather than ordinary alphanumeric characters. *No other security is provided!*

Multiple-Line Text Entry Field Objects

Multiple-Line Text Entry field objects are added with the Forms Multi-Line tool (see Figure A.20). The Forms Multi-Line tool appears in the Secondary tool palette when the Form tool is active. For more information about forms, see Chapter 12.

FIGURE A.20

The Multi-Line field objects Properties palette.

The Name Field

The contents of the Name field are sent to the server as the name in the component's name/value pair. The entry box's name does not appear in the layout.

The Text Field

The contents of the Text field will appear in the text field as a default entry when the reader loads the form in her browser.

The Visible Length and Visible Height Fields

The contents of the **Visible Length field** determine the width (in characters) of the text area. By default, the field is ten characters wide. The value in the Visible Length field in no way limits the length of text that the reader may enter.

The contents of the **Visible Height field** determine the height (in lines of text) of the text area. By default, the field is ten lines high. The value in the Visible Length field in no way limits the length of text that the reader may enter.

List Box and Drop-Down Menu Objects

List box and drop-down menu objects are both added with the Forms Combo Box tool. (See Figure A.21.) The Forms Edit tool appears in the Secondary tool palette when the Form tool is active. For more information about forms, see Chapter 12.

FIGURE A.21

The Combo Box Properties palette, a drop-down list, and a list box.

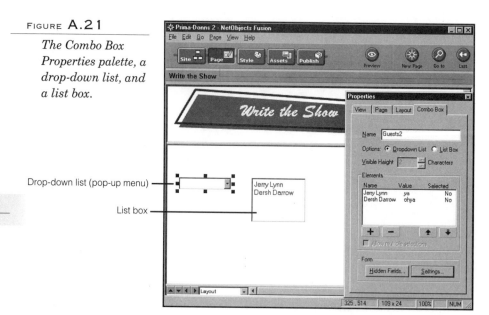

Drop-down list (pop-up menu)

428

List box

The Name Field

The contents of the Name field are sent to the server as the name in the component's name/value pair. The entry box's name does not appear in the layout.

The Drop-Down List/List Box Radio Buttons

A combo box can appear as either a drop-down list or a list box (see Figure A.21). You may change from one format to another at any time by selecting the appropriate radio button from this menu. Altering the combo box's format does not affect the contents of the box in any way.

The Visible Height Field

The value in the visible height field displays the number of lines of text a list box displays in the layout. A drop-down list only displays one list item at a time, no matter how many members the list contains, and so this field is inactive when the drop-down list radio button is selected.

The Elements Group

The Elements group contains controls for adding items to the list used by the combo box.

- **The Name/Value Window** contains a list of all the members of the list. To edit a list entry, double-click its name in the window. The Name entry for a particular list item is the text label displayed on-screen, *not* the name sent in the name/value pair. The Value entry for the list item is the value sent in the name/value pair.

- **The Add/Remove Item** buttons (see Figure A.7) are used to add parameter/value pairs to the Name/Value Window.

- **The Promote/Demote Item** buttons (see Figure A.7) change the ordering of the parameters in the Name/Value List window. Clicking the Promote button moves the selected item up in the list (that is, the second entry will become the first entry, and the first will move to second place); clicking the Demote button moves the item down in the list (that is, the second item will become the third item, and the third will move to second place.)

- **The Allow multiple selections** check box is only active when the combo box is in list box form. When checked, readers may choose more than one list box entry to be submitted with the form.

429

Header Objects

A Header object is a named layout that may be added to the top of any NetObjects Fusion page. By default, all the pages in a NetObjects Fusion use the default Header1 header; however, users may create their own headers and assign different headers on a page-by-page basis. Every page must have a header, if only a blank one (see Figure A.22). For more information about headers, see Chapter 4.

FIGURE A.22

The Header Properties palette.

The Name Field

The Name Field is inactive in the latest version of NetObjects Fusion.

The Add to Header Group

The Add to Header group contains a set of controls for adding objects that behave in special ways within the context of a header.

- **The Navigation Bar button** adds a navigation aid to the header. (The navigation aid may take the form of a navigation bar or a set of text links.) The user may add as many navigation aids as desired; a new aid is added every time the Navigation Bar button is clicked.

- **The Banner check box** toggles the display of a page banner in the header. Only one banner can be added to the header with the check box.

Layout Object

A layout object, or more properly, a layout style, is a template for the body of a NetObjects Fusion page (see Figure A.23). Every page that uses a particular layout style shares the same basic layout attributes. Layout styles can be saved by names and applied to individual pages. By default, all of the pages in a Fusion site use the layout style "layout."

The Layout Properties palette.

The Layout Name Field

The Layout Name field is used to save the current layout style. User-defined layout styles are added to the pop-up menu at the bottom of the status bar at the bottom of the Site View window.

The Width and Height Fields

The Width and Height fields control the size of the NetObjects Fusion layout style, as measured in pixels. The dimensions of the layout are used only as guides for the page designer; objects placed outside the grid area of the Fusion layout *will* appear when the page is previewed or published.

The Background Group

The Background Group controls the display of the background color of the page, including the background color of attached headers and footers.

- **The SiteStyle background radio button** sets the layout style to the default background color specified in the site's SiteStyle. (See Chapter 6 for a description of Style view.)

- **The Solid Color radio button** sets the layout style to the color indicated by the color swatch. To change the layout's color, click the Color button, which brings up the standard color picker.

- **The Picture radio button** sets the background of the page to an image specified by the user. If the browser window is larger than the image, the image is tiled to fill the window.

The Header/Footer Group

The Header and Footer Group controls enable the user to specify the named header and footer objects that are used with the layout style. By default, the default Header1 and Footer1 are used. The New button next to each control saves the current header or footer with a new name.

Footer Objects

A Footer object is a named layout that may be added to the bottom of any NetObjects Fusion page. By default, all the pages in a NetObjects Fusion use the default Footer1; however, users may create their own footers and assign different footers on a page-by-page basis. Every page must have a footer, if only a blank one. For more information about footers, see Chapter 4.

The Add to Header Group

The Add to Header group contains a single button, Add Navigation Bar, which adds a navigation aid—either a bar or set of text links—to the footer. A footer can contain as many navigation aids as desired; one additional navigation aid button will be added every time the button is clicked.

Banner Objects

Banner objects are added to the layout with the Banner check box in the Header tab in the properties palette (see Figure A.24). A banner displays the name of the page that contains it. Banner objects may be cut and pasted, exactly like ordinary layout objects.

The default base image used to construct the banner is the banner image specified in the site's SiteStyle. See Chapter 6 for more information about Site view.

The location of the base image used in the current header is displayed in the banner's Property tab. The base image may be changed by clicking the Browse button, which invokes the standard Open Image dialog box. Changing the base image only changes the appearance of the banner in the current header style; *it does not change the SiteStyle's banner image.*

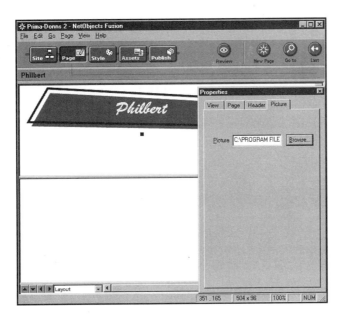

The special Picture Properties palette used for banners.

Navigation Aid Objects

Navigation Aids are added with the Add to Header/Add to Footer controls in the Header and Footer Tabs in the Properties palette (see Figure A.25). Navigation aids can appear as either an array of button images or a set of text links. Navigation aids can be cut and pasted, like ordinary layout objects.

FIGURE A.25

The special Picture Properties palette used for Navigation bar button.

The default base images used to construct the navigation bar are the primary, primary highlighted, secondary, and secondary highlighted images specified in the site's SiteStyle. See Chapter 4 for more information about Site view.

Each button in a navigation bar has its own Picture tab. The base image used to create the button may be changed by clicking the Browse button, which invokes the standard Open Image dialog box. Changing the base image only changes the appearance of the button in the current header style; *it does not change any of the SiteStyle's banner image*

Control over the Navigation bar's basic appearance is controlled by the Nav. Bar Tab in the Properties palette (see Figure A.26).

The Buttons Group

The Buttons group contains a set of radio buttons used to specify how the links in the navigation aid appear.

- When **the Primary Buttons radio button** is selected, the primary buttons specified in the site's SiteStyle are used.

- When **the Secondary Buttons radio button** is selected, the secondary buttons specified in the site's SiteStyle are used.

- When **the Text radio button** is selected, the links are displayed as a series of text links.

The Show Group

The Show group contains a set of radio buttons used to specify which pages in the site are included in the navigation bar.

- **The First Level radio button** specifies that all the pages in the first level of the site tree are included in the navigation bar.

- **The Parent Level radio button** specifies that all the siblings of the parent of the page that contain the navigation bar are included in the navigation bar.

- **The Current Level radio button** specifies that all the siblings of the page that contains the navigation bar, and the page itself, are included in the navigation bar.

- **The Child Level radio button** specifies that all the child pages of the page that contains the navigation bar are included in the navigation bar.

435

The **Include Home Page check box** is physically outside the Show group, but it is functionally related to the Show buttons. When the Include Home Page check box is checked, the site's root page is included in the navigation bar, no matter where the page that contains the navigation bar is positioned in the site tree.

See Chapter 4 for an explanation of root, parent, sibling, and child page concepts.

The Use Highlighted Buttons Check Box

When the Use Highlighted Buttons check box is checked, the page that contains the navigation bar is represented with a special highlight button in the navigation bar. The highlight button for primary buttons and secondary buttons is specified in the site's SiteStyle.

Setting Up a Web Server

Let's say you need to set up a server from scratch. Maybe you're doing a whole site by yourself—perhaps at your arctic research station—or you need to set up the test server without the Webmaster's help.

An incredibly wide range of servers is available with a wide range of feature sets. (The last chart I looked at, which was not a complete list of all the available server systems, had *92* separate packages.) Before you read about some of the packages that are available, here are a few issues to consider when you're looking at servers:

- **Price.** Web server packages have wide variations in prices. Some of the most widely used and reliable servers are free. The extended features and technical support offered by commercial servers, however, can cost thousands of dollars.

- **Speed.** Server software packages vary in speed, especially when the server is under a significant load. Vendors who claim a speed advantage will offer some sort of benchmark test results. Different tests seem to yield different results, and there's no widely accepted agreement about which test is best.

- **Compatibility with Existing Resources.** If you already have a significant investment in something like a 4D database, or a Microsoft Backoffice server, you will no doubt want to use a server that can take advantage of the tools you already have.

  The MacOS-based WebServer 4D and NetWingz servers, for example, both work together with 4D databases, and NetWingz can even serve the contents of the database directly as Web pages. (It's similar to what NetObjects Fusion does with databases, actually.) If you don't have a 4D database already, this might not be interesting, but if you've already made a significant investment in 4D technology, it makes these servers attractive.

- **Support for other Internet Services.** You might need to set up other kinds of servers when you're establishing your Internet presence: your own email server, for example, or a news or FTP server. There are many packages on the market, such as Netscape's SuiteSpot package, that offer several kinds of servers bundled together into an integrated package.

- **Security Features.** In order to provide the kinds of security features that I covered in Chapter 3, you must use a server that supports security features. A security-enabled browser such as Netscape Navigator can't create secure connections by itself. Both ends of the transaction must support the same security protocol.

- **Technical Support.** As anyone who has crashed any kind of software hours before a critical deadline knows, technical support is important, and it's a big part of what you're paying for when you buy commercial software.

A great place to find out more about the various server packages that are available is the giant chart of servers that I mentioned at the beginning of this section. The chart is put out by i-world, and contains links to every vendor included on the chart. Point your browser at `http://webcompare.iworld.com/compare/chart.html` to find it.

Setting Up FolkWeb

For those of you Windows users who are just getting started, I've included a copy of the shareware server FolkWeb on the *NetObjects Fusion Handbook* CD-ROM. FolkWeb isn't right for every situation—it doesn't have security features, for example—but it's a good server for a first-time Webmaster and small trial sites on your own machine.

438

I've included a copy of the shareware application FolkWeb on the *NetObjects Fusion Handbook* CD-ROM. You can try it out for free, and it won't expire, but if you keep it, you should pay for it. You can download the most recent version of FolkWeb from `http://www.ilar.com`.

Configuring the Software

After you've downloaded the FolkWeb software, double-click it to unzip it. (If nothing happens, you'll need to find and install WinZip or another Zip-handling utility on your machine.) WinZip will decompress a group of files to a temporary folder, and offer you the opportunity to install the software.

Here's the procedure for installing the software:

439

1. FolkWeb Setup will prompt you for the name of your network. Enter the name of your network here, or if you don't know it, use your IP address. If you aren't attached to a network at all, enter 127.0.0.1 and see the section called "loopback" below.

2. Setup will prompt you for an email address. It doesn't necessarily need to be an address on the same network as the server.

3. Setup will prompt you for a directory name. This will be the directory where the server software resides, not necessarily the folder from which the files were served. (Normally, files are served from a folder *inside* the FolkWeb directory.)

After everything is installed, go ahead and launch the FolkWeb application, which you'll find in FolkWeb/bin. The application starts minimized, and doesn't have a display window. (If you click the program's name in the Taskbar, all you'll see is an "about-this-software" box.)

FolkWeb comes preconfigured with sensible defaults. If you point your browser to http:// + your server's address, it will serve up the example home page at FolkWeb/Pages/default.htm (see Figure B.1).

Loopback

Sometimes, you'll want to run server software on a machine that isn't connected to a network. (If you didn't buy your laptop to take it to the beach, why *did* you buy it?) This way, you can test your CGIs and other network-dependent site features on a single machine that runs both your client and server software.

Using loopback on a Windows 95 machine is quite a bit simpler than setting it up on a Mac. After your server is running, you can use the magical loopback address http://127.0.0.1 to access your server. Suppose that you've published your Fusion site to the FolkWeb/Pages folder, and your site's home page is called welcome.htm. To load your page in the browser, enter http://127.0.0.1/welcome.htm in the browser's location field.

Setting Up MacHTTP or WebSTAR

MacHTTP and WebSTAR are both from the same company, StarNINE technologies, which is now a division of Quarterdeck corporation. MacHTTP is the shareware version of WebSTAR. The two programs are similar in interface, and completely compatible. However, WebSTAR is significantly faster than MacHTTP, allows remote administration, and offers the use of CGI-like plug-in extensions for the server.

> **TIP**
>
> Although MacHTTP and WebSTAR are fine to use as a staging server, and especially if you're setting them up on your own machine, the most reliable test server is the same software as the final server, running on the same platform and hardware configuration as the final server.

Getting the Software

Both a trial version of WebSTAR and MacHTTP are available for download from StarNINE's site. To download WebSTAR, use the following steps:

1. Fill out the form at http://emod.starnine.com/evals/evals.html and submit it. Be certain to fill in an email address—you can't get WebSTAR without one.

2. Download the WebSTAR.sea.hqx.

3. A CGI at the StarNINE site will process the form and email you a message that confirms that they received your form information. Normally, this should only take a few minutes.

4. The email will also include a key, a string of nonsense characters something like sd5f-sa2f-we1r-55f8-d7gy. (I just made that up…don't use it as a key!) Cut and paste the key from your email client to the MacOS Notepad under the Apple menu.

5. When the WebSTAR is finished downloading, your Web browser should unpack it automatically. Look for a folder called "WebSTAR Install" and run the application Installer inside the WebSTAR Install/Installer folder.

6. Copy the key from the MacOS Notepad.

7. Find the WebSTAR™ folder and launch the WebSTAR application that's inside. The WebSTAR application will prompt you for a password. Paste in the key by pressing Command-V.

To download MacHTTP, use the following steps:

1. Fill out the form at `http://www.starnine.com/machttp/machttp.html` and submit it. Be careful to enter your email address.

2. A CGI at the StarNINE site will process the form and email you a message that confirms that they received your form information. Normally, this should only take a few minutes.

3. The email will also include an URL from which you can download MacHTTP. Cut and paste the address from your email application to your browser's location field.

4. After the page is loaded, download the MacHTTP.sea.hqx software.

5. The email from StarNINE also contains a password. Copy it from your email software.

6. When your browser launches StuffIt Expander (or whatever it uses) you will be prompted for a password. Paste it in with Command-V.

Configuring the Software

Both MacHTTP and WebSTAR just seem to work by magic. When you launch either application, the software can serve anything that's in the same folder as the application.

Both applications come with a set of default html documents, which, handily enough, provide some basic instructions on how to use the software. To see the server in action, use the following steps:

1. Make sure that MacTCP or Open Transport are installed and running on your machine.

2. Launch MacHTTP or WebSTAR.

3. Launch your browser.

4. Enter "http://" + your IP address in the browser's location field. (Remember, you can always find your IP address by looking in the MacTCP control panel, or, if you're running under Open Transport, in the TCP/IP control panel.)

5. The server's default page loads in the browser window (see Figure B.1).

FIGURE **B.1**

The default page that comes with WebSTAR.

6. The server's window registers your activity in the WebSTAR window (see Figure B.2). The same information goes into MacHTTP log, by the way.

Remember, for security reasons, MacHTTP and WebSTAR only serve files that are in the same folder as the application, or in a folder in the application folder's hierarchy. To serve your NetObjects Fusion site with one of these servers, you must publish it somewhere inside the server's folder.

```
┌─────────────────── MacHTTP 2.2 Status ───────────────────┐
Connections : Total 7671  Max 10  Listening 6  Current 0  High 12  Busy 4  Denied 0  Timeout 223
Free Memory : Max 812720  Current 752252  Min 575060  Sent :102954.7K  Up Since : 07/24/96 :10:52
ᴜᴢ4ᴚᴛ
08/30/96  12:20:40  OK    utproduction.uchicago.edu.  :catalog:aa.Front.96.html-4
8341
08/30/96  12:20:51  OK    s23-pm08.ucr.campus.mci.net.  :housing:max_mason.jpeg
4096
08/30/96  12:20:52  OK    s23-pm08.ucr.campus.mci.net.  :housing:maclean.jpeg 8192
08/30/96  12:20:52  OK    s23-pm08.ucr.campus.mci.net.
:housing:housing_cover.jpeg 61440
08/30/96  12:21:27  OK    utproduction.uchicago.edu.  :catalog:aa.Front.96.html-3
30705
08/30/96  12:36:45  OK    cliff.chem.purdue.edu.  :home_page:original_nameplate
29822
08/30/96  12:37:54  OK    cliff.chem.purdue.edu.  :AMF.html 8243
08/30/96  12:38:40  OK    cliff.chem.purdue.edu.  :home_page:original_nameplate
8192
08/30/96  12:43:01  OK    cliff.chem.purdue.edu.  :AMF.html 86752
08/30/96  12:55:40  OK    cliff.chem.purdue.edu.  :home_page:original_nameplate
29822
08/30/96  12:56:46  OK    cnotes66.wpic.pitt.edu.  :catalog:catalog.html 2244
08/30/96  12:56:57  OK    cnotes66.wpic.pitt.edu.
:catalog:catalog.updates.spr.96.html 1618
08/30/96  13:06:37  OK    ubppp-074.ppp-net.buffalo.edu.  :catalog:catalog.html
2244
08/30/96  13:07:01  OK    ubppp-074.ppp-net.buffalo.edu.
:catalog:aa.Front.96.html-4 8341

WARNING: Can't open file! (File not found) Path=:Error.html
Bad URL reference received from:
http://www-upubs.uchicago.edu/catalog/aa.Front.96.html-4
08/30/96  13:07:24  ERR!  ubppp-074.ppp-net.buffalo.edu.  :catalog:GS 0
08/30/96  13:08:38  OK    ubppp-074.ppp-net.buffalo.edu.  :catalog:NCD.96.html
4172
08/30/96  13:10:14  OK    ubppp-074.ppp-net.buffalo.edu.  :catalog:Cin&Med.96.html
4096
08/30/96  13:10:39  OK    ubppp-074.ppp-net.buffalo.edu.  :catalog:Cin&Med.96.html
11214
08/30/96  13:11:54  OK    ubppp-074.ppp-net.buffalo.edu.
:catalog:Cin&Med.96.crs.html 13533
08/30/96  13:12:19  OK    ubppp-074.ppp-net.buffalo.edu.
:catalog:aa.Front.96.html-4 4121
08/30/96  13:24:43  OK    proxy2.cc.stevens-tech.edu.  :an.intro.html 41902
08/30/96  13:33:42  OK    proxy2.cc.stevens-tech.edu.  :catalog:catalog.html 2244
08/30/96  13:36:23  OK    17.18.218.205.in-addr.arpa.  :catalog95:NCD.95.html 6526
08/30/96  13:40:36  OK    ntcs-ip6.uchicago.edu.  :catalog:catalog.html 2244
08/30/96  13:41:02  OK    ntcs-ip6.uchicago.edu.  :catalog:aa.Front.96.html-4 8341
08/30/96  13:41:24  OK    ntcs-ip6.uchicago.edu.  :catalog:English.96.html 4099
08/30/96  13:41:58  OK    ntcs-ip6.uchicago.edu.  :catalog:English.96.crs.html
28978
08/30/96  13:46:43  OK    quads.uchicago.edu.  :housing:housing.html 62437
08/30/96  13:50:24  OK    fly1mac.bsd.uchicago.edu.  :catalog:catalog.html 2244
08/30/96  13:50:42  OK    fly1mac.bsd.uchicago.edu.  :catalog:aa.Front.96.html-4
8341
```

FIGURE **B.2**

*The server shows
the hit in the server
window.*

443

Loopback

Sometimes, you'll want to set up your test server on a machine that has no
connection to a network. I try to work on my PowerBook in a restaurant as often
as humanly possible, for example, but I seldom have the chance to dial up my
ISP from the table.

It's a little tricky, but you can set up your Mac so that it's running a server even
if it's hooked up to a network. (I pretty much stole these directions from Stewart
Buskirk's *Web Server Construction Kit,* by the way.)

WARNING

Before you do this, make sure that you have a record of your MacTCP settings. Open
the MacTCP control panel, click the More button, and take a screenshot with
Command-shift-3, or save your settings with the MacTCP Switcher utility, which you
can find at ftp://ftp.acns.nwu.edu/pub/jlnstuff/mactcp-switcher.

Here's the basic idea: you're going to force MacTCP and the browser into looking for addresses in a file in the System folder, rather than on an address server on the Net. Our file in the system points back to the current machine, so that's where the browser will look for the page. Here's how you do it:

1. Open the MacTCP control panel. Click the More button.

2. Check the Manually radio button in the Obtain Address: group.

3. Enter 0.0.0.0 in the Gateway Address field in the Routing Information: group.

4. Select C from the class pop-up menu.

5. Delete all the entries in the Domain Name Server Information: group. (This is what forces MacTCP to look in the System folder.)

6. Click the OK button to return to the main MacTCP window.

7. Click on the LocalTalk icon in the MacTCP window.

8. Enter 192.0.1.2 in the IP Address: field.

9. Launch a text editor, such as SimpleText or BBEdit. Create a new file, and enter

    your server name   A   192.0.1.2.

    (Substitute the server name you plan to use on your final server for *your server name,* of course.)

10. Save the file as text only in the top level of the System folder, with the name "Hosts."

11. Open the Chooser (under the Apple menu) and turn on AppleTalk, if it's not on already. (Don't worry if you're not connected to an AppleTalk network— you *are* the network.)

12. Restart your Mac.

To see this work, make sure that the server is running and then enter http:// + whatever you entered for *your server name,* or if that doesn't work (it doesn't work with every configuration of Macs and browsers) http://192.0.1.2. Your browser will load the server's default page.

A

ActiveX Control Downloadable software components that can extend the functionality of Microsoft Internet Explorer. ActiveX controls can function like self-running programs that run inside the Explorer window (like Java applets) or as an extension of Explorer's basic capabilities (like a Netscape Navigator plug-in).

Adobe Acrobat A suite of related products for creating, editing, and viewing files in Adobe's cross-platform Portable Document Format (PDF).

AIFF Audio Interchange File Format. A commonly used sound file format. See also MPEG and .AU.

Animation Any number of techniques for creating movement on Web pages, including Animated GIFs, Macromedia-based content, Java applets, or ActiveX controls.

Animated GIFs A variant on the basic GIF format, consisting of a series of frames loaded in quick succession, creating the illusion of movement. Animated GIFs are probably the easiest (and smallest sized) way to add simple animation to a Web page.

Assets Components of your NetObjects Fusion site listed in Fusion's Assets View window. Assets include external files (such as images and multimedia) included on the pages, links to pages on the site or to other Web sites, and Fusion's special database-binding tool, Data Objects.

Asset View One of NetObjects Fusion five basic "views" of a site. Shows the files, links, and Data Objects used to construct the site. See also File Assets, Link Assets, and Data Object Assets.

.AU A UNIX-based commonly used sound file format. Also called u-law and mu-law. *See also* .AIFF and MPEG.

AVI Audio-Visual. Windows 95 based video file format.

B

Browser A software application, such as Netscape Navigator or Microsoft Internet Explorer, that fetches files from HTTP servers and displays them as Web pages. Modern browsers perform other tasks as well, such as running applets and providing email client services.

C

CGI Common Gateway Interface. A protocol for communication between server software and scripts or application that assists the server with information processing tasks. CGI is also commonly used to refer to the scripts or applications that use the CGI interface.

CGI-bin Common Gateway Interface Binaries. The name used by many server software packages for the directory that contains the CGI applications recognized by the server.

Character styles Styles applied to individual characters of text, including font, size, color. *See also* Paragraph styles.

Client-side imagemaps An imagemap that's processed by the Web browser, rather than by the server software, which therefore frees up processing time and power for the server to do other jobs. *See also* imagemap and server-side imagemap.

D

Data Field A NetObjects Fusion picture box or text box that contains data from a database. Each Data Field contains one field from one record of a database record.

Data List A table in a Web page that indexes the contents of an internal or imported database.

Data Object NetObjects Fusion's format to represent both internal databases and imported external databases.

Data Object Assets A list of the Data Objects used in the current site, displayed in Assets view. *See also* Assets, Data Object.

Data Page A Web page that contains data from a database. Each Data Page represents one record in the database.

Dingbat An iconic ornament used to decorate a Web page. A collection of dingbats is bundled with NetObjects Fusion.

DNS Domain Name Server. Software that "looks up" Internet addresses in DNS database components distributed over the Internet (or intranet); also part of the distributed database. DNS servers are called by both Web servers and Web browsers.

E

Executable Code Software applications. Strictly speaking, executable code refers to programs that are in machine-readable code (or virtual machine readable bytecodes), *not* source code that is run by an interpreter. Modern browsers can run executable code *inside* the browser window.

External Links Links to pages (or other kinds of URLs, such as newsgroups or email addresses) that are on servers other than the Web server.

F

File Assets Files (such as images or Java applets) placed in the NetObjects Fusion Web site.

Footer A template added to the bottom of pages of a NetObjects Fusion site. A site may have several footers defined, and each page can use a different footer. *See also* Header.

G

GIF Graphics Interchange Format, developed by CompuServe Information Service. An image file format widely used to add images to Web pages, and supported by virtually all Web browsers.

GIF89 A variant on the GIF format developed in 1989. The GIF89 format supports transparent pixels in an image.

Grid A set of guidelines that appear in NetObjects Fusion Page View. The grid is used to organize the design of the page, and does not appear in the finished page that appears in the browser window.

H

Header A template added to the tops of pages of a NetObjects Fusion site. A site may have several headers defined, and each page can use a different header. *See also* Footer.

Hit Count The number of transactions that take place between server software and Web browsers. A single page can yield several hits.

Home Page The Web page designed as the "front door" of a site; usually the first page that visitors to the site will load. Also commonly used to refer to individuals' personal pages.

447

Hotspot A rectangular, oval, or polygonal region of an imagemap. Each hotspot, when clicked, links to a page on the site, or to an external URL. *See also* Imagemap.

HSB model Hue-Saturation-Brightness model. A system for specifying a wide range of colors using a set of three numbers. Also called the HSL model, for Hue-Saturation-Lightness.

HTML HyperText Markup Language. HTML is the system for creating Web pages; basically, it's a simple declarative language for controlling Web browsers. NetObjects Fusion creates Web pages by generating HTML code to describe each page.

HTML tags HTML code instructions embedded in a Web document, marked with pointy-brackets, like so: <tag>. Tags are often used in pairs to surround a string of text, like so: <tag> *string-of-text* </tag>

HTTP HyperText Transport Protocol. The commands and data-packaging standards for passing information back and forth between Web servers and clients. HTTP commands are invisible to end users and HTML authors.

I

Imagemap An image file used as a navigation aid. Different regions of the imagemap, called hotspots, are linked to different pages or external URLs. *See also* Hotspot.

Interlaced GIF A variant on the GIF format. Interlaced GIFs are organized so that the GIF's entire image area appears quickly in the browser window at low resolution, and gains resolution as the GIF loads.

Internal Links Hypertext links from one page of your NetObjects Fusion site to another page in the same site.

J

Java A programming language developed by Sun MicroSystems. Java applets can run inside a browser window. Java programs can run as stand-alone applications.

JavaScript A programming language developed by Netscape Communications, Inc. JavaScript scripts run only in the window of a JavaScript-savvy Web browser.

JPEG Joint Photographer's Experts Group. "JPEG" is used to designate the image file format developed by the Joint Photographer's Experts Group. JPEG files are small, and support a wide color gamut. They are widely used on Web pages.

Justification The way a block of text is set. A block whose lines are all of the same length, or measure, is said to be justified. Justification is not supported in the current implementation of HTML.

L

Leading The space between two lines of type, usually measured from baseline to baseline. Control over leading is not supported under the current implementation of HTML.

Link assets A list of all the links in your NetObjects Fusion site, including both links to pages in the site and links to pages on other sites. Link Assets are displayed in Assets View.

Logical styles HTML tags that instruct the browser to display the tagged text with special typographic treatment. How the browser displays the style can (sometimes) be controlled by the browser's user; that is, type marked with the logical style called "emphasis" might be rendered with bold type in one browser, and with italic type in another. *See also* Physical styles.

Lossless compression File compression techniques that temporarily reduce the size of a file without discarding any of the file's data. Lossless compression changes file sizes less dramatically than lossy compression, but it maintains file integrity. *See also* Lossy compression.

Lossy compression File compression techniques that reduce the size of a file by discarding part of the file's data. Used for image files and sound files, where the lost data is not critical. Lossy compression compresses file sizes more dramatically than lossless compression.

M

MPEG Motion Picture Experts Group. "MPEG" is used to designate the compression algorithm developed by the MPEG committee. MPEG compression is used for both audio and video files. *See also* AIFF, AU, AVI, and QuickTime.

N

\ A vertex between edges on a tree diagram. In NetObjects Fusion, each node in Site View's tree diagram represents a page in the Web site.

P

Padding The space between cells in a table. *See also* Spacing.

Page view One of NetObjects Fusion's five main "views" of a site. Page View is used to edit the layout of the site's individual pages.

Paragraph styles Type attributes that are applied to an entire paragraph of text, rather than to individual characters. Paragraph styles are defined by the user; NetObjects Fusion includes a set of pre-defined paragraph styles. *See also* Character styles.

Physical styles HTML tags that instruct the browser to display the tagged text with a particular

449

typographic treatment. Physical styles are always displayed in the same way by every browser. *See also* Logical styles.

Pixel Picture Element. The smallest component of a computer monitor's display. Each pixel in the monitor can be set to a different color.

Plugin A software module that extends the basic capabilities of a Web browser. In most cases, the plugin enables the browser to display a new file format (for example, Shockwave movies).

Publish view One of NetObjects Fusion's five main "views" of a site. Publish view is used to send a completed site to a staging server or the final server.

Q

QuickTime Apple's video technology developed on Macintosh, also used on the Windows platform. *See also* AVI and MPEG.

QuickTime VR Apple's "virtual reality" technology, based on QuickTime, that allows users to interactively examine a 360-degree panorama image, or rotate an object image.

R

RealAudio: Perhaps the most widely used technology for "streaming" an audio signal. RealAudio files are

played as they download, so that large files can be played immediately by the browser. *See also* Streaming.

Root The node of a tree diagram from which all other nodes are descended. In NetObjects Fusion Site View, the node represents the home page of the site.

S

Server A software application that "listens" for requests for Web files, and transfers the requested files to the browser.

Server-side imagemap An imagemap processed by a CGI or Web Server, rather than by the Web client. *See also* Client-side imagemap and Imagemap.

Shockwave A suite of technologies used to deliver content created with Macromedia, Inc.'s multimedia editing tools over the Web. The family of Shockwave plugins plays files in Shockwave format inside the Web browser window.

Site A collection of Web pages connected by a common navigational framework, usually (but not necessarily) served by a single server.

Siblings On a tree diagram, two nodes that share the same parent.

Site view One of NetObjects Fusion's five main views of a site. Site view is used to edit the site's overall organization.

450

SiteStyle A set of basic page elements and a color palette that can be applied to every page of the NetObjects Fusion site. Use of SiteStyles gives the Fusion site a consistent look and feel throughout.

Smart links *See* Structural links.

Spacing In a table, the space between the edge of a cell and the cell's content. *See also* Padding.

Staging server An intermediate server, used to privately test a server over a network before the site is made publicly available on the final server.

Streaming Technology that allows multimedia content to be played while it downloads. *See also* RealAudio.

Structural links Links from one page in the NetObjects Fusion site to another. The target page is defined by its relationship to the page that contains the link; not by the name of the page. Also called Smart links.

Style view One of NetObjects Fusion's five main views of a site. Style View is used to view the various SiteStyles available to the user, and to apply SiteStyles to the pages of the site.

T

TCP/IP Transmission Control Protocol/Internet Protocol.

Transparent GIFs *See* GIF89.

U–W

URI Universal Resource Indicator. *See* URL.

URL Universal Resource Locator. The "address" of a Web page or other Internet resource, such as a newsgroup.

VBScript Visual Basic Script. A scripting language developed by Microsoft. VBScript scripts may be embedded in Web pages, and are executed by the Microsoft Internet Explorer browser.

Video A video signal, stored in digital format. *See also* Animation, AVI, MPEG, and QuickTime.

Web page An HTML document, as displayed in a Web browser. A Web page can contain text, images, multimedia content, and executable code. The same page may appear differently in different Web browsers.

Web Server *See* Server.

World Wide Web Almost, but not quite, the Internet. A set of interconnected HTTP servers that serve graphical pages in HTML formats; each HTML document can provide links to pages on other servers, creating an intricate web-like network of cross-references. The Web is often referred to as a "graphical front end" of the Internet.

451

Index

A

454

455

K-L

457

Q-R

S

W-X-Y-Z

What's on the NetObjects Fusion Handbook CD

The *NetObjects Fusion Handbook* CD includes the following software:

- 30-day trial version of NetObjects Fusion software (for Windows 95 and Windows NT) with README instructions file.

- Complete copy of the URL roundups mentioned in the book for easy browser access.

- Templates designed by Clement Mok studios especially for this book.

- Example sites, including:

    a. Tree.nod in the folder /Book/Sites/Tree. You can use this file to practice tree-pruning.

    b. Story.nod in the folder /Book/Sites/Story. An example of literary magazine online.

    c. Layouts.nod in the folder /Book/Sites/Layouts.

    d. Solitaire in the folder /Book/Sites/Solitaire. You can use this site to practice placing images.

    e. Imagemap in the folder /Book/Sites/Imagemap.

- Set of reusable GIFs in the /Book/Animated GIFs/Frames folder.

- *Adire* style in the folder /Book/Styles/Adire. You can play with it before you build your own components.

- An example movie, Klassy Karl.qt file in the /book/multimedia folder.

- Doublecheck.txt in the Book/Executables folder, which is a compilation of JavaScript code for easy plug and play.

- An example sound file (AIFF), Nina.aiff, featuring my very good friend Nina Koroma saying "Moo, moo, how are you doing?"

- An example 401 (k)alculator Shockwave application, 401.dcr in the Book/Multimedia folder.

- Katipo application.

- Freeloader application.

- FolkWeb, a shareware server.

- MacPerl.

- Preflight checklist for best Web-page publication results.

Pop in the CD, and then start the README file, which will guide you through the installation process.